# Designer's Guide to Furniture Styles

**Third Edition**

*Treena Crochet*

**Allied ASID**

**Illustrated by**

*David Vleck*

**PEARSON**

Boston   Columbus   Indianapolis   New York   San Francisco   Upper Saddle River
Amsterdam   Cape Town   Dubai   London   Madrid   Milan   Munich   Paris   Montréal   Toronto
Delhi   Mexico City   São Paulo   Sydney   Hong Kong   Seoul   Singapore   Taipei   Tokyo

**Editorial Director:** Vernon Anthony
**Acquisitions Editor:** Sara Eilert
**Editorial Assistant:** Doug Greive
**Director of Marketing:** David Gesell
**Executive Marketing Manager:** Harper Coles
**Senior Marketing Coordinator:** Alicia Wozniak
**Marketing Assistant:** Crystal Gonzales
**Project Manager:** Alicia Ritchey
**Associate Managing Editor:** Alexandrina Benedicto Wolf
**Operations Specialist:** Deidra Skahill

**Art Director:** Jayne Conte
**Cover Designer:** Suzanne Behnke
**Cover Image:** DK
**AV Project Manager:** Janet Portisch
**Full-Service Project Management:** Element LLC
**Composition:** Element Thomson North America
**Printer/Binder:** LSC Communications
**Cover Printer:** LSC Communications
**Text Font:** Frutiger LT Std

Credits and acknowledgments borrowed from other sources and reproduced, with permission, in this textbook appear on the appropriate page within the text. Unless otherwise stated, all artwork has been provided by the author.

---

**Library of Congress Cataloging-in-Publication Data**

Crochet, Treena.
 Designer's guide to furniture styles/Treena Crochet.—3rd ed.
  p. cm.
 Includes index.
 ISBN 978-0-13-205041-8
 1. Furniture—Styles. I. Title.
 NK2235.C76 2012

749.09—dc23

2011045211

ISBN 10:    0-13-2050412
ISBN 13: 978-0-13-2050418

To my mentor, Jan Parker, FASID

# CONTENTS

# Chapter 2    CLASSICAL GREECE AND ROME    30

# Chapter 3    THE MEDIEVAL PERIOD    52

# Chapter 4    FIFTEENTH AND SIXTEENTH CENTURIES    68

# Chapter 5    THE SEVENTEENTH CENTURY    88

# Chapter 6    THE EIGHTEENTH CENTURY    110

## Chapter 7

### THE LATE EIGHTEENTH AND EARLY NINETEENTH CENTURIES   138

## Chapter 8

### THE NINETEENTH CENTURY   164

# Chapter 9   THE TWENTIETH AND TWENTY-FIRST CENTURIES   190

# Chapter 10    FURNITURE CONSTRUCTION    228

As a practicing interior designer, I place great importance on telling my students about the experiences I've encountered in the field with contractors, clients, and vendors. They have heard just about all of it—the good, the bad, and the ugly. I stress to my students that, although they can never know it all, they can acquire a basic knowledge of many things. My goal is for students to learn as much as possible while they are in college, yet know where to go to find answers once they graduate and begin working with clients on their own.

Although the selection and specification of interior furnishings and accessories are only one aspect of interior design, these finishing touches often determine the success or failure of the entire job. Like color, interior furnishings create a mood or feeling in the space regardless of style or design. Although there is so much to learn about the decorative arts, I recommend that any student of design begin with the most rigorous art history classes. Completion of a thorough art history course covering the Paleolithic period to the present gives the student of design a firm foundation for further study. It is not the goal of this book to teach students the history of art and architecture.

*Designer's Guide to Furniture Styles* presents significant movements in the evolution of the decorative arts including furniture, design motifs, and accessories relative to interior design and architectural settings from the Neolithic age to the current century. This book is intended to augment the study of art and architectural history by discussing the function (often the driving force in development) and aesthetic purpose of furniture, pottery, glassware, lighting, textiles, mirrors, metalworking, clocks, and wallcoverings and their integration into interior design. Furniture styles evolved as an integral part of the architecture within and coordinated with a wide array of decorative accessories. As a pretext to stylistic development, information on political and social events and the technological advances that influenced the design trends of the period are addressed.

Furthermore, comparisons are made between objects from different periods, showing the progression of an idea or concept through the object's stylistic development. Descriptions of period room settings provide the context of how the collective decorative arts complement the architecture and interior design. This book includes a listing of valuable websites for students of design to view more objects held in museum collections all over the world. Finally, the glossary highlights key vocabulary, and bibliographic information inspires further reading. This book is a handy resource for future designers or a refresher for those already in practice.

## DOWNLOAD INSTRUCTOR RESOURCES FROM THE INSTRUCTOR RESOURCE CENTER

To access supplementary materials online, instructors need to request an instructor access code. Go to www.pearsonhighered .com/irc to register for an instructor access code. Within 48 hours of registering, you will receive a confirming e-mail including an instructor access code. Once you have received your code, locate your text in the online catalog and click on the Instructor Resources button on the left side of the catalog product page. Select a supplement, and a login page will appear. Once you have logged in, you can access instructor material for all Prentice Hall textbooks. If you have any difficulties accessing the site or downloading a supplement, please contact Customer Service at http://247pearsoned.custhelp.com/.

## ACKNOWLEDGMENTS

I am continually grateful to the people at Pearson/Prentice Hall who support me in writing textbooks on subjects that not only are interesting to me, but also benefit those students studying interior design. Vern Anthony, the editor-in-chief, is unwavering in his support of my work, and I thank him for everything he has done for me over the past 10 years. Thanks also go to acquisitions editor, Sara Eilert, who smoothed out many rough patches throughout this project. Without Doug Greive, my paper trail would be a tangled mess; thanks, Doug, for keeping things organized! Much appreciation is extended to those responsible for the production of this book. In conclusion, I wish to thank those reviewers who offered extensive commentary for making this a better book: Denise Bertoncino, Pittsburg State University; Peter Dedek, Texas State University, San Marcos; Michael Dudek, Kansas State University; Jeannie Ireland, Missouri State University; Sarah A. Lichtman, Parsons The New School for Design; LuAnn Nissen, University of Nevada, Reno; and Lisa Tucker, Virginia Tech.

## ABOUT THE AUTHOR

Award-winning and bestselling author Treena Crochet, Allied ASID, is the Assistant Dean for the School of Architecture and Design at New York Institute of Technology, Bahrain. She has over 25 years of teaching experience on specialty subjects, including the history of design, architecture, and art, and has written six books on architecture and design. Also a practicing designer, her work appeared in *The Boston Globe* and *Yankee Magazine*. Contact her with questions regarding any of her books at www.TreenaCrochet.com.

Regardless of the label historians use to describe a style, period, or movement for a particular time or culture, by studying the history of the decorative arts, we learn that humans have an inherent desire to beautify their environment while satisfying the need to perform domestic duties. How a given culture at a given time chose to do so depended on social, economic, and even political factors. Over the centuries, ingenuity overcame limitations and each culture adapted household objects to fit its changing lifestyles.

Early humans survived the elements by living in makeshift shelters such as caves or huts, fed themselves by forming weapons to hunt animals for food, and eventually, devised tools used for planting and harvesting crops. Objects we take for granted today, such as a warm bed throw, a bright reading lamp, or a cleverly designed cooking pot, were, in the beginning, developed out of the most basic need for survival. Animal skins provided warmth as clothing and bedding materials whereas grass or straw spread on the ground kept the chill and dampness of the ground away from their bodies. Hollowed-out tree branches and logs were used to store food, and dried gourds or animal skin pouches held water. Over the course of time, humans developed these necessary items into well-designed objects made from whatever materials were available, and each generation of workers perfected their craft by making furniture, containers, textiles, and lamps better than the previous.

Archaeological excavations tell us that as far back as the third millennium BCE interiors were outfitted with drapes, rugs, beautiful pottery, decorative figurines, furniture, lamps, and artwork. Pharaohs, kings, and the nobility found great pleasure in amassing teams of artisans whose sole purpose was to create the most beautiful functional objects, which were then flaunted as symbols of their wealth. Historically, the designers of these objects were merely creating to fulfill the wants and desires of their patrons rather than following their own inspiration and need for artistic expression. Throughout most of ancient history, designers were looked upon as mere craftsworkers. Often the craftsworkers executed these projects while getting little or no recognition, and in many cases, their ideas were ridiculed and rejected by the elite patrons who employed them. During such times designers had to also overcome obstacles of social class to be recognized and respected for their work.

During the medieval and Renaissance periods, utilitarian objects became more decorative as workers perfected their craft, introduced new technologies and materials, and provided well-designed domestic objects for an emerging middle-class society of trade merchants and bankers. At this time, the formation of guilds set the standards for quality in artisanship through regulation, training, and apprenticeship programs, and established fair pricing for the goods produced and sold.

By the mid-18th century, elaborate furniture, fine porcelains, delicate glassware, and superb repoussé metalwork fulfilled functional purposes while contributing toward a luxurious interior décor. Fashionable interiors of the aristocracy symbolized their status in society. In the 19th century, the height of the Industrial Revolution introduced advanced production methods and techniques, breaking the boundaries of class and wealth by providing the public with inexpensive machine-made objects. Before the end of the century both supporters and detractors of the machine were debating the issue of the quality of handmade objects versus those that were mass produced. The debate over which objects were better—handmade or machine made—continued into the 20th century.

Because they were more expensive than those made by machine, handmade objects in the early styles of the 20th century, such as Art Nouveau and Art Deco, perpetuated the gap between wealthy and middle-class consumers. Enthusiastic designers eager to shed the past developed new styles for a technologically modern age, and often opposed those who chose to preserve the artistry of handmade objects. These early 20th-century "modernists" designed products that reflected the progress of the machine age. They not only explored new methods of production with industrialized machinery, but also utilized unconventional materials while seeking to break from the past.

By the mid-20th century, modern culture moved to embrace the machine age and newly introduced synthetic materials, such as plastics. Furthermore, innovative designers embraced new synthetic materials and used mechanized processes that enabled them to bring high style to mass populations. At the end of the century, clever marketing strategies by big-box department stores brought everyday household objects created by world-renowned designers to all classes of society. Those designers specialize in creating objects that fulfill both an aesthetic function and a practical solution at a reasonable cost.

During the last 30 years we began to think of designers a little differently, perhaps as visionaries. Now, they are the creative people who forecast the kind of houses we will live in, the clothes we'll wear, or the type of car we will drive. The choices are entirely up to us, yet we are limited to what the designers have to offer us. They shape our basic wants and needs based on what we perceive as the latest trends in the design community, be it an ergonomically designed office chair, the slimmest cellular phone model, or perhaps the colors for new sports utility vehicles.

Who can predict what the new styles of design will be for our 21st century? As the world is linked through satellite television and the Internet and globalization continues, styles merge and evolve as each culture takes what it needs from popular culture and adapts it to meet its own unique lifestyles. Will history books of the future still separate styles by country as we do now? Or will 21st-century design culture become one global melting pot? After living in the Middle East for several years, I realize that the creative possibilities of blending and merging cultural styles are endless. Perhaps this era of globalization is our Silk Road for the 21st century.

| Period | Significant People or Events | Creative Accomplishments |
|---|---|---|
| **PALEOLITHIC** | | |
| 30,000–25,000 BCE | Neanderthal species is replaced by Cro-Magnon. | Small statuaries depict female nude as fertility goddess, sculpture *Venus of Willendorf*, c. 30,000–20,000. |
| 15,000–10,000 BCE | Nomadic humans find shelter in caves and prepare temporary shelter. | Prehistoric cave paintings record life of early Homo sapiens. Lascaux Cave paintings are made, c. 16,000–10,000. |
| **MESOLITHIC** | | |
| 8000–7000 BCE | Humans begin cultivating crops and raising animals. | Settlement at Jericho shows development of architecture and pottery. |
| **NEOLITHIC** | | |
| 6500–5700 BCE | Humans establish permanent settlements. | Settlement at Catal Huyuk documents use of tools, furniture. Pottery and textile weaving are developed. |
| 4000–3000 BCE | Advanced settlements develop along the Nile River in Africa. | Mud brick is used in architecture; post-and-lintel architectural construction methods evolve. Cuneiform writing develops. First earthworks projects begin on Salisbury Plain in England (remade with stone in 1800). |
| **ANCIENT EGYPTIAN PERIOD** | | |
| 3000–2000 BCE | King Narmer unifies Upper and Lower Egypt. Old Kingdom begins, 2800. | Great Pyramids at Giza are completed, c. 2500. Evidence of elaborate furniture designed with animal legs, paw feet, gilding, and inlay is seen. |
| 2000–1000 BCE | Middle and New Kingdoms thrive. Pharaoh Tutankhamen reigns, 1333. Moses leads Israelites out of Egypt, 1250. | Temples, palaces are built using post-and-lintel construction methods. Temple at Luxor is built, c. 1417–1397. |
| 1000–500 BCE | Ethiopian kings rule Egypt. | |
| **ANCIENT AEGEAN PERIOD** | | |
| 3000–2000 BCE | Early Minoans settle on the island of Crete. | Evidence of basic furniture items such as stools, tables, chests is seen. Cycladic Idols appear, 2500. Palace of Knossos is built with indoor plumbing, c. 2500–1400. |
| 2000–1000 BCE | Middle and Late Minoan civilization begins. Mycenaean culture occupies mainland Greece, 1300. King Agamemnon defeats Trojans, 1200. | Linear A and Linear B script is in use, 1500. Lion Gate is created at Mycenae, 1300. Citadels flourish until 1200 BCE; beehive tombs; cyclopean architecture, keystone arch. |

| Period | Significant People or Events | Creative Accomplishments |
|---|---|---|
| **ANCIENT GREECE** | | |
| **2000–1000 BCE** | Dorians invade Greece, 1200. | |
| **1000–500 BCE** | Archaic period begins. | Stone replaces wood as architectural material. |
| | | Doric, Ionic, Corinthian orders of architecture. |
| | | Literature of Homer, *The Iliad* and *The Odyssey*, 850–800. |
| | | First Olympic games held in Olympia, 776. |
| **500 BCE–0** | Classical period begins. | Acropolis buildings are built, 447. |
| | Persian Wars are fought, 497–479. | Furniture is designed with graceful proportions; saber legs, metal, marble. |
| | Pericles rules, 460. | |
| | Socrates condemned to death for his philosophical teachings, 399. | |
| | Hellenistic period begins under rule of Alexander the Great, 332. | Plato publishes his philosophies in *Republic*, 360. |
| | | Aristotle writes *The Athenian Constitution*, 350. |
| | Alexander the Great conquers Egypt and Persia. | |
| | Greece becomes a Roman province, 146. | Sculpture *Nike of Samothrace*, c. 190. |
| **ANCIENT ROME** | | |
| **1500–500 BCE** | Etruscans move into Italy. | Trabeated architecture develops further with design of Etruscan temples. |
| | Mythical Romulus and Remus found Rome, 753. | |
| | Roman Republic is established, 510. | |
| **500–0 BCE** | Julius Caesar is assassinated; Octavius (Augustus) establishes Roman Imperial period, 44. | Construction begins on Colosseum in Rome, 70. |
| | | Furniture incorporates disc turning, massive proportions. |
| | | Virgil writes *The Aeneid*, 29. |
| | | Vitruvius completes his *Treatises on Architecture*. |
| **0–500 CE** | Jesus is crucified, 30. | Tuscan and Composite orders of architecture appear. |
| | Christians are persecuted; Emperor Trajan reigns, 98–117; Emperor Hadrian reigns, 117–138. | Concrete, arches, and dome are developed; Pont du Gard Aqueduct is built, c. 1st century. |
| | | Mount Vesuvius erupts, 79. |
| | | Construction begins on the Pantheon in Rome, 118. |
| | Late Imperial period begins, 235. | |
| | Diocletian divides Empire, 285. | |
| | Constantine legalizes Christianity through Edict of Milan, 313. | |
| | Seat of Roman Empire is moved to ancient site of Byzantium in Turkey; city is renamed Constantinople, 330. | Construction begins on the first St. Peter's Basilica in Rome, c. 333. |
| | Sack of Rome occurs, 410. | |
| | Roman Empire ends in the West, 476. | |
| **THE MIDDLE AGES** | | |
| **500–1000 CE** | Emperor Justinian rules the Eastern Roman Empire, 527–548. | Hagia Sophia, Istanbul, is constructed, c. 532–537. |
| | Prophet Muhammad dies, 622. | Islamic religion spreads throughout region. |
| | The Moors invade Spain, 711. | Illustrated Manuscript of the New Testament, the *Gospels of St. Augustine*, is completed, c. 597. |
| | Papal States are formed by the Holy Roman Empire, 756. | |

| Period | Significant People or Events | Creative Accomplishments |
|---|---|---|
| | Charlemagne, King of the Franks, is crowned Holy Roman Emperor of the West by Pope Leo III, 800. | Basilican church building thrives, Palatine Chapel, Aachen Germany, 792–805. |
| | The Franks develop the feudal system, establishing hierarchy of kings, barons, noblemen, and serfs (peasants), 800. | |
| | Egbert, King of Wessex, is the first king to rule all of England, 828. | |
| 1000–1400 CE | Leif Erickson explores the North American Continents, 1002. | Walled-towns are built throughout Europe. |
| | The Crusades take place, 1096–1204. | The crafts guilds are established; the Romanesque style develops, 1000. |
| | | St. Sernin Cathedral is constructed, Toulouse, France, 1080. |
| | | Gothic style of architecture first appears in France, 1150. |
| | Cambridge University is established, 1209. | Notre Dame Cathedral in Paris is completed, 1285. |
| | Marco Polo leaves for China, 1271. | Giotto begins painting the Arena Chapel in Padua, Italy, 1303. |
| | The Black Death plague sweeps Europe claiming 25 million lives, 1328–1351. | Dante writes *Divine Comedy*, 1306. |
| | | Chaucer writes *Canterbury Tales, 1387.* |
| | | Furniture incorporates oak, tracery, wrought iron hinges, trefoil, quatrefoil, linenfold panels, pointed arches, bracket feet. |

| Period | Significant People or Events | Creative Accomplishments |
|---|---|---|
| 1400–1500 | Plague breaks out in Europe, 1400. | Roman architect Vitruvius's architectural treatise, *De Archtitectura,* is rediscovered and published in 1414. |
| | Cosimo de Medici rules Florence, 1434. | Van Eyck paints *The Arnolfini Wedding*, 1434. |
| | The Byzantine Empire is over thrown by the Turks, 1453. | Brunelleschi completes dome on the cathedral in Florence, 1436. |
| | Ottoman Empire begins. | Gutenberg perfects the printing press using moveable type, 1454. |
| | Astronomer Copernicus reveals theory that planets orbit the sun, 1473. | Botticelli paints the *Birth of Venus*, 1485. |
| | Christopher Columbus explores the West Indies, 1492. | Durer begins woodcut series for *The Apocalypse*, 1496. |
| | | Leonardo da Vinci paints *The Last Supper, 1498.* |
| 1500–1600 | King Henry VIII rules England, 1509–1547. | Hampton Court Palace is constructed, 1514. |
| | | English renaissance Tudor style furniture incorporates oak, strong Gothic influences, Tudor arch, Romayne work. |
| | Copernicus writes his treatise on the solar system, *Commentariolus*, 1512. | Michelangelo sculpts *David,* 1504. |
| | Lorenzo de Medici becomes Pope Leo X, 1513. | Hellenistic sculpture of the *Laocoon* is discovered and brought to Rome, 1506. |
| | | Italian renaissance furniture incorporates walnut, heavy carving, pietra dura, intarsia, classical motifs based on Roman design. |
| | King François I rules France, 1515–1547. | French renaissance furniture in the Francois I style incorporates oak, strong Gothic influences, diamond point patterns, bun feet, limited classical detailing. |
| | Portuguese explorer Magellan sails to the Pacific Ocean from Spain, 1519–1520. | Martin Luther writes his *95 Theses*, launching the Counter-Reformation, 1517. |
| | | Michelangelo begins designs for the dome on the new St. Peter's basilica in Rome, 1546. |

| Period | Significant People or Events | Creative Accomplishments |
|---|---|---|
| | King Henry II rules France, 1547–1559 and marries Catherine de'Medici of Italy. | French renaissance furniture in the Henry II style incorporates oak and walnut, heavy carving depicting classical motifs brought to France by Italian craftsmen, and Burgundian influences. |
| | | Lavinia Fontana, first woman to paint publically commissioned art, is born, 1552. |
| | King Philip II rules Spain, 1556–1598. | Spanish renaissance furniture incorporates decorative wrought iron work, geometric designs based on Mudéjar influences, enlarged nail heads, decorative front stretchers, and crest rail. |
| | Queen Elizabeth rules England, 1558–1603. | William Shakespeare writes *Romeo and Juliet*, 1594. |
| | | English renaissance Elizabethan style furniture incorporates oak and walnut, carving, bulbous forms including cup and cover turning, intarsia, limited classical details. |
| 1600–1700 | British East India Trading Company is established, 1601. King James I rules England, 1603–1625. | Caravaggio paints *Conversion of St. Paul*, 1601. |
| | | English renaissance Early Jacobean style furniture maintains oak and walnut woods, bead turning, baluster forms, and limited classical details. |
| | | Miguel De Cervantes writes *Don Quixote*, 1605. |
| | | Sir Francis Bacon writes *The Advancement of Learning*, introducing theory of inductive reasoning, 1605. |
| | | Jamestown, Virginia, is established as first British Colony in North America, 1607. |
| | | Second British colony is established in North America, Plymouth, Massachusetts, 1620. |
| | King Louis XIII rules France, 1610–1643. | Rembrandt paints *The Night Watch*, 1642. |
| | | French Baroque furniture in the Louis XIII or Louis Treize style incorporates walnut, Burgundian-influenced heavy carving, bead and baluster turning, stretchers, Flemish S and C scrolls, transitional style. |
| | King Charles I rules England, 1625–1649. | |
| | Giovanni Branca invents the steam turbine, 1629. | |
| | Commonwealth governs England under the leadership of Oliver Cromwell, 1649–1660. | Bernini begins the colonnade at St. Peter's in Rome, 1656. |
| | King Charles II rules England, 1660–1685. | Vermeer paints *Girl with a Pearl Earring*, 1665. |
| | King James II rules England, 1685–1689. | English Baroque furniture in the Late Jacobean style incorporates walnut and some oak, heavy carving, cane back and seat, barley sugar twist turning, Flemish S and C scrolls. |
| | | Great Fire razes parts of London, 1666. |
| | | Milton writes *Paradise Lost*, 1667. |
| | | Sir Christopher Wren begins St. Paul's Cathedral, 1675. |
| | King Louis XIV rules France, 1643–1715. | Construction begins on the Palace of Versailles, 1669. |
| | Sir Isaac Newton introduces new theories on gravity, 1687. | French Baroque furniture in the Louis XIV or Louis Quatorze style incorporates walnut and some oak, heavy carving, gilt furniture, saltire stretchers, square pedestal legs, tall rectangular-backed chairs, ormolu, Boulle work, classical motifs. |
| | | Pachelbel composes *Canon in D*, 1680. |
| | William and Mary rule England, 1689–1702. | English Baroque furniture in the William & Mary styles incorporates walnut, strong Dutch influences, extensive veneering, oystering, seaweed marquetry, burl walnut, bell or inverted cup turning, trumpet turning, japanning, chinoiserie, Spanish or paintbrush foot, baluster forms. |
| | Witchcraft trials begin in Salem, Massachusetts, 1692. | |

| Period | Significant People or Events | Creative Accomplishments |
|---|---|---|
| | American Colonies are established under British law. | American furniture in the Early Colonial style incorporates local woods (oak, pine, maple), utility furniture, puritan economy; resembles English Jacobean, William and Mary styles, 1640–1720. |
| 1700–1800 | Queen Anne rules England and Scotland, united as Great Britain, 1702–1714.<br><br>Atmospheric steam engine is patented by Thomas Newcomen, 1712. | English Rococo furniture in the Queen Anne style incorporates walnut; spoon-back chair with vase or fiddle splat; cabriole legs; pad, club, or claw and ball feet; delicate proportions; bracket feet on case furniture, bonnet top; cockle shell motif. |
| | King George I rules Great Britain and Ireland, 1714–1727. | English Rococo furniture in the Early Georgian style incorporates mahogany and walnut, heavy proportions, heavy carving, cabriole legs with carved bracketed knees, hairy paw feet, and designs of William Kent.<br><br>Construction begins on Chiswick House, 1725. |
| | Regent Philippe d' Orleans rules France, 1715–1722. | French Rococo furniture in the Regénce style incorporates tall rectangular back chairs, cabriole legs, saltire stretchers, classical and foliate motifs; transitional style has both Louis Quatorze and emerging Louis Quinze characteristics. |
| | King Louis XV rules France, 1722–1774. | French Rococo furniture in the Louis XV or Louis Quinze style incorporates mahogany, walnut, ebony; chairs have shorter backs in cartouche shape; more curves including bombé, serpentine; cabriole legs with scroll feet, no stretchers; anticlassical motifs; oriental influences, chinoiserie, gilt furniture, ormolu. |
| | King George II rules England, 1727–1760.<br>John Key invents the flying shuttle, improving speed in textile production, 1733.<br>Excavations begin at Herculaneum, 1738.<br>Anders Celsius develops thermometer scale, 1741.<br>Benjamin Franklin discovers the properties of electricity, 1752. | Vivaldi composes *Four Seasons*, 1725.<br>Jonathan Swift writes *Gulliver's Travels*, 1726.<br>Handel performs the *Messiah*, 1742.<br>William Hogarth paints *Marriage à la Mode*, 1743.<br>John Cleland writes *Fanny Hill*, an erotic epic banned by the King of England, 1748.<br>Diderot publishes his *Encyclopedie* in France, 1751.<br>Elisabeth Vigée-LeBrun, royal painter to Marie Antoinette, is born, 1755. |
| | King George III rules Great Britain and Ireland, 1760–1820.<br>Industrial Revolution begins, launching mechanization and mass production, 1760.<br>Mechanization of textile industry begins, 1764. | Voltaire writes *Candide*, 1759.<br>Fragonard paints *The Swing*, 1767.<br>English Rococo Chippendale style furniture incorporates mahogany; French, Chinese, and Gothic influences; pierced carving, fretwork, tracery; cabriole legs with claw and ball feet; Marlborough legs.<br>English Early Neoclassic furniture designs are influenced by designers Adam, Hepplewhite, and Sheraton. Sheraton style furniture incorporates mahogany and satinwood; square-backed chairs with trellis, lattice work, urn splats; quadrangular front legs with spade or sabot feet; saber back legs; bell flower motif on legs.<br>Hepplewhite style furniture incorporates mahogany and rosewood; shield, oval, heart, wheel-shaped backs; quadrangular front legs with sabot or spade foot, saber back legs; classical motifs, wheat, urns, swags, Prince of Wales Plume; oval panels.<br>Gainsborough paints *The Blue Boy*, 1770. |

| Period | Significant People or Events | Creative Accomplishments |
|---|---|---|
| | King Louis XVI rules France, 1774–1792. | First bridge in iron is constructed, 1779. |
| | Reign of Terror in France begins under direction of Maximilien Robespierre, 1792–1795. | French Early Neoclassic Louis XVI or Louis Seize style furniture incorporates walnut, beechwood, mahogany, satinwood; classical motifs based upon Pompeii; geometrical designs, ovals, arcs, medallions, squares; reeded or fluted round tapered legs with thimble feet; painted finishes, ormolu, gilding. |
| | | David paints *The Death of Marat*, 1793. |
| | American Revolution occurs, 1775–1783. | American Late Colonial furniture incorporates walnut and mahogany; refined craftsmanship; resembles Queen Anne and Chippendale influences, 1720–1785. |
| | James Watt perfects the steam engine, 1775. | |
| | First crossing over the English Channel in air balloon is made, 1785. | Mozart composes *The Marriage of Figaro*, 1786. |
| | French Revolution occurs, 1789–1799. | |
| | Eli Whitney invents the cotton gin, 1793. | |
| | George Washington becomes the president of United States of America, 1789–1797. | American Federal style furniture incorporates mahogany, cherry, walnut, and maple; resembles styles of Hepplewhite and Sheraton, 1775–1783. |
| | Thomas Jefferson presides as president of the United States, 1801–1809. | |
| | | American Empire furniture style incorporates mahogany, painted beechwood; strong Greek and Roman influences using klismos forms, saber legs, rolled crest rails, saber front and back legs. Furniture designed by Duncan Phyfe includes lyre forms, cornucopias, and pedestal bases, 1815–1840. |
| | The First Republic of France is established, 1792–1804. | French Late Neoclassic Directoire style furniture incorporates mahogany, some painted beechwood; strong Greek and Roman influences using klismos forms, saber legs, rolled crest rails, saber front and back legs. |
| 1800–1900 | French Empire begins under Napoleon I, 1804–1814. | French Late Neoclassic furniture in the Empire style incorporates mahogany and rosewood; strong Roman influences with Greek and Egyptian motifs; saber back legs, term front legs with paw feet, rolled crest rails, ormolu ornamentation, limited carving. |
| | The United Kingdom is formed, 1801. | English Late Neoclassic Regency style furniture incorporates mahogany and rosewood; heavily proportioned furnishings with strong Greek, Roman, and Egyptian influences; some gilding, limited carving. |
| | Regent rules England, 1811–1820. | |
| | Riots erupt in England over mechanization of the textile industry, 1811. | |
| | United States and Britain become involved in War of 1812. | Jane Austen publishes *Sense and Sensibility*, 1811. |
| | First steam railroads operate in England, 1825. | Jean-Auguste Dominique Ingres paints *Grande Odalisque*, 1814. |
| | | John Nash begins renovation on the Royal Pavilion in Brighton, 1815. |
| | | Beethoven composes *Ninth Symphony,* 1824. |
| | Queen Victoria rules England, 1837–1901. | Furniture incorporates eclectic forms including Greek, Gothic, Renaissance, and Rococo revival. |
| | | Charles Dickens writes *A Christmas Carol,* 1843. |
| | | Charlotte Brontë publishes *Jane Eyre,* 1847. |

| Period | Significant People or Events | Creative Accomplishments |
|---|---|---|
| | Karl Marx writes *Communist Manifesto* with Friedrich Engels, 1848.<br>Great Exhibition opens in London at the Crystal Palace, 1851.<br>The principle of fiber optic technology is introduced, 1854.<br>First transatlantic cable is laid, 1858–1866.<br>United States Civil War is fought, 1861–1865. | Arts and Crafts style furniture is influenced by paintings of the Pre-Raphaelite Brotherhood and designs of William Morris.<br>Furniture incorporates oak, simplistic forms with rustic appearance, large brass hinges, limited inlay, 1860–1900.<br>Charles Darwin publishes *Origin of the Species,* 1859.<br>Victor Hugo writes *Les Misérables,* 1862.<br>Manet paints *Luncheon on the Grass,* 1863.<br>Lewis Carroll writes *Alice's Adventures in Wonderland,* 1865. |
| | Alexander Graham Bell invents first successful telephone, 1876.<br>First gasoline-powered automobile is introduced, 1888. | Dutch painter Vincent Van Gogh finishes *Starry Night,* 1889.<br>Thomas Edison patents motion picture camera, 1891.<br>Art Nouveau movement, 1895–1905.<br>Victor Horta completes Tassel House, 1895.<br>Art Nouveau furniture incorporates exotic woods, nature-inspired motifs.<br>H. G. Wells writes *War of the Worlds,* 1898. |
| 1900–1920 | World's Fair is held in Paris, 1900.<br>Orville and Wilbur Wright conduct the first controlled airplane flight, 1903.<br>Albert Einstein presents his *Theory of Relativity,* 1905.<br>First newsreels are shown in movie theaters in Paris, 1909.<br>Marie Curie wins Noble Prize for chemistry, 1911.<br>World War I begins 1914, ending in 1918.<br>First radio broadcast occurs, 1920. | Giacomo Puccini composes *Madame Butterfly, 1904.*<br>Matisse and other Fauve painters exhibit in Paris, 1905.<br>Frank Lloyd Wright's *Prairie Style* architecture is established, 1909.<br>Picasso paints *Les Demoiselles d'Avignon*, introducing Cubism, 1907.<br>First skyscraper is built in Manhattan; it rises 47 stories, 1908.<br>Robert Weine debuts his film *Cabinet of Dr. Caligari,* 1919.<br>De Stijl movement, 1917–1934, is influenced by Piet Mondrian's *Composition* series in red, blue, and yellow. De Stijl furniture incorporates geometric shapes.<br>Bauhaus and the International Style, 1919–1933, furniture introduces the use of tubular steel. |
| 1920–1940 | The first rocket is launched, 1926.<br>First television is introduced, 1927.<br>The Great Depression begins, 1929.<br>Hitler is appointed Chancellor of Germany, 1933. | Art Deco and Art Moderne, 1920–1940, furniture incorporates rates exotic inlays and woods.<br>Exposition des Arts Décoratifs is held in Paris, 1925.<br>F. Scott Fitzgerald publishes *The Great Gatsby,* 1925.<br>Empire State Building is completed as world's tallest building, 1931. |
| 1940–1960 | Ballpoint pens are introduced, 1944.<br>World War II begins 1939, ending in 1945.<br>Color television is introduced, 1951.<br>Video tape recorder is introduced, 1951.<br>Francis Crick and James Watson discover the "double helix" of DNA, 1953.<br>Russians launch the first satellite, *Sputnik,* into space, 1957. | Hemmingway writes *For Whom the Bell Tolls,* 1940.<br>Contemporary Design, 1945–1960, furniture incorporates laminated wood, fiberglass, and plastics.<br>Jackson Pollock initiates Action Painting, 1951.<br>John Cage composes *Music of Changes,* 1951.<br>J. D. Salinger writes *The Catcher in the Rye*, 1951. |

| Period | Significant People or Events | Creative Accomplishments |
|---|---|---|
| 1960–1980 | IBM introduces System 366 computer, 1964.<br>First ATM machine is introduced, 1968.<br>Man lands on the moon, 1969.<br>The first Boeing 747 crosses the Atlantic, 1970.<br>Greenpeace movement is established, 1971.<br>First video game, *Pong,* is introduced, 1972.<br>Barcode is invented, 1974.<br>Apple Computer is introduced, 1976.<br>Microsoft is formed, 1977. | Harper Lee writes *To Kill a Mockingbird*, 1960.<br>Pop, 1960–1975, Andy Warhol and the "Factory" produce commercialized art *Campbell's Soup Cans,* 1962. Furniture incorporates laminated wood, plastics, and motifs from popular culture.<br>Michael Crichton writes *The Andromeda Strain*, 1969.<br>Alvin Toffler writes *Future Shock,* 1970.<br>I. M. Peii designs the East Wing of the National Gallery of Art in Washington, DC, 1978.<br>Philip Johnson wins the first Pritzker Prize for his Glass House in New Canaan, Connecticut, 1979. |
| 1980–2000 | IBM introduces the world's first personal computer, 1981.<br>Space Shuttle Columbia is launched, 1981.<br>MTV is first televised, 1981.<br>Tim Berners-Lee creates the World Wide Web, 1989.<br>Pathfinder unmanned spacecraft lands on Mars, sends photographs back to Earth, 1997.<br>First Social Networking sites are created, 1997. | Postmodern, 1980–2000, Michael Graves's Portland Public Office Building, 1980; furniture incorporates full range of styles from traditional to modern with new interpretations.<br>Ettore Sottsass forms Memphis, 1981.<br>Alice Walker, author of *The Color Purple,* wins Pulitzer Prize, 1983. |
| 2000–2010 | iPod is introduced, 2001.<br>Hybrid automobiles are introduced, 2003.<br>YouTube is launched, 2005.<br>3-D Television is available, 2010. | Gehry Tower is completed, 2001.<br>Mitch Albom writes *Tuesdays with Morrie*, 2002.<br>Translucent concrete is invented, 2004.<br>Zaha Hadid is first female architect to win the Pritzker Prize for Architecture, 2004. |

# The Ancient World

## The Prehistoric Period

The life of early humans existing more than 35,000 years ago during the Stone Age predates recorded history, so little is known about their existence and culture. The Stone Age is categorized into three main periods: the Paleolithic, the Mesolithic, and the Neolithic. The distinction between one period and the next is determined by particular advancements toward a civilized or orderly existence. Scholars such as archeologists, art historians, and anthropologists have reconstructed the lives of our primitive ancestors through thorough analysis of the artifacts they left behind. During the Paleolithic period, early nomadic humans foraged for food and traveled on foot following migratory animals, the mainstay of their food supply. The Mesolithic period developed from around 9000 BCE and is marked by the establishment of transitional encampments and the beginning of social hierarchies within tribes.

Marking the beginning of the Neolithic period, tribes of people occupying Europe, Africa, and Asia began using metal tools to make life easier. As they began cultivating crops and raising animals, they established permanent settlements. Scholars studying Neolithic culture through architectural remains, *fresco* fragments, sculptures, and a wide range of household objects, reasoned that these early artifacts fulfilled both spiritual and practical purposes. Excavated burial sites filled with tools, *anthropomorphic pottery* jars, and small figurines (perhaps deities) suggest these people believed in an afterlife, burying their dead with the things they will need in the next life.

Artifacts from the Neolithic period show some highly ornate objects whereas others are quite simple in design and decoration. In studying the development of various artifacts throughout time, historians have concluded that during prehistoric times, those who owned functional objects of great artisanship and beauty had wealth, social standing, and a high level of sophistication or taste.

As more advanced civilizations evolved, individuals instinctively brought beauty into their daily existence. In fact, throughout history, humans have surrounded themselves with beautiful objects, announcing their wealth and status to others. Higher social standings led to the refinement of the decorative arts as each generation attempted to live a better lifestyle than the previous one.

# Prehistoric Architecture

Paleolithic huts dating back to 27,000 BCE, made from the bones of the woolly mammoth, reveal early humans' attempt at building a protective shelter. The design of these huts formed an almost domelike structure. Large bones were stacked one row on top of another in circular arrangements, with makeshift columns supporting a curved roof (Figure 1.1). The bones were then covered with grasses, hides, or mud to provide protection from weather. The hut could be dismantled and transported to the next encampment.

Portable shelters improved over time as tentlike structures appeared. Thin tree branches stripped bare of limbs and leaves were arranged in a broad circle and *splayed* toward the top, where they were tied together with either rope or animal tendon. The sloped branches and narrow apex stabilized the frame and became the structural support for a protective covering made of grasses or hides. These building materials were readily available, and it took the ingenuity of early humans to design a type of shelter that was sturdy and could be taken apart easily and carried with them on their hunt for food. The timber frames for these tents were lighter than carrying around a lot of woolly mammoth bones, which made them easier to transport from place to place.

The resourcefulness of Neolithic humans and their experimentation with the available materials surrounding them informed the designs of more permanent shelters. Grasses were woven, bundled, or braided together for roofs and wall coverings on huts, whereas bricks—made from mud mixed with straw and set in the sun to dry—provided structural building blocks. The process of stacking these bricks one on top of the other proved to be a relatively quick and easy method of construction (Figure 1.2). Mud bricks were built in several *courses*, and openings for doors and windows were reinforced by placing logs overhead as a structural *beam*. Lightweight thatch was used for covering the roof. Mud brick houses proved to be permanent structures best suited in those areas where the weather was dry.

In climates where rainfall came with the spring and summer seasons, stone proved to be a more suitable and long-lasting building material. Stone, quarried in close proximity to the settlements, was cut into uniform blocks and set in courses, one on top of the other, without the use of a *mortar* bond. The mere weight and size of each stone kept them in place and made the walls strong. A thatched roof

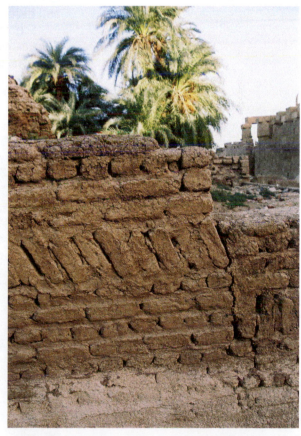

**FIGURE 1.1** A drawing of a Paleolithic bone hut shows how animal bones were arranged to create a supporting structure for a hide covering to offer shelter to its inhabitants. © Ray Grinaway, Dorling Kindersley.

**FIGURE 1.2** The remnants of a mud brick wall still stand in Egypt as a testament to its strength and durability as a building material in hot, dry climates. Reprinted with permission. © Treena Crochet.

**FIGURE 1.3** Prehistoric houses in the village of Breuil, France, feature stone walls and a thatched roof. © Anyka/Shutterstock.

with small openings allowed for smoke from the hearth to escape from the interior (Figure 1.3).

Jericho, located in the Jordan River Valley, is the oldest settlement discovered thus far, dating from around 8000 to 7000 BCE during the Mesolithic period. The layout of the town is haphazard, lacking any attempts at organizing roads and houses. At Jericho, little survives to tell the story of its ancient culture. Only remnants of the original stone foundations and mud brick houses remain, with little else besides some traces of *plaster* covering floors and walls. No *pottery shards* were found in Jericho, or any other forms of household furnishings other than grinding stones for grain, and stone bowls. Because this settlement predates recorded history, only these few artifacts recovered from excavations inform scholars how members of this ancient culture might have lived their daily lives.

The best example of a somewhat preserved Neolithic settlement was found in Catal Huyuk located in present-day Turkey (Figure 1.4). The town of Catal Huyuk dates back to 7000 to 6500 BCE. By farming the land and keeping livestock, ancient Anatolians put down their roots and developed a town structure with row houses built side by side and back to back. The one-story homes were supported by wooden *posts* and beams, and walls were filled with mud brick covered with plaster. The houses had high windows and featured flat roofs with openings for access into the dwelling.

Artifacts unearthed during excavations at Catal Huyuk indicate that the residents of this town made useful objects for themselves and decorated their homes with bright and colorful wall paintings. Those living at Catal Huyuk created drawings and paintings depicting animals and humans. In addition, landscape paintings decorating the walls of their homes and fragments of patterned *textiles*, woven mats, and decorated pottery were found there.

Scholars agree that the artifacts found at Catal Huyuk served practical functions as well as aesthetic ones. Most of the artifacts discovered at this site fulfilled domestic purposes, yet their decorations were coordinated with those used in the

**FIGURE 1.4** The archeological site at Catal Huyuk reveals foundations and lower walls of what was once housing for Neolithic Anatolians. Visible in the center of this picture, an excavated room features a raised platform at one end, with recesses where wooden columns once stood. Arlette Mellaart © Dorling Kindersley.

interiors. Remarkably, textile fragments had traces of geometric patterns corresponding to painted wall designs. In addition, woven floor mats and baskets, pottery, and wooden and stone boxes feature geometric designs, a testament to the creation of an item not just for human comfort, but with a deliberate consideration of aesthetics.

Who knows for sure why the potter began to decorate the surface of the clay or why landscapes were painted on the interior walls of houses? However, from these ancient prehistoric settlements, arise the humble beginnings of the decorative arts. How each culture coordinated design elements within the built environment resulted in unique stylizations of furniture, textiles, architecture, and art. These elements help us distinguish one cultural period from another and gain insight into our own sense of aesthetic purpose.

**FIGURE 1.5** This copy of a small sculpture believed to represent a fertility goddess, as evidenced by her swollen breasts and protruding belly, was taken from excavations at Catal Huyuk. The woman is seated on a chair flanked by lions. The lion, which appears in the furniture design of the Egyptians, Greeks, and Romans, is a symbol of power.
Arlette Mellaart © Dorling Kindersley.

# Prehistoric Furniture

It is not known when the first humans sat on a rock to rest their tired bodies. Whenever it occurred, it must have been an improvement over sitting on the ground, because this unrecorded event eventually led to the evolution of furniture design and construction. Furniture items were found in Catal Huyuk, although scholars are not sure whether these items are the earliest examples. Excavations of houses revealed built-in reclining couches—beds made from plaster attached to the walls on three sides of the room. Presumably, these couches were used for lounging or sleeping, yet human skeletal remains were found buried below them. This discovery is perplexing and suggests that the couches may also have functioned as family burial shrines, supporting the notion that they believed in an afterlife.

Along with these couches, evidence of other types of furniture were also found at Catal Huyuk. Small clay statues recovered from grain bins depict female figures, possibly fertility goddesses, seated on stools or in chairs (Figure 1.5). Although primitive in artistic technique, these sculptures clearly show another form of seating furniture used by this Neolithic culture. The findings at Catal Huyuk, along with similar sculptures discovered across Europe dating from the fifth and fourth millennia, establish a precedent for furniture design and document the advances made by Neolithic cultures.

# Prehistoric Accessories

## VESSELS AND CONTAINERS

The need to collect and store water, grains, and other foods led to the development of a variety of vessels and containers, almost all of which—discovered to date—feature a swelling or *bulbous form*. Early storage vessels were made from woven reeds in the form of baskets or hollowed-out gourds. The gourd, with its rounded shape and tapering end, provided the perfect design for storing and pouring liquids.

Containers made from hollowed-out logs, and stone carved into variety of shapes proved more durable and long-lasting than the more fragile gourds. Well after they discovered pottery making, Neolithic people continued to use wood and stone vessels for food storage, preparation, and serving. Wooden examples are scarce because of the natural decomposition of their organic material, but bowls and jars made from stone have been found in several excavated sites throughout Europe, Asia, and the Americas.

Pottery containing food, grains, and wine were imported and exported freely among neighboring cultures in Late Neolithic society, and drove economic growth in regions between Mesopotamia and Egypt. Scholars are unsure of how the process of pottery making evolved, although *ceramic* bowls, cups, jars, and vases have been unearthed from several prehistoric cities throughout the world. Typically in Neolithic culture, women reared the children, and their roles naturally catered to domestic responsibilities, including making household objects. Scholars agree that pottery making was probably first performed by women in efforts to make their domestic lives easier and more productive.

Although some of the earliest pottery dating back to 6900 to 6800 BCE lacks any kind of surface decoration, pottery shards discovered dating to around 6000 BCE show simple geometric designs. Early potters used clay-rich soil that they shaped by hand into pots using a coiling method, or by pressing wet clay into a mold. Many of the examples excavated so far show embossed patterns, indicating that the wet clay was pressed into a woven basket that acted as a mold. Making pots using the coiling method was time-consuming. Clay was rolled into long, ropelike coils and then concentrically wrapped one row on top of the other while the vessel was slowly turned. Variations in the diameter of these concentric bands gave the pot its shape. The surface was then smoothed to mesh the coils together, and then covered with a fine *slip*, a creamy mixture of clay and water. The piece was then fired at high temperatures to make the clay stronger and virtually watertight once cooled. More than likely, the first clay vessels were laid in the sun to dry and harden in the same manner as sun-dried bricks were made for building houses. During the Late Neolithic period in Egypt, tomb paintings show pottery baking in a large *kiln*.

Painted decorations were applied to the surface of the clay with a brush, using a slip mixed with natural minerals added for coloring. Once fired, these minerals changed into brilliant colors (Figure 1.6). Other methods of ornamentation seen on various examples found in Mesopotamia, Africa, and the Mediterranean include both *incised* and *relief* designs. Incised designs were created while the clay was still wet. A sharp tool was used to draw designs into the surface of the clay before firing. For relief work, separately formed designs from wet clay were applied to the pot using a slip to bond the ornament to the surface of the pot.

The shapes and sizes of pottery produced during the Neolithic period were determined by their function. For storage of liquids, the vessels had a base with a handle for gripping, and a long neck or spigot for easy pouring. A drinking cup had two handles and a broad, basinlike bowl that was supported on a footed base to keep the cup from tipping over. Wide-mouth jars had tight-fitting lids to store grains, and many bowls and saucers have been found.

Other domestic vessels discovered from Neolithic sites include lamps. Made from either hollowed-out stone or pottery, the lamps were shaped into bowls and filled with oil or animal fat. The oil or fat supplied fuel to a wick made from twisted grass or reed, which absorbed the oil and kept the lamp alight. These early lamps were small enough to be carried from place to place, and were used both inside and outside the home. From this simple bowl-type shape, more practical designs developed, such as those with folded edges to keep the oil from spilling. Others were molded with narrow spouts or funnels to keep the wick in place, and still others were designed with carrying handles (Figure 1.7).

## WEAVING AND TEXTILES

Textiles used during the Paleolithic period consisted of animal skins laid on the floors for warmth. With the discovery of ivory or bone needles threaded with stripped animal tendons, these skins were sewn together to make the earliest form of clothing. Textile weaving developed much later during the early Neolithic period, although the process of weaving is thought to date back to the Stone Age. Weaving

**FIGURE 1.6 This piece of domestic pottery features two handles, and decorative designs painted on its surface.** © Judith Miller/Dorling Kindersley/R & G McPherson Antiques.

**FIGURE 1.7 This ancient ceramic lamp features a wide bowl for holding oil and a formed spout for securing a twisted fiber wick.** Dave King. © Dorling Kindersley, Courtesy of The Science Museum, London.

Two ceramic pots separated by 4,000 years of history share common design features. Both vessels have short, rounded bodies, yet their decorations are vastly different. The first pot, decorated with red and black coloring, dates from 2700 to 2200 BCE. Its mottled coloration results from a chemical reaction during the firing process (Figure 1.8).

Although the basic function and shape of pots have not changed much over time, the English teapot from the 18th century is meticulously decorated with polychrome floral designs accented in gold (Figure 1.9). As trade routes opened between Europe and China during the 18th century, drinking tea from the Orient became a fashionable pastime for well-to-do Europeans. The decorations featured on the English teapot reflect the wealth and sophisticated taste of its owner, which was meant to impress guests invited for tea. The social aspects of drinking tea led to the design of the tilt-top table during the 18th century.

**FIGURE 1.8** This early Bronze Age red and black mottled pottery vessel dating from approximately 2700 to 2200 BCE has the characteristics of a modern teapot. © Judith Miller/Dorling Kindersley/Helios Gallery.

**FIGURE 1.9** This Worcester ware teapot from the 18th century features polychrome decorations with gilt accents. © Judith Miller/Dorling Kindersley/Albert Amor.

is seen in a variety of items, including hair braiding, fishing nets, and rope. Small sculptures of female figures dating from the Paleolithic period are shown with tightly braided hair. Rope was made by twisting fibers together for strength, and fishing nets were made from interlaced plant stems. Moreover, the roofs of houses during this period were made by interlacing *thatch*, reeds, or palm fronds to protect against the weather.

The technique of overlapping fibers may have started with hair braiding or the fishing net, but basket weaving became a prolific craft in Neolithic cultures. Baskets made from the over-and-under technique of interlacing reeds and grasses gave someone the idea to take these *cellulosic* fibers and spin them into yarns for producing textiles. Evidence of flax (linen) and wool yarns in textile fragments has been found in several Neolithic sites in central Europe, the Middle East, and China. Excavations at Catal Huyuk also provided scholars with textile clothing fragments believed to date back to 5800 BCE, and sections of woven grasses that were used as floor mats (Figure 1.10). Eventually, the process of weaving became more productive around 5000 BCE with the introduction of the loom. The earliest looms were no more than a rope stretched between two trees with strings hanging down (called the *warp*) with a string woven horizontally (called the *weft*) in an over-and-under pattern. At this time, cloth was not used as an upholstery fabric on furniture, although it could have been used for cushions.

**FIGURE 1.10** This fragment of speckled black cloth found during excavations at Catal Huyuk was woven from woolen yarns. Arlette Mellaart © Dorling Kindersley.

# Ancient Egypt

As early as 4000 BCE, advanced settlements developed in the areas of Mesopotamia and Egypt. The ancient Sumerians and Egyptians are two of the most fascinating Neolithic cultures to have lived in these regions. Although there are ancient *cuneiform* writings documenting Sumerian culture, more artifacts have been found intact from the Egyptian period, preserved by the Egyptian's elaborate burial practices.

In 3000 BCE, King Narmer of Upper Egypt defeated the ruler of Lower Egypt and established the first political dynasty to rule one unified country. This cohesive government with strong military power positioned Egypt as one of the greatest nations bordering the Mediterranean. The Nile River offered fertile land for agriculture, promoting a thriving economy, and many Egyptians prospered throughout Egypt's lengthy history of 30 dynasties with such notorious rulers as Ramses I, Tutankhamun, and Cleopatra.

Generally divided into three distinct cultural periods, the Old, Middle, and New Kingdoms of Egypt reflect a unique stylization of art, architecture, and decoration distinct from their Mesopotamian neighbors. During this time, large-scale building projects took place, many of which survive to this day. The Great Pyramids near Giza, Queen Hatshepsut's Temple outside of Luxor, and the numerous burial tombs in the Valley of the Kings and Queens are only a few examples of the large architectural projects by the ancient Egyptians. Excavations at these and other sites have yielded thousands of artifacts that reveal how the ancient Egyptians once lived.

The accomplishments of ancient Egyptian craftsmen and -women influenced and inspired architects and designers throughout history. Napoleon's campaigns into Egypt during the late 18th century contributed to the revival of Egyptian–based design *motifs* and characteristics seen in interior design of the period. More recently, early 20th-century designers incorporated Egyptian design motifs into the Art Deco style prevalent during the 1920s and 1930s after the discovery in 1922 of King Tutankhamun's tomb, still full of ancient antiquities preserved after thousands of years.

# Egyptian Architecture

The types of structures built during the Old, Middle, and New Kingdoms included burial tombs, temples and monuments, palaces for the pharaohs, villas for the wealthy, and mud brick houses for skilled laborers and townspeople. Ziggurat-shaped architectural design concepts borrowed from the Sumerians inspired Egyptian builders to create distinctive pyramidal burial tombs during the Old Kingdom. Egyptian burial practices ensured that their cultural history would not be forgotten; the Great Pyramids on the outskirts of Giza are a testament to the immortality of Old Kingdom pharaohs (Figure 1.11).

The builders of the Great pyramids at Giza combined the forces of workers and leverage to position 2.5-ton blocks, one on top of the other, to form the structures. More than two million limestone blocks comprise the largest of the pyramids—the Great Pyramid of Khufu—which was constructed around 2600 BCE and reaches more than 450 feet into the air. Rock was quarried and transported to the construction site from miles away. The blocks were shipped on barges down the Nile River during flood season, when water levels were high, then were brought to the Giza plain on rope-pulled sleds. When onsite, the blocks were cut to precise measurements. Workers then used a series of ramps and ropes to pull the blocks into position, forming each new coursing.

**FIGURE 1.11** The Great Pyramids at Giza, built between 2570 BC and 2500 BC, are monumental examples of burial tombs from the Old Kingdom in Egypt. All three pyramids were covered with limestone after construction was completed, which gave the sides a smooth surface and reflected the intensity of the setting sun. The larger pyramid belonging to Cheops still has traces of the limestone. © Treena M. Crochet.

The afterlife was an important component of Egyptian culture because they devoted themselves to preparing for the afterlife where the spirit, or *ka*, would live for all eternity. Elaborate tombs for royalty and the nobility were also a symbol of status. Walls inside burial tombs were plastered and painted with scenes of Egyptian life, both carnal and spiritual. Lavishly decorated scenes narrate the life of the deceased and include images of their rites of passage into the afterlife. Along with wall paintings, jars of food and wine, furniture, perfumes, jewelry, clothing, and sometimes boats and chariots were placed in the tomb for enjoyment in the next world.

Vast architectural complexes used for religious practices and funerary purposes were built during the Middle and New Kingdoms. Constructed to honor the gods and having to stand for all eternity, temples were built of limestone, sandstone, and granite. The temples were adorned with artwork that reflects important gods and goddesses, and the accomplishments of the pharoah. These scenes were painted in bright colors, and the temples featured elaborate designs on floors and ceilings.

New Kingdom Egyptian temples like those in Karnak, built from 1408 to 1300 BCE, were designed as trabeated structural systems consisting of columns and lintels. A series of columns arranged in close proximity to the main *hypostyle hall* were 75 feet high and had diameters of 6.5 feet. Perimeter columns and the inner columns of the hypostyle hall were massive, supporting the weight of a sandstone roof; however, their robust diameters significantly reduced the amount of usable interior space (Figure 1.12). The massive stone columns were made of individual cut stone *drums*, which were designed with interlocking joints. A large hoisting device similar to a pulley system was used to lift the drums, placing one on top of the other to create the column (Figure 1.12). Interlocking joints between each drum stabilized the columns.

**FIGURE 1.12** This drawing shows how a large mechanical hoisting device was used to lift each section of a column into place during the building of the Temple at Karnak. Reprinted with permission from Pearson Education.

The oversized columns of the hypostyle hall supporting the temple roofs were inscribed with *hieroglyphics* painted in bold color so that the text could be easily read and interpreted. Many of these ancient temples still exist, preserved by the hot, arid climate of Egypt and offer clues to the past with their informative hieroglyphics and colossal statues adorning them. Hieroglyphics were undecipherable until the discovery of the Rosetta Stone in 1799. This stone tablet had both Greek and Egyptian hieroglyphs which allowed scholars to break the code. Since the breaking of the code, archaeologists are able to read these ancient symbols and gain greater insight into ancient Egyptian culture.

Sophisticated town planning created a clear distinction between rank and social class by providing housing in separate sectors of the city. Within the main sector of town, merchant classes occupied single-story row houses arranged back to back and in close quarters. By the New Kingdom, these dwellings rose to a height of two or three stories. The layout of each house followed a similar plan; the living area was located near the entrance, with a kitchen and open-air courtyard to the rear. A staircase accessed the second level, which led to the bedrooms, whereas the third level, or rooftop, served as a terrace or place for storing grains.

For privacy, windows on the street side were shielded with palms or protected with plaster *tracery* or wooden shutters. Made from sun-dried mud bricks, all that remain of these types of dwellings are their foundations, with

**FIGURE 1.13** This drawing of a reconstructed street scene depicts typical multistoried housing for middle class Egyptians living during the New Kingdom. © David Vleck.

**FIGURE 1.14** An ancient Egyptian house is shown in this cross-section diagram. Notice the functions of separate rooms and use of the roof by servants.
Sergio © Dorling Kindersley.

some wall and floor fragments. Painstaking reconstruction of these fragments shows that the façades were brightly painted, with the door and window openings in contrasting colors (Figure 1.13).

Palaces and villas proved to be much more luxurious than row houses, and they varied in size depending on the wealth and social status of their owners. Most Egyptian palaces were located near the religious temples and housed pharaohs whereas wealthy priests and noblemen lived in large compounds. These compound estates had gardens, granaries, and outbuildings that allowed their residents to be self-sufficient. Built of fired brick, remnants of palaces and villas have been excavated, although none has survived completely intact. Foundation, wall, and ceiling fragments unearthed from sites in Amarna and Thebes date back to the New Kingdom, and, after thorough analysis of wall and foundation fragments, archeologists and art historians were able to reproduce these ancient structures in drawings or models (Figure 1.14).

Excavated fragments show that plaster was commonly used to cover the floors and interior walls, and many examples show traces of decorative painting. The geometric patterns used around window and door openings were often accented with design motifs modeled after plant and animal forms. Along with these paintings, household inventories—maintained by scribes in hieroglyphic-filled texts listing the interior furnishings and possessions—provide valuable references for researchers.

Worker housing was built from sun-dried mud bricks. All that remain of these types of dwellings are their foundations, with some wall and floor fragments. These houses were furnished with the essentials for domestic life. The Egyptian working class was considered important to society, as tomb paintings display colorful

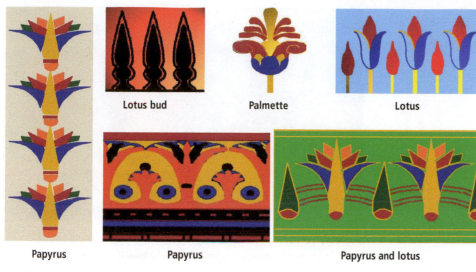

Rosettes

Guilloche

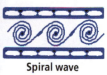
Rosettes and spiral wave   Guilloche and rosettes

Spiral wave

Rosettes and spiral wave

**FIGURE 1.15** Floral-based Egyptian design motifs feature lotus, papyrus, and palmettes. © David Vleck.

Lotus bud   Palmette   Lotus

Papyrus   Papyrus   Papyrus and lotus

scenes of workers at their tasks of making wine, fishing, herding cattle, and making pottery. These scenes prove that the Egyptian economy was dependent on a large workforce, and their images are immortalized within the tombs.

**FIGURE 1.16** Stylized designs were taken from the natural surroundings as seen in these motifs. © David Vleck.

# Egyptian Design Motifs

Design motifs adorning furniture, lamps, textiles, and the interiors of tombs and temples were inspired by surroundings of Egypt's life-blood: the Nile River. Lotus and *papyrus* blossoms, flowering roses, and the river's fluid waters were simplified into stylized renditions and used in decorations, with some motifs fulfilling symbolic purposes (Figure 1.15). For example, lotus and papyrus flowers are seen consistently throughout the Egyptian period, and these designs once symbolized Upper and Lower Egypt, respectively. Consequently, when the two regions were unified by King Narmer, the intertwining of the lotus and papyrus was frequently used to represent a united Egypt. Other floral motifs appearing in the artwork from ancient Egypt include palmettes and blossoming roses. Palmettes are stylizations of intertwining lotus and papyrus blossoms fashioned into the shape of palm trees.

Rosettes featured a simple flower designed with a contrasting center and radiating petals (Figure 1.16). The rosette motif was used repeatedly as border decorations on the walls, floors, and ceilings of tombs and temples, and appeared on the surfaces of decorative accessories. It is a design motif that also appears in ancient Mesopotamia, a connection made between cultures through economic trade. Motifs appearing on the walls and ceilings of temples and burial tombs were painted with bright colors to enhance their presence as seen from a distance (Figure 1.17).

Many motifs had symbolic meanings. Egyptian spirituality was based on a system of gods and goddesses who ruled over the earth and the heavens (Figure 1.18). The sun god Re was supreme, Anubis was the god of mummification, and Osiris ruled the underworld throughout eternity. These gods were represented as mythical figures. For example, the falcon or hawk is a symbol for the sky god Horus, who, along with the sphinx, protected the reigning pharaoh (Figure 1.19). Like the sphinx, the griffin symbolized protection and

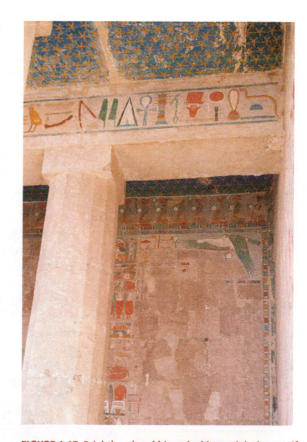

**FIGURE 1.17** Brightly colored hieroglyphics and design motifs decorate the entrance hall to a temple near Luxor. The barrel vaulted ceiling is painted with a dark blue background, with stylized gold stars representing the night sky ruled by the goddess Nut. Geometric patterns create border designs around wall panels. © Treena M. Crochet.

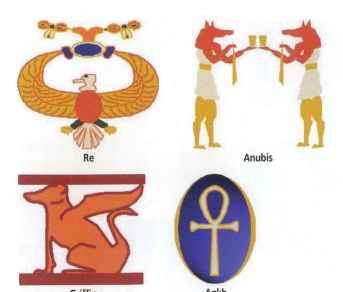

Re

Anubis

Griffin

Ankh

**FIGURE 1.18** Religious deities were believed to hold special powers. © David Vleck.

**FIGURE 1.19** The colossal figure of the sphinx (half man, half lion) stands guard in front of the Great Pyramids at Giza. © Treena M. Crochet.

appeared in artwork as a winged lion. The ankh symbolized eternal life; its design is an abstraction of the womb and birth canal.

Geometric designs were plentiful and were used extensively inside tombs and homes as border designs or loose abstractions of natural elements (Figure 1.20). The spiral wave was an abstraction of the swiftly moving water of the Nile, rendered as swirling spirals. The chevron motif featured rows of zigzags, indicating the movement of the Nile's forceful current, and it is the hieroglyph for water. The fret motif symbolized the cresting waves of the Mediterranean Sea running in succession to the shore. Artisans used checkerboard patterns and wide bands of alternating colors to fill in around landscape paintings and paintings of scenes of daily life inside tombs (Figure 1.21). Often, various motifs were combined and repeated to create ornate patterning for walls, floors, and ceilings.

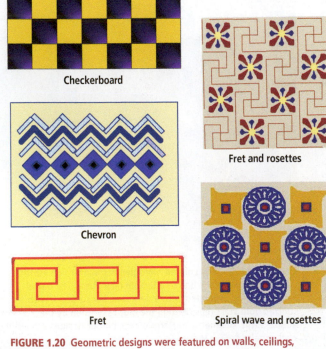

Checkerboard

Chevron

Fret

Fret and rosettes

Spiral wave and rosettes

**FIGURE 1.20** Geometric designs were featured on walls, ceilings, and floors. © David Vleck.

**FIGURE 1.21** The interior of this Egyptian tomb shows ornately decorated walls with an array of design motifs. © airphoto.gr/Shutterstock.

# Egyptian Furniture

During ancient times, there was not an abundance of furniture items, and most Egyptians, from both the lower and upper classes, had only basic pieces. Stools, chairs, chests, and tables were used the most, and the artisanship varied depending on the owner's wealth. Most of the furniture was constructed out of wood, but sycamore and palm were also available locally and used by Egyptian furniture makers. At great expense to the owner, finer woods were often imported, like ebony from Nubia and cedar from Lebanon.

In most cases, household furnishings used by the residents of the row houses were minimal and strictly utilitarian. Furniture items consisted of wooden tables and folding stools with cloth seats, or three-legged stools (similar to a milking stool) with wooden or *rush* seats. Family members slept on straw-stuffed linen mattresses placed directly on the plastered floor. Occasionally, some residents had built-in plaster couches similar to ones found in Catal Huyuk. Physical examples of furniture and household objects dating from the Old and Middle Kingdoms are scarce; however, objects used during these periods can be seen in numerous wall paintings, relief carvings, painted papyrus, and *sarcophagi* details.

The discovery of King Tutankhamun's tomb in 1922 by the British archaeologist Howard Carter was one of the most spectacular events of the 20th century. Sealed away in the king's tomb since 1325 BCE, and preserved against centuries of decay-causing elements, the artifacts recovered from the tomb are some of the best examples in existence from the New Kingdom and give a complete picture of the opulent possessions of the pharaohs. Now on display in the Egyptian Museum in Cairo, artifacts taken from the tomb include chairs, beds, tables, lamps, and chests, along with a multitude of floor coverings, fabrics, and vases. These collections of furnishings are a testament to the refinement of royal possessions and to the skill of the ancient Egyptian artists in construction methods, materials, and decoration.

The artifacts found inside King Tutankhamun's tomb were made in royal workshops and show a range in artisanship from the most elegant (for the pharaoh's use) to the most basic (for his domestic servants). Those objects made for the pharaoh were carved from wood and incorporated design motifs made more vibrant through *gilding*, a process of applying gold to the surface of an object (Figure 1.22). A fine example of a stool from King Tutankhamun's tomb was made from locally harvested acacia and *gilt* by first covering the surface of the wood with *gesso*, and then applying gold leaf (Figure 1.23). Hammered gold and silver were also used to make dazzling coverings over wooden chests and boxes. The creamy white of carved *alabaster* vessels was contrasted against gold-painted designs. Other forms of decoration included inlaid designs of semiprecious stones, bone, ivory, and *faience*, a glasslike substance made from silica.

Although the tombs yielded many examples of the types of household furnishings the royal court enjoyed, most of the population had simply designed,

**FIGURE 1.22** A highly decorative throne chair found in the tomb of King Tutankhamun features design motifs with spiritual significance. A falcon with its wings spread wide and the solar disk, symbolizing the sun god Re, appear on the crest rail to offer protection to the pharaoh. Other motifs decorating the chair include lotus and papyrus blossoms, rosettes, and checkerboard patterns. Robert Harding, World Imagery.

**FIGURE 1.23** This fine example of a double-cove, fixed-seat stool was found in the burial tomb of King Tutankhamun. Made from acacia, a local wood, the furniture maker painted the surface of the stool with gesso then applied gilding to the decorative details. The ornamental grille work incorporates the symbol for unification—the intertwined lotus and papyrus stems—in its design. Animal legs with paw feet face forward, indicating which side the pharaoh was to sit. Robert Harding World Imagery.

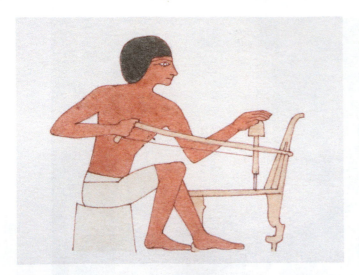

FIGURE 1.24 An illustration from a tomb painting shows a furniture maker using a hand drill to make a hole in the seat rail of a chair. A wooden dowel is inserted into the hole to keep the two pieces of wood joined with a secure bond. Brian Delft © Dorling Kindersley.

functional furnishings. Hieroglyphic texts that document extensive inventories of more modest homes for tax purposes list chairs, tables, beds, lamps, vases, kitchenware, woven mats, and cushions as part of the household.

The most basic furniture item found in the Egyptian home, whether row house or palace, was the stool. In general, there were two types of stools: a folding type used mostly by men, and a fixed type that varied in design and decoration. The folding stool had an X-form base designed to collapse. The construction of the X-form stool was simple. A bow saw was used to shape pieces of wood into rounded spindles (Figure 1.24). Artisans used *mortise-and-tenon* joints or *dowels* to secure the legs to the *seat rail* whereas the legs were secured with dowels. Linen cloth or leather was stretched over the seat rail, which made collapsing the stool much easier. Folding allowed the stool to be moved easily from room to room or stored.

Folding stools were favored by the Egyptians for use in private chambers, as is often represented in tomb paintings. Hair grooming and the application of kohl—a makeup used to line the eyes—aided by a handheld mirror made from polished copper, would be done as

## COMPARISONS     X-Form Stools

**S**uccessive cultures borrow what they need from previous ones while developing their own unique interpretations. The lasting effects of Egyptian design can be seen in many furniture styles throughout history. Compare the Egyptian X-form stool (Figure 1.25) with the modern example shown in Figure 1.26.

What do these items have in common? Certainly the X-form base has been used in these examples, but how did each designer reinterpret this design characteristic while supporting a variety of functions?

The Barcelona stool designed by Mies van der Rohe in 1929 reflects a 20th-century modernist approach in its design and fabrication (Figure 1.26). The Egyptian X-form stool and the Barcelona stool each fulfill a

practical purpose, are simple in design, and exemplify the materials and production methods prevalent during each period. Mies van der Rohe's version embodies the simplistic delicacy of the Egyptian's X-form base, while providing a modern rendition using stainless steel. The Egyptian example was used by the pharaoh for nonritualistic purposes; however, Mies' stool was designed in conjunction with official ceremonies for the King and Queen of Spain. This is only one example of how the creativity of Egyptian craftsmen and -women influenced designers from different cultures. Can you think of others?

FIGURE 1.25 A drawing of an Egyptian, X-form folding stool based on examples found in King Tutankhamun's tomb.

FIGURE 1.26 The X-form base of this stool, designed by Ludwig Mies van der Rohe for the 1929 World Exposition, was manufactured from flat steel bars that required precise welding where the members intersect. Height, 14.5 inches; width, 21.2 inches; depth, 23.2 inches. © Treena M. Crochet.

the pharaoh sat on a stool before a toiletry chest. More refined fixed-type stools afforded by wealthier Egyptians were reserved for high officials of the palace court or important invited visitors. A stool found in King Tutankhamun's tomb imitated the folding type by using an X-form base with each leg carved into the delicately shaped head of a duck. Additional types of fixed stools had four legs extending straight down from the seat to the floor.

Because stools were used most often in daily activities, side chairs or armchairs were reserved for special occasions; however, the basic design of fixed stools, side chairs, and armchairs was similar. Animal legs, either lions or panthers, terminated into a paw foot that rested on a block of tapered wood referred to as a *drum* (Figure 1.27). (Historians believe that the use of the drum dates back to a period before plaster floors were commonly used in Old Kingdom palaces and earthen floors were covered with straw.) Animals either represented spiritual beings or were believed to possess supernatural powers. Egyptians hypothesized that their virtues were conveyed from the god or animal to the person seated in the chair. In this case, it was necessary to raise the paw above the straw-covered dirt floor. Even after more advanced floor covering methods were developed, the drum remained at the base of the leg and foot as a design characteristic. Lion legs and paw feet appeared on chairs and stools made for the Pharoahs as a symbol of

**FIGURE 1.27** A modern papyrus painting taken from scenes inside an ancient tomb shows figures seated on a side chair and stool. A table laden with food is placed before them, and all furnishings are reinforced with stretchers and struts.
© Treena M. Crochet.

# A CLOSER Look

## Hetepheres Gold Chair

**FIGURE 1.28** A drawing of a gilt chair belonging to Queen Hetepheres I, c. 2600 BCE.

Rare examples of Old Kingdom furniture were discovered in the burial chamber of Queen Hetepheres I at Giza dating from around 2600 BCE. The mother of Cheops, Queen Hetepheres was buried in an elaborate tomb near her son's pyramid. This drawing of a ceremonial chair (Figure 1.28) was reconstructed based on hammered gold casings recovered from her tomb that had once covered the now decomposed wooden frame. The furniture maker constructed the chair by using mitered joints at the *crest rail* with mortise-and-tenon joints and dowels attaching the legs to the seat rail. A wooden seat was dropped into place, providing support for a loose cushion. Three lotus flowers, a symbol of lower Egypt, act as a support for the armrest. Although the backrest is perfectly straight, the back legs are shorter than the front, creating a slight pitch that allowed the queen to sit in a less-than-erect position. The chair measures 76 centimeters high, 71.2 centimeters wide, and has a depth of 65.6 centimeters. The front legs measure 28 centimeters high, whereas the back legs are 25.8 centimeters.

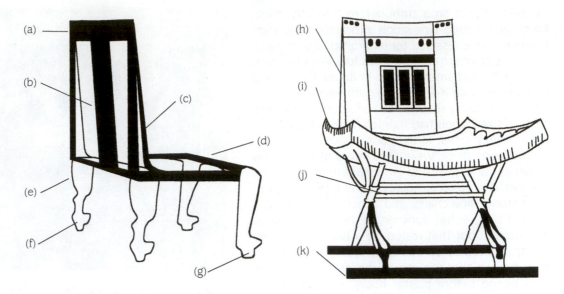

**FIGURE 1.29** These drawings of Egyptian–style chairs illustrate technical terms applied to most seat furniture: (a) crest rail, (b) vertical slats, (c) raking or slant back, (d) seat rail, (e) animal leg, (f) paw foot, (g) drum, (h) uprights or stiles, (i) double-cove seat or dipped seat, (j) stretchers, (k) runners. © David Vleck.

their strength and power as leaders of their country. Furniture designers from the Greek and Roman periods continued to use the animal leg as a symbol of power, but without the drum.

Egyptian crafts workers reinforced the structural frame by adding *stretchers*, *continuous stretchers*, or *runners* to the legs of stools and chairs (Figure 1.27). Occasionally, *struts* were also added between the stretcher and seat rail for extra stability and strength. Seats were made out of either rush or wood. Wooden seats were ergonomically shaped to follow the contour of the body, creating a *double cove* or dipped seat (Figures 1.22 and 1.23). Because upholstered furniture was not in use at this time, a loose cushion was placed on top of these dipped seats to make the seat more comfortable.

The Egyptian chair exemplifies another aspect of ergonomically designed furniture. Instead of a straight back positioned at a 90-degree angle to the seat, a slanted or *raking back* was added. The angled back was supported by three vertical slats that extended from the crest rail to the seat rail (Figure 1.29). Motifs such as native plant forms, religious deities, and figures representing the owner were then painted, carved, or gilded on the backrests.

During important religious rituals or official coronations, armchairs would be used instead of side chairs. Considered the highest seat of honor, the armchair was reserved for the pharaoh and was richly decorated. An established hierarchy developed with the evolution of various seating units. Social prominence determined on what piece of furniture the Egyptian sat. A stool was better than sitting on the floor, but a side chair had a back on it and was much more comfortable.

The highest ranking Egyptian would sit in an armchair, because this type of chair had the comfort of both back and arm supports. Moreover, the political hierarchy of seat furniture continued into the Greek and Roman periods with authoritatively designed throne chairs. The armchair was also a seat of prominence during the Medieval period. When receiving visitors to the manor house, the lord sat in a massive armchair with the lady of the manor seated in a side chair. During banquets, the lord and lady sat side by side while their guests sat on benches, or stools, some of which were brought by the guests themselves. A form of hierarchical seating continues today in the formal dining room. Armchairs are placed at each end of the table for the host and hostess, whereas guests sit in side chairs.

Perhaps the most common furniture item used by all classes of society was the chest. Designed with removable lids, chests varied in size, construction techniques, and materials. Common ones were made out of woven papyrus reeds similar to *wicker* baskets. These types of chests were generally used by the lower classes for storage of household objects, although specimens of reed chests were recovered from King Tutankhamun's burial tomb. More complex chests were made of wood and differed in shape, size, and artistic expression, depending on the contents they held. Many included panels of detailed narratives and had the same motifs that were used on stools and chairs.

Nearly all the larger chests had straight or tapered legs and were designed to rest on the floor rather than on a table. One chest taken from King Tutankhamun's tomb featured a barrel-shaped lid and two knobs that worked as a fastener. A second barrel-shaped chest discovered in his tomb was made from acacia wood and featured elaborate inlay designs showing the boy king riding a chariot. The frame's construction was secured with mortise-and-tenon joints and was reinforced with dowels. Although elaborately designed chests were discovered in King Tutankhamun's tomb, simple chests were used by all societal classes (Figure 1.30). To lock or secure the chest, two knobs attached to the lid and side of the chest were tied together with twine in a figure-eight style to ensure that the contents were not tampered with. The string was then secured with melted wax and embossed with an official seal bearing the emblem of the owner. As long as the seal remained intact, the contents were assumed to be safe.

Smaller chests called *caskets* were either made of wood or alabaster. A casket found in a tomb in the Valley of the Kings dating form the reign of Thutmose III shows extraordinary cabinetmaking skills. The furniture maker used cleats on the lid to ensure a tight fit. Dovetail joints are used to hold cypress panels together, creating the body of the chest. The bottom is secured with two dowels whereas concave *shoes* are added for legs. Two knobs fastened to the lid and side were used as a locking device. Designed to hold toiletry items, jewelry, linen, and other valuables, caskets were also sealed with encrusted wax for security purposes.

Egyptian tables were designed for a variety of uses, and most were small. Table-like stands supporting alabaster vases and pottery containing precious *unguents* were recovered from King Tutankhamun's burial tomb. These stands had four splayed legs and continuous stretchers with struts (Figure 1.30). Numerous tomb illustrations from the Old, Middle, and New Kingdoms show small pedestal-supported tables laden with food—presumably as offerings for the gods—or for feasting. Unlike dining habits today, Egyptians did not sit around a large table to eat. Guests sat on stools, chairs, or floor cushions while attendants served food and wine from small tables placed in front of them. Greek and Roman cultures followed these dining practices with minor modifications.

Beds or reclining couches were rare, because most people could not afford such luxuries. Several beds were discovered in King Tutankhamun's tomb, and they indicate how the wealthier classes lived. Most beds or couches were constructed from wood with stuffed linen mattresses supported by *webbing* material placed on top for added comfort. Painted tomb illustrations reveal an unusual Egyptian sleeping habit; they slept with their heads elevated as a symbol of resurrection. A separate headrest, called a *yoke*, was positioned at the base of the neck and raised the head 6 to 7 inches above the shoulders (Figure 1.31). This unnatural repose of the body necessitated the use of a footboard placed at the opposite end of the bed. What some mistakenly identify as the headboard on an Egyptian bed is actually the footboard.

Although most reclining couches were used for sleeping, tomb paintings show that low beds with flat surfaces were used as a sort of bench-type seating (Figure 1.32). In addition, scholars believe that two specific examples from King

**FIGURE 1.30** A scene from inside the tomb of Sennefer in the Tombs of the Nobles in Luxor shows workers carrying a chair, tables, and chest into the burial chamber. Alistair Duncan. © Dorling Kindersely.

**FIGURE 1.31** Certain African tribes still use the Egyptian yoke for sleeping. This example is made from carved wood and dates from the 20th century. © Treena M. Crochet.

**FIGURE 1.32  A scene from a tomb painting now housed in the Egyptian museum in Cairo features three figures seated on a bed with animal legs and paw feet.**  Alistair Duncan © Dorling Kindersley, Courtesy of the Cairo Museum.

Tutankhamun's tomb were ceremonial in purpose. Carved out of wood and covered with gilt, one bed was in the shape of a lion and the other, a panther. Ceremonial beds similar to those found in King Tutankhamun's tomb are frequently seen in tomb painting illustrations. Among the beds found in King Tutankhamun's tomb was one specifically designed for traveling. Similar to a cot, these beds could be easily folded and taken from place to place. Most traveling beds were used by military personnel and continued to be used by the Roman army centuries later.

# Egyptian Accessories

Numerous vases, *chalices*, and lamps have also been recovered from Egyptian burial tombs. Several examples have decorations depicting religious themes whereas others display geometric designs and plant motifs. Wealthy Egyptians could afford to have many of these essential articles made from molded glass, carved alabaster, hammered gold, or rare silver. Vases made to hold expensive perfumes and unguents resembled animal or plant forms in shape and design.

Aesthetically designed yet practical, these objects show how crafts workers coordinated each item with its architectural setting; motifs mimicked decorations that were painted on interior walls and seen on woven rugs or rush mats. The artists themselves were regarded as mere craftsmen and -women. Utilitarian objects such as these were not intended to be works of art; they were necessary items designed to be functional. Every article had a purpose, whether spiritual or domestic.

## EGYPTIAN VESSELS AND CONTAINERS

As early as the Old Kingdom, Egyptian artists were applying a colorful glaze over earthenware objects, ranging from jewelry to *amulets*. Known as *faience*, the glaze made from a silica-based material gave the appearance of glass when fired. Glass-making techniques traced back to the ancient Egyptians included both the core forming and mosaic methods. Core forming (Figure 1.33) involves the application of molten glass over a core of formed *clay* and sand, or animal dung. After the desired colors are applied over the core's surface, the glass is cooled and the inner core is dug out with a stick or long tool.

FIGURE 1.33 This whimsical fish made from the core method of glass making stored scented oils or cosmetics. Dorling Kindersley Peter Hayman © The British Museum.

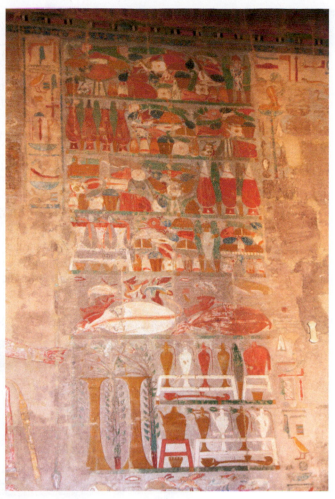

FIGURE 1.34 A tomb painting from the New Kingdom in Egypt shows an assortment of colorful pottery jugs, bowls, and vases placed on tables and stands. © Kokhanchikov/Shutterstock.

Mosaic glass, produced in Egypt after 1390 BCE, became a leading export to other regions of the Mediterranean, even though these regions had knowledge of glass-making processes. The mosaic glass-making method created multicolored designs on the surfaces of vases and bowls. Glassmakers positioned an assortment of hardened glass rods and beads on a ceramic surface, and then placed this ceramic palette into a furnace to soften and fuse the rods and beads together. Working the glass while still soft, glassmakers shaped the malleable glass and created surface patterns by dragging a tool across the fused rods and beads, producing swirls of brilliant color. To avoid breakage, the glass was cooled slowly.

Like other ancient cultures, Egypt relied on ceramic production to provide the necessary household vessels for food storage, eating, and drinking. The advent of the potter's wheel, at first a primitive wooden turntable, has been traced back to at least 3000 BCE, with evidence verified through potsherds discovered in Mesopotamia. In fact, Egyptian tomb paintings discovered in Beni Hasan dating to around 1900 BCE document the business of manufacturing pottery for both domestic and export markets. Egyptian pottery depicted in tomb paintings is plain and undecorated, yet examples found in excavated sites show some elaboration (Figure 1.34). Geometric designs were painted on the clay's surface with a mineral-enriched slip, and the pieces were then fired to harden the clay and bring out the color of the slip.

Vessels found inside King Tutankhamun's tomb held a variety of goods, from foodstuffs to perfumes to kohl. Ordinary ceramic jars, beakers, and *amphorae* were found among chalices, unguent jars, and *canopic* containers carved elaborately from alabaster. A triple design lamp carved from alabaster and found in the tomb of King Tutankhamun exemplifies the craftsman's reverence for the plant life of the Nile, as well as harmony and elegance in design. Today, modern artisans in Egypt carve and chisel alabaster into beautiful vases for the tourist industry using methods dating back to these ancient times. Because alabaster has a translucency that allows light to filter through it, it is the perfect material for making lamps (Figure 1.35). Animal fat or plant oils kept a wick, made from twisted linen cloth or flax reed, burning. Alabaster was later used for windows before glass panes become affordable.

## EGYPTIAN METALWORKING

Leaving the Stone Age behind, people during the Neolithic period made impressive technological advances in metallurgy, and the developing Bronze Age and Iron

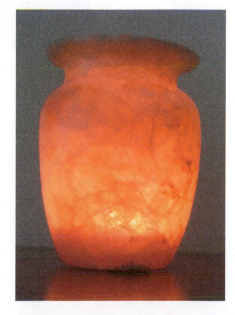

FIGURE 1.35 The translucent qualities of alabaster are shown in this lit candle vase from modern-day Egypt. © Treena M. Crochet.

Canopic jars discovered in ancient Egyptian tombs were integral to the mummification process as receptacles for the deceased's internal organs. Many unearthed examples have lids fashioned into either a likeness of the deceased or a rendition of a sacred deity. The canopic jar shown in Figure 1.36 is simple in its design, and it features colorful geometric bands encircling its bulbous form. A rudimentary likeness of the deceased is fashioned into the lid.

When Napoleon's troops invaded Egypt as part of his military campaigns during the 18th century, Egyptian–inspired design became fashionable in Europe because his troops brought back souvenirs of their conquests. The *jasperware* vase made by English potter Josiah Wedgwood

(1730–1795) was designed much like the originals discovered in Egypt (Figure 1.37). The lid is fashioned into the image of a pharaoh wearing an official headdress, yet curiously, concentric bands of Egyptian hieroglyphics appear with Greek and Roman mythological figures around the base of the vase in white relief over a blue background.

These combinations of Egyptian, Greek, and Roman design motifs are indicative of the mood of the Neoclassic period in Europe during Napoleon's reign. The Wedgwood factory produced jasperware, which was sought after by wealthy British patrons. Whether these well-to-do Londoners would have wanted these jars decorating their interiors had they known the originals held internal organs from humans is questionable.

**FIGURE 1.36** This canopic jar from ancient Egypt features a stylized head of the deceased. © Rachelle Burnside/Shutterstock.

**FIGURE 1.37** This Wedgwood jasperware jar dates from the Neoclassic period. © Judith Miller/ Dorling Kindersley/Woolley and Wallis.

Age supported increased mining for iron, copper, and tin. Ancient Egyptians made weaponry, jewelry, and domestic objects; and evidence of their skills as metalworkers has been traced to around 4000 BCE. Metalworking developed into a recognized art form as objects were created either by hammering sheets of metal into desired shapes or by smoothing thin sheets of metal over wooden forms—a form of gilding. The practice of smelting raw ores and the methods of mold casting developed during the New Kingdom.

Indigenous to Egypt, copper was plentiful and greatly exported to other regions around the Mediterranean. Gold, reserved for the pharaohs, was used freely on their household furnishings and jewelry. Domestic objects fashioned from metal included mirrors that reflected images from their polished surfaces. Mirrors were small and handheld, and were very expensive; thus, they became a luxury of the wealthy. Bronze, an alloy of copper and tin, proved suitable for making lamps because the

**FIGURE 1.38** A bronze lamp fashioned into three arms for holding wicks, with a hinged lid encircled by hieroglyphics for holding the oil. © Judith Miller/Dorling Kindersley/Sloan's.

**FIGURE 1.39** This 2,300-year-old Egyptian rug depicts an image of a sacred cat. Linda Whitwam © Dorling Kindersley.

metal was more durable than ceramic (Figure 1.38). Amulets, also made from bronze, were fashioned into deities that were believed to bestow protective and spiritual powers.

## EGYPTIAN WEAVING AND TEXTILES

Fiber baskets made using either the coiled, plaited, or braided methods were plentiful, allowing households to run efficiently by storing a variety of food stuffs and domestic wares. In fact, found inside the tomb of King Tutankhamun were several baskets containing remnants of flowers, fabrics, and grains. Woven floor mats became more common in Egyptian households by the New Kingdom, replacing the earlier practice of scattering straw over the beaten earth floors. Woven from cellulosic fibers such as flax, floor mats ranged from those with simple designs to those embellished with colorful patterns (Figure 1.39).

Textile production during the Ancient Egyptian period yielded beautiful linen garments that were worn by men and women, as depicted in tomb paintings. Egyptian law declared that all garments had to be produced from linen to support the local flax crop. The flax fibers were colored using natural dyes to produce bright reds, blues, and yellows. Egyptians used a *spindle* for twisting the flax fibers into yarns, and textile production was made faster by using a loom. Tomb paintings reveal that there was a booming textile industry in Egypt, with a variety of clothing styles, draperies, and chair cushions. The tombs themselves yielded many still-intact mummy masks and body coverings, including those made from wool.

# Ancient Aegean Cultures

Between the Mediterranean and Aegean seas, a mountainous mainland and cluster of small islands were home to Mycenaean and Minoan settlements. The region's history can be traced back to 3000 to 2500 BCE, at the end of the Neolithic period and the start of the Bronze Age in Europe. The Greek culture evolved from the coalescence of the Mycenaean peoples who lived on the Peloponnesian mainland, the Minoans who lived on the island of Crete, and the tribes who traveled from Anatolia and settled in the nearby Cycladic islands.

Over several centuries, cataclysmic events like earthquakes and volcanic eruptions weakened the endurance of these civilizations. Around 1500 BCE, a volcanic eruption on the island of Thera (now Santorini) sent tidal waves throughout the Cycladic islands and into Crete. Many historians believe the location of the lost city of Atlantis, described by Plato, is ancient Thera.

Earthquakes following the eruption destroyed Minoan settlements and weakened the defenses of the Cretans. The Mycenaeans took advantage of this opportunity; their armies invaded the islands, and the displaced Minoans were assimilated into Mycenaean culture. The Dorians—a tribe from the north of present-day Greece—invaded the Mycenaean mainland in 1150 BCE. Subsequently, by 1100 BCE, Ionian tribes traveling from the east reestablished the island population. Ultimately, by 776 BCE, the Dorian and Ionian tribes merged to form distinctive city-states extending from mainland Greece and the islands into ancient Mesopotamia, Italy, and eventually Egypt.

**FIGURE 1.40** The Palace of Knossos on the island of Crete, shown in this partial reconstruction interpreted by Sir Arthur Evans, has red-painted columns with flared black capitals and circular relief carvings on the frieze. © Treena M. Crochet.

# Aegean Architecture

Remains of architectural foundations, wall fragments, pottery shards, and funerary and other religious objects excavated from Minoan and Mycenaean sites revealed advanced skills for the period. The most significant discovery of Minoan cultural remains occurred in 1900, with the excavation of the Palace of Knossos on the island of Crete (Figure 1.40). English archaeologist Sir Arthur Evans (1851–1941) accomplished the first successful excavations of the palace after attempts during the 19th century failed.

The Palace of Knossos dates to 1600 BCE and was the royal residence of the mythical King Minos. The legend of the labyrinth is thought to have evolved from the palace itself—with 1,500 rooms spread over three stories, it was easy to get lost in its vastness (Figure 1.41). The architecturally advanced palace complex had light courts that illuminated rooms on all three levels. In addition, sophisticated engineering skills are evident in an elaborate underground plumbing system that brought running

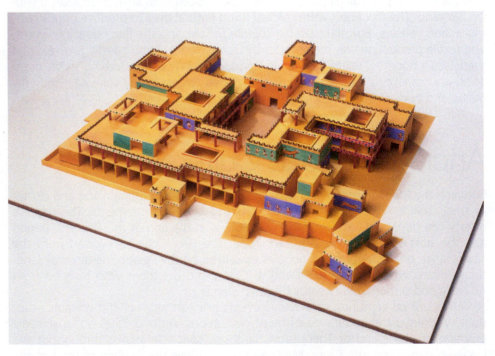

**FIGURE 1.41** This model shows the Palace of Knossos with its central courtyard and interconnecting buildings. Mark Hamilton © Dorling Kindersley.

water into rooms through a complex network of interlocking clay pipes. Inside the queen's bedchamber are the remains of a bathroom equipped with a flushing toilet system (although primitive by today's standards) and a stone bathtub.

Evans reconstructed sections of the palace based on his findings, although this work is highly criticized today. Support columns and door and window frames originally made from wood were replaced with plaster replicas, whereas large stone walls were put back in place according to how they had fallen onto the foundations. He instructed artists to paint murals on the reconstructed walls based on fresco fragments discovered during excavations. Most of these murals depicted scenes from religious ceremonies and popular sporting events or depicted scenes inspired by the Aegean Sea. Native animals, plants, and sea creatures were framed within geometric patterned borders colored in bright blues, reds, greens, and gold that complemented the tranquil waters of the Aegean Sea.

Door frames and windows in the rebuilt sections of the palace were painted in bright red following examples seen in the fresco fragments (Figure 1.42). Unlike Egyptian painting techniques in which the crafts workers applied pigment to dry plaster, Minoan artists painted directly onto prepared wet plaster. Because the plaster dried quickly, the artisan had to have an adept hand and be more spontaneous with the rendering of the subject. This approach resulted in a more durable surface finish because the pigment was indelible after the plaster dried.

Consequently, this technique contributed to the quantity of fresco fragments that have survived with original colorations for more than 3,000 years. Evans used these fragments to reconstruct in brilliant color how the rooms inside the Palace of Knossos might have appeared. Inside the royal throne room, walls feature bright red frescoes with mythical griffins and abundant plant designs framed by built-in benches and an alabaster throne chair (Figure 1.43).

On the island of Crete, city planning was not practiced because the towns grew haphazardly from the center of the large palace complex. Recognized as the official seat of government, the complex provided living quarters for the royal family, housed the servants and guards, and functioned as a religious center. Public officials, noblemen, priests, and priestesses lived in the villas and country estates that surrounded the palace, whereas townhouses accommodated the merchants, mariners, and scribes of the town.

Lower classes lived in densely packed, single-family dwellings. Made out of fired bricks with wood framing around door and window openings, these houses rose to a height of two or three stories. Small faience plaques excavated from Knossos show examples of the decorative designs painted on the façades of these houses (Figure 1.44). Excavations of the town are incomplete; therefore, little is known about the interiors except that a storeroom was located on the ground floor with the living quarters above.

Another significant ancient Minoan archaeological site was discovered on the island of Santorini and first excavated in 1967. Dating to 2000 to 1650 BCE, the city of Akrotiri was instrumental in providing scholars with the understanding of what a typical town of the period looked like. Sophisticated city planning with carefully laid out streets and public squares, multiple-story houses, and shops revealed a highly developed culture. Like the Palace of Knossos, the town of Akrotiri was equipped with underground plumbing that furnished hot and cold running water. Unfortunately, the warm thermal springs feeding into the public water system were an early indicator of an impending volcanic eruption, which eventually destroyed the city in 1500 BCE.

FIGURE 1.42 Sir Arthur Evans used fresco fragments like these as a visual guide during the rebuilding of the Palace of Knossos. The fragments seen here in darker coloration document the type and color of the original wooden columns used to support the palace roof and walls. Checkerboard patterns frame a row of rosette motifs.
© Treena M. Crochet.

FIGURE 1.43 The throne room in the Palace of Knossos reconstructed to show colorful walls and elaborately painted griffins. © Pietro Basilico/Shutterstock.

FIGURE 1.44  These reconstruction drawings show the painted Reprinted with permission. © David Vleck only for use in projects by Treena Crochet fronts of Minoan houses. The illustrations are based on small faience plaques excavated at Knossos.  © David Vleck.

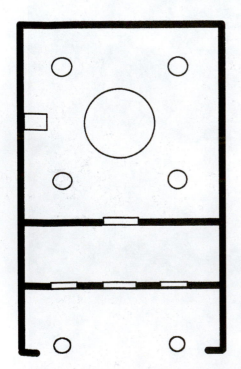

FIGURE 1.45  A drawing of the floor plan from the Megaron at Tiryns shows an entrance porch supported by two columns, an antechamber with three openings into the inner sanctuary, where four columns support the ceiling and frame a large central basin. The rectangular altar on the left wall was used for holding offerings.  © David Vleck.

Under constant threat of marauding troops, the Mycenaeans built their palaces on high ground, overlooking the surrounding mainland, as a form of defense. These citadels offered the most protection for the kings and princes who ruled from within the massive rough-cut stone walls of the palace complex. Similar to Knossos, the vast citadels of Mycenaean culture were self-sufficient. Running water was channeled in from a local source, and food supplies were kept in underground storehouses.

The plan for the Mycenaean citadel revolved around the Megaron, a rectangular building accessed through a covered entrance porch (Figure 1.45). The porch was supported by columns, and visitors entered through an antechamber before progressing through to the inner sanctuary. The inner sanctuary served as a stately throne room for the official business of the king, and it was used for religious sacrifices as well.

In 1939, in the Peloponnesian town of Pylos, excavations uncovered evidence of a great palace. Further work at this site yielded artifacts from the Palace of Nestor, including several fresco fragments. Reconstructions of these wall fragments dating from around 1200 BCE reveal ornate interior decorations, including narrative scenes, and animal forms surrounded by geometric borders. Excavations at Pylos, Tiryns, and Mycenae have revealed much about the culture of the people that lived on the mainland. Townspeople lived in small houses along the sloping hillside that led to the citadel, outside the protective walls of the compound. Houses were either circular or rectangular and had flat roofs made from clay-covered thatch. Simple in construction and design, these houses provided modest living quarters for the crafts workers, merchants, and laborers of the town.

# Aegean Design Motifs

Minoan and Mycenaean artists created spectacular displays of color and movement in their fresco designs that feature a wide range of design motifs. Many of the Minoan motifs celebrated the surrounding marine life, and combined playful water creatures such as cuttlefish and octopi, seaweed patterns, and coastal plant life,

Octopus

Banded rosette

Allover geometric

Marine plants

Fret-designed labyrinth

Spiral wave

Rosettes

**FIGURE 1.46** A variety of design motifs used by Minoan and Mycenaean artists. © David Vleck.

**FIGURE 1.47** This dolphin fresco was reconstructed from the original fragments found in the Queen's hall at the Palace of Knossos. The overlapping of both spiral wave and rosette decorative borders indicates the room had undergone redecoration throughout the centuries of Minoan occupation. © Karel Gallas/ Shutterstock.

with strong geometric patterning (Figure 1.46). Dolphins appear as playful creatures, commonly swimming in opposite directions within the same composition (Figure 1.47). More common motifs found in rooms excavated at the Palace of Knossos included rosettes, circles or *guilloche* patterns, frets, and spiral waves. These motifs appear as allover decorations on floors and ceilings, or were contained within small bands bordering the perimeters of rooms, doors, and windows.

Egyptian in nature, the lotus, zigzag, and rosette were found on Mycenaean artifacts. Similarly, Minoan spiral waves and fret designs were stylized variations on the theme. Moreover, like the Egyptians, the Aegeans favored designs with symbolic or spiritual meanings. Animal motifs such as griffins and bulls were plentiful. The bull was a precious sacrifice offered to the gods, and its representation in murals depicting sacrificial rites speaks to the legend of the Minotaur (Figure 1.48). The griffin, introduced to the Mediterranean regions from Persia, was a symbol of strength to the Minoans. The throne room in the Palace of Knossos depicts these winged creatures flanking the throne and protecting the king (Figure 1.43).

**FIGURE 1.48** The leaping of the bulls, an event that took place during Minoan funerary rituals, is represented in this fresco taken from the Palace of Knossos. Pearson Education U.S. ELT

**FIGURE 1.49** The front of the H. Triadha sarcophagus excavated from Knossos depicts a religious scene contained within checkerboard and rosette borders. Spiral wave motifs run along the length of each side.
© Treena M. Crochet.

# Aegean Furniture

Unlike the airtight tombs of the Egyptians that preserved ancient artifacts, the humid climate surrounding the Aegean Sea contributed to the decay of furnishings from this culture. Furthermore, burial sites yield few artifacts from this period because the practice of entombing the deceased with all their worldly possessions was specific to Egypt. Other than royals, most Mycenaeans cremated their dead by placing the deceased and their possessions on a funeral pyre.

Evans' excavations of the Palace at Knossos yielded a few examples of furniture. In the throne room, an alabaster side chair was found placed against one wall and resting on a raised platform or *dais* (Figure 1.43). The back of this chair is designed with scalloped edges and incised patterning that is also repeated on the legs and front stretcher. Unlike Egyptian raking-back chairs, this chair has a tall, straight back. The absence of the raking back on this chair indicates that it was intended to be placed against the wall at all times, affirming that it was designed for ceremony and not for comfort.

Low plaster benches built around the perimeter of the throne room apparently established the same type of seating hierarchy practiced by the Egyptians. In an antechamber to the throne room, Evans discovered charred wooden debris from another chair. He reconstructed this chair in wood using the alabaster chair as a reference and placed it in the antechamber during his excavation and rebuilding of the palace. It is uncertain that this copy is an accurate depiction of the original.

Other examples of seat furniture recovered from Knossos are two stone specimens of X-form chairs designed with tall backs. Their height of 5 inches suggests that these chairs were used as some sort of shrine for a small statuette, although this is speculation. Unlike Egyptian tomb paintings that show the pharaoh surrounded by luxurious furnishings, fresco fragments excavated from the Minoan period rarely show furniture items. Only two illustrations recovered from Knossos depict furniture. In the *Camp Stool Fresco,* Cretan men are shown seated on X-form folding stools similar to Egyptian prototypes. The discovery of this fresco clearly establishes the use of portable furniture in Minoan culture.

The second example of furniture illustrated in artwork from Knossos is seen painted on the H. Triadha sarcophagus (Figure 1.49). Within the context of religious ceremony, a sacrificial bull is tied to a table as an offering to the gods. The artisan's depiction of the table reflects tapered legs that mimic the structural columns used in the construction of Knossos (Figure 1.50). From this illustration, it is difficult to know for sure whether the table was supported by two pedestal-type supports or four turned legs.

In establishing a precedent for Greek furniture design, apparently one Aegean culture built upon another. Most of what we know about Mycenaean furniture comes from an ancient form of writing. Used as a means of communication similar in concept to Egyptian hieroglyphics, the Mycenaeans inscribed clay tablets with ideograms or pictures that represented words or thoughts. These tablets, classified as *Linear B texts,* have been translated and provide written accounts of household inventories. They list chairs, stools, tables, beds, footstools, and chests. Although Linear B texts do not give any reference to furniture size, some ideograms show chairs with footstools, indicating that the seats were quite high (Figure 1.51).

Furniture items made from ebony, sycamore, and yew are described in these texts as having decorative spiral patterns of inlaid silver, bone, and ivory. Chests are also mentioned and

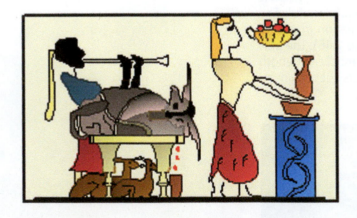

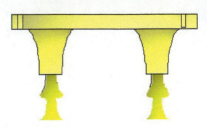

**FIGURE 1.50** (a) Illustrated details from the H. Triadha sarcophagus show the sacrifice of a bull laid out on a table. (b) Details of the table show shaped legs resembling the columns used in construction at the Palace of Knossos. © David Vleck.

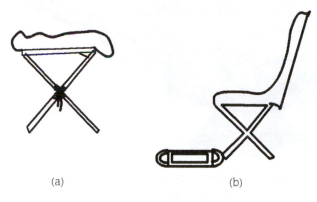

(a)                    (b)

FIGURE 1.51 (a, b) Ideograms from Linear B tablets show a folding stool (a) and a chair with a footstool (b). © David Vleck.

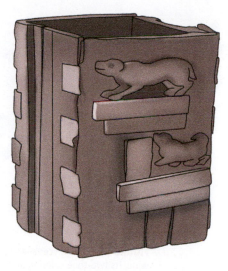

FIGURE 1.52 Rudimentary dovetail joints were used to connect the sides of a Mycenaean wooden jewelry box dating from around 1550 BCE as seen in this drawing.

were used to store jewelry (Figure1.52). Locking devices similar to the two-knob system used by the Egyptians were discovered. Only a few bronze hinges and looped handles recovered from Knossos remain as evidence of chests, although one rare example of a wood and gilt jewelry box was discovered in a Mycenaean royal tomb, and the remains of a charred wooden box were recovered from a funeral pyre.

There are no specific references to the sleeping habits of the Aegeans prior to Greek culture; however, plaster couches were found in the residential quarters at Knossos and were believed to have served as beds. Moreover, Mycenaean Linear B texts make references to beds in household inventories, although no visual representations exist from this period.

# Aegean Accessories

## AEGEAN VESSELS AND CONTAINERS

The development of the potter's wheel on the island of Crete traced to 2300 BCE advanced the Aegean ceramic industry into producing inexpensive containers used by all classes of society for domestic purposes. Firing the clay at high temperatures produced a vessel that would not break with normal use. Ceramic containers were an important part of daily life; they stored the food supplies of the household (Figure 1.53).

The art of Aegean pottery making became specialized, with one artist forming the clay into a variety of shapes while another applied decorations. Many examples of Aegean pottery display decorative patterns inspired by architecture. There was a deliberate effort by the crafts workers to ornament the vessels with designs that mimicked the interior décor. Designs ranged from simple geometric banding to designs inspired by nature in the form of spiral waves and plant and sea life (Figure 1.54).

By the 14th century BCE, pictorial scenes like those painted on the palace walls started to appear on the

FIGURE 1.53 Pithoi excavated from Knossos reveal typical Minoan design motifs. The vessels were decorated in relief with concentric bands on the potter's wheel, and then circular and spiral designs were painted on the surface of the clay before firing. © Andrei Nekrassov/Shutterstock.

**FIGURE 1.54** This Mycenaean buff ware footed cup with two handles was used for mixing water and wine; its two-tone coloring and geometric banding is a form of early pottery decoration. © Judith Miller/Dorling Kindersley/Sloan's.

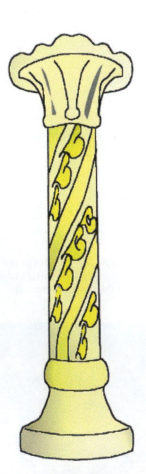

**FIGURE 1.55** This drawing of a pedestal lamp replicates one found at the Palace of Knossos that dates from c. 1450 BCE. The original was made from limestone. Lamps such as these were exported from Crete to neighboring colonies. © David Vleck.

surfaces of ceramic ware. It is widely accepted that these scenes documented historical and mythological events, including stories about the gods and goddesses, and great battles. These ceramic wares were instrumental in the home schooling of children. What better way for children to learn about their heritage than seeing these dramatic narratives on the family milk jug?

A collection of unusual containers made from ostrich eggs was discovered in excavations at Thera, Knossos, Zakros, and Mycenae. The impractical delicacy of the eggshells has led scholars to believe these vessels were used in religious ceremonies rather than as domestic objects. Furthermore, examples of ostrich egg vessels also appeared in Egyptian culture, and were thought to represent life and creation. The egg motif appears throughout ancient and modern history, incorporated into the design of Greek and Roman temples, Christian churches, and Islamic mosques. Although religious practices have changed throughout history, the symbolic meaning of the egg has remained a part of our modern culture.

Candle stands and lamps were also widely used in the Aegean household. These objects were shaped into columnlike pillars and were molded from clay or carved from limestone. Designs were then painted or carved along the length of the shaft. Several examples of Minoan-designed lamps have been found throughout the Aegean region, suggesting that Cretan artists produced these accessory items for export (Figure 1.55).

## AEGEAN METALWORKING

The Aegean Bronze Age, dating between 3200 BCE and 1050 BCE, is marked by the introduction of smelting copper and tin imported into the region to produce bronze. Artisans used bronze in the production of weaponry, vessels, and jewelry, and their craft was widely exported. Artifacts excavated from royal burial tombs in Mycenae and Pylos included jewelry, amulets, and vessels used in offerings to the gods, such as cast and hammered-gold cups, rhytons (drinking cups), and plates (Figure 1.56).

## AEGEAN WEAVING AND TEXTILES

Although small fragments of textiles have been found in gravesite excavations (mostly the remains of funerary shrouds), the best documentation of the Aegean textile industry comes from ancient Minoan and Mycenaean writing tablets. Woolen fibers taken from gravesites, and shearing tools found in other excavations show evidence of a woolen textile industry, although most of the fiber fragments found from this period were made from flax. Like the Egyptians, the Aegean cultures grew flax to produce linen textiles.

FIGURE 1.56 A solid gold death mask with the relief image of the Mycenaean king, Agamemnon. © Nick Pavlakis/Shutterstock.

Furthermore, the discovery of loom weights made from stone and ceramic reveals that the use of the loom was active in these regions. The frescoes unearthed at the Palace of Knossos show figures outfitted in colorful costumes with lively patterns (Figure 1.57), and written tablets describe the textiles used in the making of clothing and bed linens.

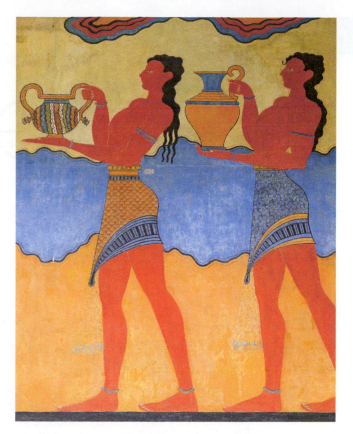

FIGURE 1.57 A reproduction of a fresco from the Palace of Knossos shows a man wearing a colorful loincloth decorated with design motifs. The figure is carrying a ceramic vase with lively geometric designs painted on its surface. © Ralf Hirsch/Shutterstock.

# Classical Greece and Rome

## Ancient Greece

Around 1150 BCE, Dorian tribes from the northern regions of the Aegean Sea pushed south into central Greece and brought significant changes to Mycenaean and ultimately Minoan cultures. The Dorian civilization instituted political and social reforms that replaced the former monarchical systems with the beginnings of a more democratic system of government. Property was owned by all citizens, and the first city-states were organized around 750 BCE. These changes brought a more equalized distribution of social rank and class. Four cultural periods shaped the remainder of Ancient Greek history—specifically, the Geometric (900–700 BCE), Archaic (700–500 BCE), Classical (500–300 BCE), and Hellenistic (300–100 BCE).

During the Archaic period, land was divided among members of a territorial aristocracy that forced workers and merchants to rent property from them or move to the outlying regions of the cities. Throughout Greek history, wars affected the region, and the country suffered from constant Persian invasions. Finally, the Persians were defeated during the fifth century BCE, and Pericles of Athens established a new form of government ruled by the people. He instituted democratically governed city-states and undertook ambitious building projects. The beginnings of the Classical period marked the greatness of Athens as a port city that also had the largest population in the region.

In 447 BCE, construction began on the Acropolis, a site for building a collection of temples honoring the Greek gods and goddesses. Religious practices were celebrated by all the people through festivals, sacrificial offerings, and prayers to their sacred deities. The role of the priestess of Apollo in Delphi as deliverer of the Oracles, which told of prophesies in vague terms that could be interpreted in any manner, endured for a thousand years, until the religion of the ancient Greeks submitted to Christianity.

The following Hellenistic period was dominated by the military strength of Alexander of Macedonia (called "Alexander the Great" by western historians). This young king invaded Greece and Persia, and led an attack against Persian–occupied Egypt. By the second century BCE, Alexandria became a key port city on the Mediterranean, and a new Macedonian Empire was established. The power of the empire was overtaken by the Romans in 146 BCE, who claimed the region as their own.

The Romans adopted much of the Greek way of life, including its religious practices, architectural styles, and artistic skill. The synthesis of Greek and Roman aesthetics into an established design tradition is seen throughout the history of western decorative arts. The resulting *Greco-Roman* style of art and design is considered one of the most enduring of all historical styles, and these designs continue to influence designers today.

# Greek Architecture

The Greeks planned their cities systematically, considering the natural topography of the surrounding region. Streets were organized on north–south and east–west grid patterns, *amphitheaters* were built into hillsides, and sectors of the city were zoned for sacred temples, public and municipal buildings, and private housing. People gathered in public buildings for assemblies and cultural events, market centers were located nearby, and freestanding houses reflected the social prominence of its citizens. Temples were built for worshiping the various gods and goddesses who ruled spiritually over the laws of nature.

The plan of the Greek temple was based on the Mycenaean megaron (Figure 1.45). Steps led to a portico-covered entrance, and an antechamber directed worshippers to the inner sanctuary. The construction of Greek temples followed the same trabeated systems used by the Egyptians, but the Greeks made an important engineering improvement; the diameter of the structural columns was smaller, which allowed for more usable interior space. Perhaps the Greeks discovered that Egyptian temples were over engineered, with massive columns filling the interior space of the hypostyle halls (Figure 1.12). Large temples had *gabled* roofs supported by a system of beams and columns (Figure 2.1). Perimeter columns and strategically placed interior columns along with interior load-bearing walls supported the roof (Figure 2.2). Lintels spanning these columns, and load-bearing walls supported timber rafters that defined the shape of the roof. These rafters became the foundation for supporting roofing materials made from terra cotta tiles or stone.

During the Classical period, styles emphasized *Doric* and *Ionic* orders of architecture for exterior columns whereas the more delicate acanthus leaf capitals of the *Corinthian* order were used on the interior (Figure 2.3). The Doric, Ionic, and Corinthian orders of architecture developed at various time periods during Greek history. The Doric order is the oldest of the three and is seen on the earliest archaic temples. The Ionic order appeared on many Classical and Hellenistic buildings, and the Corinthian order developed sometime during the fifth century BCE. The appearance of the Corinthian order is regularly seen on Roman architecture. Last, the Greeks introduced *caryatid* forms, a structural support fashioned into the shape of a clothed female (Figure 2.4).

Many of the middle-class merchants and artisans rented from the aristocratic town dwellers or moved to newly developed districts outside the city. Common Greek townhouses were usually two to four stories in height, and more upscale homes had interior wall paintings and *mosaic* floors. Geometric patterning made

**FIGURE 2.1** The Parthenon in Athens represents architectural achievements in Greek design. Its refined proportions and manipulation of proportional ratios created a visually perfect structure. © Vladimir Mucibabic/Shutterstock.

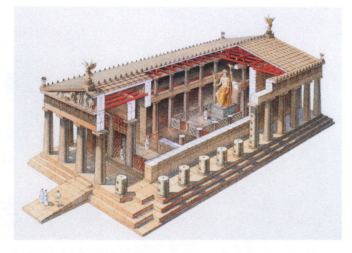

**FIGURE 2.2** A reconstruction drawing shows the interior structural system for a typical Greek temple. Kevin Goold © Dorling Kindersley.

**FIGURE 2.3** The three orders of Greek architecture shown from left to right are the Doric, Ionic, and Corinthian, respectively. The Doric column is broad and flat, and its shaft rests directly on the floor, or stylobate. A volute capital and column base was used on the Ionic order, and the Corinthian order is recognized by its acanthus leaf capital and flared base. © David Vleck.

**FIGURE 2.4** Caryatids from the Erectheum at the Acropolis in Athens were originally painted with realistic colors. First used as an architectural support column, this vertically erect figure became the source of inspiration for furniture ornamentation. © Georgescu Gabriel/Shutterstock.

from black, white, and red *tesserae* created floor mosaic patterns that followed the perimeter of the room and accentuated the position of furniture. The Greek writer Homer, who lived during the Geometric period, wrote about a "lovely dwelling full of precious things" in his book *The Odyssey*. These elaborate interior furnishings are seen in numerous pottery paintings that confirm the Greeks owned sophisticated furnishings with embellished details.

Housing for the working-class population was made from mud bricks. Unfortunately, severe winters and humid summers deteriorated most of the mud brick houses as well as the interior furnishings. Farmhouses outside the city were simple structures with a main floor and upper sleeping loft (Figure 2.5). Wooden shutters covered windows, and wooden doors closed the house from the outside.

**FIGURE 2.5** A cutaway model shows the interior of what a typical Greek farmhouse might have looked like with its vast interior courtyard and upper-level sleeping lofts. The dwelling features a red-tile roof, and the exterior walls are covered with stucco. Bill Gordon © Dorling Kindersley.

# Greek Design Motifs

Like their Aegean predecessors, Greek artisans incorporated design motifs into their work that featured strong geometric patterning, nature-inspired stylized designs, and animals that conveyed their spiritual beliefs. Decorations on buildings, furniture, pottery, wall paintings, mosaics, and textiles all featured similar motifs that unified the design scheme. Spiral waves, fret borders, and rosettes reappear in Greek design, borrowed from the Egyptian and Aegean cultures (Figures 2.6 and 2.7).

Floral designs include the anthemion, a motif based on variations of the Egyptian palmette flower, along with variations of the palm frond (Figure 2.8). *Antefixes* positioned at the ends of gabled roofs often incorporate these stylized floral designs and, along with honeysuckle patterns and all over floral designs, appear in the entablature sections of temples and civic buildings. These architectural details were painted in bright reds, blues, greens, and golden yellows so the designs could be seen more clearly from a distance (Figure 2.9).

Additional design motifs based on mythological creatures like the griffin, and minor deities that were half animal and half human, such as the Greek sphinx and triton, or merman, represented spiritual beliefs and were thought to possess special powers (Figures 2.10 and 2.11). Furthermore, Greek artists incorporated human representations of the Olympian gods and goddesses into designs that celebrated their spiritual existence and powers on earth. Sometimes these deities were referenced symbolically, like the grape bunch and vine motif, which represented Dionysus, the god of wine.

**FIGURE 2.6** A painted vase from ancient Greece features a spiral wave motif, a common design pattern used by cultures surrounding the Mediterranean. © Kamira/Shutterstock.

**FIGURE 2.7** The fret motif, also referred to as a "Greek key," appears frequently on artifacts from ancient Greece and Rome. © David Vleck.

Frieze detail

Entablature

**FIGURE 2.9** This rendering of frieze area details shows the bright colors applied to design motifs, which gave them a strong visual presence from the street below. ©David Vleck.

Antefix with palmette

Anthemion

Palmette and honeysuckle

Leaf and vine pattern

**FIGURE 2.8** These drawings represent design motifs commonly used as decorative embellishments on Greek temples, vase, and wall paintings. ©David Vleck.

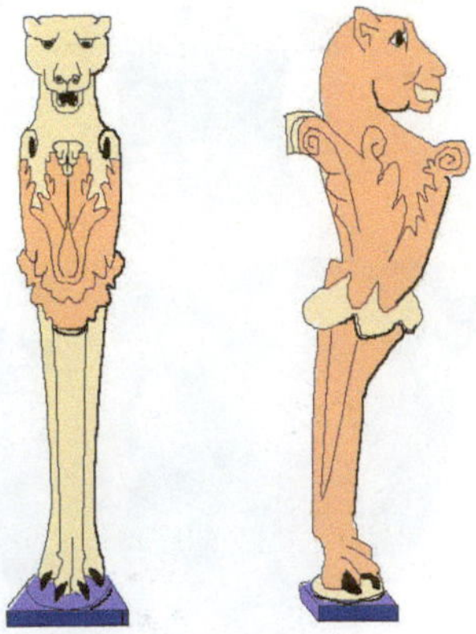

# Greek Furniture

Unlike the Egyptians, the Greeks did not entomb their dead with all the possessions they would need for a comfortable afterlife. Rather, the personal possessions of the deceased were placed along with the body on a funeral pyre. As a result, examples of furnishings from this period are scarce, and the only furniture that still survives from the Ancient Greek period are those items made from bronze or stone. However, pottery scenes provide the best examples of what was fashionable for the period. These paintings feature designs with graceful proportions and minimal ornamentation. Designers emphasized the sweeping curves of chair backs and legs rather than applied decorations, and the quality of furniture construction was more advanced, eliminating the need for runners or stretchers.

Stools were owned by all classes of society, and were the most common piece of furniture found in Greek homes because they were easily moved from room to room at a time when people did not own a great deal of furniture. The Greek *curule* form stool called a "diphros okladias" resembled the Egyptian X-form folding stool (Figure 2.12). Other types featured four legs that extended straight down from the seat rail to the floor. Greek furniture makers, like Egyptian crafts workers, used a *lathe* to turn blocks of wood into rounded spindles to use as legs on stools and tables.

The hierarchical status that was once associated with seating furniture became less significant to the Greeks, although a special armchair called a *thronos* was used for important occasions (Figure 2.13). These throne chairs had high backs with elaborate carving, and records indicate the chairs were used by state officials and by the deliverer of the Oracles at Delphi. The thronos featured a wide seat and arms with lion-shaped legs and large paw feet.

The *klismos* chair was a popular style of side chair, designed with slender proportions, a curved crest rail, and *saber legs*. This distinctive style of chair was carved from stone for the box seats at theaters and stadiums, which were reserved for political officials (Figure 2.14). Dowels were used to attach the delicate saber legs to the seat rail and were also used to attach the uprights to the crest rail. Woven grass, called *rush*, was used for the seat, and a loose cushion made it more comfortable. Artwork shows women sitting in klismos chairs doing household tasks like spinning yarn or attending to their daily toilette of hair styling.

Working-class households had only those furnishings necessary to perform daily domestic tasks—primarily, stools and tables. Artwork from the period depicts people sitting on floor cushions rather than on furniture. More affluent households could afford stools, tables, chairs, chests, and reclining couches. These upscale items were decorated with gilding, fine carvings, and inlay. Tables were either square or rectangular with four sturdy legs. They were used to prepare meals, and were where children and slaves ate their meals. Small round tables were used for serving wine. These small *tripod tables* were supported by three legs fashioned into the legs of goats, lions, dolphins, and geese, and were usually made from stone or bronze (Figure 2.18). Greek furniture makers also realized that by designing furniture with three legs instead of four, they were much more stable when placed on uneven plaster floors. These tripod forms included stands for pottery jars, stools, and tables. In fact, when the working classes sat around a table to eat their meals, people usually sat on a tripod stool because it was more stable on their uneven plaster floors. Pedestal tables, those with one central support rather than individual legs, also appear in pottery scenes shown in a variety of sizes.

**FIGURE 2.10** The griffin appears as if its wings are made from acanthus leaves. © David Vleck.

**FIGURE 2.11** Slightly different from Egyptian examples, Greek and Roman artists depicted the sphinx as a female head on the body of a lion with the wings of an eagle. © Tatiana Popova/Shutterstock.

**FIGURE 2.12** This pottery painting shows a figure seated on an X-form folding stool with the seat legs fashioned with animal forms and paw feet. © Koroleva Katerina/Shutterstock.

**FIGURE 2.13** The remains of a Greek thronos from the ancient theater of Dionysus in Athens. © Ariy/Shutterstock.

Although most working-class Greeks ate their meals at a table while seated on stools, the wealthier classes took their meals while reclining on a couch or bed. Designed for lounging and sleeping, a *kline* was raised high off the ground and required the use of a step- or footstool to get onto the mattress (Figure 2.19). Cushions propped up the left elbow, supporting the body as the person dined. A table where a servant placed trays of food and beverages was placed in front of each kline, and small tripod tables were placed nearby for serving wine. These short tables were small, and simple in construction. Their size allowed servants to slide the table under the kline after the meal to clear the room for the entertainment by musicians and dancers while guests remained on the kline throughout the rest of the evening. Owning a bed showed high social standing and

**FIGURE 2.14** Although worn with time, the distinctive shape of the klismos chair is still seen in these stone box seats in an ancient Greek theater. © Ariy/Shutterstock.

## COMPARISONS  Greek Chairs

During the Classical period in Greek history, furniture makers had refined the design for a wooden chair by slenderizing its proportions and using dowels to reinforce its construction. The design for the wooden klismos chair, and its distinctive features such as the front and back saber legs and a concave crest rail, was often duplicated in bronze and stone. The chair's concave crest rail and back support had the right degree of curvature, making the klismos one of the earliest examples of an ergonomically designed chair.

Compare Figures 2.15 and 2.16. What similarities are seen between the chair depicted in the Cycladic sculpture of the seated lyre player and the klismos chair featured on the Greek grave stele? The Cycladic chair, dating from 2000 BCE, has four straight legs that extend from the seat rail to the floor, with two sets of side stretchers shaped into gentle sweeping forms. Could the design of these stretchers have influenced the design of the delicate saber legs used on the Greek klismos chair dating from the fifth century BCE?

What are the similarities between the Greek klismos chair and the English Regency–style side chair from the 19th century (Figure 2.17)? The English chair features a lyre-shaped back and has Greek key motifs surrounding the crest rail, which prompts the question: What were the historical events that led to the reintroduction of Greek design during this time period? If the furniture makers during the 19th century were influenced by Greek design, were they acting alone or did architecture also express an interest in reviving the Greek style? Throughout history, it was common practice for designers and architects to create new styles based on a blending of elements from the past. How does the Regency–style chair in Figure 2.17 capture the spirit of the klismos chair in Figure 2.15, but in a new way?

**FIGURE 2.15** A grave stele depicts a woman seated in a klismos chair while her attendant holds a jewelry box. © Jozef Sedmak/Shutterstock.

**FIGURE 2.16** This cycladic sculpture of a lyre player shows an early chair design. © John Bigelow Taylor / Art Resource, NY.

**FIGURE 2.17** This lyre-back chair dates from the early 19th century and is typical of furniture from the English Regency style. © Judith Miller / Dorling Kindersley / Wallis and Wallis.

**FIGURE 2.19** This funerary stele with a banquet scene dates from 480 to 450 BCE and shows the deceased on a mattress-covered kline. A small table is placed before him while a woman is seated on a straight-backed armchair. A servant refills an amphora from a large wine urn placed on a pedestal support.
© Faraways/Shutterstock.

**FIGURE 2.18** This tomb carving shows a family gathered around a small tripod table placed in front of reclining couch, or kline.
© mountainpix/Shutterstock.

was therefore considered to be an important piece of furniture. For those who could not afford a bed, a stuffed mattress was placed either on the floor or on a raised plaster platform.

Chests made of cedar were in great demand and were used to store clothing and small valuables. These low-to-the-ground chests were fixed with short legs and had a hinged lid (Figure 2.20). Pottery paintings show examples with a variety of decorations. The myth of Perseus describes him being placed in an elaborately designed chest and set afloat in the sea, and the writings of the ancient Greek poet Homer refer to carved, gilt, and inlaid chests containing fine cloth.

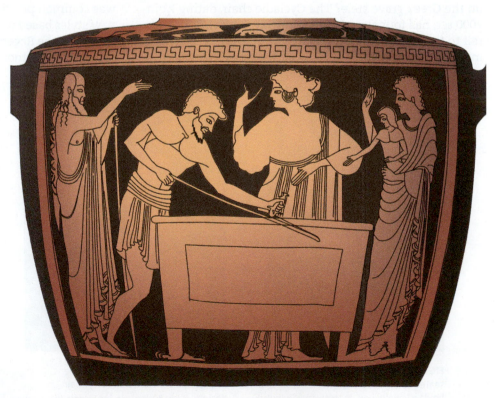

**FIGURE 2.20** A pastel drawing based on a fifth-century BCE Greek vase painting shows a carpenter making a chest.

# Greek Accessories

## GREEK VESSELS AND CONTAINERS

Accessory items used in the Greek home were essentially functional objects necessary for daily life. Pottery vessels were the most commonly used domestic items found in any home, regardless of wealth or social standing. The craft of Greek pottery making was very similar to Egyptian pottery making. Firing the clay at high temperatures produced a vessel that could withstand breakage through normal use. Various shapes and sizes of containers served many purposes; *hydria* for water, *amphora* for wine, and *lekythos* for oils. The *kylix* was a

**FIGURE 2.21** Drawings show the most fundamental shapes of Greek pottery. From left to right are the kylix, krater, amphora, hydria, and lekythos. © David Vleck.

two-handled drinking cup, and a footed vase fitted with handles, called a *krater*, stored grains and other food items (Figure 2.21). In addition, pottery was used to store perfumes and cosmetics.

Although Greek pottery was made for utilitarian purposes, the surface of the clay was lavishly decorated with motifs corresponding to architectural details. Artists who specialized in pottery painting used brushes to paint colored slip on the surface of pots. *Black figure technique* on pottery dates back to the Greek Geometric period with the positive image of the scenes painted over the clay with slip. Firing at high temperatures and no oxygen brought out the deep black of the designs. *Red figure technique* developed during the beginning of the Classical period. Iron-rich clay was painted in the reverse, slip was applied to the background, and the positive images were created by the exposed areas of the clay. Controlling the amount of oxygen in the kiln turned the clay bright red. Narrative scenes painted on the clay depicted religious themes, historical events, and daily tasks, and these scenes were used as a way to teach young children about their heritage. Moreover, like Egyptian tomb paintings, these pottery scenes document the life of this ancient culture.

Before the Hellenistic period, most glass objects used in Greek households were imported from the Phoenicians who excelled in glass-making techniques. Only those

## COMPARISONS — Trophy Cups

The first Olympiad was held in Greece in 776 BCE, and it was customary to crown the heads of the winning athletes with laurel wreaths as a symbol of honor. The expression "resting on your laurels" originated from this custom. Over time, these games became an integral part of Greek culture, and a more lasting commemorative gift in the form of a trophy cup was bestowed on the winning athletes. These two-handled ceramic cups depicted scenes of athletes receiving their crowns of glory from Nike, the mythological goddess of victory (Figure 2.22). Although silver has replaced ceramic, the symbolic gesture of presenting winners of golf tournaments, car races, and the like with these kind of trophy cups is still practiced worldwide (Figure 2.23).

**FIGURE 2.22** The scene on this red figure technique vase shows Greek athletes running in a marathon. The winners are crowned with a wreath of laurels. © topal/Shutterstock.

**FIGURE 2.23** A silver trophy cup with a footed base is designed to commemorate special occasions or accomplishments. © HomeStudio/Shutterstock.

**FIGURE 2.24** A bronze cauldron dating from the fourth century BCE in Greece features animal legs with large paw feet. © Olemac/Shutterstock.

**FIGURE 2.25** The handle of this bronze mirror is fashioned into a standing woman flanked by winged gods representing Eros. The copper, added to the tin to produce bronze, has oxidized over the years, leaving a green patina.
Nick Nicholls © The British Museum Dorling Kindersely.

with wealth owned glass. The delicacy of glass plates, drinking cups, amphorae, and cosmetic jars in transparent colors with gilt accents were a reflection of great taste and social standing. Locally made glass objects were either faience or were made by molding or coiling soft glass into the desired shape. Glass-blowing techniques introduced at the end of the Hellenistic period allowed Greek artisans to produce vessels and beakers more efficiently.

## GREEK METALWORKING

The Greeks were the first to strike silver coins as early as the seventh century BCE, an inventive form of metalworking that introduced a new way to pay for goods. Greek sculptors practiced metallurgy as they mixed copper and tin to make bronze for casting life-size statues using the lost wax method. Therefore, it is no surprise that a variety of household objects, including vessels for serving water and wine, oil lamps, and furniture, were made from metal.

Silver, gold, and bronze hydria and amphorae were embellished with decorative details such as rosettes, egg-and-dart banding, human figures, and mythical creatures created by casting molten metal into clay molds and then working the cooled material to eliminate seams and polish the surface (Figure 2.24). Also, handheld mirrors were made from polished silver or bronze, and examples dating back to the seventh century BCE feature graceful caryatids as handle supports or incorporated mythical creatures in their designs (Figure 2.25). The disk of the mirror was polished to a high shine. However, like all metals, these surfaces would tarnish easily.

Greek lamps were mostly made from ceramic because the material was inexpensive and easy to make (Figure 2.26). Finer lamps were made out of metal—bronze oil lamps fashioned into a variety of shapes and sizes. A basin held oil, and a wick made from twisted fibers soaked up the oil for burning when it was lit. Small lamps designed with carrying handles could be moved around the house easily and carried outdoors. Placing these smaller size lamps onto stands or torchères raised the light source high into the room, allowing more light to filter through the room. Small figurines fashioned into dogs and other animals, people, and mythical creatures were created as votives, or gifts, to the gods. Many bronze examples have been recovered from the sites of ancient temples and treasuries.

## GREEK WEAVING AND TEXTILES

The spinning of woolen and flax fibers into yarns, and the efficiency of the loom enabled the Greeks to produce a myriad of textiles for fine clothing and household accessories. Weaving was done by all social classes of women, producing cloth for

**FIGURE 2.26** This ancient Greek lamp made from blackware pottery features embossed designs on its top and sides, and dates from the third century BCE. © Judith Miller / Dorling Kindersley / Ancient Art.

**FIGURE 2.27** A cosmetic jar with a removable lid shows scenes of women making textiles in the home. The women are seated on furniture, with curtains and other objects hanging on the walls. The white background of the ceramic gives stark contrast to the red and black coloration of figures and decorative details. Ivor Kerslake © The British Museum Dorling Kindersley.

use inside their households. Ancient texts of Greek mythology describe how the goddess Athena, who was the goddess of both war and weaving, wove the cloth for making her tunic. Examples of clothing and the domestic use of fabrics appear in pottery paintings that show a wide range of chair and bed cushions, wall hangings, and draperies (Figure 2.27). Decorative stripes, polka dots, and Greek key motifs appear in these pottery scenes, confirming that bold patterning was preferred to plain cloth. In addition, period wall paintings show that cloth was dyed in bright colors.

# The Roman Empire

By the eighth century BCE, Greek settlements had expanded into southern Italy and the coast of Sicily. In northern Italy, a tribe known as the Etruscans had settled in the area between the Tiber and Arno rivers. Originally from Asia Minor, the Etruscans spoke a language unfamiliar to the Greeks, which limited cultural exchanges between the two cultures. In fact, the Etruscan form of writing has evaded translation by scholars to this day, which has contributed to the lack of detailed information about this ancient culture. The Greeks viewed the Etruscans, along with other cultures in the northern regions of Europe, as barbarians—crude people with uncivilized ways, ignorant of the refinement of Greek customs and culture. Little is known about the Etruscan way of life and its people because most of their cities were not abandoned, but were assimilated by encroaching Roman culture.

The establishment of Rome on the south bank of the Tiber River on the Italian peninsula dates to 753 BCE. This area was first called "Latium," from which the word Latin was derived. Myths, developed many years later, credited the founding of Rome to Romulus and Remus, twin sons of Mars, the god of war. The first laws of the empire were established during the Roman Republic period in 510 BCE. At that time, monarchical control was replaced by patrician rulers, or those with aristocratic upbringings. A network of sophisticated highway systems, including roads and waterways, kept the city of Rome connected to expanding regions of the empire. Considered one of the greatest political nations in the western world, the Roman Empire held political control for nearly a thousand years and ruled geographic regions as far north as the British Isles, and into Egypt, Greece, and parts of Asia Minor.

The Greek city-states finally fell to Roman rule in 146 BCE. Over time, the Romans meshed with the highly developed Hellenistic culture by adopting Greek religious beliefs. The rise of the Imperial period in Roman history occurred after the assassination of Julius Caesar in 44 BCE. At this time, Caesar's great-nephew Octavius expanded territorial holdings through a vast army and navy, and by 27 BCE, the emperor and his consulates maintained autocratic control through a centralized government. Highway and bridge construction kept all outposts of the empire within manageable traveling distance to Rome. For most of the western world, all roads led to Rome.

The Late Imperial period lasted from 284 to 395 CE, during which time Rome was under constant threat from advancing forces from the north. The division of the empire into western and eastern regions (the eastern seated in Constantinople, which is present-day Istanbul) divided the imperial army and weakened the control of the emperor in Rome. The city of Rome fell to plundering northern Goths in 410 CE, and in 476 CE, the western Roman Empire had collapsed. The eastern empire continued to exist until overtaken by Ottoman control during the 15th century.

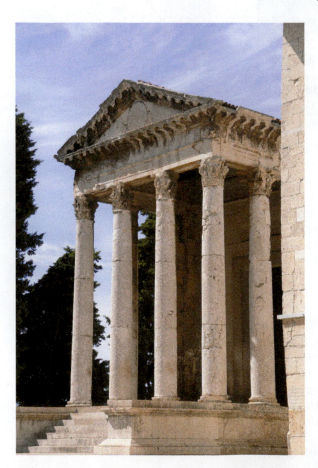

**FIGURE 2.28** This Roman temple, built c. 2 to 14 BCE in present-day Croatia, features magnificent Corinthian columns on its portico and is well preserved for its age. © robert paul van beets/Shutterstock.

# Roman Architecture

Great building projects dating back to the Roman Imperial period featured vast temples and civic buildings modeled after Greek prototypes in the design of the floor plans, exterior facades, and interior decoration (Figure 2.28). Remains of these structures built with trabeated support systems used throughout the first half of the Ancient Roman period appear in all regions of the former empire. Evidence of the use of large cranes to hoist marble building elements in place appear in a relief carving dating from the first century CE (Figure 2.29).

The Romans introduced two new architectural orders to the post-and-lintel support systems: the Tuscan and Composite orders (Figure 2.30). The Tuscan order was based on Etruscan examples and resembled the Greek Doric order, but with a smooth columnar shaft rather than a fluted one, and the column rested on a base. The Composite order was recognized by its capital, which combined both volutes and acanthus leaves supported on a slender, fluted columnar shaft.

Although trabeated architectural systems were the prevailing structural support methods for early buildings, roman engineering skills were further advanced through the extensive use of concrete. By mixing volcanic ash, or pozzolana, with loose aggregate, water, and lime, the material dried to a rock-hard substance suitable for use as a building material. Pozzolana acted as a binding agent similar to cement. The reliance on concrete as a building material by using poured-in-place concrete allowed Roman builders to perfect an arcuated architectural support system that enabled the construction of large-scale building projects and domed structures. Arcuated architecture systems use arches or vaults as load-bearing supports that the Romans then stabilized with concrete. What remains of these domed

FIGURE 2.29 This relief dating from the around 100 CE documents the use of a large crane to build a Roman temple. The great wooden crane was powered by a multitude of men who worked the wheel like a giant treadmill. Simon James © Dorling Kindersley.

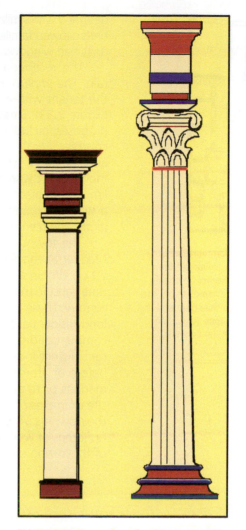

FIGURE 2.30 New orders of architecture used by the Romans include the Tuscan and Composite orders. © David Vleck.

buildings, aqueducts, and massive amphitheaters can be seen throughout the former Roman Empire and are a testament to Roman engineering achievements.

Roman towns and cities were dependent on aqueduct and a highly developed water system that brought water into towns from local aquifers (Figure 2.31). This water system brought hot and cold running water into the public baths and, for those who could afford it, into private homes as well. With the building of aqueducts, it was no longer necessary for towns to develop only along rivers and lakes. Temporary wooden *formwork* supported the weight of stone blocks until the uppermost block, called a *keystone*, was inserted and the concrete mortar hardened. After the arch was stabilized, the formwork was moved to create the next arch.

In addition to the numerous temples and civic buildings built throughout the empire, thriving cities had residential districts that included townhouses and private villas (Figure 2.32). Families of wealthy patricians could afford a villa with land apart from town. These homes were self-sufficient, and many homeowners maintained vineyards, owned livestock, and had storehouses full of grain. The Roman working class lived in town, often renting an apartment in an *insula*, or owning a unit similar to today's townhouses. Ranging in height from two to five stories, most townhouses were

FIGURE 2.31 An aqueduct built by the ancient Romans still stands in Istanbul. © Treena M. Crochet.

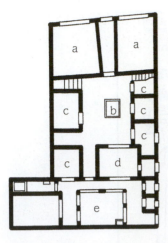

FIGURE 2.32 This floor plan represents the House of the Tragic Poet excavated from Pompeii. Typical of many homes belonging to wealthy Pompeians, the layout shows the proximity of the atrium to the street and the peristyle to the rear. (a) Shops. (b) Atrium. (c) Bedrooms. (d) Tablinum. (e) Peristyle.
© David Vleck.

designed with similar characteristics and layouts. A block of vertically arranged individual units allowed families privacy while sharing common walls. These long, narrow dwelling units had windows on the street side with an entry that led to a reception room.

The reception room had an open-air atrium that allowed in both sun and rain. The *impluvium*, a recess built into the floor, collected rainwater and provided the tenant with a convenient water source separate from the public water supply (Figure 2.33). Smaller rooms arranged around the atrium were used for a variety of purposes, including sleeping or eating. To the rear of the unit was a larger open-air courtyard, or peristyle. The expansive openness of the peristyle allowed for greater air circulation, which made this area the center of activity during the hot summer months. Because the restrictive qualities of apartment buildings and townhouses limited the placement of windows to the street sides only, resourceful artists found a way to expand the sense of space in these dwellings by painting *trompe l'oeil* landscape scenes that provided windowlike views.

The towns of Pompeii and Herculaneum, located south of Naples along the Mediterranean Sea, were buried in volcanic ash when Mount Vesuvius erupted in 79 CE. Within a day, these two cities were entombed by volcanic debris creating a time capsule that was forgotten until they were accidentally rediscovered in the 18th century. These two resort towns along the sea feature streets laid out on a grid with long residential blocks that were cross-accessed by busy traffic avenues that led to commercial districts and civic centers (Figure 2.34). In Pompeii, there was a restaurant district located near a coliseum and stadium where people could get a meal before or after events or games, and a forum where people came to the open-air markets or to attend political events. Excavations from both towns revealed exquisite examples of architecture, furniture, wall paintings, and mosaics once enjoyed by their owners. Archeologists have been able to remove and document systematically hundreds of well-designed and crafted artifacts, a reflection of the wealthy lifestyles of those who once lived during the Roman Imperial period.

FIGURE 2.33 The atrium view of a Pompeian insula shows the impluvium built into the floor to collect rainwater from an opening in the roof. A marble table supported by massive trestles with paw feet is placed at one end. © Treena M. Crochet.

FIGURE 2.34 A street in excavated Herculaneum features a row of townhouses that reveals the façade of the Trellis House, a two-story, multifamily dwelling with walls comprised of wood and reed laths, lime masonry filling the frame, and a balcony supported by brickwork columns overhanging the sidewalk. © kated/Shutterstock.

**FIGURE 2.35** The Villa of the Mysteries, originally built in the third century BCE, is indicative of working estates owned by wealthy Roman citizens. Located on a terraced hillside overlooking the Bay of Naples, the interior of this *domus* was elaborately decorated with brightly colored frescoes and detailed mosaics. © Treena M. Crochet.

**FIGURE 2.36** Bright and colorful wall paintings line the corridor of the logia inside the Villa of the Mysteries. Demetrio Carrasco ©/Dorling Kindersley.

The Villa of the Mysteries excavated in Pompeii is an example of a well-preserved country home (Figure 2.35). Located outside the city, the large, multiroom villa was designed around a central peristyle and had been expanded since it was first built during the second century BCE. The villa featured a bakery, a wine press room, kitchens, servant's quarters, living and sleeping areas, dining rooms, and private baths. The logia surrounding the peristyle featured colorful wall paintings, as did other rooms inside the villa (Figure 2.36). The most elaborate frescoes feature bright red walls painted with Dionysian cult practices set against a black-and-white mosaic floor (Figure 2.37).

In residences of the wealthy, whether in town or out in the country, the decoration of interiors did not depend on furnishings, but rather emphasized elaborate

**FIGURE 2.37** Inside one of the rooms in the Villa of the Mysteries, a colorful wall painting depicts a scene from Dionysian cult practices. © Treena M. Crochet.

**FIGURE 2.38** A colorful wall mosaic taken from a house during excavations at Herculaneum features the mythical King and Queen of the Sea. The scene is framed by an interesting juxtaposition of motifs, including a shell design with a spiral wave pattern, Corinthian columns, fluid arabesques, and flat bands of blue and green. © kated/Shutterstock.

trompe l'oeil frescos and mosaics. Mosaics made with tesserae (small pieces of colored stone) were inlaid into a cement binder, and covered floors and walls. Colorful wall mosaics depicted scenes from mythology, history, and domestic life. Often, decorative mosaic borders delineated the placement of key furniture items like beds or reclining couches, whereas the repetition of coordinated design motifs that appeared in the floor and wall mosaics unified the interior design. One example found inside a home in Herculaneum features the mythical King and Queen of the Sea, framed by an interesting array of design motifs including shells, spiral waves, Corinthian columns, fluid arabesques, and flat bands of blue and green (Figure 2.38). In addition, the ancient Roman city of Ephesus in present-day Turkey featured elite shopping districts with mosaic sidewalks, a tribute to the wealth of the town's populace.

# Roman Design Motifs

Roman design motifs decorating buildings, interiors, and decorative accessories incorporated many of the same characteristics of those favored by the Greeks. Although many of the design motifs were taken directly from Greek sources, the techniques of the artisans varied. The primary difference between Roman and Greek artisans rests in their execution of the design pattern. Greek artists rendered their designs freehand, then hand chiseled the stone, whereas Roman artisans used precisely fabricated templates and hand-powered drills.

Motifs inspired by nature included the rosette and floral patterns depicted in arabesque and rinceau designs (Figure 2.39). The classical arabesque featured a symmetrically arranged vertical panel of flowers and fauna, often embellished with minor deities. Rinceau motifs highlighted asymmetrically arranged flower and vine patterns repeated to create borders in architectural friezes (Figures 2.40). Entablatures of buildings incorporated many Greek motifs, including dentil moldings, and the egg and dart, which was an ancient symbol of life and death.

Arabesque with
griffin and cupids

Stylized "grapevine"

Rinceau

**FIGURE 2.39** Design motifs like these were used as carved embellishments on buildings, and were painted in bright colors. ©David Vleck.

Mythical creatures, gods and goddesses, and minor deities seen in Roman design motifs are representative of Roman religious beliefs. Grape clusters on meandering vines represented Dionysus and Bacchus, the Greek and Roman gods of wine. Other motifs with connections to religious deities include representations of cupid shown as a winged baby or young man, Pegasus depicted as a winged horse, and the head of Medusa with hair of serpents, believed to turn those who looked upon her face to stone (Figure 2.41). In addition, the sacrificial ram frequently adorned the frieze areas of temples, where these rites were held (Figure 2.42). Roman artists accentuated these decorative motifs on buildings with colorful paint.

**FIGURE 2.40** This relief carving taken from the frieze area of the Altar of Augustan Peace in Rome depicts the family of Marcus Agrippa. The figurative scene rests on a band of Greek key motifs, and free-flowing vines and flowers of the rinceau pattern appear below. © Ariy/Shutterstock.

Cupid

Pegasus

Sacrificial rams

**FIGURE 2.41** These drawings illustrate a few of the mythical figures found in Roman art and design. Cupids are the featured motif in this border design surrounded by anthemion and rinceau patterns whereas Pegasus leaps over swirling vines and is placed next to a ram symbolizing virility. ©David Vleck.

**FIGURE 2.42** The skulls of a sacrificial ram are often depicted on architectural entablatures as relief details, and also appear as carvings on sarcophagi. ©David Vleck.

FIGURE 2.43 This reproduction of a typical Roman kitchen features a "cup board" for storing pots, two work tables, and an assortment of pottery. John Chase © The Museum of London Dorling Kindersely.

# Roman Furniture

As in earlier periods, furniture used by the Romans was designed to be practical and utilitarian (Figure 2.43). Most households had the usual supply of stools, tables, and reclining couches, and artwork shows that they were simply designed out of wood with minimal decoration. Finer examples made from bronze and stone were excavated from Pompeii and Herculaneum, and featured more elaborate designs.

Most furniture items were based on Greek examples, like curule-form stools, small tripod tables, and reclining couches. Although Greek and Roman furniture designs share similar characteristics, such as animal legs, paw feet, and disk turning, Roman furniture often lacked the delicate proportions perfected by classical Greek artisans. Turned legs made in a variety of shapes adorned stools, chairs, and beds. The use of a lathe, introduced by the Greeks, enabled Roman artisans to turn rectangular blocks of wood into rounded forms much faster than carving them by hand. This technique is called *disk turning*. The most common shape resembled a spindle of flattened disks.

The Roman *sella curulis* was a stool fashioned after the Greek *diphros okladias*, or a folding stool in the curule form. Easily transported, this piece of furniture varied in style and decoration, and became a symbol of dignity used by patricians. Standard-type stools with straight, disk-turned legs appear in frieze reliefs and wall paintings, and are often shown with loose cushion seats (Figure 2.44).

Many chairs were fashioned out of wood with turned legs and ladder back-styled slats. The design of the crest rail and uprights often had *finials*, sometimes carved into the shapes of figures or animals. These chairs had loose cushions placed over the back and seat for added comfort. Draped fabric often concealed the frame and cushions, giving the appearance of a modern overstuffed chair. Chair seats were quite high by modern standards, and most were accompanied by a footrest. In contrast to wooden chairs, the wicker tub chair was the most economical chair to produce because the reed was inexpensive to obtain and easy to weave; thus, the chair was commonly found in most households. Moreover, its lightweight construction allowed the chair to be moved from room to room. Comfortable and practical, the tub chair was favored by women while nursing or attending to their toilette.

The Roman use of the Greek thronos was not common until the Imperial period, when government control was placed in the hands of an emperor. The emperor and his consulates sat in armchairs when attending to official business. Occasionally the *solium*, or throne chair, was placed on a dais that elevated the emperor to a position higher than anyone else in the room, which was a way of establishing his importance as ruler. In this example of a solium, the seat of power is supported on both sides by oversized lion legs and paw feet (Figure 2.45). The use of the dais continued into the Renaissance period of the 16th century as a symbol of authority.

FIGURE 2.44 A relief carving from a Roman sarcophagus shows a man sitting on an X-form folding stool fashioned with large animal legs and paw feet. The importance of the man is established by the placement of the stool on a dais. © Valery Shanin/Shutterstock.

FIGURE 2.45 A Roman throne chair features lion paw legs and armrests, a seat of honor inside this theater in Turkey. © Valery Shanin/Shutterstock.

Large tables were used as a preparation area for meals whereas smaller round tables called *mensae*, were centered between dining couches placed in the *triclinium* (Figure 2.46). Small tables were found in many roman households. Roman tripod tables incorporated a practical improvement over Greek designs; a raised edge, or gallery, followed the circumference of the top, preventing the wine-filled amphora from falling over the side. In addition to the three-legged tripod forms, satyr, goat, or lion legs rested on a *plinth*, or base, that stabilized the weight of the tabletop.

FIGURE 2.46 A small round table used for dining is seen here in what used to be the triclinium of a Pompeian home. Three dining couches were placed around the table in a U formation, with food and beverages served from the table. © Treena M. Crochet.

## COMPARISONS   Tripod Tables

The Greek and Roman designs for tripod tables were adapted by other cultures for their own specific and unique purposes, making slight modifications to the forms as needed. The tables presented here have similar qualities and characteristics, even though they were designed several hundred years apart.

The Roman tripod table seen in the fresco in Figure 2.47 was made from cast bronze. The details feature a small gallery edge with legs fashioned into animal leg forms ending in small paw feet. Ornate stretchers connect the legs, which stabilized the table. This table was used for serving wine. The pair of mahogany tripod tables dating from the Victorian period of the 19th century, shown in Figure 2.48, was also

designed for serving wine. Compare the earliest of these forms with those designed in later centuries, and discuss what changes were made to the table.

- How has the original tripod table changed over time?
- Why is there a need to have a special table for serving wine?

These tables from the late 19th century Victorian era (Figure 2.48) have circular tops supported by spirally fluted, urn-shaped pedestals attached to a tripod base. The tripod base is carved with *cabriole legs* that terminate into *claw-and-ball* feet. The design of the cabriole leg was inspired by the leg of a goat, whereas the claw-and-ball form was influenced by Chinese designs that resembled bird talons clutching a pearl.

FIGURE 2.47 A Roman tripod table is seen in this fresco excavated from Pompeii. © kated/Shutterstock.

FIGURE 2.48 A pair of Victorian wine tables made during the second half of the 19th century. © Judith Miller / Dorling Kindersley / Lyon and Turnbull Ltd..

**Pilaster table support**

**Lion form table supports**

**FIGURE 2.49** These drawings show the designs carved for use as trestle supports for marble tables, and feature pilaster and lion forms. © David Vleck.

Marble tables were discovered at Pompeii in the outdoor peristyle area of the home where the Romans took their meals during the summer. Designed to withstand the weather, the marble table, or *cartibulum*, had either pedestal, *pilasters*, or *trestle* supports often shaped like lions or griffins (Figure 2.49). The trestle supports, two slabs placed on each end of the table, were not permanently fixed to the table top. These tables remained stationary in the peristyle and atrium areas of the home, and were not intended to be portable.

Roman chests, like Greek and Egyptian prototypes, came in a variety of sizes and were designed to store articles of clothing, cloth, and valuables such as jewelry and coins. These storage chests were often basic and simple in construction materials and methods, made predominately from wood with some metal reinforcements or hinges. Large chests held clothing and other textiles, whereas small boxes were used to store coins, jewelry, and precious oils. Although sophisticated locking devices were not developed until the Middle Ages, there is evidence of a bolt-and-key locking device found on a chest excavated from Pompeii.

Some of the houses excavated from Pompeii had built-in plaster couches used for sleeping that accommodated one person. These plaster couches were located in small *cubiculums* off the main atrium. As with most ancient cultures, the upper classes enjoyed their meals while reclining. Only children and slaves ate their meals while sitting at a table. The Romans lounged on a dining couch while eating from a food-laden *mensa* placed within reach, the same eating habits established by the Greeks.

The Roman *lectus* replaced the Greek kline as a bed or resting couch. This piece of furniture provided comfort for eating, sleeping, or reclining and was made from wood, stone, or bronze, depending on its location either inside or outside the home. Like the kline, the height of the lectus from the floor required the use of a footstool. Loose mattresses were then placed on top of the lectus and overlaid with coverlets and pillows. The lectus had a *fulcrum* at one end that supported the body slightly elevated at the left elbow. The *cyma recta*-shaped fulcrum was made from the same material as the lectus. At some point, the Romans added two fulcrums, one at each end, which was a prototype for the medieval settle (a bench with a backrest and armrests similar to the modern-day settee).

# LEARN More

## Roman Interior Design

This cubiculum nocturnum, or bedroom, contains artifacts taken from ancient Roman excavations at Boscoreale. The frescoes date from the first century BCE and were taken from the villa of P. Fannius Synistor at Pompeii. Walls were frequently adorned with trompe l'oeil paintings that depicted expansive views onto an imaginary landscape in an effort to expand the sense of space. The mosaic floor and furnishings were taken from villas of a later date. The lectus set with two fulcrums has disk-turned legs with classical figures contrasted against a colorful, Tuscan red background. The height of the lectus required the use of a footstool, and a loose cushion provided comfort while sitting or reclining.

**FIGURE 2.50** A reconstruction of a cubiculum nocturnum, or bedroom, dating from the first century CE. akg-images/Werner Forman.

# Roman Accessories

## ROMAN VESSELS AND CONTAINERS

Accessories such as lamps, glassware, pottery, and bronzes coordinated with interior furnishings and were abundant during the Roman period. Pottery, still a main staple of the domestic household, now featured intricate designs created by artists' use of plaster molds. Pressing wet clay into molds was a fast, economical way of manufacturing pottery pieces in a variety of shapes and with a myriad of surface decorations. The embossed surfaces were covered with monochromatic glazes rather than the red and black figure techniques favored by the Greeks.

New glass-making techniques were introduced during the Roman period, and glass making became a valued art form. The most intricate glass objects in the possession of wealthy households were made from cameo glass (Figure 2.51). Cameo glass was made by layering different colors of molten glass into a mold, which gave the object its shape. After the glass cooled, an artist exposed the different layers of colored glass by cutting the figures or patterns in relief. White figures over a dark blue background were the most popular color combination for the period.

Making glass objects from molds yielded a wide range of vessels for domestic use including cups, bowls, and storage jars. More complex perfume bottles, beakers, and vases featuring three-dimensional relief designs were molded in two parts. The parts were then fused together before cooling. Mosaic glass was made by taking different-colored pieces of softened glass and pressing them into a mold. The object was then heated to fuse these small pieces of glass together, producing interesting colors and patterns in the final design (Figure 2.52).

With the aid of the iron blowpipe (developed during the first century BCE), glass production became more economical, and glass began to appear in middle-class households. Molten glass was affixed to the end of a long pipe and air was blown into the pipe by a glassworker at the other end. This inflated the molten glass like a balloon, and the artist could manipulate the shape by spinning the pipe and stretching the glass. Blowing glass into a patterned mold yielded a variety of surface decorations. Furthermore, by blowing glass directly into molds, glassworkers could make bottles, vases, and beakers more quickly and in consistent shapes and sizes. In fact, blow-molded glass bottles and beakers were inexpensive enough that shops set up alongside the Colosseum in Rome sold them as souvenirs to spectators.

## ROMAN METALWORKING

The casting and forging of metals during the Roman Empire produced a wide range of artifacts now housed in museum collections throughout the world. In addition to the striking of coins, Roman metalworkers kept busy producing weaponry needed for the enforcement of imperial law. So important was the role of metalworkers that, in Roman mythology, the god Vulcan protected

**FIGURE 2.51** This cameo cut-glass vase has white relief figures sculpted over a dark blue glass background.
© Kamira/Shutterstock.

**FIGURE 2.52** A small piece of ancient Roman mosaic glass features floral patterns in bright colors. Alistair Duncan © Dorling Kindersley.

FIGURE 2.53 A Roman bronze lamp, with the handle in the form of a cockerel, c. 200 to 300, shows the versatility of a Roman metalworker. © Judith Miller / Dorling Kindersley / Wallis and Wallis.

them. A wide range of household goods including, mirrors, cups, baking dishes, vases, small figurines given as offerings inside temples, and lamps were made from bronze, silver, and gold worked by artisans who mastered the skill of *repoussé* and *casting* (Figure 2.53). Objects made from gold and silver appeared in homes owned by those who could afford such luxuries (Figure 2.54). As Roman artists mastered the casting method, fine and intricate detailing appeared on goods produced for affluent households, and on fine jewelry.

## ROMAN WEAVING AND TEXTILES

The Roman Empire had a thriving textile industry. The main commodity was clothing, although only fragments of cloth made from

# A CLOSER Look

## The Silk Road

FIGURE 2.56 This illustrated map shows land and sea routes of Silk Road trading. © Dorling Kindersley.

FIGURE 2.57 A silk textile from the Han dynasty shows elaborate embroidered designs. Dorling Kindersley © Jamie Marshall.

The Han dynasty, which ruled China at the start of the third century BCE, marked the beginning of the infamous Silk Road, which linked trade between the East and the West (Figure 2.56). The term "Silk Road" is misleading because there was not one single route, but rather several roads that connected China to points west. The German scholar Ferdinand von Ritchthofen (1833–1905) coined the term in 1877 as a way of identifying the overland trade routes that existed between 206 BCE until the start of the Ming dynasty in 1368 CE. The Chinese produced silk as early as 3000 BCE, although silk did not reach the Roman Empire until the first century CE (Figure 2.57). Moreover, trading between the East and West was not limited to silk; it included a wide range of commodities. Spices, like pepper and cinnamon, were traded between countries along a route that began in modern-day Xi'an and ended in what is present-day Turkey.

Merchants trading along the Silk Road traveled in caravans with camels that carried heavy loads of goods, and were protected along the way by armed sentinels. By the 10th century, caravanserais appeared at key points

along trade routes that were determined by the distance a camel could travel in a day's time (Figure 2.58). The caravanserais were comparable with modern-day hotels; they offered food and rest for merchant travelers, and livery services for camels and other livestock. Locked treasuries ensured merchants' goods would be safe while weary travelers rested for the night. Wherever there were caravanserais, there were services for the traders, including money exchangers, barbers, and clothing and shoe repairers. In addition, nearby bazaars allowed traders to sell goods that would never reach the end routes of the Silk Road, and to bargain for goods to trade farther down the line.

Ceramics, jade, bronze mirrors, and lacquerware originating in China were traded along the route for gold, precious gems, ivory, and colored glass brought from the West. Colored glass brought to China from the Middle East was a better quality than the glass produced in China, which had a high lead content (Figure 2.59). Although jade was available in Europe, it was used to make weaponry until the Bronze Age, when metals wool and flax yarns remain from this period. Fabrics were sewn into bed coverings, drapes, and cushion covers (Figure 2.55). The Silk Road from China reached the Roman Empire by the first century CE, and imported silks were coveted by the affluent and influential of Rome, including its emperors. Most could not afford these imported silks, however. Within the empire, slaves produced fabrics on warp-weighted looms, which sped up production. In general, women continued to weave fabrics for various items necessary for their homes, mainly bedding, drapery, and cushions. The legend that Cleopatra delivered herself to Julius Caesar rolled up in a carpet is myth; rather, she wrapped herself in a swathe of bed linens.

**FIGURE 2.54** A Roman silver handheld mirror from the second century features ornate rosette and laurel leaf designs. Rob Reichenfeld © Dorling Kindersley.

**FIGURE 2.55** The marriage of the god Mars and goddess Aphrodite depicted on this ancient Roman wall fresco shows colorful fabric cloth and cushions draped over a chair and on a reclining couch.
© Image Asset Management Ltd. / SuperStock.

**FIGURE 2.58** This drawing shows the layout of the Sultanhani (caravansary) built in 1229 in Aksaray, Turkey. Steven Felmore © Dorling Kindersley.

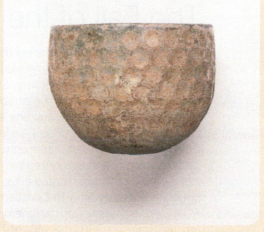

**FIGURE 2.59** A Persian glass bowl with orange and green coloration was made during the pre-Islamic period of the Sassanian Empire. Peter Hayman/Dorling Kindersley © The British Museum.

**FIGURE 2.60** This Chinese jade vase dates from the Ming dynasty, which lasted from 1368 to 1644. © Judith Miller / Dorling Kindersley / Wallis and Wallis.

were then substituted. The Chinese made jewelry out of jade, and wore it to ward off evil spirits and to guard the health of the wearer. The stone was also believed to bring good luck, and was made into vases, plaques, figurines, utensils, and tools (Figure 2.60). The technique of producing lacquerware (Figure 2.61) was specific to Asia, where the sap from the tree *Rhus verniciflua* was used as a protective coating over decorated wooden objects.

The height of Silk Road trading occurred during the seventh century during the Tang dynasty. Also at that time, Islam was brought to Asia from the Arabian Peninsula, introducing an alternative religion to Buddhism, which had entered China from India during the first century CE. By the ninth century, as sentinel protection along the road routes declined, a new sea route was established from Canton (Guangzhou), which continued to the Mediterranean Sea, reaching Constantinople (Istanbul). The tales of Marco Polo during the 13th century piqued European interest, with tales of exotic travels by the Venetian explorer. By the 15th century, European explorers attempted to find a shorter sea route to the East, which resulted in discovering new lands such as North and South America, which they subsequently colonized. The establishment of the Dutch East India and English East India shipping companies at the onset of the 17th century made trading between Europe and China more lucrative for merchants who imported spices, tea, and fine porcelain, which aided in setting a new design direction for all things *chinoiserie*.

**FIGURE 2.61** A lacquerware bowl dating from the Han dynasty features red and black designs.
David Glower/Dorling Kindersley © The British Museum.

# 3

# The Medieval Period

## The Fall of the Roman Empire

The Medieval period, often called the "Middle Ages," is the time period between the fall of the Roman Empire during the fifth century CE and the beginning of the European Renaissance in the 15th century. Several developing factors took place during the fourth century that led to the establishment of this cultural period, and it is difficult to say with certainty that any one event took precedence over another. Changes in religious practice and political leadership, however, were important catalysts. When Constantine the Great became emperor of Rome in the early fourth century, he legalized Christianity and authorized the construction of the first Christian church. This feat alone would not have merited great significance because the practice of paganism, or polytheism, coexisted with Christianity through the early fifth century.

However, when Constantine divided the Roman Empire into eastern and western territories in 330, the spilt of the empire proved to be a significant catalyst in prompting cultural change during the Medieval period. The eastern Empire, seated in Turkey, aligned itself with the ancient city of Byzantium. Under the city's new name, Constantinople continued to prosper until the 15th century. But in the West, weakening protection offered by Roman armies at the farthest outreaches of the empire led to constant invasions, and an eventual deterioration of Roman dominance. Finally, the city of Rome itself was attacked in 410 CE. After the Roman Empire lost its political stronghold in western Europe, territories were claimed by individuals who established their own laws and form of government. These "lords and ladies" of the land eventually became kings and queens, ruling over controlled lands protected by paid mercenaries, and worked by peasant serfs under feudalistic law. These small kingdoms, which later developed into larger countries, were strong unifying forces for the people who lived during the Medieval period.

During this time of political unrest, the Catholic Church gained strength as the spiritual leader of the people. The church became the source of education for the population, and pious but illiterate individuals followed liturgical teachings made visible through the artwork of the period. Strict church doctrine controlled social mores and the acceptance of what was appropriate in science, literature, and art. The Medieval period is sometimes referred to as the *Dark Ages* because, at this time, church doctrine overruled individual thinking, and progress deteriorated. A sequestering of polytheism in church libraries put an end to the classical ideologies of Greece and Rome that would not be revived again until the 15th century during the European Renaissance.

Also, Islam was introduced during the early seventh century by the prophet Muhammad, and the new religion spread into the region of the Middle East, parts of Africa, and, by the mid-eighth century, India, Portugal, and southern Spain. There are several factors that contributed to the end of the Medieval period, among them the weakening authority of the church along with new scientific discoveries that challenged church doctrine.

# Architecture

After the turn of the first millennium CE, population growth in western Europe led to expanded city centers where local trade flourished. A surge in building construction followed, with large castles built for wealthy rulers and gentry, and immense church compounds dominated the largest cities across Europe and into the British Isles. Many of the engineering advancements made by the Romans, such as an extensive use of concrete and networked plumbing systems, were not widely used. Medieval builders used stone rather than poured concrete as a primary building material. Massive churches and cathedrals were built from locally quarried stone, and in the early days of church construction, many of the ancient Roman temples and civic buildings were used as recycling sources. Furthermore, depletion of the forests for shipbuilding, and the high risk of fire, encouraged the use of stone as a primary building material for larger structures.

The Roman Catholic Church, which sponsored church building along with the decorative arts created for the interiors, dictated current style and taste. Large-scale cathedrals became the most prominent structure in town, and many were visible for miles on the horizon before evidence of a city could be seen (Figure 3.1). The development of the Romanesque style of architecture in 950 CE resulted from the transformation of the Roman basilica into Christian churches, with high-walled *naves* supported by massive vaulting systems. The towering cathedrals designed in both the Romanesque and subsequent Gothic styles utilized arcuated systems of structural support dependent on the extensive use of cross-barrel vaults. The cross-barrel vaults were made of large stone reinforced with concrete construction. As the heights of these structures rose higher and higher toward heaven (a symbolic gesture to raise eyes upward to God), the diameter of the columnar supports increased to massive sizes. These vaulting systems supported the roof over the inner nave and side aisles to carry substantial structural loads. As the heights of the nave walls pushed toward the heavens, the vaulting system on its own proved insufficient. In 1284, in the cathedral at Beauvais, France, as winds pressed against the outside structure, the 157-foot-high walls became unstable and collapsed. On rebuilding, additional supports were added to keep the walls of the nave from crashing inward. External *buttresses* were attached to the exterior walls that distributed the weight down into the foundation.

Gothic–style cathedrals appeared as early as 1150 and remained a popular style through to the 14th century. These structures featured tall spires, large arched windows with stained glass, and decorative details carved from stone (Figure 3.2). Gothic cathedrals were built with thinner walls supported by elaborate, ribbed vaulting systems on the interior and a series of flying buttresses on the exterior (Figure 3.3). With the weight of the structure distributed from the vaults to slender columned piers below, walls were opened up to large-scale stained glass windows, which allowed an abundance of light into the nave. The stonework tracery used to hold these stained glass panels in place became synonymous with Gothic decoration and appears as cut stonework all over the exterior. Vast cathedral-building projects often drained the money supply of townspeople and local parishes because everyone was taxed to pay for the construction. This left most individuals without money to build anything greater than modest shelter from the weather.

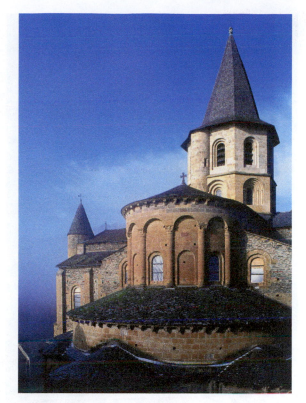

**FIGURE 3.1** The Abbey Church of St. Foy built in 1120 in France features Romanesque–style architectural details including a stone arcuated support system, tall spires, arched windows, and massive scale. Alan Williams © Dorling Kindersley.

**FIGURE 3.2** The Cathedral in Milan was begun in 1386 in the High Gothic style, emphasizing the vertical height of the structure. Rich, decorative carving on all *façades* adds textural qualities to the exterior stonework while depicting characteristic motifs for the period such as tracery, pointed arches, and towering pinnacles. © Cristian Santinon/Shutterstock.

**FIGURE 3.3** The interior of the cathedral in Milan features gothic tracery on the pointed vaulting and a decorative mosaic floor. © Julia Britvich/Fotolia LLC.

Although the claiming of land established a hierarchy of kings over gentry, the ability to maintain possession of the land ensured a forceful reign. Authority was upheld by powerful paid armies, and the protection offered by a system of fortification. Large castles with enveloping walls distinguished the political control of one landowner from another (Figure 3.4). These castle compounds were large enough to house the nobility and extended families along with the servants and mercenaries who worked for them (Figure 3.5). In addition, visiting noblemen often brought their more important servants, including personal maids or valets, with them for extended periods, so the total number of guests could exceed a hundred people at one time. The fortification of these castles depended on the strength of the defenses. Often, high walls surrounded these compounds, reached only by crossing a moat, and acted as a deterrent to keep intruders at bay. Entry was through a main door, which was large enough to allow for the passage of ox carts and horses. The door was closed at night to protect the inhabitants. The vastness of these compounds, including surrounding fortifications, reflected the power and wealth of the lords who owned them.

Early castles were stone and timber buildings with, at first, only one large room called the *great hall*. The great hall served as dining room, bedroom, and gathering room for all aspects of medieval life. Fires to warm the castle were built in the center of the room on the stone floor, and an open window provided ventilation until the introduction of the fireplace during the 14th century. To safeguard against the risk of fire, ceiling heights with their wooden timbers exceeded 20 feet above the floor. These high ceilings endured as a design feature as a symbol of greatness and wealth even after the introduction of the fireplace. The lord and lady of the castle greeted guests and attended to the official business of the manor while seated in large chairs placed at one end of the great hall. As the kingdom grew, so did the size of the castle and, eventually, separate rooms developed for different functions. Soon, the great hall became the dining or banquet room, where guests were entertained by minstrels who performed from a *minstrel gallery* above. As the lord's domain became more prosperous, the interior decoration of the castle became more elaborate. Wall hangings made from woven *tapestry* or linen cloth kept more warmth in the room and, in some regions, wood paneling carved to simulate folded linen panels was used. In homes of lesser wealth, wall paintings imitated these designs. Most floors were either stone or brick, and although woven rugs were rare at this time, a straw mat helped to keep the floors warm.

The great hall was the main gathering place inside the medieval castle or manor house. In the example shown in Figure 3.6, the structural ceiling beams affixed to the wall with large modillions, or brackets, are left exposed. Stone relief work above the fireplace features the family crest, or coat of arms, and the fireplace opening is shaped by a rounded arch. The stone floor is bare, and a long bench is placed against the wall beneath a tapestry hung for warmth. Wrought iron accessories include a large chandelier, fireplace tools, and an assortment of weaponry. The room's interior reflects the style of an affluent household of the period.

Laborers lived in mud, stone, or timber cottages with thatched roofs and beaten earth floors located outside the protective city walls (Figure 3.7). Designed to be sustaining, these dwellings were one and a half stories high, with a sleeping loft tucked into the eaves of the roof, raised above the ground floor. Merchant-class families, although a smaller percentage of the population, had better living conditions. They lived in detached homes or townhouses made of stucco and timber. The family businesses were located on the street level, usually workshops or stores, with two levels of living quarters above. Interiors featured wood floors, white-washed stucco walls, exposed ceiling beams, and windows that closed with wooden shutters. In rare cases, small panes of glass filled in the uppermost portion of the window to allow light to filter inside when the shutters were closed.

FIGURE 3.4 High above terraced walls, this Norman castle typifies the medieval fortification necessary to protect its occupants from marauding invaders. Known as *Rochester Keep,* this 12th-century castle features four tall towers, making it the tallest in England for its time. © Alan Jeffery/Shutterstock.

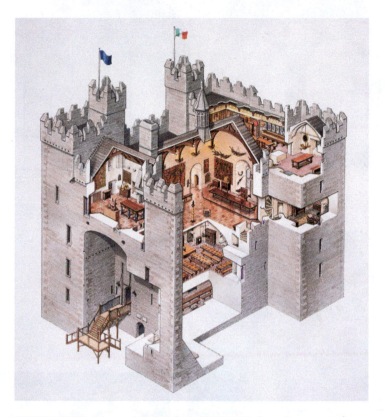

FIGURE 3.5 This cutaway drawing shows the great hall as a large, central room inside the castle. Hastings Partnership © Dorling Kindersley.

# Design Motifs

Motifs appearing as decorations on interior furnishings and decorative accessories were fashioned after the architectural styles of the great cathedral projects. Tracery patterns, strapwork carvings, *trefoil* and *quatrefoil* patterns, *crockets, pendants,* and pointed arches can be seen on the Gothic cathedral in the intricate stone carvings on

FIGURE 3.6 The great hall in this medieval castle displays an array of wrought iron objects including fireplace tools, weaponry, and a large chandelier. Geoff Dann © Dorling Kindersley.

FIGURE 3.7 This stone cottage with a thatched roof and small windows was reconstructed based on 13th-century farmhouses. Geoff Dann/Dorling Kindersley © Weald and Downland Open Air Museum, Chichester.

Stained glass trefoil

Leaded glass

Stained glass trefoil

Trefoil and quatrefoil

**FIGURE 3.8** These window designs are made up of small pieces of glass fit in lead or stone tracery. © David Vleck.

**FIGURE 3.9** Quatrefoil motifs like this one were carved on the side of the Cathedral of Seville, built in the 15th century as the largest church in Spain. © Treena M. Crochet.

walls, buttresses, and windows (Figure 3.8). Trefoil and quatrefoil patterns fashioned into the design of stained glass windows and carved decorations represented the Holy Trinity and the four evangelists (Figure 3.9).

The decoration of church buildings and cathedrals across Europe was orchestrated by the church fathers, and most of the designs conveyed spiritual meanings or were selected for their decorative appeal (Figure 3.10). Similar to the ancient Greek and Roman temples, the artwork was painted in bright colors so the images could be seen and interpreted (Figure 3.11). In Christian iconography, certain animals represented virtues and vices, and plants and flowers had special meanings assigned to them; for example, natural forms, including the grapevine, grape leaf, and grape bunch, had a special meaning associated with Christ. This motif, so far seen in the decoration of Egyptian tombs (for wine production) and Greek and Roman temples representing the gods of wine, Dionysus and Bacchus, conveyed to Medieval churchgoers the symbolic nature of the Eucharist.

The thornless rose represented the Virgin Mary, and a combined white and red rose became the symbol of the Tudor kings of England after a truce ended the War of the Roses during the 15th century (Figure 3.12). Other symbols for the Virgin Mary included a white lily as a testament to her purity; the three petals of the lily also represented the Holy Trinity. French kings used the *fleur-de-lis*, or the "flower of the lily," as an emblem of their Christian faith in flags and shields (Figure 3.13). Although the fleur-de-lis is mostly associated with the French, Elizabeth I of England incorporated the motif into insignias for the Tudor monarchy. The integration of fleur-de-lis motifs into medieval furnishings and interior design showed the owner's strong allegiance to the monarchy and Christian faith.

The crocket, a motif partly based on the hilt of the medieval sword, appeared along the rooflines of Gothic cathedrals as decorative finials. Delicate flowers intertwined with strapwork appeared in stone tracery carvings and on wall designs. Crockets and strapwork carvings did not carry any spiritual meaning, and they were applied to secular architecture where they appeared as decorative details on fireplace mantel designs, interior wood paneling, and on furniture (Figure 3.14). Figural and animal forms were used to illustrate biblical teachings through numerous narratives. The pious quickly interpreted these illustrations with their correct associations. Natural forms also dominated the intricate carvings of capitals and *impost blocks* used to support massive vaulted ceilings in a church. These designs resemble the freeform patterns used by monks in decorating the pages of illuminated manuscripts.

| | |
|---|---|
| Fleur de lis | Crocket |
| Latin cross crocket | Strapwork |
| Tudor rose | Stylized rose |
| | Rosette |

**FIGURE 3.10** Design motifs like these were featured on buildings, furniture, and decorative accessories. © David Vleck.

Wood joiners, who made furniture and wood paneling for church interiors, had incorporated these same motifs in the commissions for designing home furnishings (Figure 3.15). Panels carved to look like folded linen, and oak leaves with acorns were typically used on Gothic furniture and architectural wainscoting (Figure 3.16). The linen-fold motif represented the importance of the cloth-making trades to the medieval economy because cloth guilds were first established in the 12th century. The ease of carving the linen-fold motif onto oak panels made it a favored design for woodworkers. The oak leaf and acorn appeared on furnishings in northern Europe, with origins possibly dating to the Roman Empire.

# Furniture

Furniture from the Medieval period is directly associated with architectural design and has many *architectonic* qualities. In many cases, artisans who worked on the construction of a cathedral also designed and crafted furniture. It was natural for them to translate architectural details into carved wood decoration. Workers belonged to specific craft-related guilds that set standards for quality craftsmanship. Guild membership was earned after serving lengthy apprenticeships. Medieval furnishings and interior design dating from the 12th through the 15th centuries reveal the strong architectural influences of the

**FIGURE 3.11** A column and capital from inside a 12th-century church in France depicts the Virgin Mary shrouded in blue among brightly painted decorative carvings that include a band of rosettes, checkerboard, and lattice design. Philippe Giraud © Dorling Kindersley.

**FIGURE 3.12** This architectural carving incorporates the crown of the monarchy with carved fleur-de-lis motifs around its midsection and a Tudor rose carved with the perceived image of the Virgin Mary. Rob Reichenfeld © Dorling Kindersley.

**FIGURE 3.13** The fleur-de-lis is the central design motif in this tiled floor. Geoff Dann © Dorling Kindersley, Courtesy of Chateau de Saumur.

**FIGURE 3.14** Sweeping floral patterns painted on a white wall are surrounded by *arabesques* and a large central rosette. Dave King/Dorling Kindersley © Weald and Downland Open Air Museum, Chichester.

**Oak leaf and acorn**

**linen-fold**

**linen-fold**

**Arabesque**

**FIGURE 3.15** Popular motifs for carved details into stone or wood include strapwork, the oak leaf and acorn, and linen-fold designs. © David Vleck.

Gothic cathedral. These furnishings placed inside medieval castles were designed proportionately to interior spaces. The high ceilings of the great hall required that larger scale furniture items be used, and the introduction of tall *case pieces* and chairs with high backs was necessary to achieve a sense of balance in the interior. The fine carving on chairs, case goods, and chests was made to coordinate with interior woodworking details seen on wall paneling and staircases inside well-appointed interiors. Rooms inside medieval castles were furnished with a few furniture items including stools, large trestle tables for dining, chests, and beds.

The stool was still viewed as the most functional type of seating furniture, and stools prevailed as the most practical piece of furniture throughout the Medieval period. They were lightweight and often had built-in handles that made transporting them from room to room, or even castle to castle, much easier (Figure 3.17). Written accounts of banquets tell about guests bringing their own stools so they would have something to sit on when they arrived. Three-legged stools with short backs were easy to move about, and the three legs stabilized the stool on the uneven floors (Figure 3.18).

Medieval furniture was designed for economy as well as for its decorative value and function. Chairs often had a hollow space built beneath the seat that was used for storage. Iron hinges attached to the seat enabled it to be raised like the lid on a box, allowing access to the space below. A loose cushion placed over the seat kept the hinges hidden from view. Furniture of this sort provided a practical solution to creating multifunctional furniture. In the great hall of the medieval castle, where the lord and lady of the house received visitors and entertained guests, massive side chairs and armchairs reflected their importance and were placed on a dais in the room. These chairs had a straight back that kept the formality of the seated person in check. Carved with intricate tracery patterns and linen-fold designs, the heavy oak construction did not allow these chairs to be moved from room to room (Figure 3.21).

A new type of seating furniture introduced during the Medieval period as a precursor to the modern-day sofa was created by adding a back and arms to a long bench. The *settle* resembled a church pew; however, the settle was not used in the church because, at this time, the congregation stood during services. Made from wood and following the design of carved chairs, some settles were enclosed at the bottom and had a hinged seat that provided access to the storage space. Other bench-type seats with no backs were used around dining tables.

The great hall of the castle was used for dining. People no longer reclined to eat; during the Middle Ages, they sat at a long and narrow trestle table for their meals. Guests sat along one side of the trestle table on either a long bench or on stools. Servants brought food into the great hall from the kitchen and served from the open side of the table (Figure 3.22). At this time, it was uncommon for servants to walk behind the seated guests because constant fear of assassination cautioned people to protect their backs.

The trestle table was made from a long, narrow board placed on supports called trestles that were similar to modern sawhorses. Because the top was not permanently attached to these supports, the table could be quickly disassembled after dinner. The planks were placed against a wall with the trestle ends in front, clearing the room for entertainers or dancing. Because these tables were rudimentary, the table was covered in a cloth, a precious commodity of white linen that showed social standing. Less affluent households also used tablecloths; however, these coverings were often coarse and lacked the embroidered designs seen on more expensive ones.

Other new items of furniture, the *dressoir* and *credenza*, were also designed for inclusion in the great hall and were associated with dining. The *dressoir* was a large case piece used to store table linens and to display eating implements, usually made from *pewter* or pottery (Figure 3.23). The vertical height and massive construction of the dressoir incorporated flamboyant tracery, decorative pendants, linen-fold panels, finials, and pierced tracery, giving the piece its architectonic style. The credenza was a small table with a square top placed next to the host in the dining hall. A servant, called a "credence," placed food on this table before it was served to guests. It was the duty of the credence to taste the food to make sure that it was not poisoned, proving to everyone that it was safe to eat. This piece was eventually enlarged into the size of a cabinet or a long sideboard.

All sizes of chests were considered the most important pieces of furniture inside medieval homes, and earlier chests from this period were actually made from hollowed-out logs. It was common for chests to be taken while traveling from place to place, like today's luggage. Clothing, tapestries, and linens were stored in larger chests, whereas small caskets stored jewelry, money, gold, and silver. Strength in construction and iron reinforcements, including locking devices fitted with keys, ensured the safety of the valuables placed inside and protected the goods from theft (Figure 3.24). Chests were also given as wedding gifts to brides as part of their dowry. A chest contained a bride's possessions as she left the family home to live in that of her husband, and this is where the term "hope chest" originates. Decorations on these chests and caskets included linen-fold carving, trefoil and quatrefoil motifs, strapwork detailing, and iron reinforcements that were translated into beautiful designs (Figure 3.25).

The appearance of a chest of drawers around the 15th century was simply a chest that was raised off the floor onto legs and fitted with one drawer beneath the chest cavity. Other types of storage cabinets, such as the *armoire*, appeared during the Medieval period and were first designed to store military armor. The armoire, which was fitted with interior wooden pegs and shelves, developed into a wardrobe for hanging clothes. The cupboard became another frequently used piece of furniture in the medieval castle. Prior to the development of the cupboard as a unit of

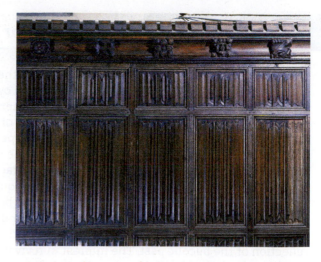

FIGURE 3.16 This section of wall paneling from a castle from the Medieval period reveals the fine linear carvings of linen-fold panels. The motif represented the cloth guild. Dave King © Dorling Kindersley, Courtesy of The Brooking Collection of Architectural Detail, University of Greenwich.

FIGURE 3.17 This small rectangular stool with trestle-type leg supports has holes cut along the long sides that provide a handgrip for carrying the stool from place to place. Geoff Dann/Dorling Kindersley © Weald and Downland Open Air Museum, Chichester.

FIGURE 3.18 A three-legged chair with a triangular seat is an improvement over the basic stool with the addition of a backrest. Geoff Dann © Dorling Kindersley.

The Gothic style of design, popular throughout the end of the Medieval period, was gradually replaced by a renewed interest in classicism that spanned the next three centuries. The resulting Renaissance period of the 15th and 16th centuries embraced a newly developed style based on Greco-Roman examples, leaving the heavily proportioned Gothic style behind. General characteristics of classicism can still be seen in the Baroque period, which followed during the 17th century. A brief attempt to revive Gothic architectural and interior design occurred during the late 18th century as a romanticized reflection of the bucolic past. The interest in revival styles continued well into the 19th century.

Compare the two chairs presented here and discuss the elements that evoke the Gothic style. The chair in Figure 3.19 was designed in 1296 as a coronation chair for the Gothic–style Westminster Abbey and was used by British monarchs throughout history. The chair is made of carved oak and shows traces of gilding. Its high back features a pointed arch with crocket finial designs. The chair is supported by two lions situated on a built-in dais, and reflects the influence of the ancient Greek and Roman throne chairs. The chair in Figure 3.20 was designed in the 1880s as a dining room chair. The set includes a second armchair and four side chairs with matching Gothic–inspired architectural details. Carved from pine, the pointed arch crest rail features crocket finials and an exaggerated trefoil motif. The back is carved with a quatrefoil motif encasing a single lily.

**FIGURE 3.19** The royal coronation chair at Westminster Abbey was inspired by the design of ancient Roman throne chairs. Stephen Oliver © Dorling Kindersely.

**FIGURE 3.20** Decorative details on this Gothic–style oak chair include a crest rail of pierced tracery, crocket-carved finials, flamboyant tracery, and linen-fold panels on the back. © Dorling Kindersley.

furniture, cups and bowls were usually placed on a narrow plank of wood attached to the wall with brackets and was called a "cup board." Other items were stored in a cupboard as well. A sacristy cupboard contained sacred books, a livery cupboard stored food, and an *ambry* held household objects (Figure 3.26). The livery cupboard was designed as a small, wide cabinet on legs that made it easier to access the interior shelves. Doors were designed with pierced tracery panels that allowed food odors to escape from the inside. The concept of the livery cupboard can be seen in the Victorian version of a pie safe.

Unlike the Romans, who preferred to sleep singly, the idea of a full-size bed originated during the Middle Ages. Before separate bedrooms were added to the design of castles, everyone in the household—from the servants to the gentry—slept

**FIGURE 3.21** A Gothic revival-style armchair features a prominent flamboyant tracery back. © Judith Miller/Dorling Kindersely/The Design Gallery.

**FIGURE 3.22** This ceramic tile from England shows a banquet scene. © Dorling Kindersely.

**FIGURE 3.23** This French Gothic–style *dressoir* from around 1500 incorporates many design characteristics found on the great cathedrals. Figural finials spaced between a row of crockets adorn the top gallery of pierced tracery, and flamboyant tracery decorates each panel on the front and sides of the piece. A lower display area is framed by pendants and columnar supports with linen-fold motifs appearing on the rear panels.

in the great hall. Although the servants slept on the floor on loose straw or stuffed mattresses called "beds," gentry slept in a large canopied bedstead fitted with drapes that were closed at night for privacy and warmth. Drapes were attached to the canopy, or *tester*, that ran the length of the bed. A frame attached to the headboard, but not the footboard, supported a mattress. This design feature made it easier for the drapes to be pulled around the mattress and frame completely without obstruction, keeping the

**FIGURE 3.24** The view inside this medieval jewelry casket shows a collection of gold rings. The body of the box is made from wood covered with leather, and the inside lid is covered with tooled leather featuring floral designs. The locking device and hinges are made from wrought iron. Liz McAulay © Dorling Kindersley.

**FIGURE 3.25** A medieval trunk with rustic features has iron reinforcing braces and lock. © Aleksandra Nadeina/Shutterstock.

**FIGURE 3.26** An illuminated manuscript shows a scribe seated on a bench in front of a writing desk. Cupboards of open shelving line the wall and are closed with curtains. Notice the linen-fold panel design on the side of the stool. Laurence Pordes © Dorling Kindersley, Courtesy of The British Library.

warmth inside. The amount of wood needed to construct the frame, headboard, footboard, and canopy, along with several yards of fabric, made the tester bed the most expensive piece of furniture listed in household inventories during the Medieval period. The tester bed was a luxury for most individuals. Even medieval kings could not afford to furnish each room with a tester bed, let alone the additional lodging places they owned throughout the region. During a trip, it was common for the king to send the royal bed ahead of him to ensure comfortable sleeping accommodations on arrival.

Similar types of beds were available to other classes, although their designs were not as elaborate. The family bed would be fitted with a canopy and plain muslin curtains (Figure 3.27). A straw mattress was supported by a network of ropes threaded through the side rails. Periodically, a wooden key was used to tighten the ropes to keep the mattress from sagging. The expression, "sleep tight; don't let the bedbugs bite" refers to the tightening of the ropes and usually insect-infested straw. Underneath these beds were smaller trundle beds on wheels that could be pulled out at night for the children to sleep.

# Accessories

## POTTERY

Medieval potters produced the usual assortment of housewares such as beakers, plates, jars, and bowls (Figure 3.29). These *earthenware* vessels were decorated with vibrant glazes in deep ultramarine, gold, crimson, and green—essentially the same bright colors seen in the stained glass windows of Gothic cathedrals. Designs included family crests and colorful coats of arms, crowns, and other symbols of the nobility who owned them. Clay tiles were also made to decorate floors, walls, and fireplaces inside more affluent households (Figures 3.13 and 3.22).

**FIGURE 3.27** A canopy bed with a straw-stuffed mattress has a trundle bed below where the children slept. Ropes were tightened periodically to keep the mattress from sagging over time. Geoff Dann/Dorling Kindersley © Weald and Downland Open Air Museum, Chichester.

# LEARN More

## Medieval Interior Design

*The Annunciation Triptych* (Figure 3.28), painted by Robert Campin and the artists in his workshop during the first decades of the 15th century, documents the interior of a home belonging to a wealthy family. Notice the following architectural details and furnishings: The ceiling is held up by large beams supported by oversized wall-mounted brackets. The walls seem to be made from plaster, and decorative tile covers the bare floor. Carpets were expensive during this period and even if owned, were never placed on the floor to be walked upon. A large hooded fireplace on the left side of the room has two small swinging iron brackets attached to its surface, designed as candle holders. Windows remain open, allowing natural light to enter the room and provide adequate ventilation to the interior. Notice that small, diamond-shaped glass panes are used only in the window's transom area of the rear and side windows because the technology for making large panes of glass does not exist at this time. When necessary, the windows are closed off by the heavy, wooden shutters seen in the painting.

The furniture shows superb craftsmanship, as each piece has detailed decorative carving. The settle, with its large blue velvet cushions, is pushed against the fireplace during the summer months and faces the fireplace during winter. To the left of the rear window, a brass kettle is placed inside a wall niche and a brass candlestick sits on the small round table in the foreground. Owning brass objects like these were a symbol of wealth.

**FIGURE 3.28** *The Annunciation,* **painted by Robert Campin during the first decades of the 15th century, documents the interior of a home belonging to a wealthy family.** Nelson Hancock © Rough Guides, Dorling Kindersley.

## GLASS

Glassware was reintroduced to Europeans after 12th-century crusaders brought back Roman glass-making techniques from the eastern empire. Although stained glass was a predominant feature of the Gothic cathedral, it was still out of financial reach for many to have glass windows in their homes. Making stained glass for the windows of Gothic cathedrals became a specialized art form. Blown glass spheres were flattened by spinning the iron blowpipe to remove the air, then flattening the glass into a small disk. The artist would then cut and piece together the cooled glass into predetermined shapes and bond them together with lead. Colorful stains were then wiped onto the glass, and black ink was applied with a brush to refine and enhance the scene (Figure 3.30). Although colorful stained glass was plentiful in Gothic cathedrals, glass windows in the home were reserved for extremely wealthy families.

Owning glassware during the Medieval period reflected refinement of taste and money. The most exquisite examples came from Venetian glass makers. The small village of Murano, an island near Venice, was well-known throughout Europe for its glass production and was visited often by wealthy merchants during the Renaissance. Venetian glassmakers experimented with using quartz to produce a clear, colorless glass. This glass known as *cristallo* (*crystal*) was extremely expensive (Figure 3.31). For those who could afford them, glass cups, beakers, and bowls supplemented pewter wares and wooden dishes in household inventories.

## METALWORKING

Although the art of *enameling* can be traced back to ancient Mycenaean culture, the craft became more popular during the Medieval period. Since the first millennium, enameling appeared as decoration on church reliquaries throughout

**FIGURE 3.29** **Glazed jugs show primitively drawn birds with an unusual humanlike head projecting from the rim of the shorter vessel. These ceramic jugs were used for serving wine and ale.** Geoff Dann/Dorling Kindersley © York Archaeological Trust for Excavation and Research Ltd.

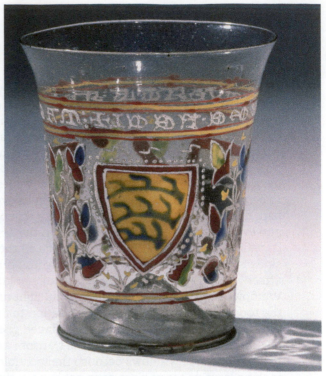

FIGURE 3.30 A pane of stained glass features a king sailing the seas. The knights with him suggest they are on a crusade. Black ink applied with a brush enlivens facial features and clothing. © Marco Desscouleurs/Fotolia LLC.

FIGURE 3.31 This Italian beaker has intricate painted designs, including a coat of arms that identifies its owner. This example of Venetian glass dates from the 1300s. Dorling Kindersley © The British Museum

FIGURE 3.32 These two metal lanterns were decorated with a punched trefoil design that allowed candlelight to filter into the room. The round ring at the top is a handle for carrying the lantern from place to place and served as a means of hanging the lantern. © Dorling Kindersley.

Europe. Enameled designs were created by applying a ground glass paste in a variety of colors to the body of either copper or brass. The object was then heated, which fused the glass to the metal and brought out the sheen of the glass. After cooling, the exposed copper or brass was polished, giving the appearance of bright gold. A form of enameling, the art of *cloisonné* was introduced into Europe from Byzantium. Thin, raised bands of copper or brass were adhered to the body of the object to define the decorative patterns. The partitions were then filled with colored enamels and heated, fusing the glass and bringing out its luster. The small partitions, called *cloisons* in French, appeared bright gold after polishing. By the 15th century, *Limoges* in central France produced some of the finest cloisonné work in Europe.

*Wrought iron* goods were produced during the Medieval period by blacksmiths, who forged the metal into a variety of usable objects by hammering out shapes on an anvil. Strap hinges and locking devices fortified doors and chests, and were held in place with large rivets (Figures 3.24 and 3.25). Window openings were secured with wrought iron bars. Lighting fixtures were made from the same iron material used for hinges on doors and case furniture. Iron was used to make light fixtures such as chandeliers, lanterns, and candlesticks.

*Torchères* were held in place by large iron rings that were mortared into the stonework or stucco, and smaller lanterns were carried from room to room where they were hung on iron brackets (Figure 3.32). Swinging candle holders were mounted on each side of fireplaces; in the open position when the candles were lit, and against the wall when they were not in use. Chandeliers hung from the high ceilings from chains that were lowered by a pulley-type system at dusk to light the candles or oil they contained (Figure 3.6). Candles made from beeswax were relatively expensive for the time, but were preferred by wealthy households because they burned clean without much smoke. Cheaper ones made from tallow, or animal fat, emitted black smoke and an unpleasant odor.

A variety of decorative accessories was found in the medieval castle, although their purpose was primarily functional. Most were household utensils fashioned out of pewter and were displayed in the great hall on the massive *dressoir*. Pewter, an alloy of tin and lead, was made into kitchen and tableware items such as pitchers, cups, plates, and bowls. Silver was a luxury enjoyed by wealthier families; pewter, with its dull finish and thicker proportions, was a less expensive substitute. By the 14th century, pewter workshops were commonplace around Europe, and artisans who worked with this metal established guilds to improve their craft.

Copper, brass, and bronze were used in the making of statuary, reliquaries, and candlesticks for the church by metalworkers using both the lost-wax and casting methods. Monumental brasses first appeared during the 13th century as effigies to deceased nobility, royalty, and papal leaders, capturing the likeness of the deceased in flat relief applied over sarcophagi. Brass was made from an alloy of copper and calamine, a material with zinc compounds. Although bronze figurines and lamps date back to early Roman times, during the Medieval period brass was favored for its coloring, which resembled gold. The establishment of guilds for metalworkers during the 13th century set standards for the artisans and workshops that regulated the quality of these goods.

## TEXTILES

First used in China and the Middle East as early as the ninth century, the spinning wheel appeared in Europe by the mid 14th century. Separate guilds were set up for those who produced the cloth—like dyers, spinners, and weavers—from those who sold the cloth. Cloth merchants quickly became the new middle class as the trade flourished throughout Europe. Most fabrics were made from linen or wool fibers, and in addition to making clothing, were used to supply homes with drapes, tablecloths, bedding, and cushions (Figure 3.33).

During most of ancient history, *embroidery* work was performed by women as part of their domestic duties. Girls were taught how to embroider, and as their skills improved, contributed to making the pillowcases, draperies, tablecloths, and seat cushions for the home. Professional guilds supplied the necessary textiles for church interiors. The most famous embroidery dating from the Medieval period comes from Bayeux, France. Misidentified as a tapestry by early scholars, the Bayeux Tapestry was commissioned to commemorate the Battle of Hastings, which occurred in 1066 between England and Normandy (Figure 3.34). Scenes embroidered into the more than 230-foot-long cloth document medieval history and include the battle itself, the construction of Westminster Abbey in London, and the passing of Halley's Comet. The embroidery was believed to have been stitched by nuns.

The art of tapestry weaving thrived during the 13th and 14th centuries in Europe, with some of the finest examples coming from France and Flanders in northern Europe. Expensive to own, tapestries were hung on the walls of the great hall, insulating the room against drafts and dampness (Figure 3.6). Tapestries made from hand-dyed woolen yarns interspersed with silk threads were commissioned that depicted landscapes, Christian scenes, and contemporary subjects in rich colors of crimson, ultramarine, and greens with yellow gold. An expensive detail in tapestry weaving were small clusters of local flora called *millefleurs*—literally, "thousand flowers"—and the quantity was agreed on in advance between weaver and patron.

**FIGURE 3.33** This gold embroidered pillow finished in gold fringe depicts an enthroned Christ. Alistair Duncan © Dorling Kindersley.

**FIGURE 3.34** The famous Bayeux Tapestry is not a tapestry at all. It is embroidery work featuring the Battle of Hastings. It was completed during the 11th century. © Image Asset Management Ltd./SuperStock.

Medieval tapestries were very expensive to produce, requiring more than a year for a workshop of weavers to complete. Woven with woolen yarns, silk threads, and sometimes gold, tapestries bore colors that were bright and vivid. The dyes used for coloring yarn came from plants, especially *woad*, which gave the medieval weaver the brilliant blue seen in many tapestries from this period.

The tapestries shown here have similar qualities, although they were woven nearly 400 years apart. The first tapestry dates from around 1511 and is one of six panels designed by a French artist and woven in Belgium (Figure 3.35). Its subject, *Lady and the Unicorn*, illustrates the five senses (touch, smell, taste, sight, and hearing); the meaning of the sixth panel is unclear. Each panel features the central figures set in a landscape of flora and fauna among a field of millefleurs with Latin inscriptions.

The Pre-Raphaelite Brotherhood of artisans, including the legendary William Morris (1834–1896), who worked during the late 19th century, sought to recreate the handcrafted quality of medieval guild workers in a time when machine-made crafts were threatening the livelihood of the artist. Morris & Company sold high-quality home furnishings all made by hand using traditional craft methods. Tapestries made for his company depicted images similar to those once popular during the Medieval period: Christian subjects, pastoral landscapes, and figures dressed in medieval clothing.

The second tapestry, designed by Pre-Raphaelite painter Sir Edward Burne-Jones (1833–1898) in 1892 and woven by John Henry Dearle (1860–1932), depicts a landscape set with flora and fauna including deer, fox, and rabbits among trees on a field of millefleurs with inscriptions appearing above (Figure 3.36). Both tapestries were woven by hand on looms using hand-dyed woolen yarns colored with natural pigments.

Although the two tapestries share similarities, their differences reveal the changes in art over the span of nearly 400 years. The scene in the earlier tapestry shows a flattened, almost bird's-eye perspective; the figures are viewed as if looking at them from straight on, and the background landscape rises up and is forced forward into the scene rather than receding toward any distinctive horizon. These contrasting perspectives are indicative of earlier painting styles of the period.

In the later example, Burne-Jones used variations in scale to project a sense of depth into the scene and used millefleurs along the bottom to anchor the figures to a ground plane. Furthermore, the animals and trees depicted in the landscape appear in scale to one another, unlike the disparity between the size of the woman and her maidservant from *The Lady and the Unicorn*.

**FIGURE 3.36** This tapestry dates from the 19th century and was inspired by those from the Medieval period with its depiction of animals in a forest surrounded by millefleurs. © Judith Miller/Dorling Kindersley/Lyon and Turnbull Ltd.

**FIGURE 3.35** This French tapestry depicts a well-dressed woman and her attendant in a forest surrounded by a field of millefleurs and animals, including the mythological unicorn. Neil Lukas © Dorling Kindersley, Courtesy of Musee National du Moyen-Age Thermes de Cluny.

# Fifteenth and Sixteenth Centuries

## The Renaissance

The word "renaissance" is derived from the French "renaitre," meaning to be born anew. The term is used to describe the cultural milieu of the 15th and 16th centuries, which many scholars consider to be the origin of modernity. Significant cultural changes took place during the last two and a half centuries of the Medieval period that led to a rebirth of classic ideology that we call the "European Renaissance." Until the 13th century, only a small percentage of people had reading and writing skills. The majority of the population received a limited education, mostly through liturgical teachings from the church. Because members of the clergy were respected as great scholars and teachers, Christian monasteries became vast repositories of ancient classical texts that predated Christianity, and professed polytheistic religions were sequestered by the church, including classical studies and the writings of Plato, Socrates, and Homer. It is not difficult to understand why classical studies were not part of the educational process.

By the end of the 13th century, England, France, and Italy had established the first universities, allowing the sons of wealthy landowners to study subjects not covered in liturgical teaching. Over time, education continued to improve. At the end of the 14th century, Greek philosophy was taught for the first time since antiquity. The establishment of Greek studies at Florence University prompted Italians to explore their heritage and rediscover the beauty of classicism that lay in ruins around them.

Other factors contributing to the end of the Medieval period occurred during the mid 15th century. The seat of the eastern Roman Empire fell to Ottoman Turks in 1453. At that time, members of the clergy fled to Europe, bringing with them ancient classical manuscripts from the libraries established by the Muslims in Alexandria. In 1454, with the invention of movable type and the printing press, these ancient texts were translated into Latin, and multiple copies were printed for distribution around Europe.

Enlightenment soon followed as western Europeans were introduced to the great philosophers, scientists, and mathematicians of ancient Greece and Rome. Educated readers thirsting for knowledge embraced the classical teaching of humanism, which encouraged free thinking and the right of individuals to determine their own destiny. These events, coupled with greater independence from strict church doctrine, enabled educated classes to experience knowledge at levels unequaled since before the fall of the Roman Empire.

# Architecture

## ITALY

The construction of churches and cathedral projects continued during the 15th century throughout Europe. In addition, with a thriving economy brought on by an increase in international trade, large-scale palaces, villas, and *chateaus* were built for the wealthier merchant classes. A shift away from the heaviness of the medieval style gave way to more unified proportions of classicism when a compilation of writings by the first-century Roman architect Vitruvius was first published in 1486 as contemporary Italian architects experimented with Vitruvian theories.

The Palazzo Davizzi, first built in the 1350s, was transformed into an upscale palace for the wealthy merchant Davanzati family, who purchased it in 1578 (Figure 4.1). The street-facing exterior resembled ancient Roman townhouses, with large ground-floor bays that led to an interior courtyard, where four floors of rooms inside the palace were arranged around its perimeter. The interior was decorated in lavish fashion for the 14th century, with decorative frescos of faux hanging cloth, coats of arms, and scenes from medieval literature (Figure 4.2). Exposed wood-beam ceilings featured painted motifs that complemented wall paintings in each room, and floors were laid in ceramic tile in a herringbone pattern. Heavy wood shutters closed off windows made of small panes of glass.

In 1570, the architect Andrea Palladio (1518–1580) published *Four Books on Architecture* in which he wrote about classic traditions in architecture and provided illustrations of architectural relics from the days of the Roman Empire. His treatise not only influenced contemporary Italian design, but influenced architects and designers throughout Europe. Palladio's design for the Villa Rotunda, built in 1567, is a testament to his exploration of classical forms. The villa established the Italian Renaissance style with its large Ionic porticoes, central dome, and monumental staircases arranged on all four sides (Figure 4.3). The villa emphasized perfect symmetry on each of its four facades and in the interior planning (Figure 4.4). Elaborate trompe l'oeil paintings, black-and-white patterned marble floors, highly ornate moldings, and classically based reliefs used in the interior scheme set the tone for interior décor throughout the next two centuries.

**FIGURE 4.1** The exterior of the Palazzo Davanzati features the family coat of arms among the rows of arched windows along its façade. An upper loggia is a significant characteristic of Renaissance architectural planning. James McConnachie © Rough Guides Dorling Kindersley.

**FIGURE 4.2** This salon from the Palazzo Davanzati shows the family wealth as seen in the elaborate decoration of the interior. Walls are painted to look like hanging cloth, and the wooden beam ceiling features painted accents. akg-images/Rabatti-Domingie.

Italian villas resembled Roman counterparts by featuring vast interior courtyards reminiscent of the garden peristyle. Many of the villas were situated on hills overlooking manicured gardens with rushing fountains. Interiors had high ceilings with windows placed at the top, leaving walls open for decoration. Intricately woven tapestries were hung against brick or stone walls to provide beautiful decoration and offer warmth to otherwise drafty interiors. In many homes, walls were plastered, allowing skilled artists to paint elaborate frescos rivaling ancient Roman examples. Trompe l'oeil scenery expanded the imagination through false representations of bookcases, landscapes, and *intarsia* paneling. By the 16th century, the Italian Renaissance style had spread to Spain, Scandinavia, the Netherlands, France, and England.

## SPAIN

Because Spain had been occupied by the Moors from the eighth century until they were driven out of power by the Christian rulers King Ferdinand and Queen Isabella in 1492, architectural styling had been greatly influenced by Arab culture and Islamic designs. These influences prevailed over Italian Renaissance design for most of the 16th century as Spanish architects gradually reintroduced classical elements. The Alhambra palace complex built in Grenada between 1338 and 1390 reflected Islamic design elements brought into southern Spain with Moorish occupation (Figure 4.5). The palace was arranged around gardens and reflecting pools, which were symbolic of heaven and paradise. Surface decoration on exterior and interior

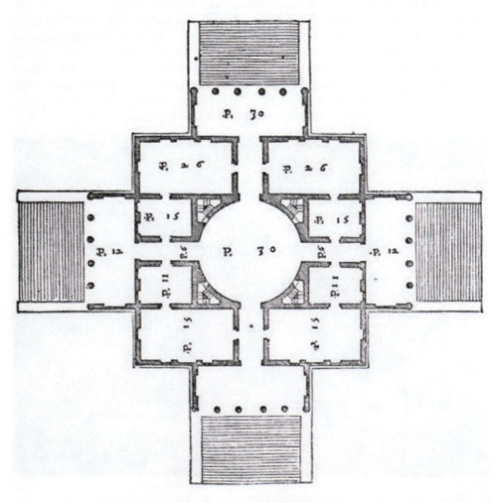

**FIGURE 4.4** The perfectly symmetrical plan of Villa Rotunda is anchored by a large, central dome.

**FIGURE 4.5** A view of one of the Moorish–designed buildings in the Alhambra.
© Philip Lange/Shutterstock.

**FIGURE 4.6** The lion courtyard inside the Alhambra is seen with Moorish arches and honeycomb vaulting in the background.
© Sillycoke/Shutterstock.

walls featured lacelike arabesque carvings and Kufic calligraphic script because early Islamists avoided representation of living beings akin to graven images. Three-dimensional honeycomb patterns called "*muqarnas*" were a key element of Islamic design based on strict geometric patterning (Figure 4.6). These elaborate patterns were adapted as applied ornamentation to vaults, walls, and capitals.

Arabian houses were designed around a central patio and water fountain, common elements for houses in regions with hot, dry climates. Iron *grillwork* in arabesque patterns of Islamic inspiration were incorporated around the loggia and on stairwells and balconies. Colorful ceramic tiles designed with highly ornate and fluid linear patterns, or those with strong geometric patterning, covered floors and walls. Similarly, the Spanish house, or "*casa*," was designed around a central patio surrounded by wrought iron grillwork resembling medieval tracery. Emphasis on this iron grillwork was repeated in the interior in the design of accessories and furniture. Interior walls and floors were covered with ceramic tiles designed with intricate geometric patterns or in the shape of an eight-point star, a definitive Moorish influence. The resulting *Mudéjar* style was a blending of Moorish and western influences (Figure 4.7).

The El Escorial, the royal palace and mausoleum built for the Spanish monarchy begun in 1563, incorporated many Italian Renaissance characteristics, including an attention to symmetry, classical detailing, and Tuscan columns (Figure 4.8). Built under the guidance of King Philip II (r. 1556–1598), the complex, which also included a monastery, was first started by Juan Bautista de Toledo. Upon his death in 1567, the project was taken over by Juan de Herrera (1530–1597). Interior furnishings featured finely designed furniture, quality textiles, and intricate decorative accessories. The king's chamber appears modest when compared with European examples, but is a fine example of Moorish influence. The antechamber features a low ceiling, plaster walls with tiled wainscoting, and a monochromatic tiled floor (Figure 4.9). A view through to the bedchamber reveals heavy wooden doors with geometric paneling that were carved in Germany, and a tester bed covered in rich red and gold embroidered bed curtains and coverlet.

## FRANCE

French architectural design remained immersed in the heaviness of the Medieval style well into the 16th century. The Italian Renaissance style of design and architecture was first introduced to French craftsmen and women when Leonardo da Vinci (1452–1519) left Italy in 1516 and traveled there on the invitation of François I (r. 1515–1547). In France, Leonardo became the king's military advisor and offered

**FIGURE 4.8** The architects Juan Bautista de Toledo and Juan de Herrera designed El Escorial, palace to King Philip II of Spain. The palace complex dates from 1563 and shows the emerging Renaissance style in Spanish architecture. © Alberto Loyo/Shutterstock.

**FIGURE 4.7** This 16th-century Spanish interior in the Mudéjar style has a heavy wooden ceiling, white plaster walls, and a hooded fireplace flanked by niches filled with decorative pottery. Placed around the dining table are two armchairs—in Spanish, *sillón de frailero*. One chair has velvet upholstery and the other is covered in leather. A fancy rug with geometric designs in the Islamic tradition covers the floor. Museo Nacional de Artes Decorativas.Madrid.

designs for Chateau du Chambord, François' palatial hunting lodge (Figure 4.10). The palace was remodeled to include classical designs mixed with medieval fortifications. It was not until François' son and successor, King Henry II, married Catherine de Medici of Italy in 1533 that the royal residence at Chambord was transformed into an Italian–inspired palace. Fontainebleau, begun in 1528, quickly became a showplace of French high Renaissance styling with the interior design completed by Italian wood-carvers, painters, and plasterers. The Italian Mannerist style of design came to France through Catherine's importation of Italian artisans who changed the royal residences from weighty medieval castles into refined renaissance estates (Figure 4.11).

**FIGURE 4.9** The interior of El Escorial shows restraint in classical designs in this view of the king's private chamber. Low ceilings, plaster walls with tiled wainscoting, and a tile floor laid in a herringbone pattern provide a simple background for leather chairs. A rather ornate chandelier hangs from the ceiling. The Art Archive at Art Resource, NY.

**FIGURE 4.10** This view of Chateau du Chambord, built from 1519 to 1547, reveals a classically appointed façade with its Palladian windows, ornate pediments, and pilasters coupled with Medieval–style turrets. © Lazar Mihai-Bogdan/Shutterstock.

## ENGLAND

The Renaissance style developed much later in the British Isles than in other countries, perhaps because of England's geographic location, separated from the European continent by the English Channel. English design characteristics borrowed heavily from other countries, including Holland and Flanders, and appropriated features from ecclesiastical models like oak paneling, stained glass windows, and vaulted ceilings. Hampton Court (Figure 4.12), home to the English monarchs beginning with King Henry VIII, featured crenellated brick walls and turrets on the exterior, with fan-vaulted ceilings, wall paneling carved with linen-fold motif, and large windows fitted with stained glass. Like those of the Medieval period beforehand, English castles built during the 15th century maintained the importance of the great hall as the most impressive room in the house, specifically designed to display the wealth of its owners (Figure 4.13).

**FIGURE 4.11** The bedroom of Catherine de Medici at Chenonceau features elaborate Italian–influenced designs. © Vladimir Korostyshevskiy/Shutterstock.

**FIGURE 4.12** An interesting juxtaposition of the various styles of Hampton Court architecture is seen in this photo. On the right, the original 1515 castle appears with its crenellated walls. The building on the left, an addition built in 1689 by Sir Christopher Wren, exhibits refined classical detailing with its balustrade roofline and prominent quoins. © Rachael Russell/Shutterstock.

**FIGURE 4.13** This great hall in the Tudor style features a high, fan-vaulted ceiling with hooded fireplace, a refectory table, and wall cupboard. Joe Cornish © Dorling Kindersley.

FIGURE 4.14 Begun in 1616, Inigo Jones's design for Queen's House in Greenwich introduced England to the classical styles of the Italian Renaissance. © aniad/Shutterstock.

FIGURE 4.15 This home in Stratford-upon-Avon in England belonged to the physician John Hall, who was the son-in-law of William Shakespeare. Although the home is modest compared with an English manor house, it is an exemplary Tudor–style house with its exposed timber framing and white stucco walls, and is typical of the physician's social class. © WH CHOW/Shutterstock.

English country houses eventually advanced from the large fortified castles, once seats of power for feudal lords, to well-proportioned estate houses. Floor-to-ceiling oak wall paneling and *pargework* ceiling designs were featured in English Renaissance period interiors. The long gallery, an adaptation of a cloistered walkway in a medieval church, was used as an activity area during inclement weather. The long and narrow room had windows that ran its length on one side, whereas on the opposite wall, ancestral portraits were hung. English designers did not adopt a true interpretation of the Renaissance style until the 17th century, when the architect Inigo Jones (1573–1652) returned from studying in Italy and introduced the style to England's King James I (Figure 4.14).

Residences built for the middle class were half-timber framed houses with stucco walls, a style often referred to as "Tudor," named after King Henry (Tudor) VIII (Figure 4.15). The timber framing clearly visible on the outside of these structures was carried through to the interior walls, which were periodically whitewashed to cover layers of soot. Rooms were small and had low, exposed-beam ceilings in-filled with plaster, wood floors, and modest furnishings.

# Design Motifs

With a renewed interest in the aesthetic qualities perfected by the Roman and Greek cultures, Italian Renaissance artisans had only to turn to the ruins of Rome for inspiration. Half buried in the earth, broken entablatures and capitals lay on the ground around the city. As excavations began and the new foundation was laid for the rebuilding of Saint Peter's church in Rome at the beginning of the 16th century, a multitude of classical artifacts were discovered that provided exquisite examples of architectural details. Motifs like dentil moldings, egg-and-dart patterns, gadroons, garlands, and guilloche designs inspired builders and artists during the Renaissance, and were incorporated as decorations in well-appointed interiors and on furnishings (Figure 4.16).

The great sculptures of Apollo and Venus, no longer idolized as gods, became sources of inspiration for perfect beauty. Gods and goddesses, including small cupids or *putti,* adorned architectural interiors and furnishings as creatures from mythology, but not as the powerful supreme beings once worshipped by the ancient Romans. Lively scenes with frolicking putti, classical goddesses, and an assortment of satyrs, griffins, and nymphs were popular subjects of tapestry weavings, fresco designs, and carved details on moldings and furniture (Figure 4.17).

Garlands

Garlands

Fleur de lis

Guilloche with oakleaf
and rosette

Laurel leaves

Rinceau

Cartouche

Arabesque

Arabesque

**FIGURE 4.16** Motifs popular during the Renaissance period feature those designs inspired by the ancient Roman past. © David Vleck.

Spanish, French, and English artists adopted classical motifs over time as the Renaissance style was introduced through Juan Bautista de Toledo in Spain, Catherine de Medici's Italian workers in France, and Inigo Jones in England. French designs focused on classical arabesques, establishing the Burgundian style of carvings, and simple geometric lozenge patterns (Figure 4.18). Spanish designs featured moderate classical ornamentation, choosing to emphasize Moorish-based geometric designs in the Mudéjar style. The octogram, or eight-pointed star pattern, was used by Moslem designers in the building of eighth-century mosques and became a symbol of Islam (Figure 4.19). The Mudéjar style, popular in southern Spain since the Medieval period, was a western interpretation of these Moorish or Islamic designs (Figure 4.20).

# Furniture

During the 16th century, an established middle-class economy enabled more people to own fine furnishings for their homes than any previous time in history. However, there was still a disparity between the classes in what they could afford when it came to quality and style. Wealthier merchant classes could afford to own furnishings designed for luxury and comfort in the latest style. Upholstered furniture first appeared during the 15th century as the cloth trade flourished throughout Europe. New types of furniture were introduced, presenting a new array of chair designs, expandable tables, and a chest of drawers.

Typically, walnut replaced oak as the primary wood used in furniture construction, and carving was the most common decorative feature. Turned *baluster* and urn shapes were used on chair and table legs, often made more decorative with carved motifs or exaggerated into swelling, bulbous forms (Figure 4.21). Stretchers continued to be used and were designed in a variety of forms, usually mimicking the style of the furniture legs. Feet were articulated with geometric designs, although use of the lion paw appeared on classically inspired pieces. Case goods were designed with more architectonic features, accentuating entablatures with frieze relief carvings.

Because furniture was more plentiful than in prior periods, the need to move items from room to room decreased and chairs were designed for specific purposes. In addition, the introduction of

**FIGURE 4.17** This detail of an architectural panel from the 15th century shows two putti holding a cartouche. Linda Whitwam © Dorling Kindersley.

Lozenge

Geometric panels

**FIGURE 4.18** Geometric design motifs like these were an Islamic influence and are seen as decoration on doors, chests, and cabinets. © David Vleck.

**Eight-point star**

**Rosette medallion**

**Eight point star with geometric pattern**

**FIGURE 4.19** Design motifs based on variations on the eight-point star are Islamic in origin. © David Vleck.

**FIGURE 4.20** Emblems of the fleur-de-lis and rosettes appear on these Spanish–made tiles. Queen Elizabeth I of England used the fleur-de-lis in her official coat of arms, and the motif was adopted by the French monarchs as early as the 12th century. Linda Whitwam © Dorling Kindersley.

**Ball foot**

**Bun foot**

**FIGURE 4.21** Common foot forms used on furniture of the Renaissance period. © David Vleck.

**FIGURE 4.22** This drawing represents an Italian *sgabello* from the early 16th century and features an exaggerated tapered back and delicate acanthus leaf carvings on the trestlelike supports, with egg-and-dart moldings and an ornately carved crest rail.

upholstered furniture made an improvement over loose-cushion seating. Horse hair padding was placed over the seat and sometimes the back of a chair, and then covered with either fabric or leather. Held in place with nails or tacks, the stretched material gave the piece of furniture a tailored look.

Chests and small caskets were an integral part of household inventories. Like those of the Medieval period, these trunks contained household valuables that were kept under lock and key. In addition to chests and caskets, cupboards and cabinets appeared in greater numbers. The design of these case goods incorporated numerous architectural elements; engaged columns supported entablatures with carved moldings, and elaborate classical motifs appeared in the frieze area. Cupboards were used in the dining hall to store linens, dishes, and glass beakers, and writing cabinets were owned by the literate wealthy.

## ITALY

Because the Renaissance basically began in Italy, it is important to look at specific examples of furniture from this country first, because the Italian style set the tone for other countries. Household inventories list two types of stools in plentiful quantities. The typical X-form folding design was still common, although a more comfortable type with a fixed back developed. A *sgabello*, which evolved from these types of stools, had a small, triangular backrest attached to the trestle-supported seat (Figure 4.22). Although these chairs were quite uncomfortable, they were small enough to be moved from the bedroom into the dining hall when necessary. Women usually sat in these chairs because the absence of arms accommodated their cumbersome skirts. Many were fitted with a single drawer under the seat that was used for storing sewing yarns.

Chairs used for ceremony were not as popular as they once had been during the Medieval period, and the few examples that still existed were ornamented with classical carvings. The box-form armchair, called a *sedia*, generally replaced these large-scale ceremonial chairs and was much smaller in size, although still rectangular in design. *Sedias* had velvet or tapestry upholstery that often featured fringe, or were upholstered in tooled leather. Finials carved into various shapes extended from the uprights, and squared legs with bracket or paw feet were connected front to back with runners or stretchers. This chair was used on a more formal basis in the *refectory*, or dining room. A *sedia* was positioned at each end of the table during the meal, and was placed against the wall while not in use. As chairs continued to be designed in smaller, more lightweight styles, upholstered armchairs and side chairs introduced during the latter half of the 16th century had shorter backs and an open frame. This style of chair was adopted by other European countries and is characteristic of more practical, less formal designs (Figure 4.23).

Another popular upholstered chair, the *Dantesca*, was named for the Italian Renaissance poet Dante. This chair was designed with front and back staves that

FIGURE 4.23 This 19th-century reproduction of a 16th-century Italian chair has a *needlepoint*-patterned fabric trimmed in fringe. The volute arms, oversized but decorative front and back stretchers, and inlaid ivory are typical features of Renaissance furniture styling. © Judith Miller/Dorling Kindersley/Lyon and Turnbull Ltd.

FIGURE 4.24 This drawing of a 16th-century Italian folding chair, called a "Dantesca," is identified by its low upholstered back, loose cushion seat, and X-form base.

were of the X form, although the chair did not fold (Figure 4.24). The two curule-form staves were connected with runners that usually had front-facing paw feet. A broad, upholstered crest rail served as the back support. Although some Dantescas had classical details carved on the frame, others were decorated with *intarsia* or *certosina*. Similar in shape, the *Savonarola*, was designed to fold. The name of this chair pays homage to the 16th-century friar who was unpopular with the Florentines and the powerful Medici family. Friar Savonarola was burned at the stake in 1498. These chairs were made from walnut and had multiple staves that enabled the chair to fold lengthwise (Figure 4.25). The crest rail was hinged on one side and clamped into place on the opposite side, maintaining the stability of the chair when it was open. In a less decorative form, the chair was popular among monks and friars, which is probably how the chair became known by the name of the infamous friar.

Derived from both the Roman *lectus* with fulcrum armrests and the medieval box-form settle, the *cassapanca* became the prototype for the modern sofa. Made entirely from wood, the *cassapanca* was attached to its own dais, had arms on both ends, and had a hinged seat that could be raised to access a concealed storage compartment. This piece was not upholstered, but like the settle had loose cushions on both back and seat.

During the Renaissance period, dining took place in a room used exclusively for eating, and a more permanent table was designed to

FIGURE 4.25 This walnut *Savonarola* is all wood with no upholstery, and its X-form base with multiple staves allows for easy lengthwise folding. akg-images/Orsi Battaglini.

In ancient Roman times, the *lectus* served as a bed and a reclining couch from which people ate their meals (Figure 4.26). The 16th-century Italian *cassapanca* resembles the design of the Roman *lectus* in form, with its fulcrum-shaped arms and raised seat (Figure 4.27). Like the *lectus*, the *cassapanca* would be covered with loose cushions to make it more comfortable, although its design did not support reclining, but sitting, like a modern-day sofa. Compare the two furniture pieces:

- How does the *lectus* influence the design of the *cassapanca* that evolved nearly a thousand years later?

- What lifestyle changes occurred to eliminate the practice of reclining while eating?
- What characteristics on the *cassapanca* were influenced by Roman design?

**FIGURE 4.26** This drawing of an ancient roman lectus features four disk-turned legs, each pair attached to runners. A fulcrum arm rest is positioned next to a short backrest.

**FIGURE 4.27** This drawing of a *cassapanca* from the 16th century features a scrolled pediment of reclining classical nudes. A loose cushion placed on top of the seat would have made the piece more comfortable.

remain in the center of the room. The refectory table was similar in design to the medieval trestle table; however, its long and narrow top was securely attached to a supporting framework, often two trestlelike ends connected with a stretcher (Figure 4.28). Also, as threat of assassination lessened, people sat on both sides of the table seated on *sedias, sgabellos*, stools, or benches. When the table was not in use, the seating furniture was either placed against the wall or returned to the rooms from which they were borrowed. In homes of the very wealthy, tapestries or Turkish carpets were often used as table covers.

At the time of the Italian Renaissance period, the medieval credenza developed from a small table-like cabinet into a larger type of storage cupboard. Placed in the refectory, this piece of furniture provided storage for eating implements. Designed with drawers in the frieze area, and doors that opened to shelving below, this cupboard was ornamented with either carved, inlaid, or painted designs (Figure 4.28). Cupboards were plentiful because there was the need for separate storage pieces used to contain a wide variety of household goods. Cupboards were designed in all sizes—small and wide, tall and narrow (Figure 4.29). Designs varied depending on which room they occupied. Simpler types were embellished with moldings whereas classical motifs were carved on friezes, door fronts, and legs.

The most important piece of furniture used in the home was the chest, or *cassone* (Figure 4.30).

**FIGURE 4.28** The banquet room from the Palazzo Davanzati in Florence features an Italian Renaissance–style refectory table carved with large paw feet. A long credenza can be seen against the back wall. © Scala/Art Resource, NY.

Renaissance versions of the medieval chest resembled Roman sarcophagi, and were decorated with classical figures rather than heavy iron strapping and crude carvings. These chests were often placed at the foot of the bed and were used to store family valuables as well as clothing.

In Italy, the winter temperatures were not as harsh as those in northern Europe. Because of this, the tester bed was replaced by a four-poster canopy bed, highly decorative in design but not necessarily outfitted with enclosing drapes. Bedrooms served as private chambers for individual members of the household, and it was not unusual for people to visit with their guests in these quarters. Bedrooms were furnished with chairs and tables, allowing for meals to be eaten in privacy.

**FIGURE 4.29** A carved walnut credenza with large paw feet features a geometric front and side panel design. © Judith Miller/Dorling Kindersley/Sloan's.

**FIGURE 4.30** This Italian *cassone* carved from walnut features an array of classical motifs including acanthus leaves, gadroons, arabesques, and laurel leaves. © Judith Miller/Dorling Kindersley/Sloans & Kenyon.

# LEARN More

## Italian Renaissance Interior Design

**FIGURE 4.31** A bedroom room from the Palazzo Davanzati features Renaissance–style furniture dating from the 16th century. Erich Lessing/Art Resource.

The Palazzo Davanzati residence in Florence was built during the 14th century as a palace for a wool merchant and his family, and was a testament to the prosperity of the cloth trade. The palace is representa- tive of homes owned by wealthy Florentines during the early Renaissance (Figures 4.1 and 4.2). The massive scale of the room and its elaborate decorations are an indication of the family's status. This bedroom boasts high ceilings, with painted wood beams supported on the ends with large *modillions*. Brightly colored frescoes are painted in the frieze area, high above a geometric border and wall pattern, and feature the narrative *Lady of Vergi*, a French romantic tale about a noblewoman and a medieval knight. The corner fireplace was used to take the chill out of the room, while heavy wooden shutters close out drafts and help to filter the light. The *terra cotta* tile floor is run on the diagonal, mocking the diamond-patterned wall painting. These architectural elements are typical of the 14th century; however, the interior furnishings date from the 16th century. The carved walnut canopy bed, cradle, and credenza depict classical motifs whereas the chair incorporates carved decorations on its oversize crest rail back.

## SPAIN

It has already been mentioned that the Italians set the stylistic direction for the Renaissance period, whereas other European countries adapted the style to fit their own unique tastes. Although there are many consistencies in the type of furnishings used, including the curule-form armchair, square-back upholstered dining chairs, and numerous chests and cabinets, there are some distinctive stylistic differences among European countries. Furniture items presented in this section reflect some of these variances. Spanish furniture craftsmen introduced a new chair designed to benefit the working class. The Barcelona *ladder back chair* was an economical chair to produce because the frame, uprights, legs, and stretchers were turned spindles held together with mortise-and-tenon joints. The backs were a series of flat, horizontal splats spaced like the rungs of a ladder, giving the chair its unique name. A rush seat provided a firm but comfortable foundation without the expense of upholstery fabric or leather.

Very similar in styling to the Italian *sedia*, the Spanish *sillón de frailero* was so commonly used by monks that the name itself is derivative of the word "friar." The back legs were one continuous piece, extending upward to create the stiles or uprights of the chair (Figures 4.7 and 4.9). A wide, ornamental stretcher was placed between the front legs and it typically mocked the design of the crest rail (Figure 4.32). This chair was usually padded and upholstered; nevertheless, folding types with a hinged frame covered with stretched leather seat and back enabled the chair to fold vertically. The furniture maker used nails with large heads to tack the upholstery fabric or leather to the seat rail and uprights. The use of large, oversize nail heads is a unique characteristic of Spanish designs. Comparable with the Italian Dantesca, although not as deep in the seat, the *sillón de caderas* (armchair hip) or *sillón de tijera* (armchair scissors) was of the curule form and was upholstered on the seat and back. Occasionally, these chairs would be designed without a back so that they resembled stools, except that the staves extended up from the front and back legs and along the sides, enveloping the sitter at the hips.

Table designs from the Spanish Renaissance period evolved from the prototype trestle table and, like Italian versions, were not intended to be dismantled and stored (Figure 4.7). The trestle supports were splayed, often in the shape of a lyre, or had decorative carvings. A common Spanish characteristic is the incorporation of wrought iron braces, a design feature that complemented the iron grillwork commonly seen in the stair railings and balconies of Spanish Renaissance homes. These underbraces were affixed to the underside of the tabletop, bent into delicate S curves and attached to the trestle ends in lieu of a stretcher (Figure 4.33).

Spanish Renaissance chests served the same purpose as other chests already discussed in this book. Most were of a box form with architectonic features like cornice-shaped lids and frieze panels, but the main difference between Spanish and Italian chests occurred in the style of the ornamentation. Even though the Italian influence reached Spain by the early 16th century, Moorish styles remained popular. Geometric patterns including lozenge or diamond shapes, radiating starbursts, eight-point star patterns, and recessed square panels appeared as carved details or were created in *taracea*, an inlay of bone, woods, metal, or ivory. A uniquely Middle Eastern

**FIGURE 4.32** This *sillón de frailero* is upholstered in leather, with prominent nail heads to keep it in place. The leather was tooled with geometric banding. The wide front stretcher is characteristic of 16th-century Spanish chair design. © Judith Miller/ Dorling Kindersley/Sloans & Kenyon.

**FIGURE 4.33** This drawing of a 16th-century Spanish table has trestle ends carved with acanthus leaf modillions and paw feet. Decorative wrought iron underbraces extend from the tabletop to the stretchers located on the supporting trestles.

**FIGURE 4.34** This antique Spanish damascene chest features an ornate eight-point star motif at its center. Max Alexander © Dorling Kindersley.

influence, Spanish *damascene*-style jewelry chests featured intricate arabesque patterns incised into iron or bronze and then gilded to bring out the designs (Figure 4.34).

The *armario*, a taller case piece designed after the medieval armoire, stored articles of clothing. Its arrangement resembles two chests placed one on top of the other, featuring architectonic qualities, carved geometric designs, or "*taracea*." These tall case pieces were also known as a "wardrobe," "linen press," or "press cupboard," and appeared in the bedroom or dining room, wherever appropriate depending on the items they stored, like bed linens, clothes, or table linens (Figure 4.35).

Portable writing desks were introduced into Spain by the Moors because their nomadic culture inspired furniture that could be transported easily from place to place. The

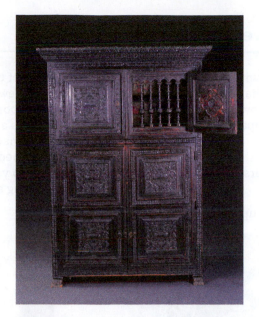

FIGURE 4.35 This cabinet is an example of a 17th-century Spanish press cupboard and features spindle turning with arabesque carved door panels. © Judith Miller/Dorling Kindersley/Sloan's.

FIGURE 4.36 This 17th-century Spanish walnut and marquetry *vargueño*, or writing cabinet, has a hinged fall-front surface for writing, and compact drawers for storing writing implements and papers. The inlaid arabesque patterns, along with the cabinet's portability, are influences of Moorish design. © Judith Miller/Dorling Kindersley/Sloan's.

Spanish *vargueño* featured two carrying handles, one on each side of a small cabinet (Figure 4.36). The interior was fitted with small drawers and pigeonholes concealed by a drop-down, front panel. When opened, the panel provided a smooth writing surface, usually covered in leather. Supporting the writing surface of the *vargueño*, two rods extended from the body of the stand to keep it in a horizontal position. In the home, the *vargueño* was placed on either a small stand called a *puente* (bridge) or set on top of a chest of drawers called a *taquillon*. These writing cabinets featured *taracea* or were carved with geometric diamond patterns. A *papelera* (from the word "paper") was used to store important papers. Like the *vargueño*, it was portable and had carrying handles at each end. Unlike the *vargueño*, the *papelera* did not have a writing surface. The *papelera* was placed on a small table or a tablelike stand.

## FRANCE

French furniture designed during the reign of François I appeared smaller in scale and was more lightweight than the preceding Gothic style. Chairs were small enough to be moved about the room and arranged according to need and function. Like most practices of the period, chairs were placed along the perimeter walls until they were needed. Ornamentation emphasized carved techniques, relying on subdued classical details, and many Gothic–inspired patterns were still somewhat fashionable. The *caquetoire*, which emerged during the latter half of the 16th century, was used as a conversation chair (Figure 4.37). *Caqueter* in French means "to chatter," and this chair, favored by men and women, featured a tall, slender back; a trapezoidal seat with the broad side positioned at the front of the chair, and *incurvate* arms. The openness of the arms enabled people to pivot left and right as they spoke with guests who were seated on either side. The back crest rail often featured a scrolled pediment, and arm posts and legs were turned into baluster or columnar shapes. The back panel often displayed carved barrel vaults or classical arabesque patterns.

Dining tables were designed with a variety of leg forms—from those with trestlelike supports to ones with distinctive shaped legs fashioned into columns, balusters, or bulbous forms. Because the table was now a stationary element in the dining room or refectory, expanding tables called "draw tables," were designed with either pull out extensions or drop leaves to accommodate more dinner guests. The extensions were fitted underneath the main tabletop and, when pulled out, were supported on wooden rods. This enabled the table to double its surface size. Gateleg tables were much smaller and were often used in the bedroom for serving

The *caquetoire* has a unique design with a tall, narrow back and a trapezoid-shape seat that narrows toward the back. Broad, rounded armrests allow plenty of room for people to move when seated. Compare the chair in Figure 4.37 with Figure 4.38.

- What characteristics do both chairs share?
- How are they different?
- Why does one chair have leather upholstery?

The design of the chair in Figure 4.38 was based on a romantic view of the past. The Arts and Crafts movement was popular in England during the 1860s as furniture makers and other artisans looked back to the quality of handmade objects in a time when mass production threatened their craft. After analyzing the 19th century chair, do you think its designer could be credited with creating a new style of furniture?

**FIGURE 4.37** This *caquetoire* is designed with classically based motifs that include arabesque carvings on the back, a scrolled pediment, turned arm posts, and columnar legs. Katarzyna and Wojciech Medrzakowie © Dorling Kindersley.

**FIGURE 4.38** An Arts and Crafts–style chair with inlaid flower designs and a leather seat. © Judith Miller/Dorling Kindersley/ Clevedon Salerooms.

**FIGURE 4.39** This French traveling chest was made from carved walnut reinforced with metal strapping on the exterior and inside the lid. A central rosette decorates the front surface.
© Dorling Kindersley, Courtesy of the Musee de Saint-Malo, France.

**FIGURE 4.40** A French provincial carved oak press cupboard has a palmette frieze cornice and foliate designs incorporated in geometric panels. It is fitted with shelves on the interior.
© Judith Miller/Dorling Kindersley/Freeman's.

light meals, like breakfast. The legs swung outward to support side leaves. When the meal was finished, the table was folded and placed against the wall.

Chests continued to be used throughout the Renaissance and served the same purpose as those from the time of the Middle Ages. Traveling chests were fitted with carrying handles, making transport much easier, and large trunks were often placed at the foot of the bed (Figure 4.39). Designs were based on the eclectic combination of classical forms initiated by Jacques Androuet du Cerceau (1520–1585) in his book published in 1559, *Livre de Architecture*, which featured designs for townhouses, gardens, and furniture that were purely geometric.

A variety of cupboards and cabinets were designed for different rooms in the home (Figure 4.40). Architectonic in structure, these case goods emphasized carved details on the entablature, engaged columns, classical carvings, and a combination of geometric designs. Dining rooms were furnished with a dressoir (Figure 3.23) for storing linens and tableware, and the *armoire à deux corps*, an armoire of two parts, was used in bedrooms to store articles of clothing. The separate top and bottom pieces made it much easier for the cabinetmaker to transport the armoire from his workshop to the chateau.

## ENGLAND

Styles in England did not immediately follow the Renaissance direction set by the Italians during the 15th century. It took time for the classical details to appear in furniture and other interior furnishings. There was more emphasis placed on turned forms rather than heavy carvings (Figure 4.41). The cup and cover turned supports typify English Renaissance design and ornamentation. English furniture designed during the Elizabethan period of the 16th century made little advancement over Gothic form. It was sturdy and rugged, and not as sophisticated as Italian or French examples. Stools usually were supported by splayed legs with baluster turning and were called "joint stools" because the components were held together with mortise-and-tenon construction.

Full skirts worn by women during this period hindered them from sitting in armchairs. The *Farthingale chair* was popularized by women's style of dress; full skirts were broadened with an underpinning of hoops in decreasing size toward the waist. Fully upholstered in *Turkey work* (large floral designs that looked like Oriental carpets), the chair had no arms, a raking crest rail back, and a shallow seat that enabled women to "perch" rather than sit. Gentlemen's versions were similar in design but had arms.

Other chairs resembled the Italian Dantesca; they had uprights, raking backs, curule-form legs, finials, nail heads, and fringe. Upholstered, this chair had thick cushions attached to the seat. The back was high with a broad crest rail. The English *wainscot chair* (Figure 4.42) was made popular through the placement of furniture tight against the wall. Its panel and frame design, taken from hay wagon construction methods, had a slightly raking, solid wood back ornamented with a scrolled pediment crest rail, modillions on the sides of the uprights, and box stretchers. These chairs were not upholstered, but were made more comfortable with a loose-cushion seat. The back panel was either carved, decorated with delicate inlay patterns, or both. Other chairs of similar type featured turned legs and arm posts, and backs had some carving if the chair was not upholstered. These turned elements were easily produced and made the furniture more affordable.

The English continued to use long tables in the dining hall, and many were fitted with expandable leaves. Draw tables featured sturdy bases that could support the extended table top (Figure 4.43). Smaller, multifunctional tables were used in other rooms. A very practical and somewhat adaptable table that unfolded and expanded as needed was introduced during the 16th century. The top had hinged leaves that could be raised onto legs that swung open for support (Figure 4.44). The gate-leg table offered the flexibility of having a larger

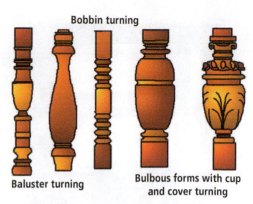

Bobbin turning

Baluster turning

Bulbous forms with cup and cover turning

FIGURE 4.41 Turned forms commonly used on furniture in the northern regions of Europe during the 16th century. © David Vleck.

FIGURE 4.42 This English wainscot chair has acanthus leaf carvings, classical putti, gadroon patterned arms, and columnar legs. Although upholstered chairs appeared in England during the 16th century, this wainscot chair would have had a loose seat cushion. Its position against a wainscoted wall gives it its name. Modillions in carved scroll patterns make the transition between crest rail to uprights. © Judith Miller/Dorling Kindersley/Hamptons.

FIGURE 4.43 This English oak refectory table has bulbous turned leg forms connected with a flat stretcher. © Judith Miller/Dorling Kindersley/Lyon and Trunbull Ltd.

FIGURE 4.44 The surface area of this English table from the mid 17th century expands as its gate legs swing open to support the drop-leaf sides. This example has turned baluster-shaped legs. © Judith Miller/Dorling Kindersley/Freeman's.

**FIGURE 4.45** An English, mid-17th-century oak court cupboard with open shelves functioned as a server in the refectory of the English home. The shelves are carved in relief and are supported with turned supports. © Judith Miller/ Dorling Kindersley/Woolley and Wallis.

**FIGURE 4.46** This English, mid-17th-century court cupboard with an enclosed top compartment was used to store eating utensils and to serve food. Similar examples are sometimes identified as hall and parlor cupboards because of their location in the home. This oak example is designed with a canted cornered top cabinet with bulbous form legs and a gadroon design along the base of the cabinet. © Judith Miller/Dorling Kindersley/Woolley and Wallis.

**FIGURE 4.47** An oak joined press cupboard, with carved frieze and panel doors, acanthus and rib turned baluster supports, and gadrooned frieze above a pair of panel doors and sides dates from the 17th century. © Judith Miller/Dorling Kindersley/Woolley and Wallis.

table for formal meals, with the convenience of a smaller table when it wasn't being used.

More refined dining practices led to a need for more formal furniture in the dining hall. The court cupboard, introduced during the 16th century, predates the sideboard or buffet that accompanied a suite of dining room furniture. It was a tiered shelving unit that acted as a food server during meals (Figure 4.45). Some court cupboards featured an enclosed cabinet top that also kept tableware when not in use (Figure 4.46). A variation of the court cupboard, called a "hall-and-parlor cupboard," was a type of a cabinet that had an enclosed section with fitted drawers and shelves concealed behind a set of decorated doors (Figure 4.47).

Chests were fashionable and varied in decoration from geometric diamond patterns to modestly decorated classical examples (Figure 4.48). Painted motifs, *Romayne* work, and family crests often ornamented the surfaces. Panel and frame construction methods were common, but unlike the medieval chest, English chests of the Renaissance period concealed the hardware on the inside of the piece, leaving the exterior surface free for decoration. Small chests raised off the ground on high legs, called "coffers," had a hinged lid, or a cabinet-type door to access the storage area (Figure 4.49). They were used to store the personal belongings of an individual, and remained popular until the chest of drawers replaced them during the 17th century.

More ornate than previous Gothic examples, the English tester bed (Figure 4.50) emphasized bulbous-form supports, usually turned in a cup-and-cover design or melon turning. The bed featured extensive carving on the headboard. The tester bed was still the most expensive furniture item found in upper class homes during the Renaissance period. The fabric canopy and side drapes, along with the quantity of wood and costly workmanship, reflected the wealth of the owner.

**FIGURE 4.48** This early-17th-century English oak chest has guilloche carvings along the front with lozenge-shaped motifs on its side. © Judith Miller/ Dorling Kindersley/Wallis and Wallis.

**FIGURE 4.49** A 17th-century oak coffer has a rectangular box-form cabinet set on turned legs connected with runners. © Judith Miller/Dorling Kindersley/Lyon and Turnbull Ltd.

**FIGURE 4.50** This large-scale bedroom features an Elizabethan–style tester bed set in an interior finished with a heavy coffered ceiling design of wood, parquet flooring, a large wall tapestry, a brass chandelier, and a frieze design of patterned flowers. The room belonged to the King of Poland. Michal Grychowski © Dorling Kindersley.

# Accessories

## POTTERY

Ceramic production on the Spanish island of Mallorca introduced western Europe to the bright colors and Moorish designs of tin-glazed earthenware. The tin glazes that gave these ceramics their distinctive appearance relied on a lead-based glaze—brought to Spain from the Middle East—that gave the pottery an opaque white finish. Colorful patterns and designs were painted on the vessels, which were fired at high temperatures to make them impermeable. Mallorca exported many of its pieces to Italy, and the designs quickly became the model for Italian ceramics, spreading throughout western Europe during the late Renaissance period. In fact, *maiolica* (*majolica*) production took place in the cities of Urbino in northern Italy and Venice to the south, and these ceramics were traded across Europe (Figure 4.51).

**FIGURE 4.51** These two hand-painted storage pots date from the Italian Renaissance and feature Latin inscriptions. The vessel on the left has delicate acanthus leaf designs. Andy Crawford © Dorling Kindersley.

## GLASS

Venetian glass—and specifically examples from the island of Murano—was coveted by those who could afford it. Crystal goblets, beakers, and vases featured patterned designs enhanced with bright colors or gold leaf. During the 15th century, Murano glassmakers reintroduced the process of making mosaic glass called "Rosetta" that dated back to Hellenistic and Roman times. Slender rods of glass were made from concentric bands of color, giving the appearance of small flowers after the rods were cooled and cut. The cross-sectioned pieces with intricate floral designs, or rosettes, at their center were then fused together to create a variety of objects with millefiori, or thousand flowers, patterns (Figure 4.52).

**FIGURE 4.52** These millefiori glass beads are cut crosswise to reveal the floral designs within their core. Andreas Von Einsiedel © Dorling Kindersley.

## MIRRORS

In addition to glassmaking, mirror making flourished during the Renaissance. Adding to the stock of handheld mirrors, wall-hung looking glasses were made by applying a coating of tin and lead to the back side of either convex or flat glass. Elaborate frames held the mirrors, and themes varied from religious and classical figures to simple geometric designs (Figure 4.53). Convex mirrors reflected small and distorted images, whereas flat mirrors were more accurate in their reflection. Large-scale mirrors were scarce and very expensive because making large panes of glass was a difficult task.

## METALWORKING

*Silversmiths* and *goldsmiths* working during the Renaissance made a range of goods for wealthy patrons who could afford these precious metals—the church and the nobility. Ecclesiastical objects for the Eucharist, such as chalices, basins, and platters, were handcrafted for these special purposes. Domestic wares for the nobility included drinking cups, spoons, salvers, or serving trays, and the newly introduced fork.

**FIGURE 4.53** In this painting, a framed convex mirror gives a distorted view of the room's interior, including a fancy brass chandelier. Michael Crockett © Dorling Kindersley.

COMPARISONS **Commemorative Plaques**

To commemorate a special event, person, or accomplishment, wall plaques made from metal, wood, or ceramic were popular throughout the Renaissance. Memorial plaques featured historic and religious figures, events in history, and events with meanings important to the families who commissioned them. The example shown in Figure 4.54 is from northern Europe and dates from around 1600. Made from silver, the plaque depicts a hunting scene rendered in detail; a dog handler reins in his hounds to the left while a man on horseback on the right rides with a falcon on his wrist. Finely dressed women in the background are observing the hunt from inside a carriage, and castles and other buildings appear faintly in the distance.

The pewter wall plaque from 1905 (Figure 4.55) shows the bust of a woman with long, flowing hair wrapping around her torso. Poppies connected by sinuous vines encircle the rim, and the entire scene is anchored at the bottom with an acanthus leaf. The design and subject matter of this plaque are typical of the Art Nouveau style that was popular from 1895 to about 1905 in Europe. The plaque was designed for decoration rather than commemoration, and was purchased for its aesthetic value.

**FIGURE 4.54** A hunting scene appears in this silver wall plaque dating from 1600. Geoff Dann © Dorling Kindersley, Courtesy of the Wallace Collection, London.

**FIGURE 4.55** This pewter wall plaque from 1905 features a woman with flowing hair surrounded by vines and poppies. © Judith Miller/Dorling Kindersley/Titus Omega.

**FIGURE 4.56** This lantern made from gilt bronze with leaded glass insets is from Seville and dates from the 16th century. Neil Lukas © Dorling Kindersley.

## LIGHTING

Only wealthy households or the church could afford candles made of beeswax. Most homes used candles made from tallow and, by the 15th century, cotton had replaced grass or rush as a wick. The wick would be dipped several times in tallow, coating the wick and building up the candle to the desired size. Oil lamps were used by those who could not afford the luxury of candles. Lighting an interior was relegated to carefully placed chandeliers, candlesticks, and lanterns that were fashioned from bronze, brass, or wrought iron (Figure 4.56).

## CLOCKS

First introduced during the 14th century, the mechanical clock—too expensive for most middle-class households—became a status symbol of the rich. Improvements in clock making during the early 15th century resulted in the introduction of spring-coil pocket watches. By mid century, clocks with minute hands were introduced. The cases designed to hold the clock's mechanical workings became highly elaborate, embellished with designs popular during the Renaissance period. A bracket clock, a small clock that was hung on the wall, appeared at this time. By the end of the century, table clocks, pocket clocks, and wall clocks adorned many interiors, and by the 17th century, the invention of the swinging pendulum made them more accurate.

## TEXTILES

Merchants who dealt in cloth, like those who lived during the Medieval period before them, had wealth and status in the community. Cloth incorporated into clothing, upholstery, and bed drapes reflected the wealth of its owner in its refined quality and quantity. Expensive Italian–cut *velvet*, which hung on the walls of the finest palazzos, was highly prized throughout Europe. The introduction of flocked wallpapers during the 17th century offered an inexpensive substitute. The tapestry-weaving industry continued to prosper in Brussels, Flanders, and France throughout the Renaissance (Figure 4.57). Aubusson, a small town in France, earned a reputation for producing the finest designs in Europe. By the 17th century, Aubusson was declared the royal manufacturing center for textiles for King Louis XIV. The carpets (*Aubusson*) and wall hangings from these workshops were made with a flat weaving process and had no pile. Tapestry designs of the Renaissance period emphasized more pictorial representations as many painters created the *cartoons* for their weaving.

Embroidered cushions, wall hangings, table and bed linens, and clothing were more plentiful in merchant-class households, with some of the finest needlework coming from Italy. An offshoot of embroidery, *lace* became fashionable during the mid 16th century with the establishment of a lace-making industry in England. Handmade lace, called "needle lace," was very expensive; only royalty could afford it. *Bobbin lace*, developed during the latter half of the 16th century, was constructed using a weaving process. It was used as edging on table linens, garments, and bed linens. Fine handmade lace also showed the wealth of those who could afford its delicate luxury.

**FIGURE 4.57** **This French tapestry depicts peasants making wine among a field of millefleurs.** Ranald MacKechnie © Dorling Kindersley, Courtesy of the Musee des Thermes et de 1'Hotel de Cluny, Paris.

# The Seventeenth Century

## The Baroque Period

The first use of the term "Baroque" appeared in late-18th-century texts as writers attempted to chronicle significant cultural changes that took place during the centuries following the Renaissance period. Although the term "Renaissance" embodied the rebirth of classical ideologies and expanded learning in the arts and sciences that had been suppressed since antiquity, the French term, *baroque*, translates as "irregular." The term was used to describe a change in artistic style that emphasized lively patterns, superfluous ornamentation, and contrasting textures. By the mid 16th century, considerable changes were occurring in religion and politics. Intellectually, attitudes toward God, science, and human existence were more rational, which liberated culture from spiritual dominance by the church.

Prompted by the writings and actions of Martin Luther and John Calvin, a new Protestant religion was introduced that sought religious reform and freedom from the papacy of the Roman Catholic Church. The ensuing wars, instigated by the Reformation movement in 1517 and the Counter Reformation in 1560, finally ended around 1650. Furthermore, the Thirty Years Wars fought among the major powers of Europe lasted from 1618 to 1648. By then, European countries were divided by religious alliances, either Protestant or Catholic. Throughout the religious wars, Europeans saw merciless battles among fellow compatriots. Compensating for these internal religious insurrections, respective monarchies attempted to create a profound sense of nationalism, promoting an allegiance to country rather than faith. The ruling monarchs strengthened absolutist control and took precautionary measures to reinforce their political power. Absolutism and internal trading resulted in greater economic opportunities for individuals, and the merchant classes rose to the ranks of upper society.

Another important result of the religious wars and the quest for absolutism was an increase in imperialism as the first permanent English colonies were established in North America. In 1607, John Smith and a small group of English adventurers seeking gold and religious freedom settled Jamestown, Virginia. Thirteen years later, in 1620, the *Mayflower* set sail from Plymouth, England, and established the second settlement in Plymouth, Massachusetts.

From the beginning of the 17th century until after 1666, there was a cultural lull as England experienced turbulent political change. Absolutism under James I was threatened when Parliament refused to support the king on matters of state. Further troubles followed under the kingship of James' son and successor to the throne, Charles I (r. 1625–1649). A bloody civil war led to the execution of Charles in 1649 and the dissolution of the monarchy. The following period of the Commonwealth was led by Oliver Cromwell and was governed by Parliament. The regime lasted until 1660, when a newly elected Parliament reinstated the monarchy under Charles II (r. 1660–1685), who had been in exile in Holland. This period of the Restoration established the balance of power between king and Parliament. With the restoration of the monarchy, the second half of the 17th century ushered in new optimism for individual freedom and wealth, which was exemplified by vast building projects undertaken by private patrons.

Although Italy was the seat of the papal states, France became a leading political force in Europe when five-year-old Louis XIV (r. 1643–1715) ascended the throne. Much too young to rule, Louis XIV's mother acted as regent until 1661, when he took control of the affairs of state. By this time, France was already the wealthiest and most populated country in Europe. As king, Louis XIV made many progressive reforms, including the implementation of a standardized money system and a consistent method of determining weights and measures. Trade was encouraged within the French borders, and Louis XIV viewed this as a means of building a greater tax revenue base. An increase in local trade supported the growth of a wealthy middle class, the bourgeoisie, that outnumbered the aristocrats.

# Architecture

## ITALY

Although the political power of the Catholic Church diminished significantly during the Baroque period, its religious strengths brought on by the victory of the Counter Reformation and the endurance of the papal states (Italy, Spain, Portugal, and France) was reflected in the construction of new churches. In Italy, the Baroque period emerged as a more passionate and expressive extension of the 16th-century Italian High Renaissance style. Designs for new Catholic churches emphasized magnificent size and scale, and exaggerated ostentatious decorative details replaced the simplicity of classical elegance used by Renaissance architects. Baroque architectural style was, in essence, a highly articulated extension of Renaissance classicism. Columns, pediments, pilasters, and rounded arches balanced energetic sculptures influenced by the Italian artist Gian Lorenzo Bernini (1598–1680) (Figure 5.1).

Bernini dazzled Italy with his work at St. Peter's in Rome (Figure 5.2). The large piazza featured bracing arms of colonnades that welcomed the people into the plaza,

**FIGURE 5.1** Bernini drew the original sketch for the Trevi Fountain in Rome during the 17th century, yet work was not begun until after his death. Taking over the project in 1732, Nicola Salvi (1697–1751) maintained the spirit of Bernini's original design, completing the fountain in 1762. The fountain is positioned in front of the façade of the Palazzo Poli, with its oversize cartouche and Corinthian columns. © littlewormy/Shutterstock.

**FIGURE 5.2** The central piazza in front of St. Peter's basilica in Rome features colonnaded walkways that lead to the front steps of the church. © Iwona Grodzka/Shutterstock.

and the *baldachin* he designed for the church interior forced the eyes to glance upward toward Michelangelo's grand dome. The grandiose nature of St. Peter's and other ecclesiastical accomplishments prompted monarchs and aristocrats to adopt this new style in the construction of their own private estates and palaces. First seen in the interior of the Italian Palazzo Farnese in Rome, the development of the Baroque style evolved in the gallery space designed by Annibale Carracci (1560–1609). His work on the gallery from 1597 to 1604 epitomizes the lavishness of the Baroque style: Pilasters with gilt Corinthian capitals flank wall niches articulated with classical moldings, and the upper walls and ceilings are covered with trompe l'oeil paintings compartmentalized by plaster moldings.

Architects and designers working with the new influences of the Baroque period placed importance on the coordination of architectural structure, paintings, and sculptures into a single cohesive unit. Fresco painting and plaster relief works were used as backgrounds for exquisitely crafted furnishings. Accessory items completed the room design and ranged from pedestals used to display fine vases and sculptures to expertly crafted clock cases. Mirrors were more abundant during the 17th century and were placed above console tables and over fireplace mantels, serving as necessary reflectors of candlelight. The skill of the Italian craftsman was celebrated throughout Europe. Traveling in almost all the papal states to meet the demands of aristocratic patrons, these Italian artisans inspired architects in the 17th-century Baroque style, including many of the French.

## FRANCE

The chateau at Fontainebleau, built in 1528, underwent a number of renovations as monarchs changed. Various rooms feature the emerging styles popular between the 16th and 18th centuries. The Salon of Francois I features Renaissance architectural details, Baroque furniture, and Neoclassic chandeliers and carpet designs. The gilt-coffered ceiling, doors, and wall panels date from the Renaissance period and prominently feature the emblem for Henry II, a cartouche with a gold crown above the initial *H*. The Italian influence in France during the Baroque period continued with the marriage of Henry IV (r. 1589–1610) to Marie de Medici of Italy, keeping Italian taste at the forefront of French fashion. Moreover, Chateau de Chambord's Italian-influenced architecture and interiors were updated during Louis XIV's reign with furnishings in the emerging baroque style (Figures 4.10 and 5.3).

**FIGURE 5.3** The bedchamber at Chambord for King Louis XIV's Queen shows interior furnishings in the emerging baroque style. © Steve Vidler/SuperStock.

It was King Louis XIV, however, who took the initiative to develop art and culture in France, contributing greatly to its advancement. With an increase in revenue, he funded public works projects in an attempt to create a French national style. In 1667, Louis XIV organized the workshops at the *manufacture des Gobelins* (established in 1633 by the Minister of Finance, Jean-Baptiste Colbert (1619–1683) to provide furnishings for the royal palaces) under the leadership of Charles LeBrun (1619–1690).

The following year, LeBrun found himself in charge of his most celebrated achievement—the interior decoration of a new palace for the French monarchy located outside of Paris in Versailles (Figure 5.4). An existing 1624 chateau built for King Louis XIII (r. 1610–1643) was to be transformed into the new royal palace (Figure 5.5). In addition to LeBrun, Louis XIV assembled under his patronage the leading architects of the period—Louis Le Vau (1612–1670), Jules Hardouin-Mansart (1646–1708), and André Le Nôtre (1613–1700)—to design the palatial residence and gardens. A garden façade setback designed by Le Vau and enclosed by Hardouin-Mansart held the most impressive room in the palace—the Galerie des Glaces, or the Hall of Mirrors.

The Hall of Mirrors, designed with 17 lunette windows overlooking the garden, featured equal-size mirrors hung opposite each window (Figure 5.6), which created a room bathed in sunlight. Each morning, the room served as the site of Louis XIV's morning processional because his royal apartments connected to this hallway. Just as the sun is at the center of the solar system, Louis XIV considered himself to be at the center of the French state. He viewed himself as the "Sun King," and, unequivocally, Hardouin-Mansart's design had complemented the king's perception of himself.

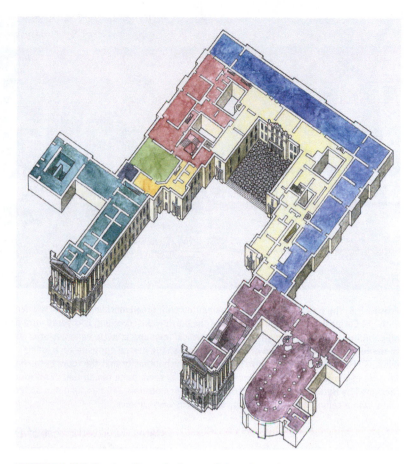

**FIGURE 5.4** This drawing shows the layout of the Palace of Versailles. © Dorling Kindersley.

**FIGURE 5.5** The façade of the Palace of Versailles, designed by Jules Hardouin-Mansart, reveals Baroque styling with its projecting bays, Ionic columns, pilasters, and monumental sculptures running along the roofline. © onairda/Shutterstock.

**FIGURE 5.6** The Hall of Mirrors was ornamented with green marble pilasters crowned with gilt Corinthian capitals. The length of the barrel-vaulted ceiling is covered with fine oil paintings surrounded by gilt putti and classical festoons. Lunette windows offer views to the formal gardens. Mirrors of similar size and shape placed opposite each lunette window reflect the light back into the hall with such intensity that the room became the favorite of the Sun King. No expense was spared, as seen in the famed Hall of Mirrors (designed by Hardouin-Mansart in 1677). The room measures 240 feet long and 34 feet wide, with a ceiling height of 43 feet. © Jose Ignacio Soto/Shutterstock.

LeBrun attended to the interior details of Versailles. He directed teams of artisans in the design and execution of paintings, tapestries, furniture, and decorative accessories, achieving complete unity in the palace. Along with tapestries, fine embroideries, and velvets, gold and silver gilt furniture played an integral part of the interior scheme at Versailles (Figure 5.7).

Ultimately, Versailles became the envy of Europe for its beauty and lavish social events. Celebrations and festivals lasted for days, and ballets and performances entertained numerous guests. Court life was poetic for everyone; it was carefree and leisurely. The completion of Versailles established France as the cultural leader in Europe during the 17th century. French was the fashionable language to speak, and French court fashion provided a model for aristocrats and the middle-class bourgeoisie alike.

## ENGLAND

England and the rest of the predominantly Protestant countries were not immediately influenced by the Baroque style of the papal states. Unlike the rest of Europe during the 16th century, England had not yet fully embraced the Renaissance style. Inigo Jones' contributions toward bringing the High Renaissance style to England during the early part of the 17th century led the way for the Baroque style later during the century (Figure 4.14). It was he who introduced Palladianism to King James I (r. 1603–1625) and all of England with his design for Banqueting House built in 1619. *Palladian* influences abound as its façade reiterates the unified proportions of Italian Renaissance architecture through the rhythmic placement of windows, engaged columns, and pilasters. Festooning delicately ornaments the architrave beneath the balustrade and cornice of the roof. Interiors featured elaborately carved and gilt moldings, and ceiling panels painted by the Flemish artist Peter Paul Rubens (1577–1640).

After the Great Fire in 1666 destroyed most of London, King Charles II set out to rebuild London in grand style, and appointed Christopher Wren (1632–1723) as surveyor to his court. St. Paul's Cathedral in London, begun in 1667, was Wren's first royal commission (Figure 5.8). Wren had traveled to Paris in 1665 and returned to England with countless engravings depicting the ornate French Baroque style. The grandiose nature of the French Baroque style had impressed the king; however, it was too flamboyant for London. An English national style developed through Wren's achievements, and he was knighted for his architectural accomplishments.

Grinling Gibbons (1648–1720), working under Wren's charge and independently, mastered the skill of wood carving and transformed the English interior. For both monarch and gentry, Gibbons' creations reflected an exuberance not typically seen before in English style. The staunch oak paneling and plaster pargework ceilings of the Renaissance were replaced with

**FIGURE 5.7** The salon of Apollo in the Palace of Versailles includes rich fabric-covered walls, green marble accents, gilt architectural moldings and ceiling panels, and a large Savonnerie carpet. © Summer/Shutterstock.

highly elaborate wood carving and detailed classical molding. Cupids, fruits and flowers, birds, and foliate patterns adorned paneled walls, door frames, mantels, and staircases (Figure 5.9). Gibbons' decorative carving, typical of Jacobean interiors, became less fashionable toward the end of the 17th century, when more simplistic classical motifs increased in popularity and ceiling paintings came into vogue.

Wren's interpretation of the high Baroque style supplanted excessive Baroque ornamentation with classic Palladianism. Wren continued work under two additional monarchs: James II (r. 1685–1689) and husband-and-wife rulers, William of Orange (r. 1689–1702) and Mary (r. 1689–1694, daughter of James II). Unlike her predecessors, Queen Mary took a keen interest in architecture and the arts, and she commissioned Wren to expand Hampton Court Palace with a wing designed in this new style (Figure 4.12). The interior of the formerly austere Hampton Court, under Wren's direction, was remodeled into a stately residence for the king and queen. Perhaps because of William's puritanical upbringing that defied luxury and excess, the interior of the transformed Hampton Court was more restrained in appearance and execution than the exuberantly carved Jacobean interiors that were popular at the time. Characteristics of the period included *wainscoted* walls with tapestries hung above, ceiling frescos framed by gilt woodwork, and wood plank floors covered with carpets (Figure 5.10).

## AMERICA

The style of 17th-century American architecture was quite different from the Baroque style expressed in European churches and country houses. English ships sailed for America with a wide range of passengers aboard, but with little provisions. Upon their arrival, the first settlers' primary concerns were to build sufficient shelter from the weather, and to cultivate the land and prepare for the winter. As each independent colony developed, the most fundamental methods of architectural construction were used. Although some basic tools were brought with the settlers, other goods had to be imported from England on ships that were costly and took months to arrive. The

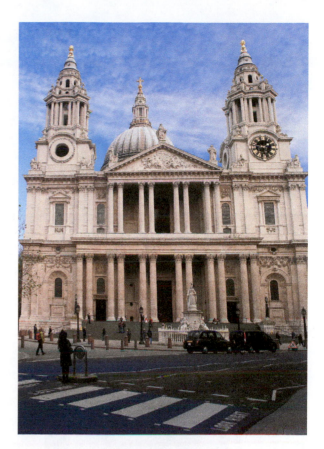

FIGURE 5.8 Sir Christopher Wren's design for St. Paul's Cathedral, begun in 1675, reflects strong allegiance to Michelangelo's dome of St. Peter's in Rome, built during the Italian Renaissance period. Wren's façade and dome reflect the English Baroque style, which never fully embraced the energetic sense of movement seen in Italian Baroque architecture.
© Kamira/Shutterstock.

FIGURE 5.9 English wood carver Grinling Gibbons created his classical details—such as rinceau patterns, oak leaf and holly designs, and pineapple finials carved out of pine, ash, and oak—that capture the exuberance of the Baroque period. This molding detail of Gibbons' work features an elaborately carved putti wrapped in gilt laurel leaves.
Stephen Oliver © Dorling Kindersley.

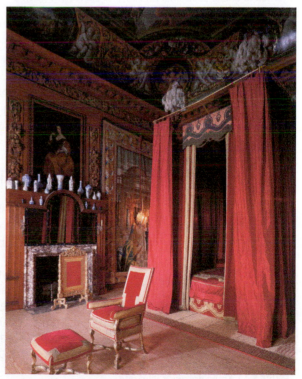

FIGURE 5.10 The state bedroom in Hampton Court Palace is decorated with Baroque ceiling paintings, and a tall canopy bed complete with crimson bed hangings. © Massimo Listri/CORBIS.

**FIGURE 5.11** This 20th-century recreation of 1627 Plymouth, Massachusetts, accurately depicts the architecture of the first English settlers in America. Based on English examples, these houses were made from timber, with thatched roofs and interior walls of wattle and daub. © Treena M. Crochet.

**FIGURE 5.12** This recreated interior of the Stephen Hopkins House from Plimoth Plantation shows a low beamed ceiling, wattle-and-daub walls, a beaten earth floor, and sparse furnishings. A collection of pewter ware sits on the "cup-board" attached to timber posts on a wall beyond the table. David Lyons © Dorling Kindersley, Courtesy of the Plimoth Plantation, Plymouth, Massachusetts.

**FIGURE 5.13** These drawings illustrate a design motif typically used during the Baroque period. © David Vleck.

small but accommodating houses were made from wood planks that were felled, planed, and cut from the abundant supply of oak trees (Figure 5.11). These early settlements resembled European country villages rather than sophisticated cities such as London or Paris.

Homes in America had one or two rooms, with loft spaces used for storage. Beaten earth floors and *wattle-and-daub* walls provided shelter from the elements, but lacked aesthetic detailing. The interiors were furnished with utilitarian items, most of which were made by local joiners or were shipped from England at great expense (Figure 5.12). Shortly after the establishment of the Jamestown and Plymouth settlements, the Dutch, Spanish, and French also came to the New World. By 1630, towns sprang up all along the eastern seaboard. A developing economy dependent on tobacco and rice exported to Europe brought wealth to the American colonists, and towns continued to grow and prosper. By the end of the 17th century, larger and more comfortable colonial homes dominated the American landscape.

## Design Motifs

Key design elements found consistently in architectural interiors and subsequently incorporated into furniture designs reflect the Baroque adherence to classic inspiration. These classically based designs were more elaborate during the Baroque period, when interiors were filled with rich decorations. Acanthus leaves, shell motifs, griffins, pilasters, classical arabesques, garlands, and cupidlike figures appeared in design details along with lively botanicals (Figure 5.13). As in the Renaissance period beforehand, putti were popular; they appeared on furniture, wall paneling, textiles, and decorative accessories.

Localized to the French decorative arts, the symbolic emblem of the Sun King, featuring a masklike face with radiating rays behind it, appeared throughout the Palace of Versailles (Figure 5.14). Botanical designs, especially the iris, lily, and tulip, appeared in plaster relief work and wood carvings. These intricate and ornate floral designs were brought to France by the Dutch during the religious crusades and were made popular in England after the royal marriage of William of Orange to Mary Stuart. Moreover, these floral patterns appeared in *marquetry* designs on furniture tabletops, drawer and door fronts, and *longcase clocks*. Influenced by an increase in trade with China, chinoiserie motifs—those that depict Chinese landscapes and figures—became popular in England by the end of the 17th century.

## Furniture

The wealth and social status of individuals in 17th-century Europe were measured by the size of the estate and the quantity and quality of the furnishings within it. The large but sparsely decorated and furnished chateaux, country houses, and villas were filled with matching suites of furniture produced for comfort and function, the best tapestries and carpets, and crystal chandeliers, all a reflection of the owner's wealth. Each country adapted the Baroque style of architecture to suit its regional preferences; the furniture was also modified in style. The celebrated furniture designs of André-Charles Boulle (1642–1732) for the completion of Versailles established France as the new trendsetter for interior furnishings.

Although still highly decorative, furniture became less architectonic in styling and much more comfortable. The introduction of more specific-use furniture rather than multifunctional furniture revealed greater individual wealth as interiors provided satisfying accommodations to the inhabitants. New items introduced during the 17th century included a chest of drawers in an array of heights and sizes, the *sleeping chair*, cabinets, console tables, the sofa or settee, and bookcases with glazed panels. In England in the late 17th century, sleeping chairs were used for convalescing. Distinctive side panels kept drafts away from the face, and an adjustable ratcheted back enabled the occupant to recline comfortably.

Attesting to the skill of the cabinetmaker, exuberant carvings and delicate inlay patterns decorated furniture made during the Baroque period. Inlay of intricate marquetry patterns became a popular surface treatment for cabinet doors, tabletops, and drawer fronts. The variety of *fruitwoods*, imported ebony, *mother-of-pearl*, and *ivory* used for these inlays underscored the wealth of the owner. These better made pieces were often signed by the cabinetmakers, whose reputations were known through their "trademark" marquetry patterns. *Pietra dura*—inlay using marble, granite, and other semiprecious stones—created beautiful mosaic botanical patterns on tabletops and cabinet doors. *Tortoiseshell*, perhaps the most exotic new material used to ornament furniture, was heated then flattened and used as a veneer. Often, the shell was covered with a thin glaze of red paint to make it glow under a protective layer of *chased* metal.

By the 1680s, the Chinese export trade flourished, bringing Turkish and other Middle Eastern goods to Europe, including exquisite enamels, lacquered cabinets with chinoiserie patterns, and fine Oriental porcelains. These imported treasures were enjoyed by the wealthy, who could afford such extravagances. Lacquered cabinets with chinoiserie patterns were quickly imitated by local cabinetmakers, offering their customers a less expensive alternative to veneer.

The majority of country furniture was still made by joiners using the standard mortise-and-tenon method of construction. Toward the end of the 17th century, as the use of oak lessened and more walnut was used, the dovetail joint became a more suitable method of joining two pieces of wood. Also, the practice of veneering grew rapidly as furniture makers used walnut—known for its richness of color and grain—from France, Spain, or Virginia.

## FRANCE

The Italian influence in France during the Baroque period continued with the marriage of Henry IV to Marie de Medici of Italy. Upon the death of Henry IV, Marie became regent to the heir, Louis XIII. Furniture designed during the first half of the 17th century is usually categorized as the Louis XIII style, and the designs were influenced by both Italian and Flemish Baroque styles. Louis XIII–style furnishings featured turned forms, often spiral, on chair and table legs. Chairs had high backs and included stretchers, as did most tables. Interiors were brighter than those from the Renaissance period and featured painted wall paneling, wood floors, and finished ceilings (Figure 5.15).

Scholars attribute the height of the French Baroque period to the reign of Louis XIV and the development of the Louis XIV–style of furniture (Figure 5.16). Moreover, the completion of the Palace of Versailles established French design as the standard of fine quality and taste for the rest of Europe. Charles LeBrun directed the completion of the palace interior, and the workshops of the Gobelins produced some of the finest examples of interior furnishings made during the 17th century in the Louis XIV, or Louis Quatorze, style. Because the scale of the palace was monumental, the furniture was proportioned accordingly. Louis XIV himself stood an astounding 6 feet 3 inches (unusually tall for the period), and because his comfort was a primary concern for LeBrun, chairs were adequately oversized and not scaled for normal stature. Furniture details

**FIGURE 5.14** The face superimposed on a sun burst was adopted as the symbol of King Louis XIV of France, who was called the "Sun King" after the Roman god Apollo. The sun mask motifs, along with sculptures fashioned to represent Apollo, are a common element in the interior design of the Palace of Versailles, and as seen on this gate. © fdimeo/Shutterstock.

**FIGURE 5.15** This room featured in the Musée Carnavalet in Paris features richly painted wall paneling, Louis XIII–style chaises, a small center table, and two gueridons with brass candlesticks. A large, gold-framed mirror reflects details of the marble fireplace mantel and a variety of *objets d'art*. © Travel Division Images/Alamy.

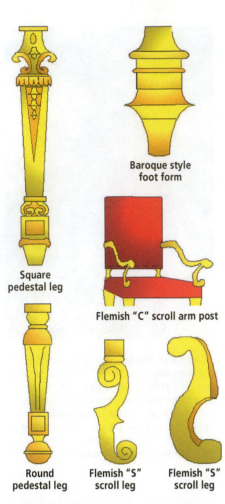

**Baroque style foot form**

**Square pedestal leg**

**Flemish "C" scroll arm post**

**Round pedestal leg**

**Flemish "S" scroll leg**

**Flemish "S" scroll leg**

**FIGURE 5.16** These drawings indicate the typical leg, foot, and arm forms used on French Baroque furniture in the Louis XIV style. © David Vleck.

**FIGURE 5.17** This luxurious bedroom designed for King Louis XIV at Chateau du Chambord features gilt plasterwork, a crystal chandelier, a large carpet over a parquet floor, and a majestic bed with gold-embroidered draperies. The railing serves as the separator between the King's private sleeping area and the more public receiving room. It was not uncommon for the King to receive his invited guests while still in bed. The two fauteuils upholstered in red, and the gilt tabourets are designed in the Louis XIV style. © SOMATUSCAN/Shutterstock.

**FIGURE 5.18** This drawing of a Louis XIV–style fauteuil features a tall rectangular back with square pedestal legs and a saltire stretcher. Floral printed upholstery covers the armrests, back, and seat.

focused on more angular shapes, straight legs with the occasional S and C scroll forms, and carved wood decorations (Figure 5.17).

A typical French Baroque armchair, or *fauteuil*, has a tall rectangular back framed by carved wooden arms. The back and seat were usually upholstered; however, some chairs had cane backs. The arms were placed lower toward the front of the chair than at the back, which allowed for a more relaxed positioning of the arm. Various leg forms were used; however, the square pedestal type was more common. Because some fauteuils weighed a hefty 60 pounds each, stretcher systems, either saltire or H form, were necessary to support the massive carved legs and frames (Figure 5.18). Although the frames for chairs and other furniture items made for Versailles were of carved wood, most were gilded with either gold or silver. Written accounts specifically refer to furnishings made exclusively of silver. Unfortunately, the solid silver items were melted down when France suffered an extreme financial burden late in the century.

The *bergère* was similar to the fauteuil, but was completely upholstered, including the sides and the arms. Another popular type of chair developed during the Baroque period was the wing chair. This chair, designed with extensions that shielded the face from drafts, was referred to as a "confessional" (derived from ecclesiastical types) or a "sleeping chair," because the back also reclined. The number of fauteuils and bergères was limited at Versailles, but stools with either upholstered seats or removable cushions were in greater abundance. Louis XIV kept with traditional seating hierarchies by "permitting" guests to sit on stools, or *tabourets*, by his command. *Placets* or *ployants* are French X-form folding-type chairs. It was not unusual for people in the king's presence to be denied a place to sit. The evolution of the settle into the settee occurred during the reign of Louis XIV. Not to be confused with an appetizer, the French *canapé* was the first introduction to the formal settee (Figure 5.19). These early examples were usually upholstered and designed to match en suite with the fauteuils and tabourets. The uncomfortable upright back forced the sitter into an erect and formal position.

Tables were designed to suit a variety of functions; some were strictly decorative whereas others were quite practical. The console table was developed during the Baroque period (Figure 5.20). It had a carved wooden frame with legs and stretchers that matched those of the fauteuils. With *aprons* on three sides, these small tables were designed to be placed against the wall, usually in front of a large mirror. Although expensive, mirrors were necessary because they aided in reflecting light back into the room. Illumination came from richly decorated *candelabras* and sconces. A marble top protected the surface of the console table from dripping candle wax Other types of tables included those for dining, playing cards, dressing, and working. Writing tables were in greater use during the 17th century as both men and women of the court were highly educated, and written correspondence was maintained on a daily basis. Some were simply tables fitted with a single center drawer, like the *bureau plat*, whereas desks were fitted with side drawers as well as tabletop compartments. The *bureau Mazarin* was a small-scale desk fitted with drawers and a recessed center panel often referred to as the "knee hole" that provided space for sitting close to the desk for writing (Figure 5.21).

The medieval or renaissance chest was transformed into the more popular commode of the Baroque period. Commodes were a chest of drawers placed on short legs. They were either fitted with two horizontal drawers or cabinet-type openings, and they were used as storage pieces. André-Charles Boulle is credited with designing the first examples of this type of furniture for Versailles. Boulle's grandfather was furniture maker to King Louis XIII, and it was only natural for the younger Boulle to be appointed to the commission of Louis XIV in 1672. Original commodes designed for Louis XIV introduced Boulle's specialized trademark marquetry designs. His name sometimes is used generically; *boulle work* indicates marquetry patterns that resemble his style. Thin sheets of brass, copper, or pewter were cut in foliate patterns and applied to the surface of the furniture. Both positive and negative metal images were used to create impressive "matched" designs for the suite of furnishings. Not only were two furniture items perfectly paired in their design, but all the precious metal was used without waste. This metal marquetry was laid over a body of ebony and tortoiseshell, creating dramatic detailing over these rich veneers. Boulle work marquetry appeared on a variety of objects, including commodes, cabinets, armoires, clock cases, and accessory items.

French Baroque furniture of the court and aristocracy was stately, formal, and richly decorated. Secondary storage units, such as the cabinet on a stand, were not simply functional, but reflected the wealth of the owner. These cabinets were made

FIGURE 5.19 A French canapé from 1715 to 1723 in the Louis XIV style is designed with a rectangular back framed by carved and gilt wood; a squared seat with a carved, decorative apron; and eight pedestal legs connected by saltire stretchers. Classical detailing can be seen in the carvings and the Beauvais tapestry upholstery.

FIGURE 5.20 Gilt console tables with square pedestal legs, saltire stretchers, and elaborately carved aprons are arranged in the hall at the Palace of Versailles. Oversize gueridons appear in the background topped with brass candelabra. © Summer/Shutterstock.

FIGURE 5.21 This bureau Mazarin, or kneehole desk, features boulle work marquetry on ebony. It has square pedestal legs with saltire stretchers, which are typical Baroque period details seen in the furnishings made for the Palace of Versailles. © Steven Belanger/Shutterstock.

# A CLOSER Look

## A Commode for the King

In 1687, King Louis XIV commissioned Jules Hardouin-Mansart to begin construction on a retreat pavilion near the grounds of Versailles as a place to escape from court duties. The Grand Trianon was finished the next year, and the commode shown in Figure 5.22 was designed by Boulle for the King's bedroom in 1708. The design of the commode features a marble top, roman sphinxes, elaborate marquetry, and *ormolu* appliqués. The body of the commode was made of walnut, veneered with ebony and tortoiseshell. The marquetry consists of thin sheets of brass that were carefully cut into elaborate classical arabesque and foliate patterns and applied over the ebony and tortoiseshell veneers. The bronze ormolu, although highly decorative, served a practical function as well as a decorative one. Placed on the commode's corners, on the feet, and drawer edges, these mounts protected the veneered surface from scratches, kicks, and bumps. The craftsmanship of the ormolu, was executed by specialists trained in metallurgy rather than cabinetmaking.

**FIGURE 5.22** A French Louis XIV–style commode created by André-Charles Boulle between 1708 and 1709 for Versailles features ebony veneer on walnut with marquetry of engraved brass over a tortoiseshell background. Classical elements appear on the commode in the form of gilt bronze Roman sphinx-fashioned figures, guilloche-patterned ormolu, and a green marble top. Authors Image/Robert Harding.

from ebony, and the cabinetmakers that specialized in this material became known as *ébénistes*. The cabinet doors displayed richly detailed *pietra dura* or *intarsia* botanical patterns. The stands were equally ornate, carved with classical figures, saltire stretchers, or aprons. Armoires continued to be used for clothes storage. As in the past, furniture usually lined the perimeter walls, leaving the center of the room open. The arrangement of furniture in the room varied with purpose and function, and chairs and tables were relocated to the center as needed. In the larger French chateaux, people resided in small apartments or suites of rooms that became their living quarters. In many cases, the apartment was nothing more than a bedroom (Figure 5.3). At Versailles, the bed was placed against one wall separated from the rest of the room by a railing. The railing acted as the formal barrier between the public and private space, as it was customary to receive visitors and dine in this room. Because the boudoir was both bedroom and primary living quarters, a new piece of furniture was introduced around 1625. The daybed, or *chaise longue*, was placed transversely at the foot of the canopied and draped four-poster bed, and was used for afternoon napping. This kept the linens on the *lit à colonnes* neat and orderly throughout the day.

Another side of French furniture not represented here is worthy of mention. Not everyone had the wealth of the aristocracy. In the villages, domestic homes contained tried-and-true examples of utilitarian furnishings including tables, chairs, stools, beds, and chests. Items created by local craftsmen were copied from previous styles, perhaps with only slight modification. In discussing any period of furniture history, readers must realize that with the introduction of new styles, old ones still remained popular for quite some time. It was not uncommon for rooms to be decorated with a variety of different styles because furniture was still quite expensive to own.

## ENGLAND

Typically, there are three prevalent English furniture styles that developed during the 17th century: Early Jacobean, Late Jacobean, and William and Mary. In most examples, the style of Early Jacobean furniture followed the influences of the Elizabethan Renaissance style with little change in design. Early Jacobean–style furniture was

# LEARN More

## French Baroque Interior Design

This room from chateau Fontainebleau (Figure 5.23) is from the king's grand apartments that were first built during the reign of Francis I. However, the interior details reflect stylistic changes that occurred during the next three centuries. This room features Renaissance architectural details, Baroque period furniture, and Neoclassic chandeliers and carpet designs. The coffered wood ceiling exhibits *parcel gilding*, and from it hangs later style chandeliers that date from the time of Napoleon I. Furniture placed in the room is from the Baroque period and includes various-size fauteuils, a long settee, a center table, and an ebonized cabinet. The carved and gilt chairs and settee are upholstered in fine *petit point* needlework that features bouquets of flowers that match the fabric on the oversized canapé. The massive size of the canapé is supported by 10 square pedestal legs connected with saltire stretchers. An ebonized cabinet on a stand includes spiral turned legs and carved classical details on the cabinet compartment. Common to the era, these furnishings line the walls, except for the prominent positioning of a center table. The heavily carved and gilt center table has legs in the shape of Classical *term-figures*, and the stretcher features a robust putti-shaped finial. On top of the table and above the ebony cabinets are *Sèvres porcelain* vases with ormolu and gilding.

A large *Savonnerie carpet* almost covers the room from wall to wall. Its design features classical motifs, including the lyre, Roman soldiers, and laurel leaves, and dates from the Neoclassic period. Crystal chandeliers in the Empire style hang from the ceiling accompanied by Baroque period wall sconces. Last, Flemish tapestries from the 17th century cover all walls and dominate the interior décor.

**FIGURE 5.23** This salon at Fontainebleau features Flemish tapestries, Louis XIV–style furniture, and crystal chandeliers. Source: Gianni Dagli Orti / The Art Archive at Art Resource, NY.

designed for utility, and featured restrained decorative details. English furniture design began to incorporate characteristics of the Baroque period in furnishings after the restoration of the monarchy under King Charles II and James II. The style of design that developed is referred to as "Late Jacobean," and it follows the trends set by Sir Christopher Wren and Grinling Gibbons. This style of furniture is characterized by high-relief carving and pierced carving that imitates the complex patterns achieved in Gibbons' woodworking skills.

English Baroque furniture had incorporated a Dutch and Flemish influence as a result of England's close alliance with Holland even before William of Orange took the throne in 1689. The Flemish–influenced carved S and C scrolls were used frequently on Late Jacobean furnishings (Figure 5.24). Chair and table legs featured a form of turning resembling a

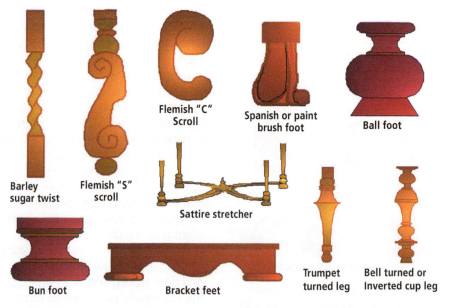

Barley sugar twist

Flemish "S" scroll

Flemish "C" Scroll

Spanish or paint brush foot

Ball foot

Sattire stretcher

Bun foot

Bracket feet

Trumpet turned leg

Bell turned or Inverted cup leg

**FIGURE 5.24** These drawings illustrate the more common furniture details for the Late Jacobean style. © David Vleck.

FIGURE 5.25 A Late Jacobean–style bench made from walnut features spiral turned legs and stretchers. *Judith Miller/ Dorling Kindersley /Gorringes.*

FIGURE 5.26 A set of 17th-century-style ebonized oak chairs, by James Shoolbred & Co. of London, each with velvet carpet-style upholstery, and tassels on the square back and seat, raised on turned and blocked legs with rosette carving and spiral turned stretchers. *© Judith Miller/Dorling Kindersley/Lyon and Turnbull Ltd.*

FIGURE 5.27 A small table made from yew has bobbin turned legs attached with a saltire stretcher and ball feet. *Judith Miller/Dorling Kindersley/Sloan's.*

**Tear drop pulls**

**Bonnet or hooded pediment**

**Double bonnet or hooded pediment**

FIGURE 5.28 These are the most common features of English Baroque furniture details for the William and Mary style. *© David Vleck.*

string of beads, sometimes called "bobbin turning." or "spool turning." Furniture legs and stretchers with the most carving were fashioned into spiral turned columns called "barley sugar twists," with uprights, stretchers, and arm posts equally designed with ornate carvings (Figure 5.25, 5.26). After the Great Fire of 1666 that destroyed most of London, furniture makers were busy filling orders for inexpensive furniture, especially chairs. Consistent with Dutch and Flemish chairs of the period, the English adapted tall, narrow-back chairs with a heavily carved crest rail. Although not a new material, woven cane replaced the more traditional leather or upholstered seats and backs, providing a more cost-effective substitute.

Small dressing tables and writing tables were simple and functional, emphasizing turned forms rather than carved details (Figure 5.27). Gateleg tables were still quite popular and were used for eating small meals or taking tea. Tea bricks were imported to England from India as early as 1660 during the reign of Charles II and tea drinking became a popular pastime. By the end of the 17th century, tea tables designed specifically for the task become an important piece of furniture during the Rococo period of the 18th century. Moreover, successful trading as early as 1601 between England and Holland with the Far East and India encouraged an Oriental influence in design trends. Soon, lacquered cabinets, tables, and small boxes made their way onto the continent.

Sir Christopher Wren's transformation of Hampton Court from an Elizabethan–Gothic palace to a more classically defined residence for England's new reigning monarchs, William III and Mary II, influenced changes in furniture design during the last two decades of the 17th century. The ornate carving on Late Jacobean furnishings no longer fit into a much simpler, classical interior, and carved details became less exuberant (Figure 5.28).

The English Baroque period is often called the Age of Walnut. Walnut replaced oak during the second half of the 17th century as the prevalent cabinetmaking material. Various types of walnut, such as black walnut or burl walnut, were chosen for color and grain, and were veneered to less attractive woods. They were then finished with a paste wax and buffed to a high sheen. As the art of veneering improved with the development of better adhesives, new marquetry patterns were introduced. Characteristic seaweed marquetry and oyster patterns adorned tabletops, drawer and door fronts, and side panels. Seaweed marquetry, appropriately named because the curvilinear cut slivers of colored wood resembled tangled seaweed, and oyster marquetry was a strong characteristic of the William and Mary style. "Oystering" was created by cutting small branches crosswise to show the small pith and growth rings, which were then applied as a veneer in matched pairs to look like opened oysters. These new marquetry patterns were interspersed with panels featuring French foliate patterns made from wood, mother-of-pearl, and ivory.

Moreover, the excessive carving seen on chairs of the Late Jacobean style was replaced by more subtle decorations. The periwig chair, a chair specifically designed with an elaborate crest rail that emphasized the fashionable wigs worn by men and women, introduced gentle curves and scrolls rather than deep carving (Figure 5.29). Flemish S and C scroll legs terminating into Spanish or paintbrush feet were used less frequently as straighter, tapering legs were introduced. Trumpet or inverted-cup turned legs were more typical of the William and Mary style, and the use of the stretcher continued throughout the 17th century.

Small side tables were introduced as tea tables, writing tables, worktables, and curio tables. A wide variety of styles and ornamentation individualized these tables to suit their specific functions, but all retained the characteristic trumpet or inverted-cup turned legs and saltire stretcher (Figure 5.30). Cabinetmakers were quick to imitate the colors, patterns, and high-gloss finishes used in Oriental lacquering. Because true Oriental lacquering processes were unknown to European cabinetmakers, they improvised by painting finished cabinets, armoires, and chairs in dark green, crimson, or black. The piece was then decorated with either inlaid or painted chinoiserie motifs and varnished. This technique was appropriately dubbed *japanning*, and its process was documented in a published treatise by Stalker and Parker in 1688 (Figure 5.31).

Instrumental in introducing the French style to William III, the Paris–born architect Daniel Marot (c. 1666–1752) fled to Holland along with other French Huguenots during the 1685 Protestant persecutions. He went to England in 1694 and remained in the service of the court until 1698. William III, not to be outdone by King Louis XIV and Versailles, continued to develop English high style even after Mary's death in 1694. The French Baroque style of furniture was favored by wealthy English gentry, and fine examples of gilt items, including rare examples of silver-gilt furniture, survive today. Cabinets on stands were used both for storage and for display of the owner's porcelain collection. Like their French counterparts, some cabinets were decorated with inlay of mother-of-pearl, ivory, colored woods, or semiprecious stones; however, seaweed marquetry dominated the design of many English Baroque examples (Figure 5.32). Seaweed marquetry duplicated the intricate designs of Boulle work marquetry.

Unique to English and eventually American furniture are the highboy, lowboy, and tallboy. These pieces replaced the low, horizontal chest and introduced a more practical means of storing clothing in drawers. The lowboy was a low table fitted with a single drawer, and was used as a dressing table (Figure 5.30). A highboy was simply a chest of drawers raised off the floor on tall legs (Figure 5.33). Both highboy and lowboy were supported by columnar-type legs with trumpet or inverted-cup turning more typical of the William and Mary style. Flemish scroll legs were still used occasionally; however, they were flat and not turned or carved in

FIGURE 5.30 A lacquered low table in the William and Mary style features gilt chinoiserie designs on its door panels and drawers. Chinoiserie is the name given to describe design motifs fashioned after Chinese landscapes and teahouse scenes. Steve Gorton © Dorling Kindersley.

FIGURE 5.31 This late-17th-century red japanned cabinet on a gilt stand is decorated with scenes seen in Stalker and Parker's publication, *Treatise on Japanning*. The pair of doors is fastened with gilt brass pierced and engraved strapwork hinges, and features drop handles at the sides, enclosing an arrangement of eight large drawers around three smaller recessed central ones. It features four C scrolled legs, splayed at the front with scroll toes, formerly silvered. Judith Miller/Dorling Kindersley/Wallis and Wallis.

**FIGURE 5.32** This 17th century English cabinet on a stand features ornate floral marquetry designs. Cabinet with floral marquetry, late 17th century, English School, (17th century)/Victoria & Albert Museum, London, UK/The Bridgeman Art Library International.

**FIGURE 5.33** This English William and Mary–style highboy is designed as a chest on a tablelike stand. Both sections are fitted with drawers articulated by decorative moldings. Notice the shaped stretcher, bell turned legs, and bun feet. The flat cornice is characteristic of 17th-century case pieces. © Judith Miller/Dorling Kindersley/Sloan's.

**FIGURE 5.34** A walnut veneered chest of drawers features teardrop-shaped drawer pulls. Chest of drawers, c.1695, English School, (17th century)/Private Collection/The Bridgeman Art Library International.

**FIGURE 5.35** A William and Mary–style kneehole desk made from burr walnut has a banded top and bracket feet. © Judith Miller/Dorling Kindersley/Lyon and Turnbull Ltd.

a decorative fashion. All legs were joined with some type of stretcher system, usually a saltire. Like the Flemish scrolls, they were often flat and not carved. Only examples imitating the French Baroque style were ornately carved.

The chest of drawers gained popularity during the Baroque period. Unlike the French commode, these were always fitted with drawers and remained closer to the ground (Figure 5.34). The later developed tallboy, a name adopted by the Americans, was a chest on a chest. The base chest was supported by bracket, bun, or ball feet. Most tallboys and highboys had a flat cornice top with a slightly bulging frieze called a *pulvinar frieze*. Teardrop pulls were the typical hardware used on William and Mary–style case furniture. These small brass drops resembled a teardrop in appearance and are characteristic of the English Baroque style.

Larger writing cabinets, or *secretaries*, also appeared during the last decades of the 17th century. Flat or slanted doors concealed drawers and paper slots, and doubled as the writing surface when dropped onto supporting members. They were known as "fall-front desks" or "fall-front secretaries." A smaller desk, or bureau, featuring full drawers on either side of the kneehole space was also a new item of furniture development during the Baroque period (Figure 5.35).

# A CLOSER Look

## Marquetry Styles

Evidence of marquetry work dates back to ancient Egypt, with hieroglyphic texts documenting the process of applying or inlaying wood veneers, ivory or bone, and shell, such as mother-of-pearl, to create decorative patterns on furniture, chests, and small boxes. *Intarsia, certosina,* and *taracea* are the Latin, Italian, and Spanish equivalences, respectively, of inlay. *Intarsia* is the Latin word meaning "to insert." *Taracea* and *certosina* are the inlay of woods, bone, or mother-of-pearl. The work was inspired by the traditional inlay patterns found on furnishings and boxes from the Middle and Near East (Figure 5.36).

The popularity of marquetry work peaked during the Baroque period. Wealthy patrons commissioned objects designed with elaborate patterns created by contrasting woods, ivory, metal, shell, and colorful stones (Figure 5.37). In France, André-Charles Boulle popularized marquetry work using tortoiseshell, brass, and ebony in the furnishings he created for the Palace of Versailles (Figure 5.38). The Medici family brought

FIGURE 5.36 Detailed marquetry designs on boxes made in Morocco. © Chrissie Shepherd/Shutterstock.

FIGURE 5.37 The detail on this late-17th-century cabinet on a stand made from teak and rosewood in India for the European market features inlaid ebony and ivory. © Judith Miller/Dorling Kindersley/ Wallis and Wallis.

the Flemish master Leonard van der Vinne (d. 1713) to their Italian patronage in 1659.

In addition, William of Orange brought the Dutch and Flemish fashions for fine marquetry work to England from his native Holland. The skill level of the marquetry worker is revealed in Figure 5.39. Thin veneers of various woods chosen for either natural or stain-enhanced coloring were layered and held together with small tacks. A pattern for each part of the design was transferred onto the veneers and then carefully cut by hand with a fine-blade saw. Edges of the cut pieces were then scorched in hot sand, giving each piece the desired shading necessary for the modeling of the overall design. Pieces were then fit into a prepared background cut precisely to receive each pattern.

By the end of the century, the production of fine marquetry work increased and was made more affordable with the invention of the jigsaw, which enabled multiple layers of veneers to be cut at one time. Furnishings with intricate marquetry patterns remained popular throughout the Rococo and Early Neoclassic periods, and a revival of fine marquetry work peaked toward the 19th century. Designers seeking to bring back the beauty of hand-crafted objects incorporated more simplistic marquetry patterns in Arts and Crafts– and Art Nouveau–style furnishings (Figure 5.40). Fine marquetry details reappeared during the Art Deco style of the 1920s; however, the interest was short-lived as design shifted towards sleek, unadorned modernism.

FIGURE 5.38 Pedestals from the 19th century feature boulle marquetry over a tortoiseshell veneer. © Judith Miller/Dorling Kindersley/Sloan's.

FIGURE 5.39 Dutch marquetry detail features a vase of flowers surrounded by scrolling foliate patterns. © Judith Miller/ Dorling Kindersley/Freeman's.

FIGURE 5.40 This Arts and Crafts–style cabinet features a Glasgow rose pattern, leaf, and vine marquetry designs in light oak. © Judith Miller/Dorling Kindersley/Lyon and Turnbull Ltd.

## AMERICA

In the American colonies, some of the earliest examples of American furniture to survive come from the New England and Chesapeake Bay regions where the first colonies were established in the early 17th century. Because the pilgrims' first concern was to establish shelter and secure a supply of food, furniture developed out of necessity and function rather than comfort or luxury (Figure 5.41). Although some pilgrims brought furniture with them, usually simple chests and chairs, during the early years of North American settlement, furniture was made by immigrant joiners or turners who specialized in the craft of woodworking. The style of furniture they made was fashioned after popular styles from their native countries and reflected those typically found in small European peasant villages. The furniture's unsophisticated, pioneer flavor resembled Early Jacobean and Elizabethan examples of the English Renaissance. American furniture made at this time is known as the "Early Colonial style."

The furniture was sturdy but ruggedly made from an abundant supply of oak, maple, and pine. Crafted using the most simplistic methods, ornamentation was limited to turned pieces, *scratch carvings*, or painted designs. Chairs made during the 17th century were usually of the turned type. Two of the more common examples from this period are the Brewster and Carver chairs, named after their original owners—William Brewster and John Carver—who came to America on the *Mayflower*. Both types of chairs were constructed out of spindles turned on a lathe and, although simple in their methods of construction and decoration, were reserved for the master of the house (Figure 5.42).

Throughout most of the 17th century, houses remained small. Adaptable, multifunctional furniture accommodated these modest quarters by their flexibility of use and size. The table–settle easily converted into a seating unit after the evening meal, and smaller ones converted into chairs. Most were fitted with a drawer or drawers that provided storage compartments for linens or utensils. The back of the chair was lowered onto the armrests of the settle or chair to support the table top (Figure 5.43). Other tables resembled the trestle type and were easily transportable. Smaller gateleg tables were in frequent use because they could be folded or expanded easily. These were fashioned after the English versions; however, the butterfly table is more uniquely American. When opened, the distinguishing support wings resembled those of a butterfly.

The Early American blanket chest was slightly taller than its English counterpart and was usually fitted with a low set of drawers positioned under the hinged lidded chest (Figure 5.44). The height of the chest made it practical to use as a small table or bench if necessary. Most furniture lacked extensive carving, and were often decorated with painted motifs. If carving was used, it was very shallow, or low relief, scratch carving.

The press cupboard resembled an Elizabethan court cupboard and was one of the more elaborately decorated pieces of Early American furniture of the 17th century. A variety of bulbous turnings were used for supports, and separate pieces of wood shaped as split spindles or lozenges were added for ornamentation. Some cupboards incorporated low-relief carving in floral or arcade patterns, and many were painted in bright colors. Cupboards were simple in design, made with

**FIGURE 5.41** A bench placed outside a recreated 17th-century dwelling at Plimoth Plantation in Plymouth, Massachusetts, reflects the crude craftsmanship of early Colonial furniture and emphasizes the extreme utility of such items made for necessity rather than luxury. © Treena M. Crochet.

panel-and-frame construction, and featured solid or fitted glass doors (Figure 5.45). Glass-making began in Jamestown as early at 1608.

Beds were usually straw-stuffed mattresses placed on a platform or bedstead. A bedstead was fitted with holes through which ropes were passed. A key at the side of the bed rail was used to tighten the ropes and keep the bed from sagging (Figure 5.12). There were no separate bedrooms in the first homes established in the two pilgrim colonies. In some cases, a sleeping loft was built into the upper rafters of the roof trusses that were left open to the pitch of the roof.

Toward the end of the 17th century, the colonists developed their own distinctive regional cultures, and, with increased prosperity, homes were furnished with finer crafted goods either made locally or imported from England. At the close of the 17th century, Early American furniture began to keep pace with European styles, largely as a result of an increase of imported furniture and widely circulated pattern books.

# Accessories

## POTTERY

Prior to the 17th century, the Portuguese capitalized on trade routes between the western coast of Europe and parts of North Africa and India. By 1600, the British East India Company chartered by Queen Elizabeth I, and the Dutch East India Company in 1602 imported exotic goods from the Far East. Goods coveted by Europeans from the East Indies included spices such as salt and cinnamon, cotton for cloth making, and indigo for making a deep blue dye. From China, trading companies brought back exquisite examples of porcelain, a type of pottery with a translucent, creamy white appearance. The techniques for making fine porcelain were unknown to Europeans at that time. Chinese export porcelain featured a white background and had bright blue designs decorating its surface (Figure 5.46). In fact, when Queen Mary took an active role in the transformation of Hampton Court, she became an avid collector of porcelain, and the new interior style for the palace relied greatly on Oriental accents.

The Dutch, in an attempt to copy Chinese porcelain, set up a pottery factory in Delft, Holland, in 1605. Known as *delftware*, the pottery had the same bright blue designs over a white background, but it lacked the translucency of real porcelain. The Delft trademark blue-on-white and polychrome decorative designs appeared

**FIGURE 5.42** A late-17th-century Carver armchair from Connecticut has turned ash and hickory spindles, which give the chair its distinctive shape. The structural members and spindles are turned into a variety of shapes; on this chair, the baluster is more prominent. Seats were made from rush or woven splints, and were covered by a large cushion for added comfort. © Judith Miller/Dorling Kindersley/Wallis and Wallis.

**FIGURE 5.43** The table–settle offered both a table and a chair, allowing for more flexibility in American Colonial homes. © Treena Crochet.

**FIGURE 5.44** The blanket chest served multiple purposes during the American Colonial period. This New England–designed chest was also used as a table. The chest is fitted with a lower drawer with scratch carving, and the uppermost chest compartment is panel-and-frame construction. © Judith Miller/Dorling Kindersley/Pook and Pook.

**FIGURE 5.45** An early 17th-century yellow pine corner cupboard made in New York has a molded cornice with dentil frieze positioned over a pair of glazed doors. Inside are three shaped shelves, and a pair of recessed panel doors below open to reveal a single shelf. The cupboard sits on straight bracket feet. © Judith Miller/Dorling Kindersley/Freeman's.

**FIGURE 5.46** This beautiful domed-lid vase from the Vung Tau cargo for the Dutch market indicates a flourishing trade market catering to middle- and upper-class households. The scene depicts the canal houses typical in the Netherlands, although styled with overtly Chinese pagoda rooftops. The vase dates from between 1690 and 1700. © Judith Miller/Dorling Kindersley/R & G McPherson Antiques.

on a variety of vases, pots, beakers, and bowls, and on tiles applied to walls and fireplaces (Figure 5.47). By the mid 17th century, England began producing its own version of delftware.

## GLASS

Venetian glass continued to be the most desired all over Europe during the early 17th century. Only the richest could afford the luxury of drinking from a crystal goblet embellished with 24-karat gold filigree. The glassmakers in Murano introduced colored glass into their filigree work, and the stunning combination of red glass and gold filigree increased the desirability of Venetian glass throughout Europe (Figure 5.48). Although Venetian glass maintained its popularity in the European market during the Baroque period, political upheavals in 1797 brought about its decline. By the end of the 18th century, Bohemia and Moravia had taken over as leading producers of fine glass; both countries produced fine crystal with hand-cut designs.

## MIRRORS

Larger wall mirrors were produced during the 17th century, and owning one was a sign of great wealth (Figure 5.49). Venetian glassmakers manufactured these mirrors by casting molten glass onto flat tables to produce larger sheets of glass, which were then coated with a mixture of tin and mercury. The largest Venetian mirror made at that time measured 45 inches by 25 inches. Wall mirrors were imported throughout Europe, and local artisans made elaborate frames in the current styles of the Baroque period. For the Hall of Mirrors at the Palace of Versailles, Colbert authorized the establishment of a glass factory in France to produce the 357 mirrors necessary to line the 340-foot-long gallery. The mirrors were the largest ever made when the gallery was completed in 1685, and the most expensive for the period (Figure 5.6).

## LIGHTING

In 1676, Englishman George Ravenscroft (1632/3–1683) added lead to his glass-making techniques and developed a type of glass called *lead crystal*. Lead added to glass made this type of crystal much stronger than the *cristallo* produced by the Venetians. By the 18th century, the lead crystal industry thrived throughout Europe, with factories established at Baccarat (France), Waterford (Ireland), and Bohemia. Lead crystal's highly reflective qualities and sparkle were beneficial to the design of light fixtures. Small lead crystal prisms were attached to chandeliers, candelabras, and wall sconces to refract the light from candles and provide greater illumination to interiors (Figure 5.50).

## METALWORKING

The skill of the metalsmith in detail and precision is evident in metalwork from the Baroque period. Repoussé work and chasing were the two most popular methods used by silversmiths for creating domestic objects. Repoussé work is made by hammering a soft metal from the reverse side, giving shape and pattern to the object's outer surface. Chasing was a technique applied to the

**FIGURE 5.47** This fireplace from an 18th-century farmhouse features delftware tiles in blue and white. Paul Kenward © Dorling Kindersley.

surface of the preformed object; a sharp tool was used to crease, incise, or indent the metal, giving the object design and pattern. Chasing was a technique used by Boulle to create his unique marquetry patterns (Figures 5.21 and 5.22). Baroque designs ranged from simple classical motifs to more complex landscapes, figural groupings, and foliate patterns.

## CLOCKS

Clocks were increasingly popular during the 17th century, although expensive, and came in a wide variety of models. With the invention of the pendulum clock in 1656 by Christiaan Huygens, clocks were more accurate in keeping time. Clockmakers teamed with cabinetmakers to create casings to house the intricate mechanical workings. The casing designs for tabletop clocks, mantel clocks, and longcase clocks incorporated popular motifs seen in Baroque interiors, including classical figures, ornate marquetry designs, and chased metalwork (Figures 5.51 and 5.52).

## TEXTILES

Jean Gobelins established the *Manufacture des Gobelins* when he came to France from Flanders during the 1400s. The factory became known for its rich dyes and intricate tapestry weavings. In 1667, the *Manufacture des Gobelins* was acquired by Minister Colbert for King Louis XIV to provide tapestries for the royal palaces. Other fine-quality tapestries came from Amiens in France, Flanders, and Brussels. Tapestry designs included scenes from history and mythological subject matter. These tapestries appeared more like paintings, with finer details and subtle color changes, and the new style was to include borders woven to look like ornately carved and gilt picture frames. The art of embroidery continued to flourish throughout the Baroque period, and these textiles appeared on bed hangings (Figure 5.17), upholstery, and wall hangings (Figures 5.3 and 5.53).

A former soap factory building called the "Savonnerie" (the French word for "soap") was converted into a weaving shop to produce the carpets for rooms in the Palace of Versailles. Savonnerie carpets were made with a tight weave—a knotted pile that measured 90 knots per square inch. Designs for the Palace of Versailles featured classical motifs, including acanthus leaves,

**FIGURE 5.48** A large Venetian ruby glass goblet and matching dish are decorated with wide gilt bands of Cupid and Psyche amid scrolling foliage in a scene based on the Baroque paintings by Giovanni da San Giovanni (1592–1636). © Judith Miller/Dorling Kindersley/Woolley and Wallis.

**FIGURE 5.50** This view into the Hall of Mirrors at the Palace of Versailles highlights a series of glass chandeliers with small prisms. © Rémi Cauzid/Shutterstock.

**FIGURE 5.49** Mirrors from the Baroque period line the walls in this Viennese museum. Peter Wilson © Dorling Kindersley.

**FIGURE 5.51** A small late-17th-century ebonized bracket clock by Richard Colston of London has a fine repoussé basket top surmounted by a decorative carrying handle surrounded by four finials in the emerging Rococo style. The clock sits on brass bun feet and an engraved back plate is decorated with chased tulip designs. © Judith Miller/Dorling Kindersley/Wallis and Wallis.

**FIGURE 5.52** This late-17th-century longcase clock has Baroque styling with a floral marquetry case and barley sugar twist motifs framing the face of the clock. © Judith Miller/Dorling Kindersley/Lyon and Turnbull Ltd.

scrolls, and botanicals, befitting the rooms that were named after Roman gods and goddesses such as the Salon of Venus and the Salon of Apollo (Figure 5.7).

French Huguenots, fleeing to England to escape religious persecution, set up weaving shops in Wilton, where they began producing cut pile carpets at the end of the 17th century. Wilton carpets featured a low-loop pile and were woven from woolen yarns. As early as the 16th century and continuing into the 17th, embroideries, *brocades*, and *damasks* were fashionable textiles used for upholstery, draperies, and bedding. Woven from silk on a loom, brocade fabrics have the appearance of fine embroideries, with raised foliate patterns in gold or silver threads enhancing the decorations (Figure 5.54). Damask features flatly woven floral designs, fruits, and animal forms in silk, gold, and silver yarns.

The lace-making industry prospered during the 17th century, with a variety of designs and patterns produced all over Europe. Each country created its own unique patterns. To protect the industry, many regions imposed bans on the importation of lace from other countries. Almost all laces featured flowers—some flatly woven, some raised, and others padded to create a three-dimensional look. Names associated with specific regions and designs include *gros point* and *rose point* from Venice, *point de France* named by King Louis XIV, and *point d'Angleterre* from the Netherlands (Figure 5.55). Lace adorned the edges of bedding and table coverings, as well as clothing, and was very expensive.

## WALLPAPER

The practice of covering walls with fine cloth began during the Italian Renaissance period and, for those who could afford to do so, the trend continued into the 17th century (Figure 5.7). Wallpaper appeared in homes before the 17th century, and it

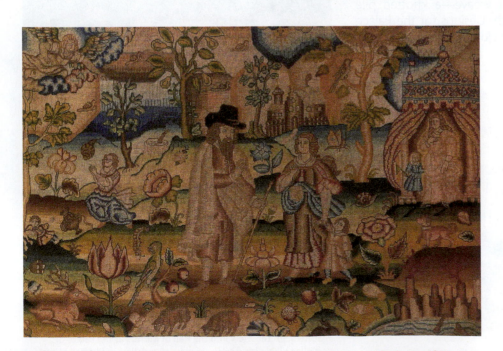

**FIGURE 5.53** A 17th-century linen and silk embroidered panel depicting the biblical story of Abraham, Hagar, and Ishmael, executed in bold colors of blues, reds and greens, was used as a wall hanging. © Judith Miller/Dorling Kindersley/Freeman's.

**FIGURE 5.54** The brocaded upholstery fabric on this 17th-century chair is woven from silk. Matthew Ward © Dorling Kindersley, Courtesy of the Central Museum Utrecht.

was either hand painted or printed using wooden blocks on small sheets of paper—a costly and time-consuming process. The French sanctioned the first paper-hanging guild in 1599; workers were trained to affix these decorative papers to the wall using paste. Wallpaper production increased during the 17th century after a French engraver, Jean Michel Papillon, used wooden blocks carved with repetitive patterns to print continuous rolls of paper. In an attempt to create the look of Italian velvet wall hangings, in 1680, the English invented a flocked paper as a less expensive substitute.

**FIGURE 5.55** This lappet from the 17th century shows a scalloped edge and a small, slightly raised flower design of point de France lace. The lace was a popular trim on linens as well as clothing. © Judith Miller/Dorling Kindersley/Mendes Antique Lace and Textiles.

# The Eighteenth Century

## Political Conditions

The 18th century was eclipsed by political upheavals that brought about wars and revolutions in Europe and in America. In England, Queen Anne (r. 1702–1714), the last reigning Stuart, took the throne in 1702 after the death of William III. In 1707, an Act of Union between Scotland and England formed Great Britain, combining the two parliaments into one unified government. Queen Anne was succeeded by George I (r. 1714–1727), elector of Hanover (Germany), followed by George II (r. 1727–1760) and then George III (r. 1760–1820) at the time of the American Revolution.

After the death of Louis XIV in 1715, the Regent Duke of Orleans (r. 1715–1723) managed the affairs of state for five-year-old Louis XV, who was a great-grandchild of the king. By 1723, Louis XV (r. 1715–1774) had assumed power and engaged France militarily in the Polish succession of 1733 and the Austrian succession of 1740. In addition, France entered into war with England in 1756 over control of territories in North America and India. Also involved in the conflict were Austria, Russia, Sweden, Hanover, and Prussia. This struggle, referred to as the "Seven Years' War" by Europeans (called the "French and Indian War" by Americans, and the "Intercolonial War" by Canadians) finally ended with the signing of the Peace of Paris in 1763 (also called the "Treaty of Paris"). This treaty settled the disputes among the countries and reorganized imperial control in North America. Britain gained Canada, the French gained Florida and territory east of the Mississippi, and Spain acquired Louisiana along with the previously French-held territory west of the Mississippi River.

As the second half of the century progressed, political unrest in America and France led to revolutions in both countries. The American Revolution developed between American colonists and British Parliament, as restrictions on imports and heavy taxation caused colonists to rebel against such actions without representation in Parliament. With increased tensions between the Crown and the colonists, King George III used British troops to enforce colonial law and secure absolutism.

Such events as the Boston Massacre in 1770, which killed five Bostonians by the muskets of British troops, and the Boston Tea Party of 1773 led the English Parliament to repress the American colonists even more by closing the harbor in Boston and rescinding the charter of the Massachusetts Bay Colony. Subsequently, in 1774, the First Continental Congress met in Philadelphia to organize a protest. The following year, American patriots fought against the British at Lexington. There on April 19, 1775, the first battle of the American Revolution took place.

France, by order of the new reigning monarch, King Louis XVI (r. 1774–1792), aided the Americans in their war against the British in 1778. Finally, in 1781, the British surrendered at Yorktown, Virginia, and the American Revolution ended with the signing of the Treaty of Paris in 1783. By the end of the decade, France would be involved in its own gruesome revolution.

# Architecture 1700–1750

Two stylistic periods developed during the 18th century as many new styles were introduced in both France and England. The first half of the century differed significantly from that of the second half, with more obvious changes seen in interior design and decoration. The first half of the 18th century ushered in a new style of design by replacing heavy Baroque features with a lighter fare. Gentle curves and ornamentation based on organic forms led to the use of the term "rococo," derived from the French *rocaille*, meaning "shell." This new style of design remained fashionable in architecture and the decorative arts until around 1750. Styles during the second half of the 18th century reverted to an interest in classicism after the rediscovery of the ancient Roman cities of Herculaneum (1738) and Pompeii (1748). The numerous artifacts excavated from these ancient sites fueled the inspiration for the Neoclassic period.

## FRANCE

The earliest expression of a Rococo–period style appeared in France as early as the last decade of the 17th century with a transitional style incorporating pilasters and columns in classical formality with more expressive façades (Figure 6.1). Although the exterior of buildings remained connected to classical detailing, as the 18th century progressed, the new modern taste in interior design replaced rectangular classical symmetry with more organic, asymmetrical curves based on nature. Smaller scale Parisian townhouses, or *hôtels* to the French, had sophisticated interiors designed for comfort and intimacy instead of grandiose Baroque–style rooms designed to impress.

As mentioned, after Louis XIV's death, a regent was appointed to monitor state affairs for the five-year-old Louis XV who was too young to rule. The regent, the Duke of Orléans, took Louis XV away from Versailles to Paris. Aristocrats wanting to stay connected to the court followed and commissioned the building of townhouses in Paris for their leisure. The regimented formality and opulence of Versailles were replaced by smaller, more intimate quarters, resulting in a style of décor taking on a lighter appearance in both ornamentation and color palette (Figure 6.2).

When Louis XV returned to Versailles in 1722, he appointed as First Architect Ange-Jacques Gabriel (1698–1782), who had the responsibility of creating more buildings on the palace grounds and rooms in

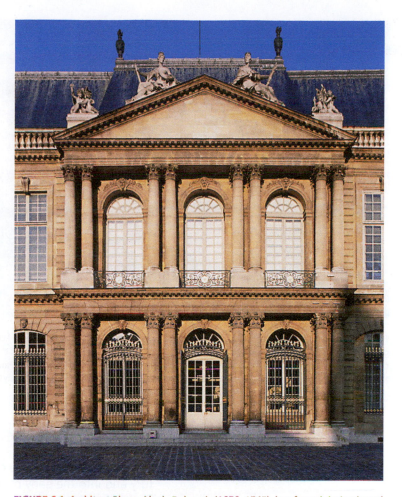

FIGURE 6.1 Architect Pierre-Alexis Delamair (1676–1745), in a formal design based on the classical symmetry of the Baroque, designed the Hôtel de Soubise in Paris in 1704. Further expansion and the interior design were carried out by Germain Boffrand (1667–1754) from 1735 to 1740. Boffrand worked on the interiors, creating oval salons, or reception rooms, designed in the new Rococo style that included curvilinear decoration, a light color palette, and asymmetrically arranged design motifs. Max Alexander © Dorling Kindersley.

FIGURE 6.2 This room setting from the French Rococo period shows restrained elegance with its needlepoint upholstered chairs, carved and pastel painted woodwork, and glass chandelier. Wall panel details feature sinuous vine patterns with subtle asymmetrical arrangements. Carpets of varying size cover a parquet floor, and a glass chandelier hangs overhead with its drop centered in front of the pier glass mirror above the fireplace. Max Alexander © Dorling Kindersley, Courtesy of Musee Carnavalet.

FIGURE 6.3 Louis XV's private study at Versailles, designed between 1753 and 1760, features gilt paneling in the Rococo manner, a large carpet with fleur-de-lis motifs, and a crystal chandelier positioned in front of an over mantel mirror above the fireplace. Louis XV's Private Study, 1753–60 (photo), Gabriel, Jacques-Ange (1698–1782)/Chateau de Versailles, France/Giraudon/The Bridgeman Art Library International.

the palace that replicated the smaller, more intimate rooms of hotels in Paris. These rooms featured exquisite ceiling frescoes depicting mythological figures, wainscoted walls painted in creamy white and embellished with gilt accents, *rocaille* (shell) motifs, and scrolls, complemented by delicate bouquets tied up with ribbons carved into molding designs (Figure 6.3).

With the introduction of pastels, paintings of pastoral or idyllic scenes depicted rosy-fleshed goddesses and putti in lush green gardens. François Boucher (1703–1770) received numerous commissions from Madame de Pompadour to paint these idyllic scenes on large-scale canvases that complemented the interior decor. Many of his designs were used as cartoons for the production of tapestries and Savonnerie or Aubusson rugs. Over time, vegetable dyes used to color the yarns have faded, leaving only a dull reminder of the original color palette. Viewing Boucher's original oil paintings reveals the soft, delicate pastel colors that once decorated the textiles.

## ENGLAND

Several variations of style existed in England during the latter part of the 17th century and into the early part of the 18th century. Following Sir Christopher Wren in pursuit of a national style, English designers vacillated between the Italian Baroque style, an emerging Rococo style, and the influence of Palladianism. Noted is Wren's design for St. Paul's Cathedral in London, which exhibits more classicism than true Baroque–influenced characteristics (Figure 5.8). For the most part, English architects rejected the inherent French Rococo characteristics for Palladianism, which had its beginnings in the work of Inigo Jones during the 17th century (Figure 4.14). Furthermore, translations of Andrea Palladio's *Four Books of Architecture*, which appeared in England in 1715, reinforced the popularity of Palladianism. Thereafter, interior design followed the classical program in every detail; columns, pilasters, and niches adorned rooms, recalling ancient Roman basilicas.

Chiswick House, built in 1729 and designed by owner Lord Burlington (1694–1753), reflected characteristics used in Palladio's Villa Rotunda by using a *piano nobile,* and symmetry was uniformly expressed (Figure 6.4). The house was built under the direction of William Kent (1685–1748). The interior design of Chiswick combined architectural symmetry with an elaboration of Baroque influences rather than contemporary Rococo styling. Kent's furniture designs featured heavy carving and massive proportions in direct opposition to the curvilinear designs of the French Rococo. His furnishings for the Double Cube room at Wilton House are more Baroque in character than Rococo (Figure 6.5).

James Gibbs (1682–1754) left his native Scotland for London in 1710 to design houses and interiors for wealthy clients. He had trained as an architect in Italy and was well studied in the designs of ancient Rome. In 1728, his portfolio of work, *Book of Architecture Containing Designs of Buildings and Ornament*, was published in London. These drawings included floor plans, elevation drawings, and details of ornamentation, and established what was more restrained than the trends favored by French aristocrats and royalty (Figure 6.6). The interior of Claydon House is

FIGURE 6.4 Palladian influences are seen on Chiswick House with its central portico and dome. © Anthony Shaw Photography/Shutterstock.

**FIGURE 6.5** First begun in 1653, Inigo Jones' interior design for the Double Cube room at Wilton House features the furniture designs of William Kent. Kent's mix of Baroque and Neo-Palladian details reflected the desire to establish a national style in England. The settees and console tables adorning the room feature ornate gilt-wood Classical carvings. The Double Cube Room, c.1649 (photo), Jones, Inigo (1573–1652) & Webb, John (c.1611–72)/© Collection of the Earl of Pembroke, Wilton House, Wilts./The Bridgeman Art Library International.

**FIGURE 6.6** Wimpole Hall in England was first built in 1643, and was expanded and changed throughout its history. James Gibbs worked on the expansion from 1713 to 1730, incorporating Rococo features, illustrated in his *Book of Architecture*, into its façade. Emily Andersen © Dorling Kindersley.

a true representation of the Rococo influences that appeared in England during the first half of the 18th century (Figure 6.7). Built in 1757, the rooms feature exuberant carving by Luke Lightfoot that incorporated Rococo, chinoiserie, and Gothic influences. Not much is known about Luke Lightfoot other than his work at Claydon House, but the new taste for chinoiserie and Gothic–inspired designs dominate the work of the cabinetmaker Thomas Chippendale (1718–1779).

## AMERICA

American architectural styles developed rapidly in the colonies as economic prosperity led to a better lifestyle than those of the early settlers. By the end of the 17th century, tobacco, rice, and sugar, among other commodities exported to England, created a boom in the American port trade business. The Georgian style of architecture emerged at the beginning of the 18th century

**FIGURE 6.7** The salon inside Claydon House in Buckinghamshire features elaborate stucco ceiling designs. Dating from the English Rococo period, these designs incorporate many Baroque features, with attention paid closely to classical elements seen here on the fireplace, door header, and windows. National Trust Photo Library.

**FIGURE 6.8** The Crowninshield Bentley House, built in 1727, reflects the American Georgian architectural style with its symmetrical façade and front door flanked by classical pilasters capped by a triangular pediment. David Lyons © Dorling Kindersley.

**FIGURE 6.9** This interior from the Cortlandt House in New York features common characteristics of Georgian period design and furniture—blue-painted woodwork and wall paneling, modest built-in cupboards flanking a fireplace set with blue and white Delft tiles, and an inlaid cabinet with Chinese export porcelains on display. The American Late Colonial style imitated England's popular Queen Anne style.
Dave King © Dorling Kindersley, Courtesy of the Van Cortlandt House Museum, New York.

**FIGURE 6.10** The crest rail on this American Late Colonial–style chair features a delicately carved shell motif referencing the rocaille (or shell) design of the French Rococo period.
© Judith Miller/Dorling Kindersley/Pook and Pook.

**FIGURE 6.11** This Worcester bowl decorated in colored enamels with chinoiserie figures, butterflies, and insects framed within a gilt cartouche on a blue background dates from 1770. © Judith Miller/Dorling Kindersley/Albert Amor.

in America, a reflection of newfound colonial wealth. Although these colonial houses were modest in size by European standards, they reflected a refinement of detail and quality based on understated classical details. Most homes were two stories, had symmetrical façades, and featured classical lintels over doors and windows. Front doors were usually flanked by classical pilasters and topped by triangular pediments (Figure 6.8).

Georgian home interiors had small rooms with low ceilings, and painted wood paneling was a prominent element of the interior architectural scheme (Figure 6.9). The colors were rich blues (influenced by the blue and white Chinese export pottery), yellow ochre, dark yellow-green, and oxblood red. Wood floors were kept natural whereas ceiling beams were painted in the same colors as the wall paneling. During the first half of the 18th century, furnishings reflected English tastes, although the American colonies lagged about 20 years behind current English style. The more affluent sailing merchants and plantation owners had the means to afford Chinese porcelains and, on occasion, Oriental rugs.

# Design Motifs

Although France and England differed in their interpretations of Rococo design elements, recurring motifs such as chinoiserie and *rocaille* united the decorative arts of these two countries (Figure 6.10). Chinese exports flooded Europe, and Oriental designs depicting dragons, bonsai landscapes, and pagoda teahouses occupied by kimono-clad figures appeared in all the decorative arts and on interior architectural details (Figure 6.11). The English adopted the use of Chinese frets, a more ornate version of the Greek key, especially used as a decorative detail on furniture and on interior millwork. There are several variations of the Chinese fret motifs, and essentially all follow a strict geometric patterning resembling fine latticework (Figure 6.12).

Idealized images of Roman gods and goddesses were replaced by *singerie* designs—frolicsome monkeys dressed in fine French fashion. Classical motifs were reduced to shells, festoons, and occasional putti (Figure 6.13). Instead, the free-flowing asymmetrical forms seen in nature, such as flowing vine patterns and foliate designs, dominated fine marquetry work, ormolu, and architectural details (Figure 6.14).

# Furniture

French aristocrats living in *hôtels* in Paris furnished their apartments with smaller scale furnishings than those found in the larger country chateaus (Figure 6.2). Chairs with shorter backs were more proportionate to lower ceilings in these much smaller living quarters, and arm pads and thicker seat cushions made chairs more comfortable. Upholstery fabrics featured *singerie* motifs or were foliated brocades or damasks in

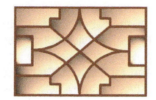

**FIGURE 6.12** Fretwork designs like these were a prominent feature of Chinese Chippendale furnishings, taking inspiration from Chinese export furniture popular in England during the mid 18th century. © David Vleck.

**FIGURE 6.13** This stone arch features three carved putti. Stephen Oliver © Dorling Kindersley.

pastel colors. Moreover, English *chintz*, French *toile de Jouy*, petit point, silk, and *taffeta* replaced the heavier needlepoint and tapestry upholstery fabrics from the Baroque period.

A variety of woods, including walnut, oak, and elm, appeared in the construction of furniture during the 18th century; however, imported mahogany gained prominence, especially in England. Painted furniture was made from beech—a strong, straight-grained wood that lacked a distinctive grain pattern. Carving and marquetry patterns provided most of the decoration. Marquetry and veneer work featured the lighter colors of fruitwoods for inlaid floral designs and chinoiserie patterns. Other decorations on furniture matched the more feminine architectural moldings; they featured sinuous curvilinear forms, delicate floral designs with graceful proportions, and light pastel colors. Tables, desks, and en suite chairs matched with settees were designed with serpentine curves on seat rails and delicately shaped cabriole legs.

Chinese lacquer work, imitated by the French and English by applying varnish over a painted surface, also became a fashionable furniture treatment during the Rococo period. *Vernis martin*, the name given to a type of shellac developed by four French brothers, the Martins, was used on a variety of case goods during the 18th century and imitated Oriental lacquer work. The application of this varnish was similar to the japanning process practiced by the English a century before (Figure 5.31).

As mentioned, seat furniture was made more comfortable than previous styles with the introduction of covered arm pads and thicker seat cushions. Upholstery fabrics in pastel colors emphasized foliate patterns either woven into the cloth, as in brocade or damask, or printed onto the surface of the cloth as in English chintz or French *toile de Jouy*. Heavy velvets, needlepoint, and tapestries used on upholstered furniture during the Baroque and Renaissance periods subsided as delicate silks and taffetas became more prevalent. Leather was still used to some extent, although it was dyed in a variety of colors, and caning continued to be used on a limited basis.

## FRENCH ROCOCO: 1715–1774

French Rococo–period furniture is comprised of two related but distinctive styles: the Régence and Louis XV. The period of time between the death of King Louis XIV and the rule of Louis XV, between 1715 and 1722, is known as the "Régence" and it marks the transformation

**FIGURE 6.14** Stucco work appearing in this staircase from the Rococo period combines foliate and shell designs with a classical putto and acanthus leaves. Joe Cornish © Dorling Kindersley.

**FIGURE 6.15** The Rococo period's subtle use of asymmetry in design is seen in this detail photo of a cartouche-shape escutcheon on a Chippendale chest. © Judith Miller/Dorling Kindersley/Pook and Pook.

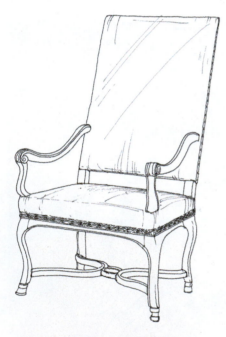

**FIGURE 6.16** The Régence style, which developed in France at the end of the 17th century, marked the beginning of the Rococo period as fluid curves replaced the straight lines and heaviness of the Baroque period. This drawing of a walnut fauteuil maintains the characteristic tall rectangular back of the Louis XIV style; however, curves appear on the armrests, arm posts, seat rail, legs, and stretchers. Cabriole legs, a common characteristic found on Louis XV–style furniture, are combined with hoof feet, and each leg is connected by a shaped saltire stretcher.

**FIGURE 6.17** A Régence–style parquetry and parcel-gilt twin-pedestal extending dining table, the top with rounded corners and a *lambrequin*-carved edge, each quadruple pedestals with incurved foliate scroll legs are centered by a foliate finial. © Judith Miller/Dorling Kindersley/Sloan's & Kenyon.

between staunch Baroque styling and the more fluid Rococo period. Régence characteristics reflect some of the heaviness of Louis XIV–style furniture, but anticipate the more delicate curvilinear style of the emerging Louis XV. Straight, symmetrical patterns were replaced with curving, asymmetrical shapes on everything from hardware to marquetry patterns and ormolu (Figure 6.15). Chairs of the Régence style were smaller in scale than those designed in the Louis XIV style, and they featured shorter backs, with slightly curved forms appearing in the shape of the back, the seat rail, and leg forms.

Curvilinear Rococo design appears during the last quarter of the 17th century with the introduction of the cabriole leg. Its use is more typical of the Rococo period and, in general, Régence–style cabriole legs terminate into a hoof, paw, or a whorl foot whereas Louis XV–style cabriole legs end in a small scroll (Figure 6.16). Régence–style chairs and tables continued to incorporate the characteristic saltire stretcher of the Louis XIV style, only with more lateral curvature (Figure 6.17). The stretchers are completely eliminated on Louis XV–style furniture. Chair backs remained somewhat tall and rectangular with a slight curvature appearing in the crest rail; however, these proportions changed by 1720 with the full development of the Louis XV style.

As mentioned earlier, as court life moved away from Versailles and into the Parisian *hôtel* or apartment, the new Louis XV style emerged. The style catered to newer, much smaller living quarters and emphasized graceful proportions and comfort over pretentiousness. Pieces of furniture that emphasized contemporary architectural spaces of the period were introduced into Rococo interiors. The *window seat* was intended to fit precisely within the windowed recessed arches of the interior, and provided a more comfortable seat than a *tabouret*. Chairs were designed with shorter backs and overall smaller proportions that fit nicely within the new, smaller scale rooms. Chair backs, seat rails, arms, and legs, along with drawer fronts, sides, and tops of tables and case goods incorporated serpentine curves into their designs (Figure 6.20). Scrolled, or incurvate, arm supports were set back from the front seat rail to accommodate the full skirts worn by ladies of the period. A small upholstered pad, or *manchette*, was added to the armrest during the early 18th century to relieve the pressure placed on the elbows, and is indicative of a greater awareness of comfort in design.

Louis XV–style furniture exemplified the almost feminine quality of the era; powdered wigs, lace, and satin were worn equally by men and women who enjoyed a life of leisure centered on active social gatherings. Evidence shows that upholstered furnishings in velvet, brocade, and satin matched the same fabrics used for clothing. Fauteuils and bergères were designed with dainty, carved cabriole legs ending in delicate scroll feet resting on shoes (Figure 6.21). Although the seat rail and apron followed a serpentine shape, more curves were repeated on the crest rail and arm supports. Wood trim extending from the arm supports to the uprights and across the crest rail framed the shape of the all-upholstered cartouche back and sides, gracefully uniting the overall design.

The 18th-century wing chair, a derivative of the 17th-century sleeping chair, protected the face from drafty interiors with side panels placed near the head and extending perpendicularly from the back (Figure 6.20). Some wing chairs were designed with mechanisms that allowed the back to recline; however, most remained stationary. The lounging chair, or the *chaise longue*, was introduced as a type of daybed and consisted of one, two, or three separate pieces of furniture, although more common examples were designed in two pieces (Figure 6.22). One section, similar to a *bergère en gondole*, was fitted to a low-back bergère that had an extralong seat. These pieces could be pushed together or separated as needed.

# A CLOSER Look

## Transitional Styles

The two French chaises presented here (Figures 6.18 and 6.19) show the transition away from the Louis XIV style toward the emerging Louis XV style. The chair in Figure 6.18 is representative of the Régence style, smaller in scale than other French chairs dating from the Baroque period, although it retains the squared-off tall and narrow back. The chair shows emerging Rococo influences with some curvature on the seat rail, and with the cabriole legs and scroll feet that rest on a small pad called a "shoe."

The walnut chair is upholstered in floral needlework. In contrast, the chaise in Figure 6.19 is smaller and features more curvature in the chair's frame. A cartouche back is pulled in at the waist and is separated from the seat with short uprights that are curved. The seat rail features serpentine shapes around the front and sides. Cabriole legs with scroll feet on shoes are longer and more slender than those on the transitional-style chair. This chair is gilded and is upholstered in solid-color damask.

**FIGURE 6.18** An transitional Louis XV walnut side chair, the back and seat upholstered in floral needlework on a yellow background, with carved and shaped seat rails standing on fairly straight cabriole legs.
© Judith Miller/Dorling Kindersley/Hamptons.

**FIGURE 6.19** A Louis XV–style chaise captures the essence of the Rococo period with full attention to the delicate curves used in the design of the chair. The frame around a shortened back is cinched at the midpoint, giving shape to what is called a "cartouche back." A full serpentine curve is given to the seat rail, and carved details include foliate patterns. This Louis XV–style French chair is small in scale, features a short back, and is carved from gilt wood. Delicately shaped cabriole legs give the chair a more feminine appearance. © Judith Miller/ Dorling Kindersley/Caroline de Kerangal.

The formal settee of the 17th century evolved into a more comfortable seating unit referred to in 18th century inventories as a "sofa." Both terms were widely used throughout the 18th century, with the differentiation that a settee was usually smaller that a sofa, which was long enough for a person to recline. The French canapé was usually upholstered and designed en suite with either bergères, fauteuils,

Cartouche back

Scrolled foot resting on a shoe

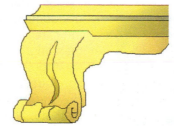

Scrolled foot

Drawer pull

Escutcheon

**FIGURE 6.20** Furniture characteristics of the French Rococo period, Régence, and Louis XV styles.
© David Vleck.

**FIGURE 6.21** A bergère dating from 1760 features a gilt-wood frame and red velvet upholstery. © Judith Miller/Dorling Kindersley/Caroline de Kerangal.

...is drawing of a French Louis ...longue, circa 1725, made of carved walnut has an ornate crest rail, winged sides to keep drafts from the face, and heavily carved aprons running along the sides and front of the piece.

**FIGURE 6.23** A late-18th-century gilt-wood canapé with a serpentine-shaped back and cabriole legs with carved foliage decorations. © Judith Miller/Dorling Kindersley/Woolley and Wallis.

**FIGURE 6.24** A Louis XV carved gilt-wood center table with acanthus leaf and C-scroll carved decorations with putti carved legs. © Judith Miller/Dorling Kindersley/Sloan's.

**FIGURE 6.25** A transitional Louis XV tulipwood and parquetry *table a jeux*. The rectangular hinged top is inlaid with a chessboard and opens to a baize-lined playing surface. The undercarriage has an accordion-action extension, the frieze has a small drawer, the restrained square-section cabriole legs with bronze doré foliate patterned sabots. © Judith Miller/Dorling Kindersley/Sloan's.

or both (Figure 6.23). The length of the canapé varied, but usually accommodated more than two people.

Console tables continued to be used primarily for decoration in rooms and were used to display candelabras or other objets d'art (Figure 6.24). Dining remained on a more intimate level and small, drop-leaf tables proved satisfactory. Many other types of tables were introduced during the 18th century, each for a variety of uses including writing, game playing, sewing, and dressing. Game tables were a prominent feature in the salons because card games were a popular form of entertainment. These tables were designed with a fold-over top so the table could be stored against the wall when not being used (Figure 6.25). A special chair called a *voyeuse* was designed with a flat pad across the top of the crest rail that enabled a spectator to watch the hand of cards of the person who was seated. The chair gets its name from the French word, *voir*, meaning "to see."

Case pieces increased in quantity and most were designed for specific purposes. Although the introduction of the commode during the 17th century was intended to raise the chest from the floor, trunks continued to be used for traveling and were easily portable. As the predominant piece of storage furniture in use throughout the 18th century, commodes, like chairs, were reduced in size to fit in smaller rooms. Maintaining the desire for curves throughout the Rococo period, commodes often had *bombé* sides and serpentine fronts. Magnificently decorated, commodes were placed against coordinating wall panels that incorporated similar floral or chinoiserie patterns. Marquetry patterns of bouquets tied with ribbons, musical instruments, and intricate vines replaced carving as the predominant ornamentation on case goods and tables (Figure 6.26).

Storage furniture increased in abundance with continued use of the armoire and the introduction of the *chiffonier*. Although the armoire stored articles of clothing, the chiffonier was used by women to store needlework and other sewing items (Figure 6.27). Adapted from the chest of drawers, this piece of furniture is an example of items designed for a specific use during the 18th century and reflects the luxury of owning such objects.

As the 18th century progressed, differentiation was made between furniture used by ladies and that used by gentlemen, leading to the introduction of more gender-specific furniture. A variety of tables and desks introduced during the Rococo period were designed specifically to meet the needs of women. Small worktables for ladies, or the *table à ouvrage*, incorporated fitted drawers or recessed compartments for storage of sewing and needlework implements (Figure 6.28).

**FIGURE 6.26** This transitional-style Louis XV commode has a marble top with kingwood marquetry patterns featuring floral designs in a classical urn. Brass ormolu mounts appear as growing vine patterns over the front and sides of the piece. © Judith Miller/Dorling Kindersley/Sloan's & Kenyon.

**FIGURE 6.27** A traditional Louis XV marble-top and parquetry *table en chiffoniere*, with a pierced three-quarter gallery, green marble top, and two drawers (28 inches [71 centimeters] high). © Judith Miller/Dorling Kindersley/Sloan's.

Tables for writing also increased in quantity and type because correspondence was maintained on a daily basis. Special desks designed for ladies and gentlemen often included secret storage compartments for the concealment of personal letters. The *secretaire, bonheur du jour, bureau à dos d'âne,* and *bureau à caissons latéraux* were types of desks commonly used by women (Figure 6.29). These cabinet-type desks featured a fall front or slant front that was designed to drop to a flat surface when opened. The inside surface of the fall or slant front was covered in leather to protect the wood and create a smooth writing surface. The *bureau plat* (a writing table fitted with a small drawer) and the *bureau à cylindre* (a rolltop desk), were much larger and preferred by men.

One of the most celebrated ébénistes of the period, Jean-François Oeben (1720–1763), produced a magnificent *bureau du roi* for King Louis XV decorated with trompe l'oeil marquetry and chased bronze (Figure 6.3). Although Oeben worked on the desk for three years, he did not live to see it completed. After Oeben's death, his apprentice and successor, Jean Henri Riesener (1734–1806), finished the desk and affixed his signature in 1769.

In the small suite of rooms or apartments taken as living quarters in the French *hôtels,* or townhouses, the bedchamber often doubled as both sleeping room and salon. Lower ceilings made the larger tester beds and four-poster types of earlier periods impractical. Beds designed with drapery that cascaded downward from large overhead canopies suspended from the headboard were more popular during the 18th century. Traversing the bed within an alcove became a popular French custom after 1755 and became increasingly popular throughout the remainder of the 18th century.

## ENGLISH ROCOCO: 1702–1760

Several distinctive styles of furniture developed during the English Rococo period. Specific characteristics that set one apart from another are subtle but noticeable as each subsequent style was greatly influenced by the previous. Queen Anne, Early Georgian, and Late Georgian furniture styles share common characteristics that classify them as products of the Rococo period. Furniture designed during the English Rococo period adopted few influences from its French neighbors across the Channel. Typical of French Rococo trends in furniture design, 18th-century cabinetmakers preferred the carved leg over the turned leg. The cabriole leg, already popularized in France during the last decade of the 17th century, was used extensively, if not exclusively, on Queen Anne and Early Georgian–style chairs, settees, and tables.

Increased trading with the Far East during the 18th century fostered British fascination with Oriental design, which influenced the style and tastes in England into the later Georgian period. Furniture imported from China, including chairs, tea tables, and cabinets, featured lacquered chinoiserie details and claw-and-ball feet. English furniture makers imitated the look of Chinese lacquer work in a technique called "japanning," essentially a red or black painted surface sealed with a high-sheen varnish. These increasingly popular Chinese characteristics dominated English furniture design by 1760.

FIGURE 6.28  (a) A lady's worktable, or *table à ouvrage,* from 1770 in the French Louis XV style features ormolu feet, and small drawers. The table is made from veneered kingwood. (b) The top has marquetry designs.  © Judith Miller/Dorling Kindersley/Wallis and Wallis.

FIGURE 6.29  This *bonheur du jour* is a small writing desk used by women whose "good hour of the day" was spent on dutiful correspondence. This example dates from the second quarter of the 18th century. This small slant-front corner desk, has a fall-front panel that is mounted with reverse hinges that support the velvet-covered writing surface when it is lowered. The cabinet's interior has shelves and fitted drawers.  © Judith Miller/Dorling Kindersley/Sloan's.

# A CLOSER Look

## Chinese Export Trade

At the beginning of the Qing dynasty (1644–1912) in China, the British and Dutch East India companies had already been trading with the former Ming dynastic rulers since 1600. Moreover, the fashions for Orientalism had already influenced interior design during the 17th century through the importation of Chinese porcelains and lacquerware. Silk, cotton, and tea were the main exports from China during the 18th century, although the Chinese saw a new market in exporting furniture. Ming dynastic furniture featured shaped, *splat-back* chairs with rounded backs and arms (Figure 6.30). The chair developed into a design that featured a taller and thinner back with a crest rail that projected beyond the sides of the uprights. The chair is often called a "hat chair" because the shape resembles the official hat worn by the emperor (Figure 6.31). This shape was commonly referred to as a "yoke back" by Europeans, the shape more reminiscent of the yoke used on oxen for hauling wagons. The influence of the yoke-back chair would play an important role in English Rococo period styles.

Furnishings exported from China for the western market featured a mix of Chinese design and European style. The *spoon-back chair*, named for the distinctive curve of the back splat, featured a curved yoke-shape crest rail, and cabriole legs (Figure 6.32). These cabriole leg forms ended with claw-and-ball feet, the Chinese motif of the talons of a bird clutching a pearl. A *rocaille* was often carved into the crest rail and on the knees of the legs.

Chinese lacquerware tables, screens, and cabinets were exported to Europe and the Americas (Figure 6.33). Owning these items showed great wealth, and these pieces were prominently displayed in the public rooms

**FIGURE 6.31** A Chinese elmwood official's hat chair with a yoke back and a spoon-shaped splat dates from 1750. © Judith Miller/Dorling Kindersley/Wallis and Wallis.

**FIGURE 6.30** A small set of Chinese furniture from the Ming period features horseshoe-shaped backs with splats, and a table designed with a large apron and bracket legs. © Judith Miller/Dorling Kindersley/Wallis and Wallis.

## QUEEN ANNE STYLE: 1702–1720

The first true style of the English Rococo period is named after Queen Anne. Unlike Queen Mary before her, who took an interest in the design of the new addition at Hampton Court and collected Chinese porcelains, Queen Anne thought little of the interior fashions of the times. Rooms added onto Hampton Court and those redecorated during Queen Anne's reign were designed in a more restrained interpretation of Rococo characteristics. Queen Anne–style furniture, however, reflects the delicate proportions and graceful curves brought on by the spirit of the Rococo movements in France (and Austria). In fact, rooms added onto Hampton Court and those redecorated during her reign maintained influences of the Baroque and Neo-Palladian styles from the previous century.

**FIGURE 6.32** This early China trade side chair brought to England from Canton, China, in 1730 is made from rosewood. The chair features Oriental details adopted by English cabinetmakers, including the shaped splat and cabriole legs with claw-and-ball feet. © Judith Miller/ Dorling Kindersley/Wallis and Wallis.

**FIGURE 6.33** A Chinese red-lacquered elmwood cabinet from 1750 features oversized brass cabinet pulls. © Judith Miller/ Dorling Kindersley/Wallis and Wallis.

**FIGURE 6.34** A late-18th-century Chinese export lacquered tea table is decorated with Oriental figures in a pastoral setting. © Judith Miller/Dorling Kindersley/Wallis and Wallis.

of the house. Chinese cabinets were more rectangular in shape, and styles dating back to the Ming dynasty show them on short cabriole legs. Ornamentation featured scenes of garden house tea parties, or the cabinet was covered with motifs that had special significance for the Chinese, such as the peony, which was the symbol of China during the Qing dynasty. The popularity of tea drinking in Europe flourished during the 18th century and tea tables, tea boxes, and other accoutrements for serving tea were imported in great numbers. A portable tea table was designed with a tilted top that could be used as a flat-surface table for serving tea, and could then be folded and pushed against the wall when finished. The surfaces were designed with beautiful scenes or bird and flower patterns inlayed with mother-of-pearl, jade, and colored woods that were shown off when the table top was tipped to show the vertical surface (Figure 6.34).

The transition away from the Baroque William and Mary styles toward the Queen Anne style resulted in a mixture of turned forms and splat-back chairs (Figure 6.35). Furniture had little carving or applied ornamentation, but maintained the current French fashion for cabriole legs. The front legs of chairs were always cabriole, but the back legs varied from cabriole to saber leg forms. The typical English cabriole leg ended in either a pad or a club foot. The cabriole leg met the seat rail at the corners and a *bracketed knee* usually carved into the shape of a shell or acanthus leaf made the transition between leg and seat. The use of stretchers disappeared around 1708 when improved craftsmanship and lighter proportions made them unnecessary.

Although French furniture of the Louis XV style was redesigned to maximize comfort, the Queen Anne and Early Georgian splat-back or spoon-back chair

**FIGURE 6.35** An early-18th-century Queen Anne chair has a vase-shaped splat back with a slight curvature to the crest rail. Turned legs and stretchers are more reminiscent of the William and Mary style in this transitional design. © Judith Miller/Dorling Kindersley/Sloan's and Kenyon.

**FIGURE 6.36** A George I armchair with open sides features a waisted back and a burr-walnut veneered splat. Each arm rest is scrolled and terminates in the shape of an eagle's head. A serpentine shaped seat rail with a drop-in cushion seat rests on cabriole legs that are carved with shell patterns at the knee and rest on hairy-paw feet. Dorling Kindersley.

**FIGURE 6.37** This English Queen Anne wing chair made from mahogany features scrolled arms and cabriole legs, and dates from 1730. © Judith Miller/Dorling Kindersley/Pook and Pook.

**FIGURE 6.38** An early-18th-century walnut-veneer lowboy has a rectangular top with a molded edge and feather banding, flanked by two deep drawers that enclose the kneehole. It is raised on slender cabriole legs that terminate in pad feet. © Judith Miller/Dorling Kindersley/Lyon and Turnbull Ltd.

offered more comfort to the sitter through shaped uprights and a back splat that followed the curvature of the spine (Figure 6.36). Sinuous uprights forming the spoon shape enclosed either a vase- or fiddle-shape splat. Rococo curves of both back and leg were carried through the design of the chair with the introduction of the *gooseneck arm*. Gooseneck arms were a common feature of Queen Anne–style armchairs and settees.

The splat-back chair, with or without arms, was frequently used for dining, and remains a favorite style in present-day reproductions. These chairs incorporated a *slip seat* or *drop seat* that allowed for more flexibility in alternating textiles with the change of seasons. A cushioned seat was covered with fabric then dropped into the seat-rail frame and secured at the corners, leaving the wood of the seat rail exposed. Other types of seat pieces were usually fitted with slipcovers that were changed in the spring and fall seasons. In rare cases, chairs might be japanned in red, black, green, or gold, with chinoiserie detailing.

The all-upholstered chair came in a variety of designs. A more basic upholstered type was designed with carved wood arms and cabriole legs. Unlike French examples from the same period, English–designed upholstered chairs connected at the juncture of the seat and back, limiting the exposed wood frame to the arms, legs, and stretchers, if used. The Queen Anne–style wing chair that evolved from the 17th-century sleeping chair is a more typical example of all-upholstered chairs used at this time. The wing chair has upholstery on the back, wings, arms, and seat (Figure 6.37). These chairs were placed in front of the fireplace, sheltering the face from drafts, while a fire screen protected the sitter from the intense heat of the fire. It is also believed that fire screens kept the wax-based makeup from melting (worn by women of the period to smooth out the skin from pockmarks).

Tables were more abundant and designed for special purposes like tea tables, game tables, and lowboys (Figure 6.38). They were designed without stretchers and featured slender cabriole legs. Queen Anne–style furniture had little carving or applied ornamentation, and tables lacked elaborate carvings or inlays other than an occasional shell motif appearing on the knee of the cabriole leg or on the apron. Moreover, the delicate floral marquetry patterns characteristic of Louis XV–style furniture were not favored by furniture makers of the Queen Anne style.

Designers relied on the beauty of wood graining as the most decorative feature on furniture. Walnut or walnut veneer was favored by most cabinetmakers until 1725, when mahogany became more fashionable. Burl walnut, a more popular finish veneer, emphasized the marbleizing effect of the wood. As the tree grew, cuts were made into the bark that caused the tree to bruise, which produced irregularities in the grain as the tree continued to grow. Lighter woods appeared as *crossbanded* marquetry applied as a decorative border around drawer fronts, door fronts, and tabletops. Although natural walnut or mahogany finishes were more common, the English court contained a few items that were either gilt or japanned (Figure 6.39). Japanning was used sparingly on most furniture types, occasionally appearing on cabinets or other case goods.

Highboys, tallboys, and chests continued to be used to store clothes (Figure 6.40). The early styles of the 18th century followed William and Mary types, featuring flat, unadorned tops, but the cabriole leg replaced bell turning while the bracket or *goddard foot* replaced the ball, or bun. The soft curves of the Rococo period were incorporated into tall case furniture through the occasional appearance of the hood or *bonnet top*. Door fronts mimicked the restrained arched shape whereas escutcheons, aprons, and feet were fashioned into undulating curves.

Trading with the Far East increased during the 18th century, and the English fascination with Oriental design and customs continued to influence furniture style and development. Tea drinking, introduced to Europeans during the 17th century, became increasingly popular with the English and Americans during the 18th century. As export porcelains were being acquired at great expense, the china cabinet became a common unit of furniture used for the storage and display of these prized possessions. Cabinets on stands were customarily ornate and modeled after French and Oriental examples. The stands depicted fine craftsmanship of elaborately carved legs and aprons, whereas the cabinets were often treated with fine japanning or burl walnut. The 17th-century writing cabinet developed into the ever-popular secretary of the 18th century. Two basic types of writing desks evolved: the fall-front and the slant-front. Slant-front writing cabinets were tall case pieces usually ornamented with some type of pediment top (Figure 6.41).

Beds in the Queen Anne style remained virtually unchanged from the William and Mary style that preceded it (Figure 6.42). Four-poster types supporting draped fabric continued to be popular, although two-poster types were introduced with a half-tester. The half-tester canopy was suspended from the ceiling and supported on posts framing the headboard.

## EARLY GEORGIAN STYLE: 1720–1760

The death of Queen Anne in 1714 left no heir to the English throne other than a distant cousin, George, Elector of Hanover (r. 1714–1727). When he was crowned King George I of England, he was 54 years old, spoke no English, brought his three

**FIGURE 6.39** A Queen Anne gilt gesso pier table has a rectangular top with a molded edge and cusped corners. The relief carving is decorated with grotesque figures on the front panel and side borders and cabriole legs feature shell designs and scroll feet. © Judith Miller/Dorling Kindersley/Wallis and Wallis.

**FIGURE 6.40** A Queen Anne walnut and burr walnut veneer chest on a stand features feather banding on the drawer fronts with crossbanding on the top. The molded top rests on an ogee cornice. Graduated drawers are supported by squat cabriole legs ending in pad feet. © Judith Miller/Dorling Kindersley/Lyon and Turnbull Ltd.

**FIGURE 6.41** This English Queen Anne–style crimson lacquer bureau bookcase features gilt chinoiserie, figural landscapes, double-hooded cabinet doors, and bun feet. © Judith Miller/Dorling Kindersley/Sloan's.

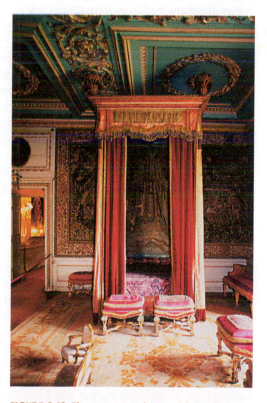

**FIGURE 6.42** The staterooms in Warwick Castle, redesigned in the current fashion for a visit by Queen Anne in 1704, reveal rich tapestries, carpet, and bed hangings, with classically designed painted and gilt ceiling moldings. Matching gilt furniture upholstered with coordinating red damask date from the Baroque period. Rob Reichenfeld © Dorling Kindersley.

FIGURE 6.43 A George I walnut stool has cabriole legs with a shell motif carved on the knee, and claw-and-ball feet. © Judith Miller/ Dorling Kindersley/Lyon and Turnbull Ltd.

FIGURE 6.45 This George I walnut-framed two-seater sofa with an upholstered rectangular back has scrolled arms and a seat raised on shell-carved mahogany cabriole legs with pad feet. © Judith Miller/Dorling Kindersley/Lyon and Turnbull Ltd.

FIGURE 6.46 The half-round mahogany table in the English Early Georgian style shown here is in a closed position with a gateleg extension. Card playing was a favorite pastime among all classes of society during the 18th century, and special tables used for this purpose were designed with folding mechanisms that allowed the table to be stored against the wall like a console table when not in use. © Judith Miller/Dorling Kindersley/Lyon and Turnbull Ltd.

FIGURE 6.44 This George I walnut corner chair from circa 1720 features curved arms attached to an overscroll crest rail supported by vase shaped splats and columns. The padded drop-in seat is supported by a combination of turned legs and block legs connected by a cross-stretcher. © Judith Miller/ Dorling Kindersley/Sloan's.

German mistresses, and had imprisoned his wife for 32 years. Although his reign was short, he was despised by his subjects. His son, George II, was 45 years old when he ascended the throne after his father's death, and he was regarded more favorably by his English subjects.

The Early Georgian style of furniture encompasses the reigns of these two monarchs. Although the actual rulers themselves took no part in the design process, the Queen Anne style appears to be more feminine in design, with its delicate proportions, whereas the Early Georgian style is more masculine. The furniture created under the reign of these two rulers took on a masculine appearance through heavier proportions, and had considerably more carving by comparison.

A shortened version of the cabriole leg was used by Early Georgian furniture designers. These legs had more carving applied to them, particularly with a lion-mask motif or the occasional shell or acanthus leaf incorporated into the bracketed knee (Figure 6.43). The claw-and-ball foot introduced in 1710 was used frequently on Early Georgian–style furniture; however, its transformation into a paw-and-ball foot was not uncommon, nor was the use of a hairy paw foot. Seats were often wider than Queen Anne types, and stretchers were used more haphazardly. Heavy carving emphasizing lion and other animal motifs, shells, and volutes appeared on furniture arm posts, armrests, and aprons. Although many furniture items were still made from walnut, mahogany became the wood of choice for most finely carved items.

The corner chair was introduced during the 18th century and was widely recorded in furniture inventories (Figure 6.44). Its design was not directly intended to fit into the corner of the room, rather, when pulled up to a desk, the unusual positioning of the front central leg allowed the person to sit closer to the desk. Like the corner chair that required the person to sit astride the central leg, a reading and writing chair designed strictly for the male gender was gaining in popularity. The sitter straddled the chair, the back of which was fitted with a book rest or writing surface, whereas armrests extended from the uprights.

Sitting rooms featured a range of chairs, stools, and settees grouped in the center of the room and arranged for conversations and taking tea. Upholstered settees were usually sized for two persons to sit in a rather formal manner because of the straight, upright backs (Figure 6.45). Settees were also favored by women, who continued to wear wide, full skirts. The formality of the social order often placed certain furnishings for either male or female use, as mentioned earlier.

The number of tea tables, toilette tables, game tables, and drop-leaf types increased during the 18th century. Designed to be portable, these tables were either small or expandable, allowing the piece of furniture to be placed in a corner or against the wall when not in use (Figure 6.46). It was not uncommon to maintain the positioning of a small, rectangular tea table in front of the settee or sofa. Unlike the low coffee tables used today, the tall legs on these tea tables allowed the person seated on the settee to reach across conveniently for a cup of tea.

Along with the small chest of drawers, the clothespress, or wardrobe, became increasingly in demand during the Early Georgian period. Smaller in scale than an armoire, the clothespress was usually fitted with a lower chest and concealed drawers located behind an upper cabinet (Figure 6.47). Clothes at this time were folded rather than hung, which is why these case pieces are fitted with multiple drawers. The more popular flat cabinet tops in the previous styles evolved into articulated pediments in a variety of forms. The bonnet top featured a wide arch often called a "hood." Swan neck-shaped broken pediment tops arched toward a central finial design that was repeated on the ends. Leg forms on case pieces featured a short bracket foot, sometimes with delicate curves carved into the shape called an "ogee bracket" or "goddard foot" (named after Townsend and Goddard, American furniture makers during the 18th century; Figure 6.48).

Although most furniture designed in the Early Georgian style evolved from Queen Anne influences, the designer and architect William Kent took a different approach (Figure 6.5). Considered a master of design, Kent's specialty was furniture and interior decoration. After studying in Rome, Kent identified with Inigo Jones' use of the Palladian style; he transformed classical forms into exaggerated, almost Baroque–like interpretations. He incorporated ormolu and gilding processes onto pier tables, mirrors, and heavily carved settees that sparsely outfitted elaborately ornamented rooms. These ornate and heavily classical designs were imitated by others who worked under the influence of Palladianism (Figure 6.49).

Apart from the exuberant furnishings of country estates, there was yet another type of furniture that dominated the English countryside. Windsor furniture, popular during the early 18th century, became recognized as a style in its own right. Made by local craftsmen, the furniture was equally stylish and included complete ensembles of chairs, tables, chests, and hutches (Figure 6.50). Made entirely from wood, its handmade quality and durability proved practical for everyday use and was quite affordable.

Efficient and utilitarian in nature, chairs with spindle backs, wheel-carved splats, shaped saddle seats, and raking backs allowed for comfort without upholstery. Most chairs were made from birch, elm, or yew; branches were turned on a lathe to create slender spindles that fit into a bow-shaped back formed under steam and pressure. The saddle seat was carved out of a single piece of wood, and splayed spindle legs were stabilized with turned stretchers. Variations in chair design incorporated cabriole legs and pierced splats, associating the piece with the more sophisticated Queen

FIGURE 6.47 A George II period mahogany linen press with a dentil cornice and inlaid foliate designs in the frieze supported on ogee bracket feet. © Judith Miller/Dorling Kindersley/ Lyon and Turnbull Ltd.

FIGURE 6.49 A George II console table clearly reflects the classically based themes of the Palladian influence inspired by William Kent. The carvings on this table are executed with an exuberance found more typically on furniture of the Baroque period. © Judith Miller/ Dorling Kindersley/Lyon and Turnbull Ltd.

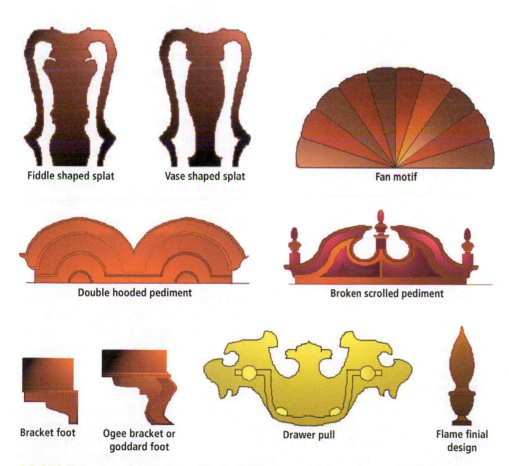

Fiddle shaped splat    Vase shaped splat    Fan motif

Double hooded pediment    Broken scrolled pediment

Bracket foot    Ogee bracket or goddard foot    Drawer pull    Flame finial design

FIGURE 6.48 Furniture characteristics of the English Rococo period, Queen Anne, and Early Georgian styles. © David Vleck.

FIGURE 6.50 Local artisans of the English countryside created a unique style of furniture that combined characteristics from the Queen Anne and Early Georgian styles with rustic ingenuity. The resulting Windsor style proved more suitable for provincial lifestyles. This Windsor chair from the 18th century has front turned legs with a characteristic Windsor–style bow or hoop back, spindles, and a saddle seat. © Judith Miller/Dorling Kindersley/Bucks County Antiques Center.

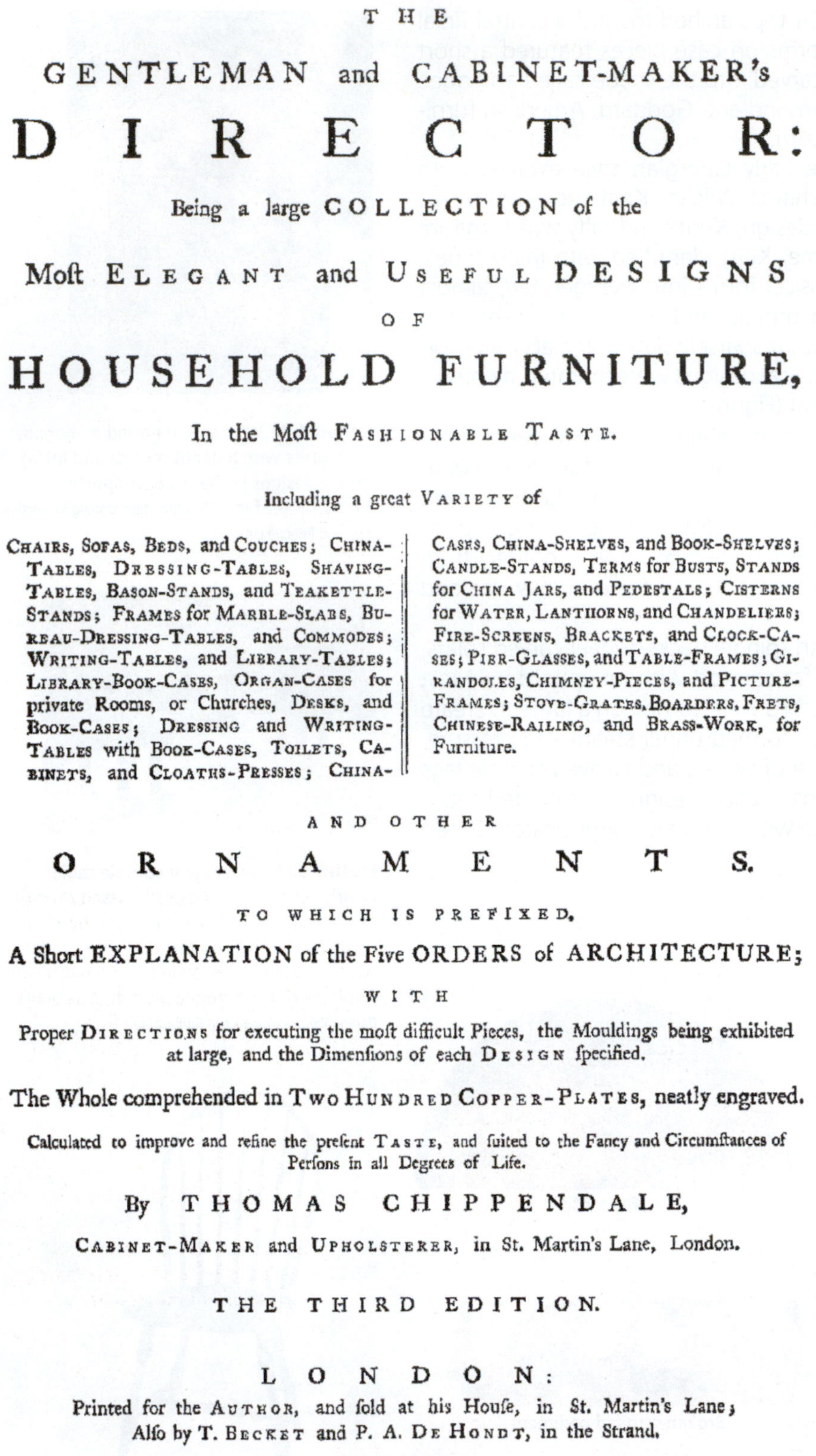

THE

# GENTLEMAN and CABINET-MAKER's

# DIRECTOR:

Being a large COLLECTION of the

Moſt ELEGANT and USEFUL DESIGNS

OF

# HOUSEHOLD FURNITURE,

In the Moſt FASHIONABLE TASTE.

Including a great VARIETY of

CHAIRS, SOFAS, BEDS, and COUCHES; CHINA-TABLES, DRESSING-TABLES, SHAVING-TABLES, BASON-STANDS, and TEAKETTLE-STANDS; FRAMES for MARBLE-SLABS, BU-REAU-DRESSING-TABLES, and COMMODES; WRITING-TABLES, and LIBRARY-TABLES; LIBRARY-BOOK-CASES, ORGAN-CASES for private Rooms, or Churches, DESKS, and BOOK-CASES; DRESSING and WRITING-TABLES with BOOK-CASES, TOILETS, CA-BINETS, and CLOATHS-PRESSES; CHINA-CASES, CHINA-SHELVES, and BOOK-SHELVES; CANDLE-STANDS, TERMS for BUSTS, STANDS for CHINA JARS, and PEDESTALS; CISTERNS for WATER, LANTHORNS, and CHANDELIERS; FIRE-SCREENS, BRACKETS, and CLOCK-CA-SES; PIER-GLASSES, and TABLE-FRAMES; GI-RANDOLES, CHIMNEY-PIECES, and PICTURE-FRAMES; STOVE-GRATES, BOARDERS, FRETS, CHINESE-RAILING, and BRASS-WORK, for Furniture.

AND OTHER

# ORNAMENTS.

TO WHICH IS PREFIXED,

A Short EXPLANATION of the Five ORDERS of ARCHITECTURE;

WITH

Proper DIRECTIONS for executing the moſt difficult Pieces, the Mouldings being exhibited at large, and the Dimenſions of each DESIGN ſpecified.

The Whole comprehended in TWO HUNDRED COPPER-PLATES, neatly engraved.

Calculated to improve and refine the preſent TASTE, and ſuited to the Fancy and Circumſtances of Perſons in all Degrees of Life.

By THOMAS CHIPPENDALE,

CABINET-MAKER and UPHOLSTERER, in St. Martin's Lane, London.

THE THIRD EDITION.

LONDON:

Printed for the AUTHOR, and ſold at his Houſe, in St. Martin's Lane; Alſo by T. BECKET and P. A. DE HONDT, in the Strand.

MDCC LXII.

**FIGURE 6.51** Thomas Chippendale's pattern book, first introduced in 1754, went into three editions. The title page shown here is from the 1762 third edition. Included within are engravings of furniture, architectural details, and decorative objects selected by Chippendale "to improve and refine the present taste, and suited to the fancy and circumstances of persons in all degrees of life." Courtesy Dover Publications Director.

Anne or Early Georgian styles. Ornamentation was kept to a minimum, and many furnishings were often painted in bright greens, reds, and yellows for added visual appeal. The Windsor style of furniture was also popular among the Americans during the pre-Revolution period.

## CHIPPENDALE STYLE: 1750–1780

In England, cabinetmaker Thomas Chippendale (1718–1779) published *The Gentleman and Cabinetmaker's Director* in 1754, which documented, through measured line drawings, the current Georgian styles of interior furnishings, including those with strong Chinese and Gothic influences (Figure 6.51). Interior furnishings featured in this portfolio incorporated distinctive Oriental designs such as pagodas, dragons, and fretwork. The style was referred to as "Chinese Chippendale." Moreover, the *Director* featured updated but romanticized interpretations of the Gothic style, with tracery, trefoil motifs, and pointed arches appearing prominently on chairs, china cabinets, secretaries, and armoires. This publication set the direction for change in furniture styles for the remainder of the 18th century.

Chippendale's publication summarized the grammar of the classical orders and provided elaborately detailed and scaled drawings of furniture and coordinated decorative accessories. The collection of drawings reflected a growing interest in culture and architectural aesthetics by educated gentlemen. New pieces introduced in the *Director* included the camel-back sofa, the triple-chair-back settee, the *breakfront* china cabinet, pagoda-top canopied beds, tilt-top tables, dumbwaiters, and Pembroke tables.

Carving was an important decorative feature of all Chippendale styles, whether Rococo, Gothic, or Chinese influenced (Figure 6.52). The Rococo-based designs used the cabriole leg, usually ending in a claw and ball, although sometimes a whorl foot was present. Bracketed knees were usually carved with an acanthus leaf or shell whereas the crest rail was formed into a yoke shape, and the uprights were an enclosed, pierced splat of unusually rich decoration. Gothic-style chairs retained the yoke back or had arched backs, but the splat was replaced by open tracery forming pointed arches. Legs generally were straight in the front, whereas extended uprights created gentle sweeping saber legs in the rear. The straighter legs often incorporated a stretcher system, although it was not necessary for strength and support.

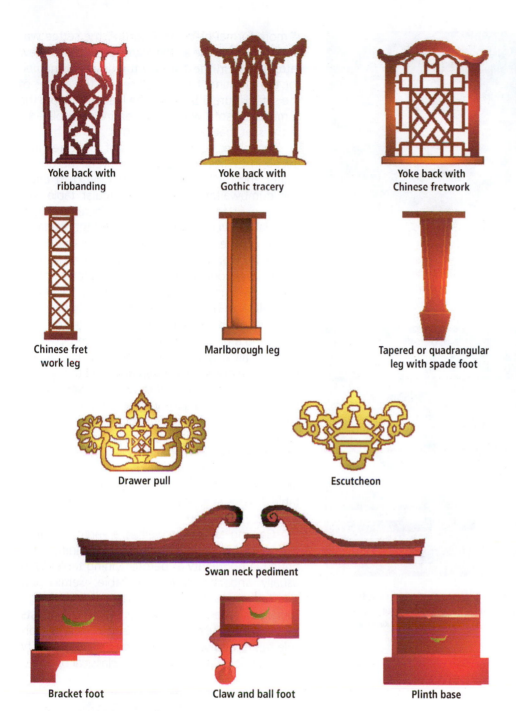

Yoke back with
ribbanding

Yoke back with
Gothic tracery

Yoke back with
Chinese fretwork

Chinese fret
work leg

Marlborough leg

Tapered or quadrangular
leg with spade foot

Drawer pull

Escutcheon

Swan neck pediment

Bracket foot

Claw and ball foot

Plinth base

FIGURE 6.52 English Rococo, Chippendale–style furniture forms. © David Vleck.

FIGURE 6.53 The fine carvings on this mahogany English Chippendale side chair, circa 1760, include acanthus leaves seen on the cabriole leg knees, along the crest rail, uprights, and pierced splat. The legs are supported by claw-and-ball feet. © Judith Miller/ Dorling Kindersley/Wallis and Wallis.

FIGURE 6.54 Chippendale–style mahogany side chairs capture current Rococo fashions. The chair on the left features strapwork carving and a quatrefoil motif on its central splat; the splat on the chair on the right features a classical urn in the Neo-Palladian style. © Judith Miller/Dorling Kindersley/Freeman's.

Chippendale included designs loosely based on the "modern" Queen Anne, Georgian, and Louis XV styles (Figure 6.53). He also introduced new styles based on romanticized representations of the Far East and the Gothic past (Figure 6.54). Interior furnishings incorporating distinctive Oriental influences such as pagodas, dragons, and fretwork became known as "Chinese Chippendale," whereas items with pierced tracery and trefoil arches reminiscent of medieval cathedrals were considered "Gothic Chippendale."

The Chinese Chippendale style continued to incorporate a straight leg in the front with saber back legs; however, the typical Marlborough leg was decorated with lattice- or fretwork (Figure 6.55). Yoke backs often reflected sweeping upward curves on the ends, imitating the effect of a pagoda top. Backs generally introduced either a pierced splat with small pagoda shapes or contained open fretwork.

Double-chair-back settees followed in the form of side and armchairs. These settees had an upholstered seat, with wood backs, arms, and arm posts (Figure 6.56).

FIGURE 6.55 This drawing is from the third edition of Chippendale's *Director*, published in London in 1762. The engraved plate is described in his book as made with cane bottoms and loose cushions. This particular chair designed in 1753 features a pagoda style back with lattice work, marlborough legs, and optional lattice arms.

FIGURE 6.56 This English Chippendale double-chair-back settee was made from mahogany veneer and includes a decorative, pierced splat; gooseneck arms; and Marlborough legs with Gothic–inspired carving. © Judith Miller/Dorling Kindersley/Wallis and Wallis.

FIGURE 6.57 This English Chippendale–style camel-back sofa, circa 1780, has high, rolled arms and Marlborough legs of carved mahogany connected with H-form stretchers. © Judith Miller/Dorling Kindersley/Freeman's.

FIGURE 6.58 A George II mahogany, three-tiered dumbwaiter with graduated circular serving trays. © Judith Miller/Dorling Kindersley/Lyon and Turnbull Ltd.

A more formal piece of furniture, the settee was not as comfortable as the camel-back sofa, a new introduction in the 18th century that was named for the prominent hump placed at the center of the sofa (Figure 6.57). Like the French canapé, the camel-back sofa was almost entirely upholstered at the seat, back, arms, and sides.

Two other significant pieces of furniture introduced in Chippendale's *Director* were the dumbwaiter and the tilt-top table with pie crust edge. The dumbwaiter was a small circular table that had two or three tiers, each in decreasing size, one placed over the other (Figure 6.58). Food was placed on the tiers then brought into the dining room and placed next to the hostess for serving. Much more popular was a type of tea table known as the "pie crust table" or "tilt-top table." This type of small table had a rounded top usually designed with scalloped edges (evoking the edges of a pie crust) and a birdcage mechanism that enabled the table to tilt (Figure 6.59). When not in use, the flat surface of the table was converted to a vertical position and placed against the wall. Rectangular tables with pierced gallery edges also served as tea tables. These tall tables were placed in front of the camel back sofa and were used for serving tea and light meals (Figure 6.60). The pierced gallery edge is reminiscent of the ancient Greek and Roman tripod tables that had incorporated the rim on their table designs in an effort to contain the amphorae that were placed on its surface.

Gaming tables, as well as a variety of other tables used in dressing, writing, and dining, continued in popularity as before. Dining tables were usually understated and portable. Semicircular side tables pushed next to a square or rectangular table created extensions for numerous guests. When not in use, the side tables became console tables and were placed against the wall. The semicircular table is a more common element seen during the Neoclassical period of the late 18th century.

FIGURE 6.59 Pie crust-edge, tilt-top tables were designed for maximum flexibility. A birdcage mechanism allowed the surface to adjust to a horizontal position at tea time, and to a vertical position when not in use. This example of an English Chippendale–style mahogany table has a tripod support with carved hairy-paw feet. © Judith Miller/Dorling Kindersley/Wallis and Wallis.

FIGURE 6.60 This Chippendale–style mahogany English tea table has pierced carving on the gallery, apron, legs, and X-form stretcher, with a flame finial. © Judith Miller/Dorling Kindersley/Lyon and Turnbull Ltd.

FIGURE 6.61 A Chippendale period mahogany veneer bombé French commode has three drawers with chased gilt brass Rococo style swing handles and escutcheons (one missing). The commode front features Rococo-inspired foliage carving, molded serpentine corners, front scrolling legs with leaf sprays emanating from cartouche shaped and knurled feet. A French table commode like this one is illustrated in Chippendale's *Director* (third edition, plate LXIV). © Judith Miller/Dorling Kindersley/Woolley and Wallis.

Chippendale's *Director* featured many commodes, some in the French taste. These commodes were based upon the Louis XV French style, with bombé sides, ormolu, and leg forms ending in a scroll foot resting on a delicate shoe (Figure 6.61). Storage items and other case pieces continued to dominate the interior scheme of a room with their immense size and exquisitely carved cornices. The popular writing cabinet, or slant-front secretary, was illustrated in Chippendale's *Director* in all three tastes—Rococo, Gothic, and Chinese.

The more exuberant Chinese style often exhibited fretwork glazing with pierced, carved pediments (Figure 6.62). Numerous glazed bookcases and china cabinets displayed interesting books and curios representative of a contemporary gentleman's intellect (Figure 6.63). The appearance of the breakfront library bookcase, which featured a tall and wide case fitted with lower concealed cabinets and glass door upper cabinets was a reflection of wealth (Figure 6.64). Highboys, tallboys, and armoires remained plentiful during the latter half of the 18th century as storage for wardrobe and linens. Chippendale styles incorporated fretwork, serpentine curves, and tracery, each reflective of its particular style—Chinese, Rococo, or Gothic. These styles can be seen in the multitude of objects illustrated in the *Director*.

**FIGURE 6.62** An 18th-century Chinese Chippendale secretaire bookcase features upper shelving in fretwork designs typical of the period. © Judith Miller/Dorling Kindersley/Sloan's.

**FIGURE 6.63** A George III inlaid mahogany bureau bookcase has a molded sloped front, fitted interior compartments, graduated drawers, columnar stiles, and splayed bracket feet. The top, added at a later date features a pair of Gothic tracery styled doors and adjustable shelves. The original piece dates from the last quarter of the 18th century. © Judith Miller/Dorling Kindersley/Hamptons.

## AMERICAN LATE COLONIAL: 1720–1785

Eighteenth-century America was a time of immense population growth brought on by increased immigration from Europe and a thriving economy through shipping industries and the exportation of cash crops such as tobacco, rice, and cod. As the modest living quarters of early colonists were replaced by much larger, multistory homes, the demand for finer furnishings followed. The increasingly larger colonial homes highlighted wainscoted walls, painted plaster moldings, and higher ceilings. Prosperous colonists sought finer furnishings that revealed their new level of sophistication.

American furniture makers in Philadelphia, Baltimore, Boston, Virginia, and Newport copied Rococo motifs and furniture designs, imitating the English Queen Anne style. American colonial furniture lagged 10 to 20 years behind its fashionable introduction in England until Chippendale's pattern books, brought to the American colonies in 1766, allowed cabinetmakers to keep current with the prevalent English styles. Motifs and designs were changed slightly to reflect the preferences of specific geographic regions by furniture makers.

Not all colonists prospered in America, and there was still a need for affordable furnishings. Windsor–type chairs with splayed legs, H stretchers, saddle seats, and spindles were used in homes of the less affluent because the furniture was made by local craftsmen and was easy to fabricate. Certain regions developed their own trademark design, whether it was a comb-back, wheel-back, or bow-back chair (Figure 6.66). Windsor–style furnishings were popular throughout the colonies and were readily purchased by all levels of society. Several pieces were purchased for Mount Vernon by General Washington.

The Queen Anne style was more prevalent in the American colonies by 1725 and became one of the more popular styles of the Late Colonial period. Spoonback chairs were more simplified versions than those in England, and kept the characteristic turned forms common to Early Colonial styles (Figure 6.67). The use of

**FIGURE 6.64** This mahogany breakfront library bookcase is designed in three parts. The central projecting panel is flanked by two recessed wings, and each section is then subdivided between the bookcase above and the cupboard below. The unit rests on a plinth base, and features Chinese fret-designed glazed panel doors, and dates from 1780. © Judith Miller/Dorling Kindersley/Sloan's.

# A CLOSER Look

## Chinese Style

The leading competitor of the workshop of Thomas Chippendale was John Linnel (1729–1796). Linnel worked with his father creating a wide range of decorative mirrors and furnishings in the Chinese style. This bedroom (Figure 6.65), designed for the apartments at Badminton House in Gloucestershire for the Fourth Duke of Beaufort, features an elaborate Chinese-theme bed. The room, completed in 1754, is testament to the popularity of Chinese taste that had been part of the English Rococo period. Chinese and Gothic styles were perpetuated by numerous publications by William Halfpenny, including his pattern book, *New Designs for Chinese Temples*, published in 1750. The great canopy bed, transformed by Chinese influence, overpowered the bedroom with its elaborately carved tester. Coordinating accessories including candle stands and mirrors complemented the

**FIGURE 6.65** A black-and-gold-lacquered bed in a Chinese style dates from around 1755. Massive in size, the bed features a pagoda canopy, dragon finials, and a fretwork headboard. V&A Images, London/Art Resource, NY.

great pagoda top, with designs incorporating dragon finials, fretwork, and other Chinese motifs. The bed is made of beech and japanned in red, yellow, and blue with gilt. Silk textiles with characteristic chinoiserie patterns made up the bed linens and drapery. Linnel designed a matching dressing table, mirrors, and candle stands.

Alternatively, under Chippendale's direction, his cabinetmakers produced fine-quality mahogany furnishings for English country houses. Sadly, only a few original pieces remain today from Chippendale's workshop. His later work was done for the architect and designer Robert Adam, and followed more closely with the developing Neoclassical style that was influenced by the excavations of Herculaneum in 1738 and Pompeii in 1748.

stretchers was more haphazard. Later during the period, these chairs were known as "fiddle-back chairs," a name adopted for the shape of the splat (Figure 6.68). As Chippendale influences reached the colonies, these cabriole legs, called a *bandy* by colonists, featured claw-and-ball feet, although the pad or club foot was preferred for its simplicity and strength.

The disparity between the introduction of new styles in England and the time it took them to reach the American colonies lessened after the publication of Chippendale's *Director*. Chippendale style is seen in America after copies of *Director* made their way to the colonies within the first year of its publication. The intricate and delicate carvings indicative of the Chippendale style necessitated the use of a harder wood, and mahogany proved more suitable. Although all three Chippendale influences were seen in the American colonies, Gothic and Chinese were less popular as the colonists embraced the more modern taste of the French Rococo influences (Figure 6.69).

**FIGURE 6.66** This American Windsor chair has a spindle back, turned legs with H-form stretcher, and a saddle seat. V&A Images, London/Art Resource, NY.

**FIGURE 6.67** An American Late Colonial–style walnut armchair incorporates many Queen Anne characteristics including the spoon-shape back and vase-shape splat. Turned stretchers and leg forms terminate on a Spanish foot. © Judith Miller/Dorling Kindersley/Wallis and Wallis.

**FIGURE 6.68** This Philadelphia walnut armchair has a serpentine crest rail with a fiddle-shape back splat, flaring arms on incurvate arm posts, and shell-carved cabriole legs on claw-and-ball feet. © Judith Miller/Dorling Kindersley/Freeman's.

**FIGURE 6.69** A Delaware Valley Queen Anne walnut side chair with a shell-carved crest rail is flanked by bold, backward scrolling ears over a pierced splat and above a slip seat that rests on a shaped apron, and cabriole legs that terminate in a three-lobe pad foot called "trifid feet." The chair dates from circa 1760. © Judith Miller/Dorling Kindersley/Pook and Pook.

**FIGURE 6.70** A mid-18th-century Queen Anne walnut drop-leaf table from Pennsylvania. The rectangular top has conforming leaves and notched corners on a shaped and molded apron. The cabriole legs end in pad feet. © Judith Miller/Dorling Kindersley/Freeman's.

**FIGURE 6.71** An American tilt-top cherry tea table has an unadorned circular top that rests on a fluted pedestal with a tripod base that ends in claw-and-ball feet. The birdcage mechanism is clearly visible in this photo. © Judith Miller/Dorling Kindersley/Freeman's.

**FIGURE 6.72** A late-18th-/early-19th-century candle stand from Massachusetts, made from mahogany over birch. © Judith Miller/Dorling Kindersley/Wallis and Wallis.

Tables and case pieces incorporated many Rococo-inspired details, including cabriole legs, serpentine curves, and scrolled pediment tops. Gateleg and drop-leaf tables were well suited to the smaller, Georgian interiors (Figure 6.70). These tables featured cabriole legs with a variety of foot forms. The more popular tea table resembled the tilt-top table illustrated in the *Director;* however, these varied in size and shape (Figures 6.71 and 6.72). Tea drinking was a habit enjoyed by the colonists, and the heavy taxes levied on its import from England led to the Boston Tea Party in 1773, when large shipments of tea were dumped into the harbor, a contributing factor toward the American Revolution.

Case goods such as highboys, tallboys, and secretaries took on characteristics of the English Queen Anne style, with flat or bonnet tops as well as those types illustrated in the *Director* (Figure 6.73). Most were quite high and nearly touched the low ceilings of American colonial homes, but they were impressive pieces and were kept in the more public rooms for guests to admire. Owning one of these case pieces in the colonies showed great wealth and was considered a status symbol.

Indigenous woods such as walnut, maple, and pine were used by most American furniture craftsmen; in rare cases, some items incorporated imported mahogany. The type of wood used to make the furniture, along with subtle nuances in design, help place pieces of furniture into respective regions. Philadelphia earned a reputation for producing some of the finest examples of furniture seen in the American colonies (Figure 6.74). The sophisticated bombé swells of French commodes translated into what the colonists referred to as "kettle shapes," and finished the sides of secretaries and tallboys which still maintained the essence of the Chippendale style, with broken pediment or scrolled pediment tops flanked by finials. Writing desks and fall front secretaries were important furniture pieces that functioned as an "office" for the owner and featured hidden compartments, cubby holes, and drawers for storing documents (Figure 6.75). Many

**FIGURE 6.73** This chest-on-chest, or tallboy, was made in Pennsylvania and dates from around 1760. Made from walnut, the piece is in two sections. It has an upper chest with drawers and a lower section with two graduated drawers. © Judith Miller/Dorling Kindersley/Freeman's.

**FIGURE 6.74** An American Chippendale mahogany scroll-top highboy, made in Philadelphia, has an upper section with a swan-neck pediment and floral terminals surmounted by three urn-and-flame finials above three short drawers. The center drawer is shell-carved above three graduated long drawers. The lower section has one long and three short drawers (the center drawer is similarly carved) above an apron on acanthus-carved cabriole legs that end in claw-and-ball feet. © Judith Miller/Dorling Kindersley/Sloans & Kenyon.

**FIGURE 6.75** A Chippendale curly-maple maple slant-front desk from Pennsylvania. The hinged lid opens to an interior with eight "valanced" pigeonholes above eight stacked drawers centering a tombstone-carved prospect door flanked by document drawers carved with wheat sheaves. The case has four graduated drawers on spurred ogee bracket feet. Minor repairs have been made to the feet, and the piece is missing brass hardware (circa 1780). © Judith Miller/Dorling Kindersley/ Freeman's.

**FIGURE 6.76** This four-poster bed with its *toile de Jouy* bed hangings reflects more refinement in furnishings for the 18th-century American home. © Treena Crochet.

slant-front desks were fitted with a bookcase-type cabinet on top, and both pieces were lockable.

Colonial beds were of the four-poster type and featured distinctive baluster-shaped turning with carved surface details like reeding or fluting (Figure 6.76). The bed drapes did not always enclose the bed completely; rather, canopies were shortened to valance-type curtains. The four posts were connected with side rails on which were placed wooden slats to support the mattress.

# LEARN More

## American Late Colonial Interior Design

The parlor presented in Figure 6.77 is of a well-to-do colonist dating between 1760 and the start of the American Revolution. The architecture of the room includes Classical-style moldings that feature a deep dentil crown and triangular pediment framed by fluted pilasters over the fireplace. Drapery made from yellow damask has classical swag valances, and gathered panels are held open with tasseled tiebacks. Chippendale–style furniture is upholstered in matching fabric and is typical for the Late Colonial period in America. Two camel-back sofas flank the hearth whereas a pair of wing chairs is set in front of a Chippendale–style highboy. The room features a tilt-top tea table and candle stands set near two yoke-back chairs. Along with English porcelains lining the mantel and on tables, a crystal chandelier hangs from the ceiling. Lighting is augmented with an array of candlesticks. A large carpet anchors the arrangement of furniture around the hearth.

**FIGURE 6.77** The Port Royal Room, now located in the Henry Francis DuPont Winterthur Museum, reveals elegant Chippendale furniture from the Late Colonial period, an ornate chandelier, sconces and candelabra, a beautifully woven floral carpet, and cascading window treatments. Courtesy, Winterthur Museum.

# Accessories

## POTTERY

Perhaps the most significant contributor to the development and refinement of a new French style was the mistress of King Louis XV, Madame de Pompadour (1721–1764). Like King Louis XIV before her, Pompadour took an active role in promoting artistic advancement at Versailles. A porcelain factory at Sèvres that she patronized supplied soft-paste plaques for furniture and dinnerware, among other objets d'art (Figure 6.78). *Soft-paste porcelain*, created in Europe, imitated true or *hard-paste porcelain* available only in Asia. Rose pompadour, the most popular color of porcelain created at Sèvres, was unique to this factory and influenced the lighter color palettes adopted by Rococo designers.

Locally made ceramics such as *bone china* and *creamware* were less expensive substitutes for Chinese export porcelain, which was very popular in Europe. In fact, the word "china" originated at this time to describe a type of ceramic meant to imitate the appearance of fine Chinese porcelain. The drawback of soft-paste ceramics was that, when subjected to high temperatures inside the kiln, the shape did not hold up well. This limited the design from anything too intricate. Transferware ceramics, such as those produced at the factory in Staffordshire, were widely distributed in England and exported to the American colonies as a middle-class substitute for fine Chinese porcelains (Figure 6.79).

At last, the Bavarian alchemist to the king of Poland uncovered the secret of making hard-paste porcelain by identifying the key ingredient—kaolin—in 1709. Soon after, factories set up in Dresden, Nymphenburg, and Meissen produced a variety of decorative objects for wealthy patrons. The modeling capabilities of hard-paste porcelain led to the design of various animal and bird forms, along with figurines brought to life with brightly colored glazes (Figure 6.80).

By 1710, porcelain factories were appearing all over Europe and the British Isles seeking to corner the market on hard-paste porcelain. Molds were made to cast the hard paste, and hand-finishing work smoothed out the seams before painting and firing. Figurines depicting aristocratic men and women dressed for a *fête galante* were popular, along with birds, animals, tableware and tea sets, and vases (Figure 6.81). By mid century, factories in Chelsea, Derby, Staffordshire, and Worcester in England had capitalized on the purchasing power of well-to-do collectors (Figure 6.11)

## GLASS

New glass factories of noteworthy importance came about during the 18th century, specifically in Bohemia, Waterford in Ireland, and Baccarat in France. Glassmakers in these regions produced fine cut lead crystal with the aid of wheel engraving. Water-powered cutting wheels allowed the glassworker to etch or cut designs into the surface of the glass, which was then polished to eliminate rough edges (Figure 6.82). With this somewhat mechanized method of decorating glass, a range of glassware featuring finely detailed designs found its way into more homes than ever before. Molded or blown clear glass decorated with painted designs was produced for middle-class patrons.

## MIRRORS

FIGURE 6.78 This Sèvres flower vase with panels of painted flowers and fruit surrounded by gilt laurel leaves on a green background dates from 1770. © Judith Miller/Dorling Kindersley/ Woolley and Wallis.

FIGURE 6.79 This Staffordshire porcelain bowl from the 18th century features a transfer pattern of an elaborate hunting scene both inside and out. A thin gold band crowns the rim. © Judith Miller/Dorling Kindersley/Clevedon Salerooms.

FIGURE 6.80 A Meissen figure of a monkey singing as it clutches a sheet of music. Dating from 1760, the colorfully outfitted monkey in contemporary clothing is a reminder of the popular singerie motifs of monkeys at play found in Rococo interior design. © Judith Miller/Dorling Kindersley/Gorringes.

FIGURE 6.81 From the 18th century, this Derby figure of a shepherd girl wearing a pink dress stands on a Rococo–style gilt base. © Judith Miller/Dorling Kindersley/Gorringes.

**FIGURE 6.82** The chinoiserie-engraved designs on this wine glass from 1780 were made using the wheel-cut method. © Judith Miller/Dorling Kindersley/Somervale Antiques.

**FIGURE 6.83** This late-18th-century mahogany Chippendale–style framed mirror from England has a scrolled pediment crest with corresponding pendant scroll below in curvilinear Rococo fashion. The glass mirror plate is a modern replacement. © Judith Miller/Dorling Kindersley/Freeman's.

Mirrors played an even greater role in completing the scheme of fashionable interiors and were more abundant during the 18th century than before. To reiterate the importance of mirrors in room design, oversized mirrors enhanced candlelight from chandeliers by reflecting light back into the room (Figures 6.2 an 6.3). Mirrors were placed strategically above the fireplace mantel and extended toward the ceiling or inset into gilt frames above the wainscoting on wall panels and doors. In addition, frame styles adopted the prevalent Rococo designs found in the room décor, usually matching the features of the furniture. Shell motifs, scrolls, and vine patterns appeared on elaborately carved and gilt frames, whereas English mirror frames reflected the delicate curves found on Queen Anne and Chippendale furnishings (Figure 6.83). Moreover, the same wheel engraving technique used on glassware was used to etch decorative designs such as leaves and flowers onto the surfaces of mirrors.

## LIGHTING

Lighting interiors during the 18th century required numerous candles placed in crystal chandeliers, brass and silver candlesticks, and wall sconces (Figure 6.86). Beeswax was favored over

---

## COMPARISONS  Reflections of Time

Reviving styles from past cultures was common throughout the history of the decorative arts, as artisans often studied the past for inspiration. Influences from the Classical past reemerged during the Renaissance and the latter half of the 18th century after excavations began at Herculaneum and Pompeii. The Victorian era, named after Queen Victoria, who ruled the United Kingdom from 1837 to 1901, witnessed more revival styles than any other period. The revivalist styles of the Victorian period were more than "inspired" by the past; rather, architects and designers recreated the past in their works, often imitating monuments seen on their "grand tours" through Europe. Greek Revival, Gothic Revival, Elizabethan Revival, and Rococo Revival were a few of the most popular styles appearing in architecture and interior design throughout the century.

However, in 1890, the Art Nouveau style emerged based on the organic forms found in nature—free-flowing vine patterns and asymmetrical arrangements—the same qualities found in designs from the Rococo period. Art Nouveau, or "new art," was created as an attempt by late 19th-century designers to introduce a new style—one classified as "universal," or not belonging to a particular place or genre.

The mirrors in Figures 6.84 and 6.85 share similar characteristics. The one in Figure 6.84 dates from the mid 18th century and features a carved and gilt frame. Characteristic Rococo motifs appear on the cartouche-shaped mirror, including its prominent *rocaille* crest and frame fashioned out of vine patterns and floral sprays. The mirror in Figure 6.85 dates from 1905 and reflects the Art Nouveau style. The mirror's frame forms a cartouche,

although it is more misshapen than the mirror from the Rococo period. Furthermore, the mirror's frame is asymmetrical and is fashioned from carved and gilt vine motifs that rise up to form the crest and flow downward to create the feet. Although the Art Nouveau style was not considered a revivalist style of the late Victorian period, designers working in this style were interested in capturing the essence of organic forms found in nature, as were those working during the Rococo period.

**FIGURE 6.84** This gilt pier looking glass from the mid 18th century has a pierced rocaille crest carved with floral sprays. Its design is balanced with pierced work on the apron skirting along the bottom and sides. © Judith Miller/Dorling Kindersley/Sloan's.

**FIGURE 6.85** This mirror in the Art Nouveau style dates from 1905 and features an energetic vine-pattern framework. The highly charged vines appear in whiplash curves fashioned asymmetrically into the mirror's frame and feet. © Judith Miller/Dorling Kindersley/The Design Gallery.

tallow (animal fat) because of its clean burn and pleasant smell; however, hand dipping candles was time-consuming. Because beeswax candles were expensive, they were found in more up-scale households. Middle-class households had pewter, wrought iron, or turned-wood candle-sticks and lanterns fit with tallow candles (Figure 6.87). As mentioned earlier, the placement of mirrors high above fireplaces and wainscoting helped to reflect light from prism-cut chandeliers back into the room.

## METALWORKING

In 1738, brass metallurgy improved when William Champion of England patented a method of producing zinc from calamine and charcoal. Brass objects made from copper, tin, and zinc were easier to form into elaborate shapes than those without the zinc alloy. Adding zinc to brass also made it less corrosive. Moreover, brass gave off the appearance of gold, but was not as expensive. Brass ormolu mounts appeared on French furniture and accessories as an integral design characteristic of the Louis XV style (Figure 6.88).

Fine dining in wealthy homes featured an elaborately laid table full of exquisite silver, including candlesticks (Figure 6.86), flatware, and *hollowware*. Silversmiths (who often worked in both silver and gold) produced accoutrements for the table that reflected the sinuous foliate and vine patterns of stylish Rococo interiors. Highly detailed designs were created through chasing or repoussé; parts of lesser importance, such as handles, were sand cast. Chased designs were created by cutting away at the metal. Repoussé is a relief design created by hammering the metal from the opposite side, or inside, of the object.

Pewterware was used on tables in more modest homes until it fell out of fashion in the 19th century. Using the sand-cast method, molten pewter was poured into molds made from sand and clay. After cooling, the piece was removed from the mold and any visible seams were polished out before the piece was finally buffed to a silvery sheen. Designs from the mold left impressions in the metal. Pewter was not malleable enough to be used with the chasing method. Hollowware pitchers, mugs, bowls, and *porringers* completed the set of pewter flatware for day-to-day use.

Other household objects made from an enameled metal called *tole* included beautifully designed boxes, platters, plates, and pitchers in painted and varnished metals. One of the first factories to produce tole was set up in Bilston, England, in 1756. Tole painting became a folk art craft in America, but the designs were not limited to metal; the characteristic polychrome flower designs on a black background also appeared on wood.

## TREENWARE

Household objects not made from pewter or other metals were fashioned from wood. Called *treenware*, objects were made by local woodworkers, who carved and hollowed out tight-grain woods to create a variety of shapes. These goods (cups, bowls, canisters, and boxes) appeared in the kitchens of households from all classes. Decorations varied from plain and unadorned to painted, inlaid, and veneered designs (Figure 6.89).

**FIGURE 6.86** This pair of candlesticks made by John Carter in London in 1770 reveals exquisite silversmith skills as seen in the sweeping gadroons that accentuate the stems and bases. © Judith Miller/Dorling Kindersley/John Bull Silver.

**FIGURE 6.87** This American folding, iron candle lantern, with six arched ribs ending in baluster-shape feet, is fixed with a carrying ring at the top. The basic form and material reflect the skill of a local blacksmith, who designed it for function rather than aesthetic appeal. © Judith Miller/Dorling Kindersley/Sloan's.

**FIGURE 6.88** This pair of brass andirons with putti and decorative swags reflects the spirit of French Rococo interior fashion. © Judith Miller/Dorling Kindersley/Sloans & Kenyon.

**FIGURE 6.89** This treenware tea caddy made from veneered hare wood and dating from the late 18th century has painted decorations of bouquets tied with ribbons, imitating tole work. © Judith Miller/Dorling Kindersley/Woolley and Wallis.

## CLOCKS

In many European villages and American colonial towns, the passing of time was announced by a striking bell clock positioned on a church or on the town hall for all to see. By the end of the 18th century, clock-making techniques had improved to the point at which clocks were no longer an exclusive status symbol for affluent families. The inner workings of clocks became more reliable and accurate with the introduction of the new noncorrosive brass, a result of Champion's process for obtaining purer zinc.

Specialized clock makers made the inner workings whereas cabinetmakers made the cases. Small mantel clocks were introduced during the 18th century and featured brass dials encased in ornate cases (Figure 6.90). Longcase clocks became fashionable with the invention of the pendulum clock during the 17th century, and these case designs continued to follow the style of the furniture designs (Figure 6.91). England banned the exportation of clockworks to the American colonies, so only entire clocks were imported until after the Revolutionary War.

## TEXTILES

Displaying tapestries on the wall continued in vogue throughout the 18th century in upscale homes. Woven designs featured colorful landscapes filled with animals, birds, and flowers along with popular *fete galante* scenes (Figure 6.92). The appearance of a woven gold frame, introduced during the 19th century, remained a conventional edge pattern on most tapestries, giving the effect of a painting.

Moreover, improvements in spinning and weaving included the *flying shuttle*, the *spinning jenny*, the water-powered spinning frame, and, by the end of the 18th century, the steam-powered loom. With these inventions, spinning and weaving went much faster and required fewer workers to run the machines, resulting in textiles produced at lower costs. Furthermore, printed cotton fabrics were being imported from India. England and France initiated bans against these foreign products to protect their own textile industries. England sent imported cotton from India to the American colonies to protect its own textile industry. Cotton gained in popularity over heavier wools, and woodblocks were used to print designs onto bolts of fabric. In addition, with the introduction of roller printing during the last quarter of the 17th century, lightweight cottons were produced quickly and economically.

Brocade, damasks, and needlework were fashionable textiles used inside 18th-century homes, and, along with velvets, were used for upholstery, bedding, drapes, table covers, and fire screens (Figure 6.93). Full drapes over windows proved effective in controlling light and providing privacy and thermal protection in more elaborate homes; these drapes gained popularity by the second half of the century (Figure 6.77). Needlework designs appeared in carpets, on upholstery, on framed pictures, and as decoration on wall paneling and fire screens (Figure 6.94).

Most common were gros point and petit point needlework made from wool and silk threads. The names refer to the size of the stitches over the canvas background; petit point is the smallest stitch and is used for fine detailing.

Needlework bobbin lace made in Chantilly, France, was traded throughout Europe and was prized for its silk

**FIGURE 6.90** This Early Georgian–style red-lacquered mantel clock features chinoiserie decorations on its casing, and a brass dial. © Judith Miller/Dorling Kindersley/Gorringes.

**FIGURE 6.91** This longcase clock dating from 1730 has tortoiseshell-inlay chinoiserie designs on its casing, and a brass Roman numeral face dial with cherubs, or putti, at the crest. © Judith Miller/Dorling Kindersley/Pendulum of Mayfair.

**FIGURE 6.92** This fine 18th-century verdure tapestry by Chaudoir was manufactured by the Schaerbeck factory in Brussels, and is signed "Mture Chaudoir" in brown in the bottom right hand corner, and includes a "CG" monogram that features a serpent coiled around a spear. This piece depicts a wild garden, although it is probably based on the garden of an estate. Giant foreground leaves create a three-dimensional effect, and there is no focal point in the composition; numerous independent vignettes combine to form a whole.

© Judith Miller/Dorling Kindersley/Jonathan Wadsworth.

threads. Silk threads were wound around wooden bobbins to keep them from tangling while the worker used pins to hold the needlework in place on top of a pillow. White-work lace was made by weaving openwork fabric on a loom. It resembled handmade laces and, because it was woven, it was less costly (Figure 6.95).

## WALLPAPER

During the first half of the 18th century, European wallpapers were either hand painted or hand blocked, and owning them declared the great wealth of the homeowner (Figure 6.96). In the American colonies, the first wallpaper-producing shop was set up in Philadelphia in 1739; before then, all papers were imported. Improvements in wallpaper production occurred in 1785 with the invention of the roller printing machine. By the end of the 18th century, wallpapers were featured in entrance halls, dining rooms, and parlors.

**FIGURE 6.93** Oyster silk damask fabric from the 18th century features floral sprigs and flowers. © Judith Miller/Dorling Kindersley/Steve Covelli.

**FIGURE 6.94** This fire screen from the George II period is covered with a silk needlework panel that depicts floral arabesque designs, urns, and birds, and it dates from 1750. © Judith Miller/Dorling Kindersley/Sloans & Kenyon.

**FIGURE 6.95** This early-18th-century example of lacework features a field of white work—threads removed from a woven cloth to give pattern or openwork designs—and threadwork flower edging. Cloths like this increased in popularity during the next century and appeared as table covers. © Judith Miller/Dorling Kindersley/Mendes Antique Lace and Textiles.

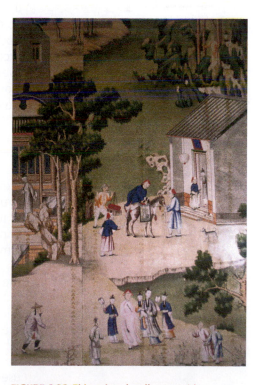

**FIGURE 6.96** This painted wallpaper with a chinoiserie design of a Chinese landscape with Oriental figures dates from the 18th century and was installed inside Westport House in Ireland. Michael Jenner/Robert Harding.

# The Late Eighteenth and Early Nineteenth Centuries

## The Neoclassic Period

The terms "Neoclassic" and "neoclassicism," first used during the 1880s, refers to the cultural period between 1750 and 1830. Significant changes in stylistic development had occurred as a result of the rediscovery of Herculaneum and Pompeii; clothing and hairstyles, and art and architecture reflected Roman inspiration. As excavations began at Herculaneum in 1738 and at Pompeii in 1748, people from all over Europe traveled to southern Italy to witness and record the event through drawings of the artifacts that were discovered there. Artifacts removed from these sites were documented in widely published treatises on ancient Roman life. Artists, architects, and scholars witnessed with great awe the removal of furnishings, household objects, and architectural elements that had been buried beneath tons of volcanic ash and debris for nearly 1,800 years.

What seemed apparent in the discovery of these ancient Roman cities was that, previously, the European idea of classicism had been based on the still-standing structures of the Italian Renaissance and the writings of Palladio. Now, classicism in its purest form could be studied, modified, and incorporated into 18th-century living. Books published at this time featured precise line drawings of the artifacts removed from the excavations.

Recapping events from the last quarter of the 18th century was a war between the American colonists and England and a brutal civil war in France. King George III (r. 1760–1820), succeeded in uniting England and Ireland, but was unable to maintain rule over the 13 American colonies. American colonists' disgruntlement about the British Crown's restrictions on imports and increased taxation without representation in Parliament was the impetus for revolution.

With increased tensions between the Crown and the colonists, King George III used British troops to enforce colonial law and secure absolutism. France, by order of the new reigning monarch, King Louis XVI (r. 1774–1792), aided the Americans in their war against the British in 1778. Finally, in 1781, the British surrendered at Yorktown, Virginia, and the American Revolution ended with the signing of the

Treaty of Paris in 1783. By the end of the decade, France would be involved in its own gruesome revolution.

By the time Louis XVI inherited the throne in 1774, problems leading to the French Revolution were irreparable. The new monarch's attempts at reform were unsuccessful. The extravagant spending of the previous two monarchs at the Palace of Versailles coupled with costly military campaigns left France near bankruptcy. Heavily in debt, French aristocrats and the monarchy lived on borrowed time. The decadent and extravagant lifestyles of an aristocratic society along with constant controversies involving King Louis XVI's queen, Marie Antoinette, resulted in the monarchy becoming a target of blame. In the eyes of the commoner, these select few lived frivolously while peasants, who comprised the majority of the population, struggled to feed their families.

Increased taxation placed on the already overburdened commoners and peasants contributed to a growing resentment of aristocratic society, and the populace eventually reacted with violence and revolution. Seeking political, social, and economic reform, on July 15, 1789, crowds of peasants stormed the Bastille, a prison for political dissidents. The mob killed the commander and his guards, parading their heads on pikes through the streets of Paris. The capture of the Bastille stood for the fall of absolutism in the eyes of the French people.

The National Assembly, composed of French bourgeois representatives, quickly passed reform laws abolishing feudalism, but the fervor of revolution could not be stopped. Even with the aid of Austria and Prussia, Louis XVI failed to maintain control and save the monarchy. Captured trying to flee France in 1791, both Louis XVI and Marie Antoinette were imprisoned, tried for treason against French citizens, and executed in 1793.

In 1794, the Reign of Terror ended with the execution of Maximilien Robespierre, a leader of the opposition against the monarchy. Political order was restored in 1795 under a new constitution enforced by a *Directoire* of five men. However, economic conditions worsened as reforms lacked cohesive leadership under the new *Directoire*. In a coup d'état, a zealous Napoleon Bonaparte (1769–1821) overthrew the *Directoire* and claimed power as consulate in 1799. By 1804, Napoleon had seized absolute control as emperor of France. For 15 years, Napoleon established peace within French borders, administered economic prosperity through progressive reforms, and maintained political order.

In an attempt to imperialize the rest of Europe and establish France as the New World Order, Napoleon led numerous military campaigns against Austria, Prussia, Naples, Egypt, Sweden, Spain, and Portugal. Defeated by the Russians, Napoleon abdicated and was exiled in 1812. In 1815, he returned to France, deposed the restored Bourbon monarch King Louis XVIII (the eldest brother of King Louis XVI), and raised an army against the British. Defeated in the Battle of Waterloo, Napoleon was exiled once again to the isle of St. Helena, where he died in 1821.

# Architecture: 1760–1830

Early manifestations of the Neoclassic movement first appeared in France as architects and designers grew tired of the exaggerated intricacies of the Rococo–based styles. In the beginning, Neoclassic elements were introduced in the design of interiors, but quickly spread outward to all aspects of the structural space. A revival of the three orders of architecture—Doric, Ionic, and Corinthian—appeared in simplistic purity of use and form, singularly arranged across vast porticoes and inside large salons.

Neoclassicism marked a return to rectangular forms, defiantly rejecting the serpentine curves and undulations typical of the Rococo period preceding it. The Neoclassic period is divided into two parts. The Early Neoclassic period coincides with the beginning of the reign of Louis XVI in France; the Late Neoclassic period followed from 1792 to 1814.

**FIGURE 7.1** The Petit Trianon by architect Ange-Jacques Gabriel was built on the grounds of Versailles in France between 1762 and 1768. The design of the west facade is reminiscent of Italian Renaissance style in its strict symmetry, fluted pilasters with Corinthian capitals, a balustrade along the roofline, and lintels with oversized keystones.
© Worakit Sirijinda/Shutterstock.

# FRANCE, 1760–1814

The Petit Trianon, designed by Ange-Jacques Gabriel (1698–1782) and built between 1762 and 1768, exemplified the transition toward synthesizing Neoclassic elements in both interior and exterior architectural details (Figure 7.1). Constructed on the grounds of Versailles and built as a personal retreat for Madame de Pompadour, the Petit Trianon's main facade is articulated by a central projection created by the symmetrical arrangement of four engaged columns. Meanwhile, at the onset of Louis XVI and Marie Antoinette's reign in France, the royal apartments at Versailles were redecorated in the newly emerging Neoclassic style, despite the finances of the country (Figure 7.2).

In 1775, Louis XVI gave the Petit Trianon to his queen, Marie Antoinette, and she began remodeling the interior in a true Neoclassic style. Interiors were designed with purely geometric shapes; arcs, rectangles, and circles organized in strict symmetrical arrangements were incorporated into wall panels, mirror frames, and floor patterns. Ceilings, door frames, and mantelpiece moldings incorporated the many Roman examples unearthed from the excavations at Pompeii and Herculaneum. Gilt swags, urns, laurel wreaths, and egg-and-dart motifs were superimposed over white, gray, or softly tinted walls.

The interior from the Musée Jacquemart-Andre in Paris reflects the transitional style of the Early Neoclassic period (Figure 7.3). The geometric paneling on the walls complements the straight lines on chair and table legs. The medallion-shaped backs on the chaises and tabletop emphasize geometry rather than Rococo curves. A bergère, chaise longue, and commode reflect the adherence to the Louis XV style,

**FIGURE 7.2** The royal apartments were redecorated during the Early Neoclassic period. The bedchamber of Queen Marie Antoinette features an elaborate *lit à la polonaise*, with gilt carvings and embroidered fabrics that match the wall hangings and furniture upholstery. The bed is flanked by two transitional-style fauteuils.. © Marco/fotolia.

**FIGURE 7.3** This interior from the Musée Jacquemart-Andre in Paris reflects a transition in style between the Rococo and Early Neoclassic periods. © Travel Division Images/Alamy.

although the folding screen incorporates a curved top with straight side rails. The marble fireplace features classical symmetry with a dentil frieze under the mantel, with carved urn sides.

Château de Malmaison, the home of the new ruler of France, Napoleon and wife Josephine, was remodeled by architects Charles Percier (1764–1838) and Pierre François Léonard Fontaine (1762–1853). After traveling and studying in Rome, the two architects returned to Paris and were appointed as "architects of the government" by Napoleon. Their designs for the remodeling of Malmaison combined Egyptian, Greek, and Roman influences reflective of the Roman Empire, with as much historical accuracy as convenient, creating dramatic interior spaces. The theme for the renovations was based on a military-style décor, with walls designed to look like tenting material. This wall treatment is seen in the council room and in Josephine's bedroom (see Figure 7.37). Interior walls were painted with Pompeian details, adorned with scenic wallpapers, or draped with fabric. Pilasters and engaged columns surrounded fireplaces, whereas cornices topped off doors and windows. Napoleon's library features vaulted ceilings with painted motifs, a tripod table, and Greek–style fauteuils. Furniture such as tables, fauteuils, and chaises reflect furniture styles derived from excavations at Pompeii, with subtle Egyptian themes blended in. The intermingling of Egyptian ornament and design into the Late Neoclassic style was influenced by Napoleon's campaigns into Egypt. At Malmaison, the pastel colors of the Rococo period were replaced with rich gold, vibrant crimson, deep blue, and dark green.

## ENGLAND: 1760–1820

Although several English architects and designers moved swiftly from Palladianism into the newly defined Neoclassical style, perhaps the most recognized was interior designer Robert Adam (1728–1792). Adam spent time in Rome studying architectural ruins, visited Diocletian's palace in Split, Yugoslavia (now modern Croatia) and traveled to France. A few years after his return to London, Adam published a portfolio in 1764 of his engravings titled *Ruins of the Palace of the Emperor Diocletian*. This work established Adam as one of the leading "antiquarians" of the day, helping to set the standard for classic revival styles in England. Along with his brother James (1732–1794) and other family members, Adam established a successful business as a designer and architect for wealthy British eager to renovate their country estates.

From 1758 to 1767, work at Croome Court in Worcestershire, England, was done by Robert Adam, French painter François Boucher (1703–1770), and cabinetmakers John Mayhew (1736–1811) and William Ince (d. 1804). Consistent with the designs of the Neoclassic period, the Tapestry room featured hearty festoons and delicate swags, palmette and honeysuckle patterns, sweeping rinceau patterns, and paterae that appeared in the design of the ceiling, carpet, and tapestries. The ceiling designed by Robert Adam was executed by artisan Joseph Rose (1723–1780), the furniture was made by Mayhew and Ince, and the wool and silk tapestries were designed between 1759 and 1767 by Boucher, and were woven from 1764 to 1771 in the workshop of Jacques Neilson (1714–1788) at the Gobelins. The estate was remodeled for George William, the sixth Earl of Coventry, and the project established the Adam style in England.

In 1761, the Adam brothers received a commission to remodel and modernize a 16th-century Elizabethan house acquired by a wealthy banking family in Osterley Park. They transformed the exterior façade by adding a vast portico supported by Ionic columns, and set the standard for neoclassicism in England. During the next 20 years, the brothers carefully designed every detail for rooms inside the house, turning them into expressions of the Neoclassic aesthetic. The grand entrance hall was laid out with a massive plasterwork ceiling, an elaborate niche fitted with classical sculptures, and large urns on pedestals. Wall paneling, ceiling designs, marble flooring, and carpets featured with Adam's signature paterae; urn and swag motifs and clocks, textiles, mirrors, and lighting fixtures coordinated with his furniture

FIGURE 7.4 Kenwood House was remodeled and expanded by Robert and James Adam in 1764. The Palladian influence is seen in the facade, which features a superimposed portico with a triangular pediment. © tonyz20/ Shutterstock.

designs. While defining the Neoclassic style in England, Adam captured the essence of the artifacts discovered at Pompeii and Herculaneum and, by 1770, his work became increasingly linear, and his stylistic development advanced to a stringent adaptation of classic conventions.

Work began in 1764 on Kenwood House, remodeling it from its 1616 Baroque style into the more current Neoclassic style (Figure 7.4). The façade now features the centralized main house with a superimposed portico created by a triangular pediment and pilasters. Side wings feature classical faux arcades with ionic orders. Hallmarks of the Adam's style were ornately patterned floors balanced by walls decorated in plaster relief, and rooms compressed by highly decorative ceilings. His most commonly used motifs—the paterae, urns draped with swags, palmettes, and classical figures—dominated the overall interior scheme.

The Royal Crescent in Bath reflects an important landmark in urban planning. The project, designed by John Wood (1728–1782) was begun in 1767 as a speculative development project arranging 30 attached townhomes in a wide arch facing a park, selling the units individually without any interior finish-out. Those who purchased the units bought the shell, and then hired architects to plan the interiors. Wood's designs for the facades reflected the Palladian influences of his father, John Wood the Elder (1704–1754).

# LEARN More

## English Early Neoclassic Interior Design

The Etruscan room at Osterley Park (Figure 7.5) was designed by Robert Adam in 1775. Adam's Neoclassic designs, although interpretive, reflect the latest trend in classicism brought on by the excavations at Pompeii and Herculaneum. This room served as a dressing room, and its decoration was inspired by scenes on ancient Etruscan and Greek pottery vases. The ceiling is painted with a central blue medallion surrounded by classical urns draped with thin swags and tied with ribbons in gold and brown. The walls feature painted scenes of classical goddesses among similar urn and swag motifs on the ceiling. These paintings are vertically arranged above a painted chair rail of rosette bands set above a blue painted wainscot. Classical statues adorn wall-lined niches (some framed by Corinthian orders) whereas door panels and a fire screen (not visible in this photo) replicate the arabesque designs of figures and urns. Adam also designed a set of furniture to match the room décor. A set of painted armchairs with urn-shaped backs and

FIGURE 7.5 This dressing room at Osterley Park in England is the work of Robert Adam, and it shows his interpretation of Pompeian–style wall paintings and classically inspired furnishings. © The National Trust Photolibrary/Alamy..

gilt bellflower motifs running along the arms, legs, and back are arranged around the perimeter of the room, along with an assortment of japanned tables.

**FIGURE 7.6** Monticello, the home of Thomas Jefferson, shows his interest in Neoclassical and Palladian architecture. Emphasizing symmetry, the central dome and large portico anchor the balanced, projecting wings. © Ffooter/Shutterstock.

## AMERICA: 1785–1830

In America, through the influence of Thomas Jefferson (1743–1826), neoclassicism was adopted as the national architectural style of the newly formed United States. Jefferson, a self-taught architect and public official, spent five years in Paris from 1784 to 1789 as the U.S. Minister to France. In Paris, he was surrounded by the Neoclassic architectural design prevalent in France at the time. While there, Jefferson was also exposed to the ruins of the ancient Roman Empire.

Monticello, Jefferson's home in Charlottesville, Virginia, reflects his exploration of classical elements (Figures 7.6 and 7.7). In 1796, he remodeled Monticello in a true Palladian sense. The home's dome, centered above a classical portico, is reminiscent of Villa Rotunda and Chiswick House (Figures 4.3 and 6.4). Jefferson's keen interest in Roman and Greek classicism is seen in his designs for the state capitol building in Richmond, built in 1789, and the University of Virginia, completed in 1826.

Jefferson's architectural achievements influenced the emerging American Federal style adopted by other notable American architects such as Charles Bullfinch (1763–1844) and Samuel McIntire (1757–1811). The American Federal home was two or three stories in height contained under a hipped roof (Figure 7.8). The symmetrical

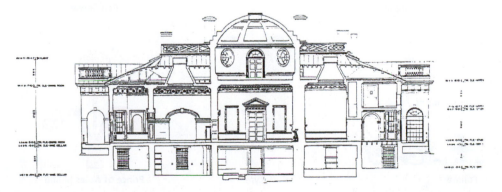

**FIGURE 7.7** This section drawing of Jefferson's Monticello shows classically inspired interior pediments, arches, and moldings. Courtesy of the Library of Congress.

facade featured a large fan light above the door with side lights. A large central hallway showed off the wealth of the owner, with elaborate plaster moldings and finely carved stair railings. At the turn of the 19th century, architects and designers turned toward more romanticized visions of the past, bringing about a number of revivalist styles including Greek, Gothic, Elizabethan, and Italianate. Moorish and Oriental influences were also included into the blending of revivalist styles, and this eclectic combination of styles became the hallmark of the English Victorian era and the Second Empire in France.

**FIGURE 7.8** An American Federal–style house from 1785 features a hipped roof with balustrade, and a prominent central door capped with a fan light and triangular pediment.
David Lyons © Dorling Kindersley.

# Design Motifs

Rosettes and medallions intertwined with Vitruvian scrolls, guilloche decorations, paterae, palmette, and anthemion, along with foliate patterns appeared as carved or inlaid decorations on architecture and furniture during the Neoclassic period (Figure 7.9). The rosette motif often appears as an ormolu mount or a carved detail on furniture, a feature of plasterwork designs, on wall paneling, and as a textile pattern. Foliate designs rendered with perfect symmetry

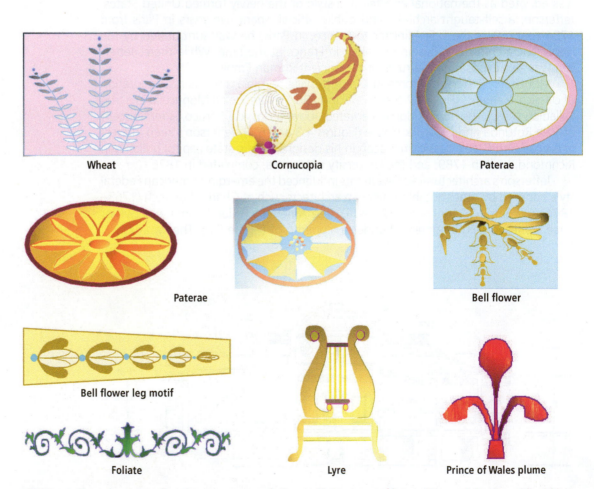

Wheat          Cornucopia          Paterae

Paterae          Bell flower

Bell flower leg motif

Foliate          Lyre          Prince of Wales plume

**FIGURE 7.9** These drawings reflect the more common design motifs incorporated into architectural details and furnishings during the Early Neoclassic period. © David Vleck.

FIGURE 7.10 Elaborate plasterwork featuring bellflowers tied with ribbons, acanthus leaves and shell carvings, and foliates frame an 18th-century seascape painting in this Early Neoclassic interior. Joe Cornish © Dorling Kindersley.

FIGURE 7.11 This plaster ceiling design of lively foliate patterns was created with wooden molds to form each section of the design. Dave King © Dorling Kindersley, Courtesy of Athelhampton House, Dorset.

FIGURE 7.12 A putti stands on a pedestal inside this wall niche painted with Neoclassical motifs, including arabesque designs, laurel branches, ribbon swags, and trompe l'oeil architectural elements in vivid red, gold, green, and blue. Joe Cornish © Dorling Kindersley.

are often seen as ormolu mounts or as inlay patterns on furniture, and also appear in plaster designs during the Late Neoclassic period (Figure 7.10). These motifs were inspired by the design motifs seen on the architectural elements, furniture, wall frescoes, and floor mosaics excavated from Pompeii and Herculaneum. Reinterpreted by the designers of the Neoclassic period, ceiling and wall designs were commonly recreated in plaster relief rather than painted finishes (Figure 7.11). Characteristic thin swags of bellflowers tied up with delicate ribbons, urns, and vases were common motifs featured on interior plasterwork.

The early Neoclassic designs appearing in Adamesque interiors included classical putti, arabesques, and paterae patterns (Figures 7.12 and 7.13). Small bellflowers tied up with ribbons were a recurring motif favored by Robert Adam, and these motifs regularly appeared on his designs for ceilings, wall paintings, paneling, and furniture (Figure 7.5). Guilloche patterns were used as decorative border designs on textiles and furniture carvings (Figure 7.14). In addition, more specific to England, the Prince of Wales plume featured three ostrich feathers arranged in a similar fashion to the fleur-de-lis.

Designers during the Late Neoclassic period used combinations of Greek and Egyptian motifs in interior fashions. Cornucopia and wheat motifs were associated with the abundance of the earth, and date back to ancient Rome. This motif was prominently featured on Empire–style furniture in France and America, particularly on legs. Moreover, from the last quarter of the 18th century and continuing through 1840, essentially all design motifs imitated those used by the ancient Romans. Decorative accessories incorporated caryatid figures, lyre forms, cornucopia, sphinxes, and representations of pharaohs into their shapes and forms. The lyre, an ancient Roman musical instrument similar to a modern harp, was commonly used as a motif on furniture during the Early and Late Neoclassic periods and was favorite of Robert Adam and the American designer, Duncan Phyfe (1768–1854).

FIGURE 7.13 Two tea caddies veneered in satinwood have painted foliate designs on their fronts, and paterae motifs surrounded by laurel branches on the hinged lids. © Judith Miller/Dorling Kindersley/Woolley and Wallis.

FIGURE 7.14 The fabrics and wall covering in this room from the Early Neoclassic period feature a guilloche border that frames a field of palmette and acanthus leaves surrounded by a border of inlaid woods. Kim Sayer © Dorling Kindersley.

# Furniture

As a whole, furniture designed in both the Early and Late Neoclassic periods did not change in proportion or scale from that of the Rococo period. Furnishings remained small in scale, and the designs moved away from organically inspired curves toward geometric shapes and symmetry, and idealized classical elements became the most decorative feature on chairs, tables, and case goods. Classicism based on historical fact was made possible because numerous pattern books published at this time illustrated with exactness the ornamentation used by the ancient Romans.

Although detailed carving was still applied to most furniture items, Vitruvian scrolls, guilloche patterns, urns, festoons, garlands, and diaper patterns were incorporated into marquetry work and ormolu mounts. New emphasis was placed on medallions, lyre forms, rosettes, and the cornucopia. In adherence to Neoclassic straight lines, legs were fashioned into fluted or reeded columns, quadrangular and tapered, or round and tapered, imitating a quiver of arrows. By 1780, most arm posts were either incurvate, straight, or fashioned into slender urns. Chair backs were oval, circular, square, or rectangular whereas seats kept a slight curvature to the front rail. Deviances from 90-degree angles were treated with an arc or canted corners.

In both France and England, furniture designed during the second half of the 18th century reflected strong Greek and Roman influences. However, toward the turn of the 19th century, designs began to include Egyptian characteristics as well. The introduction of Egyptian motifs into design during the Late Neoclassic period was a result of Napoleon's campaigns into Egypt in 1798, and marked the division between the Early and Late Neoclassic periods. In France, these later developments in furniture design are referred to as the "Empire style," whereas it is known as the "Regency style" in England.

**FIGURE 7.15** This salon in the Musée Carnavalet in Paris features French furnishings and interior paneling predominantly in the Louis XVI style. © Author's Image Ltd/Alamy.

## FRENCH EARLY NEOCLASSIC: 1760–1792

The interior decoration of Ange-Jacques Gabriel's Petit Trianon revealed the dissipation of the Rococo style. Furniture designed for the Petit Trianon was considered transitional because it blended the straight lines of the Neoclassic with Rococo curvilinearity. Interior spaces reflected his adherence to straight lines and symmetry; rooms were rectangular, and applied moldings harmonized with the angularity of the room as surface ornaments divided walls into rectangular sections (Figure 7.15).

A pure form of the Early Neoclassic style of furniture known as the "Louis XVI style," or "Style Louis *Seize*," was already being produced in the workshops of French cabinetmakers by the time Louis XVI ascended the throne in 1774. French furniture during the Early Neoclassic Louis XVI style featured straight lines and legs fashioned into fluted or reeded columns (Figure 7.16).

Chair backs were oval, circular, or rectangular, sometimes with a slight arc at the top of the crest rail. Seats and arms also featured smooth arcs, as geometric shapes prevailed over the sinuous curves of the Rococo (Figure 7.17). Most chairs and settees in the Louis XVI style were constructed from beech and were painted in light colors or parcel gilt (Figure 7.18). Those that were left in a natural finish were made out of walnut. Needlework upholstery fell out of fashion during the Neoclassic period; instead, soft pastel-colored upholstery fabrics in brocade, damask, and silk covered chairs and settees (Figure 7.19).

Console tables were designed to stand alone; however, several semicircular examples exist with the flat side intended to be placed against a wall. The use of a saltire stretcher is haphazard among console tables and side tables in the Louis XVI style, although most

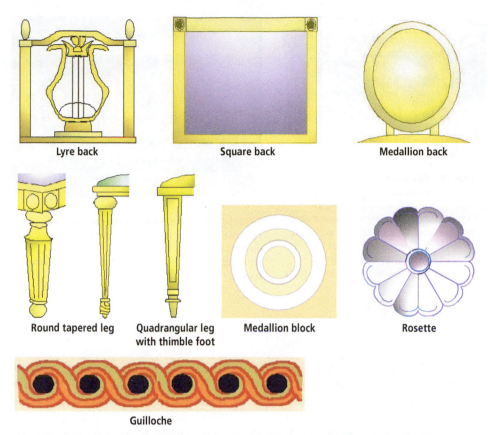

Lyre back        Square back        Medallion back

Round tapered leg    Quadrangular leg    Medallion block    Rosette
with thimble foot

Guilloche

**FIGURE 7.16** Common elements and motifs featured in the French Early Neoclassic, Louis XVI–style furnishings. © David Vleck.

**FIGURE 7.17** This Louis XVI–style chaise dates from 1770 and features a rounded back with round, tapered, and fluted legs, ending with thimble feet in the front and saber legs in the back. Rosette blocks appear at the four corners of the laurel-leaf carved seat rail. © Judith Miller / Dorling Kindersley/Caroline Kerangal.

**FIGURE 7.18** These French Louis XVI–style fauteuils made from carved and gilt beech wood feature round, tapered front legs with spiral grooves, a square back, and laurel-leaf carving on the frame. © Judith Miller/Dorling Kindersley/Lyon and Turnbull, Ltd.

incorporate a small pierced gallery that follows the perimeter surface. Small worktables, writing tables, and toiletry tables for women were designed using a variety of ornamentation, ranging from elaborate marquetry and parquetry patterns to chinoiserie and Sèvres plaques (Figures 7.20 and 7.21). Tables, commodes, consoles, and case goods were crafted using decorative veneers made from tulipwood, satinwood, ebony, and fruitwoods. Marquetry work was often used, and highly decorative effects were achieved by burning the edges of the wood in hot sand or by subjecting inlay to lime water acids, spirits of nitrate, or oil of sulfur for coloring.

**FIGURE 7.19** This gilt-wood settee in the Louis XVI style features tapered legs with carved acanthus leaf motifs and rosette blocks, and is upholstered in pink damask with patterns of tied bouquets framed by foliate medallions. © Judith Miller/Dorling Kindersley/Lyon and Turnbull Ltd.

Two celebrated cabinetmakers of the period, Jean-François Oeben (1720–1763) and Jean-Henri Riesener (1734–1806), produced some of the finest examples of French Early Neoclassic furniture in existence. Appointed *ébéniste du roi* to Louis XV in 1754, Oeben joined the workshops of the Gobelins. His mastery as a cabinetmaker was revealed through skillful marquetry work depicting spectacular floral displays combined with pictorial trompe l'oeil. While in the service of the king, Oeben completed many pieces for Madame de Pompadour. Her impeccable taste and refinement along with her preference for simplistic purity accelerated the development of what would become known as the "Louis XVI style."

In 1760, Oeben was commissioned to make a desk for Louis XV. Posthumously, the *bureau du roi* became Oeben's greatest achievement. His pupil, Riesener, not only completed the desk in 1769, but married Oeben's widow and carried on the business. In 1774, on the coronation of King Louis XVI, Riesener became *ébéniste du roi*. Riesener had a prolific career, completing several works for Marie Antoinette

**FIGURE 7.20** This transitional Louis XV–Louis XVI green marble-top and parquetry table *en chiffonière* has a pierced gallery lining three quarters of the top, a key feature of the emerging Louis XVI style. © Judith Miller/Dorling Kindersley/Sloans and Kenyon.

FIGURE 7.21 This gilt brass and Sèvres porcelain gueridon (table) incorporates many Neoclassic features, including swags tied up with ribbons, classical term figures that support the porcelain basin, and hoof-shaped feet. © Judith Miller/Dorling Kindersley/Lyon and Turnbull Ltd.

FIGURE 7.22 This drawing of a French Louis XVI–style commode attributed to Jean-Henri Riesener (1734–1806) dates from around 1785 to 1790. The commode is decorated with ebony, chinoiserie lacquerwork, and ormolu in classically inspired festoons, acanthus leaves, rosettes, and laurel wreaths. The cipher of Madame Marie Antoinette appears on the frieze.

FIGURE 7.23 A French transitional-style commode retains the cabriole leg from the Louis XV style, but features strong linear designs, which are representative of the Louis XVI style. © Judith Miller/Dorling Kindersley/Freeman's.

(Figure 7.22). He survived the French Revolution by producing rifle butts and, although the monarchy ended with the execution of the royal family, in 1794 the *Directoire* employed Riesener to remove all royal emblems from furniture of the period.

Commodes were severely rectangular in form, clearly abandoning the Rococo bombé swell. Drawers, doors, and front pieces were delineated with rectangular bands that emphasized the geometry of each piece (Figure 7.23). The bureau took on a more rectangular appearance as well. The *secrétaire à abattant* featured a box-like form with simple, classical details (Figure 7.24). Writing desks retained typical quadrangular or columnar legs, whereas ormolu patterns incorporated classical motifs such as putti, acanthus leaves, rosette blocks, and medallions. A pierced metal gallery of chased bronze was introduced on Louis XVI–style furniture and is characteristically found on case goods and tables.

Beds were smaller and had headboards and footboards, with canopies suspended overhead rather than hung on posts. As designers attempted to recreate the interiors of Roman villas, beds were placed lengthwise against the wall rather than perpendicular to the wall; a *lit à travers* is a bed that traverses the wall. Beds were also tucked away in alcoves, creating a sense of expansion in small rooms. Several *lit à la polonaise* featured upholstered headboards and foot boards with gilt frames and canopies (Figure 7.25).

## FRENCH LATE NEOCLASSIC: 1793–1814

French furniture designed during the Late Neoclassic period follows two distinctive styles: the *Directoire* and the Empire. The *Directoire* represents a transitional period between the established Louis XVI style and the emerging French Empire style (Figure 7.26). Overall, *Directoire*–style furniture reflects direct association with items excavated from Pompeii, although there is also a strong emphasis on Greek

FIGURE 7.24 A French early-19th-century *secrétaire à abattant* has a single frieze drawer above the fall-front, hinged compartment and lower cabinet doors are flanked with classical pilasters details on its canted-shaped sides. © Judith Miller/Dorling Kindersley/Lyon and Turnbull, Ltd.

FIGURE 7.25 This elegant canopy bed from the 18th century was made for a bedroom at Versailles. The design includes ostrich plume finial bedposts and elaborate embroidered bedding and drapery. © SOMATUSCAN/Shutterstock.

influences (Figure 7.27). Distinctive qualities of the Greek *klismos* and the Roman *thronos* are incorporated into the design of chairs as more attention is given to authenticity rather than interpretation (Figure 7.28). Elements of Roman and Greek design, such as rolled crest rails, volute or sphinx-shaped arm posts, and paw feet evoke the mood of the ancient past.

Georges Jacob (1739–1814), cabinet-maker to the royal family under King Louis XVI, survived the Revolution and went on to design furniture in both the *Directoire* and Empire styles. His son, François Honoré Jacob (1770–c. 1841), took over the family business along with a brother, and became Napoleon's most celebrated cabinetmaker. François adopted the name Jacob-Desmalter, and his workshop worked closely with Percier and Fontaine, fabricating furniture pieces for several of Napoleon's residences. As the new aristocracy of a prosperous France was eager to put the trepidation of the Revolution behind them, Napoleon set the direction for a return to luxurious living with the redesign of Malmaison. Furnishings at Malmaison recaptured the opulence of those at Versailles. For the aristocracy, Late Neoclassic furniture in the Empire style featured straight lines and carved details were minimized in favor of ormolu mounts.

References to Egyptian motifs appeared as ormolu mounts fashioned into the images of pharaohs or sphinxes on furniture and decorative accessories. Caryatids and term figures with paw feet were reintroduced and appear on the front legs of chairs, and sweeping saber legs support the back (Figure 7.29). Less attention was given to painted or gilt surfaces, featuring the dark graining and deep red coloring of mahogany and rosewood. Fabrics emphasized motifs more characteristic of the Roman Empire: laurel wreaths, palmettes, rosettes, and medallions.

Small tables had *pietra dura* tops with chased bronze rims and took the form of the Roman tripod, with term figures or sphinxes used as the base (Figure 7.30). Larger tables were mostly round or oval and rested on columnar or other decorative supports. A variety of other tables already in use during the 18th century took on characteristics of the Empire style. *Tables à ouvrage* and the *bonheur du jour*

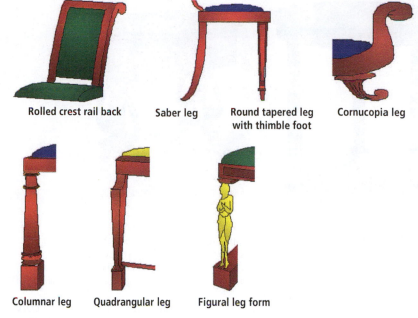

Rolled crest rail back     Saber leg     Round tapered leg with thimble foot     Cornucopia leg

Columnar leg     Quadrangular leg     Figural leg form

**FIGURE 7.26** Characteristic French Late Neoclassic–, Directoire–, and Empire–style furniture forms. © David Vleck.

**FIGURE 7.27** A pair of 19th-century Empire mahogany fauteuils, each with a slightly curved back, features ormolu laurel leaf designs on the crest rail with carved and gilt dolphin head arm posts and squared cabriole legs. © Judith Miller/ Dorling Kindersley/Lyon and Turnbull, Ltd.

**FIGURE 7.28** An early 19th-century French Empire settee made from mahogany features scrolled arms and saber legs. The upholstery features urn and foliate designs. © Judith Miller/Dorling Kindersley/ Sloan's.

**FIGURE 7.29** This tub chair followed prototypes from the period of the Roman Empire, accelerated by the ongoing excavations at Pompeii and Herculaneum. This mahogany *bergère en gondole* with laurel leaf-detailed ormolu mounts and term figure arm posts has saber back legs and square tapered front legs with paw feet. © Judith Miller/ Dorling Kindersley/Woolley and Wallis.

**FIGURE 7.30** This French Empire–style marble-top circular center table with a fossil marble top, columnar supports, and a triangular platform base has gilt-metal mounts fashioned into laurel leaves and rosettes. © Judith Miller/Dorling Kindersley/Sloan's.

**FIGURE 7.31** This early 19th-century French Empire rosewood ladies worktable, or *table à ouvrage*, has lyre-form trestle supports finished in saber legs and ormolu paw feet mounted on castors. © Judith Miller/Dorling Kindersley/Lyon and Turnbull, Ltd.

**FIGURE 7.32** This French Empire mahogany commode is fitted with three graduated drawers flanked by term figure sides, with starburst designs and paw feet. The escutcheons are fashioned into bird and foliate designs, and a laurel leaf and rosette design in ormolu appears on the plinth base of the chest. © Judith Miller/Dorling Kindersley/Sloan's.

**FIGURE 7.33** This French Empire mahogany tall chest has three drawers and a cabinet front with term figure side posts and ebony carved paw feet. © Judith Miller/Dorling Kindersley/ Freeman's.

changed from the feminine curvilinear styles of the Rococo to the more angular and straight lined influences of classicism (Figure 7.31).

Case furniture lacked the detailed carving seen in the Louis XVI style, as ormolu became the primary source of decoration on French Empire furnishings (Figure 7.32). Bronze mounts applied to mahogany-veneer surfaces were fashioned into classical goddesses, laurel wreaths, olive branches, and six-point star patterns. Term figures with caryatids, sphinxes, or pharaohs delineated the sides of *secretaires*, commodes, and cabinets (Figure 7.33).

Writing tables and *secrétaires* reflected severe geometry in design as rectangular banding followed drawer fronts and tabletops, with columnar leg forms or the round, tapered shapes popularized in Louis XVI–style furnishings (Figure 7.34). The *bureau à cylindre*, or rolltop desks that were designed for Kings Louis XV and Louis XVI, set the demand for these types of desks by the more affluent gentlemen of the period (Figure 7.35).

The *méridienne*, a new piece of furniture introduced in the Empire style, was a type of daybed used for lounging. With one arm raised higher than the other, the scrolled arms evoke the feeling of fulcrum supports found on the ancient Roman *lectus*. Similar to a *méridienne*, the *récamier* was a type of *chaise longue* that had one arm higher than the other, with an abbreviated back or no back at all (Figure 7.36). The furniture was named after the portrait of Madame Récamier by Jacques Louis David painted in 1800. The painting captures the public interest in design and culture of the Roman Empire period. Not only is Madame Récamier dressed like a Roman aristocrat, but the stage props, an Etruscan–style *torchère*, and a *lectus*-and-fulcrum-style daybed with footstool reflect Roman inspiration as well. David has positioned Madame Récamier in repose on the daybed with her left arm supported by cylindrical pillows.

**FIGURE 7.34** This French Empire writing desk has a kneehole front set on four columnar legs accentuated with cast metal and gilt capital and base designs. © Judith Miller/Dorling Kindersley/Lyon and Turnbull, Ltd.

**FIGURE 7.35** This 18th-century Directoire–style *bureau à cylindre* rolltop desk is made from mahogany and features a marble top with metal gallery edge, gold banding around the drawers, and quadrangular legs with thimble feet. © Judith Miller/Dorling Kindersley/Freeman's.

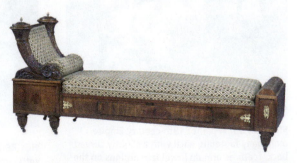

**FIGURE 7.36** A Directoire–style daybed made from carved walnut with cornucopia and ram's head details, and ormolu mounts. © Judith Miller/Dorling Kindersley/Sloan's.

Empire–style beds increasingly took on the characteristics of the Roman *lectus*. Raised on a plinth, the bed was positioned lengthwise in the room, and most were recessed into an alcove built into the wall. Those of the freestanding type often had an elaborate canopy suspended overhead. Percier and Fontaine based the bedroom at Malmaison for Josephine Bonaparte on an exotic interpretation of a military tent with Roman–influenced furnishings. The elaborately draped and carved gilt bed bears Josephine's monogram on the side rail (Figure 7.37).

Typically, accessories harmonized with the interior furnishings and completed the interior decoration of the room. Greek, Roman, or Egyptian themes were incorporated into carpets and other textiles, whereas lamps and vases were designed to imitate the urns, busts, and pottery pieces removed from Pompeii.

## ENGLISH EARLY NEOCLASSIC: 1760–1805

English furniture designed during the reign of George III is identified by three stylistic genres known as the Adam, Hepplewhite, and Sheraton styles (Figure 7.38). These styles are named after the designers who made them popular rather than the monarch who ruled at the time, although there are some references made to the George III style in auction catalogs and antiques magazines. Furniture designed by Adam was specifically for the interiors he remodeled for his clients. His association with Thomas Chippendale began in 1760, and the collaborative designs incorporated paterae, urns with swags, palmettes, and classical figures to coordinate with Adam's most commonly used architectural motifs (Figure 7.39).

The popularity of Chippendale's *The Gentleman and Cabinet-Maker's Director* published in 1754 encouraged others to produce pattern books documenting the latest styles in England. The *Cabinet Maker and Upholsterer's Guide* by George Hepplewhite (unknown–1786) and *The Cabinet Maker and Upholsterer's Drawing Book* by Thomas Sheraton (1751–1806) contained drawings representative of the current trends in furniture designs that were in vogue during the Early Neoclassic period. These pattern books perpetuated the popularity of classical designs.

Information on the life of George Hepplewhite is lacking. The *Cabinet Maker and Upholsterer's Guide* was actually published by Hepplewhite's widow, Alice, in 1788. The publication included only a few original designs by Hepplewhite; the majority of the designs were based on styles made popular by the Adam brothers and other contemporary furniture designers. The furniture illustrated in the *Guide* had classical qualities; however, the elements were synthesized in a more straightforward, simplified manner. Almost exclusively made of mahogany or satinwood, furniture items balanced straight lines with gentle curves and relied mostly on inlay rather than carving for ornamentation. Furniture designed during this period was made with East Indian satinwood, hare wood, pheasant wood, boxwood, sycamore, mahogany, holly, and thuyawood veneers and inlays.

FIGURE 7.37 This bedroom, designed for Empress Josephine at Château de Malmaison by Percier and Fontaine, features a gilt-wood canopy bed with elaborately carved swans and cornucopia legs reminiscent of an ancient Roman *lectus*. Crimson fabric embroidered in gold hangs from the ceiling in tentlike fashion and is also used for the bedding. An abundance of feminine grandeur is apparent, with the elaborately draped and carved gilt bed bearing Josephine's monogram. Max Alexander © Dorling Kindersley, Courtesy of Château de Malmaison.

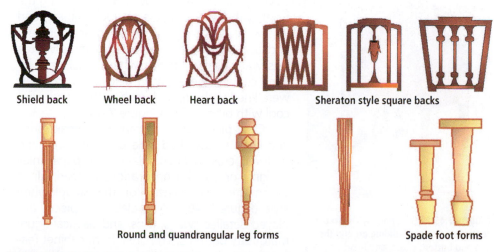

Shield back   Wheel back   Heart back   Sheraton style square backs

Round and quandrangular leg forms          Spade foot forms

FIGURE 7.38 English Early Neoclassic leg forms commonly represented on Hepplewhite– and Sheraton-style furniture. © David Vleck.

FIGURE 7.39 This wheel-back hall chair with a central pierced rosette design is attributed to Thomas Chippendale. Neoclassic elements appear in the square, tapered, fluted legs and block feet; medallion carved blocks set into the seat rail above each leg; and fluted carving on the lower back. © Judith Miller/Dorling Kindersley/ Lyon and Turnbull, Ltd.

FIGURE 7.40 English Neoclassic shield-back chairs appear in the Hepplewhite *Guide*. In this example, the back has a pierced splat designed with bundled wheat husks, and saber front and rear legs. © Judith Miller/Dorling Kindersley/Hampton's.

FIGURE 7.41 This heart-back Hepplewhite–style chair features a serpentine-shaped seat rail.
© Judith Miller/Dorling Kindersley/Pook and Pook.

FIGURE 7.42 This Hepplewhite–style chair made from satinwood features the Prince of Wales Plume on its oval-shaped back, painted foliate designs on the front seat rail, and bellflower motifs on the tapered front legs. The chair dates from 1900.
© Judith Miller/Dorling Kindersley/Sloan's.

FIGURE 7.43 This English Neoclassic Hepplewhite–style side table from the late 18th century is made from mahogany and satinwood with banding along the bow front and a paterae inlay on the top. The tapering quadrangular legs terminate in spade feet.
© Judith Miller/Dorling Kindersley/Lyon and Turnbull, Ltd.

FIGURE 7.44 A bowfront mahogany sideboard with rosewood crossbanding on the top and drawer fronts has an opening for storing a cellaret. © Judith Miller/Dorling Kindersley/ Lyon and Turnbull, Ltd.

FIGURE 7.45 This mahogany cellaret features boxwood banding around the top and bottom edges, and is set onto square, tapered legs with spade feet.
© Judith Miller/Dorling Kindersley/Lyon and Turnbull, Ltd.

Furnishings in the Hepplewhite style featured chairs, cabinets, and tables with small proportions and scant carving; decorations were either painted or inlaid. Identifying elements of the Hepplewhite style can be seen in the numerous chairs appearing in the *Guide*. Designed to be used either in the dining room or bedroom, chairs were all wood with either upholstered or cane seats. Backs were left open and formed distinctive shield, heart, or wheel shapes (Figures 7.40 and 7.41). Splats took on a variety of carved designs, including wheat patterns, arcaded tracery, urns with ribbons, and the Prince of Wales plume (Figure 7.42). Stretchers, if used, were simple H form or box form and connected to quadrangular or round tapered front legs and saber back legs.

The introduction of the half-round console table during the late 18th century influenced the design of bow-front commodes and sideboards. These semicircular tables were placed at the ends of a rectangular dining table acting as extensions when needed, then were placed against the wall after the meal (Figure 7.43). Dining rooms were also outfitted with sideboards that were used as serving tables and storage units for table linens and flatware (Figure 7.44). These case pieces featured a row of drawers along the front with lower drawers or side cabinets, and legs were quadrangular or round and tapered, and lacked stretchers. Knife boxes and silver tea sets were placed on top whereas *cellarets*, or wine coolers, were placed below. The *cellarets* were lined with tin, and wine bottles were kept cool with blocks of ice (Figure 7.45).

Case pieces such as cabinets, breakfronts, and linen presses had little or no carving, and featured cross-banded inlays, oval panel inlay designs, or painted decorations instead, all of which are characteristic of the Hepplewhite style (Figure 7.46). More elaborate pieces displayed detailed swags, urns, and classical figure marquetry patterns. The breakfront cabinet featured a projecting center panel flanked by recessed side panels, and the upper cabinet was fitted with glass front doors to show off a collection of fine porcelains or books.

Thomas Sheraton was a designer of furniture, although no records can prove that he actually was a cabinetmaker. *The Cabinet Maker and Upholsterer's Drawing Book* was published in 1791 and was widely accepted and used by cabinetmakers throughout England. Many of the examples in the Hepplewhite and Sheraton drawing books overlapped in design. Stylistically, Sheraton furniture is similar to Hepplewhite, but is more angular in appearance. Straight lines and definitive arcs replace the heart-shaped and shield-shaped backs found in Hepplewhite's *Guide* (Figure 7.47).

Sheraton's square-back chairs with carved trellis work, balusters, or urn-shaped splats were made primarily from mahogany or satinwood, although painted and gilded beech chairs were also prevalent (Figure 7.48). Incurvate arms with reeded or fluted arm posts, legs, and uprights; inlaid or painted honeysuckle; paterae; and classical swags unified chairs and settees in Neoclassic interiors. Settees featured high backs with equally high arms. Wood trim followed the edge of the back and arms, and leg forms were quadrangular with spade feet or were round and tapered with thimble feet (Figure 7.49).

Included in Sheraton's *Drawing Book* were a variety of secretaries, bookcases, dressing tables, and tables. Sheraton, a noted mathematician, designed furniture using the latest mechanical devices. Tables unfolded into library stairs, and writing tables concealed hidden compartments activated by spring locks or cranks (Figure 7.50). Small tables specially designed for women to perform daily tasks appeared in Sheraton's *Drawing Book* and an increase in the number of ladies' writing tables and bureaus emphasized the growing acceptance of educated women in society from all social classes. A Pembroke was a small rectangular-shaped, drop-leaf table fitted with a small drawer in the frieze area (Figure 7.51). The table was used for eating light meals while the lady of the house remained in bed. Winged sides were opened to support the leaves expanding the size of the table.

**FIGURE 7.46** A Hepplewhite–style mahogany cabinet on a stand with a serpentine front has a broken pediment above pair of doors that features a central marquetry paterae motif and graduated drawers. The interior is fitted with shelves and small drawers. © Judith Miller/Dorling Kindersley/Woolley and Wallis.

**FIGURE 7.47** Lattice-back Sheraton–style chairs feature squared backs with a carved crest rail centered by ribbon-tied husks. The uprights are turned with fluted detailing, saber back legs, and quadrangular front legs on spade feet. © Judith Miller/Dorling Kindersley/Lyon and Turnbull, Ltd.

**FIGURE 7.48** These Sheraton chairs feature painted designs of putti on the crest rail, bellflower patterns on the frame, a cane seat, and an urn-shaped splat. © Judith Miller/Dorling Kindersley/Lyon and Turnbull, Ltd.

**FIGURE 7.49** This square-back settee has high arms supported by turned urn posts, and reeded, round legs with brass casters.
© Judith Miller/Dorling Kindersley/Freeman's.

**FIGURE 7.50** This ladies writing table in the Sheraton style has a mechanically rising screen and spring-action pen and ink drawer to the side of the writing drawer. The piece dates from 1795 and is made from boxwood, satinwood, and rosewood, with purple heartwood inlaid top. © Judith Miller/Dorling Kindersley/Richard Gardner Antiques.

**FIGURE 7.51** A Sheraton mahogany Pembroke table with a frieze drawer (trade label for Druce & Co, Baker St, London W). The turned stems and splayed legs with brass sabots terminate on casters.

© Judith Miller/Dorling Kindersley/Woolley and Wallis.

FIGURE 7.52 This niche from an 18th-century interior features trompe l'oeil ceiling designs painted to imitate Wedgwood jasperware. Tim Daly © Dorling Kindersley.

FIGURE 7.53 A Regency–style chair from the early 19th century features a concave crest rail with saber front and back legs. The chair is beech wood painted in black with gold fret designs, and has lion-paw arm posts and a loose cushion seat. Steve Gorton © Dorling Kindersley.

FIGURE 7.54 This English Regency–style sofa has a reeded and scrolled back rail, scrolled arms, and cornucopia-shaped legs. © Judith Miller/Dorling Kindersley/Lyon and Turnbull Ltd.

FIGURE 7.55 A *recamier* in the Regency style has cornucopia legs with ormolu anthemion motifs. The fabric is not typical of the period. © Judith Miller/Dorling Kindersley/Lyon and Turnbull, Ltd.

The *Drawing Book* also set the trend of incorporating porcelain plaques into English furniture designs. This fashion had been popular in France since the early Rococo period, but was not adopted by the English until the success of Josiah Wedgwood (1730–1795). Wedgwood's factory produced jasperware, a type of pottery recognized today as pale blue with white relief classical figures (Figure 1.37). Although the pale blue is the most popular, Wedgwood china was produced in other colors, including black, green, and lavender, to coordinate with soft pastels used on upholstery fabrics, in wall paint, and on rugs (Figure 7.52).

## ENGLISH LATE NEOCLASSIC: 1810–1830

The Regency style of the Late Neoclassic period in England followed the characteristics of the Empire style that was introduced in France at the turn of the 19th century. In England, this second phase of neoclassicism identified more closely with the classical past, incorporating many of the characteristics found on furniture items excavated from Herculaneum and Pompeii (Figure 7.53). Chairs featured characteristics of the Greek *klismos*, with saber legs and concave crest rails. Some incorporated exaggerated volute arms, rolled backs, and paw feet.

Unlike the French Empire style, the proportions of English Regency–style furnishings appear heavier. Sofas took on the shape reminiscent of the Roman *lectus*, abandoning the compact designs of the camelback or clean geometry of the Hepplewhite and Sheraton styles for shapes (Figure 7.54). High arms in curving, fulcrumlike scrolls met a shorter back, and the larger proportioned sofa rested on sweeping cornucopia shaped legs. The French *recamier*, or daybed, appeared in English households, not confined to the bedroom, but also used in the parlor (Figure 7.55).

The sofa table or library table, a new piece of furniture introduced in the Regency style, was a large, rectangular table with drop leaves positioned at each of the short ends. Usually supported with trestle legs, this table was designed to be placed behind the sofa or to be used as a reading table (Figure 7.56). Another type of new table was a large mahogany pedestal type with a tripod base, with either a circular or rectangular top. This acted as a center table or console table and was often plain and undecorated, giving more attention to the accessories placed on top (Figure 7.57). Accessories included large floral arrangements in vases, candelabrums, and porcelains.

Throughout the 19th century, English design reflected an eclectic synthesis of historical elements. Although neoclassicism was one of the more popular movements of the period, other designers introduced Gothic, Turkish, and Oriental influences into their work. Thomas Hope (1770–1831) was instrumental in presenting a collection of designs based on the assimilation of divergent cultures in his 1807 publication *Household Furniture and Interior Decoration*. Inspired by his grand tour through Europe, Africa, and Asia, and his penchant for collecting ancient antiquities, Hope imitated the styles of ancient Rome. Furniture items featured Roman sphinxes, animal legs with paw feet, cornucopia leg forms, and volutes (Figures 7.58 and 7.59).

FIGURE 7.56 A Regency mahogany sofa table, shown here with dropped leaves, has boxwood and ebony stringing and rosewood crossbanding. The rectangular, hinged top with rounded angles lays above two frieze drawers opposing two dummy drawers raised over the rectangular section supports, which are linked by a stretcher between inlaid saber legs that terminate in brass cups and castors. © Judith Miller/Dorling Kindersley/Lyon and Turnbull Ltd.

FIGURE 7.57 A rosewood center table in the Regency style is inlaid with brass foliate banding, and has a reeded pedestal base with S scroll legs that terminate in brass lion paws set on casters. © Judith Miller/Dorling Kindersley/Wallis and Wallis.

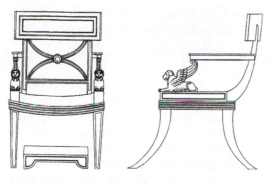

**FIGURE 7.58** This Regency–style chair designed by Thomas Hope and fashioned after the Greek *klismos* chair has a concave crest rail, saber front and back legs, and winged lion-arm supports. Dover Publications, Inc.

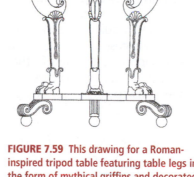

**FIGURE 7.59** This drawing for a Roman-inspired tripod table featuring table legs in the form of mythical griffins and decorated with acanthus leaf and palmette designs was taken from Thomas Hope's *Household Furniture and Interior Decoration*, published in 1807. Dover Publications, Inc.

**FIGURE 7.60** A rare Regency rosewood and ebony console table has gilt accents and sphinx-form legs ending on a plinth footed base. © Judith Miller/Dorling Kindersley/Wallis and Wallis.

Hope's travels and studies are reflected in the engraved plates of furniture, accessories, and architectural details that imitate the qualities and characteristics of each culture. As a practicing designer, Hope's completed works covered Egyptian, Hindu, Roman, Greek, Chinese, and Turkish themes. *Household Furniture and Interior Decoration* became the inspiration for incorporating a sense of exoticism into furniture designs (Figure 7.60). As the century progressed, more attention was given to the

## COMPARISONS    Reemerging Style

History repeats itself in curious ways. The two armchairs featured in Figures 7.61 and 7.62 were designed 200 years apart, yet they share many features. The more obvious are the leg forms, scrolled armrests, and shaped backs, but they share an "attitude," too. By observation alone, the two chairs appear very similar. However, researching into their histories reveals the differences between the cultural attitudes of the people who used them.

The chair in Figure 7.61 dates from the late 18th century and captures the renewed interest in ancient Roman culture brought on by the artifacts removed from excavations at Pompeii and Herculaneum. The saber back legs, and fluted and tapering front legs emulate furniture designs from this ancient Roman period. Exaggerated scrolls on the chair's arms were inventions of the 18th-century designer, who was inspired by the volute capitals seen on Roman buildings. An upholstered seat replaced the loose cushions that would have been used by the Romans and is a testament to advances in design for comfort. Although the back lacks upholstery, the slight curvature of the crest rail offers some comfort. However, the social attitudes of the time were that ladies and gentlemen needed to keep their heads high and backs straight when seated.

The Bodleian chair (Figure 7.62), designed by Robert A. M. Stern during the last decades of the 20th century, features similar leg forms, scrolled arms, and a shaped back, but its design captures the idealistic notion of the Postmodern movement popular at the *fin de siècle*. Designers of the Postmodern movement sought to abandon the Modernistic style set by the International style and the

Bauhaus from the 1920s, and turned toward the classical past in fresh and inspiring ways. Stern's chair reflects this shift toward modern design with its beautifully inspired Late Neoclassic features. The seat is upholstered in a thick cushion, and the ergonomically shaped back is padded, too. Armrests incorporate soft curves, offering a more casual pose. During the 20th century, social attitudes were more relaxed and less formal; no longer were people required to sit upright in perfectly stiff postures to impress upon their peers that they were well-heeled and refined individuals.

**FIGURE 7.61** This English Regency–style armchair with curved and fluted legs features elaborate volute, scrolled arms. The shape of the back, with its slightly concave crest rail, offers comfort without padding or upholstery. © Judith Miller/Dorling Kindersley/Gorringes.

**FIGURE 7.62** This chair, designed by Robert A. M. Stern during the late 20th century, was inspired by the late Neoclassic Regency style Bodleian chair designed by Robert A. M. Stern for HBF, 1989. Courtesy HBF.

creative reinterpretation of the past rather than its duplication, which led to the numerous revivalist styles popular throughout most of the Victorian era.

## AMERICAN FEDERAL: 1785–1820

As an independent nation under the newly established United States of America, Americans were eager to return to the more prosperous days before the Revolutionary War. Although there was a short period of economic depression, the young country recovered quickly, resuming its shipping industries along the eastern seaboard. With an increase in commerce, more people came to the United States in search of greater opportunities and fortunes. With this proliferation of wealth, homes built during the Federal period were grander than those built before the war, and more money was spent on furnishing the "public" rooms of the house. The entry hall, sitting room, and dining room were outfitted with the latest styles of furniture and accessories, and featured the first examples of wall-to-wall carpeting.

The preeminence of the Neoclassic period reached the colonies soon after the end of the American Revolution. At this time, importing furniture items made by English cabinetmakers was considered a violation of national pride, so American furniture makers captured the simplicity of Neoclassic styling illustrated in Hepplewhite's *Guide* and Sheraton's *Drawing Book* into graceful, well-proportioned chairs, settees, and case goods (Figures 7.63 and 7.64). The new style exemplified the confidence of the new republic as patriotic themes replaced more traditional ones; the American eagle appeared frequently as a decorative motif.

In addition to settees, the parlor inside the American colonial homes of the Federal period included a chair similar to the upholstered armchair seen in the English Neoclassic interior (Figure 7.65). Sturdy in its construction, square, tapered legs usually reinforced with stretchers supported a tall upholstered back and seat. The term "lolling" was given to the chair in the same context as today's easy chair; it induced relaxation. Throughout the centuries, a more popular name was used to identify this 18th-century chair, called the "Martha Washington."

One of the leading craftsmen of fine carvings for furnishings and interior millwork during the American Federal period was Samuel McIntire from Salem, Massachusetts. An architect known for his exquisite carving and exceptional skill, McIntire produced carvings for bedsteads and case goods, balustrades, mantels, and cornices for windows and doors in some of the finest homes in Salem and Boston.

Just as Windsor–style furniture satisfied the needs of the less affluent with quality furnishings at affordable prices, Lambert Hitchcock (1795–1852) produced some of the finest examples of American country chairs from his factory in Connecticut. Known as the Hitchcock chair, distinctive Sheraton styling was combined with turned legs and stretchers, a rush seat, and beautifully stenciled fruits and flowers (Figure 7.66). Widely imitated, the chair was a popular favorite seen in many homes throughout New England. The rocking chair was highly favored by the Americans, and many chairs were retrofitted with skates or rockers attached to the ends of leg forms to achieve this (Figure 7.67).

FIGURE 7.63 A pair of American Federal–style side chairs with shield backs in the manner of the English Hepplewhite designs was carved by Samuel McIntire. © Judith Miller/Dorling Kindersley/Freeman's.

FIGURE 7.64 An American Federal–style sofa with a scrolled and carved crest rail and shaped arms features turned and reeded front legs with saber back legs. © Judith Miller/Dorling Kindersley/Freeman's.

FIGURE 7.65 Furniture from the American Federal period resembles the Hepplewhite and Sheraton styles popular in England during the Early Neoclassic period. This particular style of upholstered armchair became known as the "Martha Washington" chair in America. © Judith Miller/Dorling Kindersley/Lyon and Turnbull, Ltd.

**FIGURE 7.66** Made during the early 19th century, the rounded crest rail on this example is consistent with early examples of Hitchcock–style chairs made by the Connecticut chair maker. This chair has decorative gold stenciling in grape and leaf motifs on the back slat, and a rush seat. © Judith Miller/Dorling Kindersley/Wallis and Wallis.

**FIGURE 7.67** An early 19th-century New England painted, maple wood, comb-back low rockingchair with a four-rod back surmounted by a similar headrest, down-swept arms, shaped slab seat, turned splayed legs, original floral decoration, and line work on a black background. © Judith Miller/ Dorling Kindersley/Sloans and Kenyon.

**FIGURE 7.68** A Federal–style tilt-top candle stand from Pennsylvania features a scratch-carved eagle and shield holding olive branches and arrows representative of the new symbol for the United States of America. The stand dates from around 1790. Judith Miller/Dorling Kindersley/Pook and Pook.

**FIGURE 7.69** An American Federal–style secretary from New England, made in three parts, features brass eagle and urn finial designs. © Judith Miller/Dorling Kindersley/Pook and Pook.

Case goods such as secretaries, sideboards, and cabinets featured the designs of their English counterparts in the Hepplewhite and Sheraton styles; however, these units often incorporated motifs with special meaning for America. The eagle became the national symbol for the new United States of America, and this motif was featured on furnishings as inlay, scratch carvings, or finials (Figures 7.68 and 7.69).

Sideboards became popular in American households because Federal–style homes were designed with a formal room for dining. Used as a server during the meal, the sideboard was designed with drawers and cabinets for storage of plates, cutlery, and linens (Figure 7.70). The furniture inside the dining room was intended to impress guests along with the interior design of the room (Figure 7.71).

**FIGURE 7.70** This New York Federal–style figured mahogany demi-lune sideboard with a veneered top over two graduated drawers is flanked by cabinet doors and rests on tapered legs that end on spade feet. It dates from circa 1800. © Judith Miller/Dorling Kindersley/Freeman's.

**FIGURE 7.71** A dining room designed by Charles Bullfinch of Boston for the Harrison Gray Otis House in 1796. © Kevin Fleming/CORBIS.

**FIGURE 7.72** An American Empire mahogany foot stool from Boston has a rectangular upholstered top raised on curule legs joined by a vase-and-ring-turned stretcher, and dates from circa 1830. © Judith Miller/Dorling Kindersley/Sloan's.

**FIGURE 7.73** An early 19th-century American Empire carved mahogany and upholstered settee features a scrolled backrest and arms, with bracketed lion-paw feet. The pieced is carved profusely with cornucopia and acanthus foliage. © Judith Miller/Dorling Kindersley/Sloan's.

**FIGURE 7.74** This American Empire center table has a rope-carved table edge that rests on a floral-carved and gilded pedestal base on a tripod support with heavy, carved paw feet. Judith Miller/Dorling Kindersley/Freeman's.

**FIGURE 7.75** An American Empire–style carved walnut library table, has a rectangular top, swell frieze with opposing drawers, columnar legs, and a platform stretcher. © Judith Miller/Dorling Kindersley/Sloans and Kenyon.

## AMERICAN EMPIRE: 1810–1830

The American Federal style and the American Empire style overlapped significantly because one style simply did not replace the other. The renewed interest in classical designs was reflected in interior details seen as dentil friezes below crown moldings, triangular-shaped lintels over doors and windows, furniture that incorporated X-form supports, and chairs that had a gentle roll to the back in their designs (Figure 7.72). Regal colors of blue, green, crimson, and gold, dominated interior schemes, enhancing the coloring of mahogany furniture. Scenic wallpapers featured landscapes of foreign countrysides and were often placed on walls in the entry hall or parlor for guests to appreciate. Carpet designs and ceiling medallions featured paterae, and it is during this time that carpet began to be installed wall to wall.

The American Empire style of furniture and design emerged through the work of New York cabinetmaker, Duncan Phyfe, and the Frenchman Charles-Honoré Lannuier. Phyfe immigrated to America and set up a cabinet making shop in lower Manhattan in 1791 and Lannuier came to New York in 1803 and worked as a cabinetmaker until his death in 1819. These two cabinetmakers combined English Sheraton–influenced designs with French Empire styling to form the new style which was well received by those with upper status. American Empire furnishings took on a distinctive Grecian appearance as Federal–style homes were replaced by the emerging Greek Revival style (Figure 7.73).

Center tables, ladies' worktables, along with chest of drawers, writing cabinets, and sideboards featured heavy paw feet and gilt accents in the French manner (Figure 7.74). Columns, term figures, and sphinx forms were incorporated as leg forms, and corner details were made clearer through gilt brass accents (Figure 7.75). The fashionable parlor, the equivalent of today's living room, showed off these fine furnishings to guests as confirmation of the owner's wealth and status.

## BIEDERMEIER

The Biedermeier style of furniture, popularized in Austria and Germany, offered middle-class consumers the form and style of French Empire, but it lacked the handmade quality found in fine cabinetmaking (Figure 7.76 and 7.77). Based on a popular cartoon character printed in German newspapers, the word itself as translated into English is descriptive enough: *bieder*, meaning commonplace or plain, attached to the surname, *meier*. Mr. Biedermeier represented all that was uncouth about this emerging middle-class gentleman; he was uncultured, brash, and lacked good taste. The furniture was introduced to the market through the factory and workshop of Josef Danhauser (1780–1829). Born in Vienna and trained as a painter, in 1807 Danhauser began producing home accessory items and, by 1814, had expanded the workshop to produce furniture. His workshop offered customers an array of

**FIGURE 7.76** This Biedermeier chair features a shaped crest rail back with square, tapered legs. © Prisma Bildagentur AG/Alamy.

**FIGURE 7.77** This Biedermeier mahogany loveseat with a solid rectangular form has scrolled arms, brass molded panels and fan spandrels on the back and sides, arms with rosette terminals and mahogany facings, and a seat rail with brass mounts, all on massive gilt and verdigris ball-and-claw front feet with drapery brackets. © Judith Miller/Dorling Kindersley/Lyon and Turnbull, Ltd.

carpets, glassware, and textiles for the beautification of their homes. The Biedermeier style appealed to the urbane, working middle class striving to keep up appearances.

This style of interior decoration and furniture reflected an interest in French Empire and English Late Neoclassic styling; however, it was designed to be practical and functional in smaller interiors (Figure 7.78). Detailed ornamentation was often sacrificed for painted designs and applied carvings, whereas local woods—mainly maple, birch, and fruitwoods such as pear and cherry—were used during the construction processes. Unlike the Late Neoclassic period, finer woods were seldom used for furniture. Instead, pear wood was stained black to imitate ebony, and cherry and maple replaced mahogany and satinwood, respectively.

The construction reflected the skill of the local craftsmen. Workers employed in the factories and workshops were not cabinetmakers, but semiskilled craftsmen who learned how to work with faster production methods. Standardized patterns for chair, cabinet, settee, and table designs were used, and items were often held together with glue instead of traditional joinery. Biedermeier furnishings personified the middle-class bourgeois gentleman's good taste; they were practical, comfortable, and inexpensive. As the style gained in popularity, finer examples of Biedermeier furniture with excellent quality, materials, and craftsmanship were made for wealthier clients. Most are of Russian, French, Scandinavian, or American origin.

Although most embraced these cheap imitations, a small circle of elitists reviled the shoddy, machine-produced goods. In England, social critic John Ruskin (1819–1900) feared that the machine took away the dignity of the artisan. His concerns were shared by many others during the 19th century, and the debate between handiwork and machine fabrication would not be resolved until the next century.

FIGURE 7.78 A study with Biedermeier furnishings that emphasize Neoclassical styling. © Imagno/Getty Images.

# Accessories

## POTTERY

The discovery of kaolin in 1768 near Limoges, France, prompted new factories to be built to make fine porcelain. By 1774, factories in Limoges were supplementing the output from the royal porcelain factory in Sèvres. Because of its ties to the French monarchy, the porcelain factory at Sèvres was on the verge of bankruptcy during the French Revolution. After Napoleon became emperor of France, the revitalized factory began creating pieces in the new Empire style (Figure 7.79). Included in Sheraton's *The Cabinet Maker and Upholsterer's Drawing Book* were numerous furniture items incorporating porcelain plaques into English designs. This fashion had been popular in France since the early Rococo period, but it was not adopted by the English until the success of Wedgwood.

Wedgwood's factory was known during the late 18th-century for producing fine jasperware pottery that he modeled after ancient Roman cameo designs. As mentioned earlier, classical figures in white relief appear over a soft blue background of unglazed ceramic (Figure 7.80). The much-recognized blue jasperware was most common, but green, black, and lilac

FIGURE 7.79 This two-handled Sèvres porcelain vase painted with landscape designs dates from 1793 and features extensive gilding. It reflects aristocratic taste and prosperity. © Judith Miller/Dorling Kindersley/T.C.S. Brooke.

FIGURE 7.80 Josiah Wedgwood was known during the late 18th century for the fine jasperware pottery creations he modeled after ancient Roman cameo designs. This rare Wedgwood solid-blue jasperware vase has a lift-out lid with three laurel leaf tulip holders. The white classical figures represent Apollo and the nine Muses standing above a band of trophy and lyre forms. The vase dates from between 1785 and 1795. © Judith Miller/Dorling Kindersley/Woolley and Wallis.

**FIGURE 7.81** This gilt and enamel tole box features a transfer pattern of figures in an 18th-century pastoral setting. © Judith Miller/ Dorling Kindersley/Gorringes.

**FIGURE 7.82** A pair of early 19th-century mahogany knife boxes with boxwood stringing, each with flattened bowfront and hinged, sloping lid enclosing a fitted interior. © Judith Miller/Dorling Kindersley/Lyon and Turnbull, Ltd.

backgrounds also appeared on Wedgwood pottery to coordinate with Neoclassic interior color schemes (Figure 7.52).

A porcelain factory in Derby, England, produced high-quality bone chinaware that so impressed King George III that the factory earned the Crown's endorsement. Royal Crown Derby was the only British factory authorized to use the insignia of the royal crown in its hallmark strike. In 1769, the factory in Derby acquired molds from a factory in Chelsea, and Derby–Chelsea porcelains were produced until 1784. The factory's hard-paste and soft-paste porcelain figurines, candlesticks, and dinnerware featured polychrome details with accents in 22-karat gold to compete with Sèvres porcelain.

Creamware, an opaque white glaze applied over earthenware, gave the appearance of fine porcelain, although it lacked the translucency. Middle-class households found both creamware and ironstone less costly substitutes for porcelain and bone china. Most popular was transferware, a type of creamware, which was made in a factory in Staffordshire, England. Engraved copper plates were used to transfer intricately detailed designs onto plates, cups, saucers, and vases. An engraved copper plate coated with a special ink was printed onto a thin sheet of paper. The paper was used to transfer the pattern onto the ceramic, which was then glazed and fired at low temperatures. Transferware decorated in bright blues closely resembled porcelains imported from China. Although blue was the most popular color of transferware, red on white, brown on white, and black on white were also featured (Figure 6.79). "Flow blue" is the name given to ironstone transferware that has a blurred pattern caused by a bleeding of the ink.

## DECORATIVE BOXES

Small decorative boxes made from a variety of materials were designed to contain a range of domestic and personal items including snuff, tea, wine, and face powder. Boxes in all shapes, colors, and sizes adorned tabletops, sideboards, and dressing tables, and were designed to coordinate with other interior accessories. Enameled boxes and glassware were painted to look like fine porcelain for less affluent buyers, whereas boxes made from silver, tortoiseshell, and porcelain appealed to the wealthy (Figure 7.81). Separate rooms designated just for dining were developed during the last quarter of the 18th century, and locking knife boxes and tea caddies made from mahogany or rosewood matched the suites of dining room furniture (Figure 7.82).

Inlaid boxes featured fine marquetry work in wood, shell, and *piqué*, which was inlaid silver or gold into either a tortoiseshell or ivory background. Tortoiseshell was known for its malleability and rich reddish brown color with dark veining. Fine materials such as tortoiseshell and ivory were popular among the more elite classes who could afford such luxurious items (Figure 7.83). Ivory boxes made from the bone or tusk of animals were increasing in popularity because of a burgeoning whaling industry that developed during the early 19th century. *Scrimshaw*, made from whale ivory, became fashionable in America especially. Today, it is illegal to use ivory and tortoiseshell because the animals are now protected as endangered species.

## GLASS

Glass production methods improved during the 18th century with new steam-powered equipment, high-temperature furnaces, and mechanized processes. In addition to these cost-saving production methods, wheel-cut and engraved designs and, later, press-molded glass objects made glass more affordable. The clarity and durability of the glass determined its quality, and owning lead crystal indicated

**FIGURE 7.83** This ivory box from 1820 includes a portrait of the prince regent, son of George III of England. © Judith Miller/Dorling Kindersley/Rogers de Rin.

**FIGURE 7.84** These French Empire glass vases from the early 19th century are decorated with deep-cut diamond shapes and accented with gilt palmette borders. © Judith Miller/Dorling Kindersley/Sloan's.

wealth (Figure 7.84). Colored glass came into fashion by early1800 to try to compete with porcelain accessories that currently dominated the market. In fact, opaque white glass was often painted with designs imitating those found on fine porcelains. Cobalt blue glass was a featured product of glass factories in Bristol, England. The factory, first established during the 17th century, began producing blue glass in 1780 for affluent patrons. The city became known for producing other colors such as green and purple, and exporting wares throughout Europe and the Americas.

## MIRRORS

Large sheets of glass suitable for making mirrors were made by pouring molten glass onto a frame-fitted table. The sheets were then cooled and polished by hand to give them an even surface. Wall-hung or freestanding mirrors could now be made from one sheet of glass instead of several smaller ones. Further enhancements occurred in 1835 when a German chemist developed the process of using silver to coat a plate of glass in less than a minute, replacing the formerly toxic practice of coating the glass with mercury and tin. Coating the glass with silver produced a mirror with more reflective clarity. Frames made to hold the larger panels of glass were designed to match current Neoclassic fashions. Moreover, with larger plates of glass, a new floor standing mirror called a *cheval* was introduced (Figure 7.85). The cheval mirror was hinged on a frame and could be tilted to get a better view. These mirrors were popularly used in bedrooms and dressing rooms. Decorative mirrors featured a new technique called "reverse painting," in which colorful scenes painted on the reverse side of the glass gave a glossy appearance from the front face of the mirror (Figure 7.86).

## LIGHTING

In 1780, Aimé Argand (1750/55–1803) patented a new type of oil lamp that burned more efficiently and provided stronger lighting (Figure 7.87). The lamp relied on a glass tube or shade that helped direct airflow to keep the wick burning evenly. These lamps were more expensive than other types, and were out of the financial reach of the middle-class consumer. As before, the style of candleholders followed the leading interior fashions of the period (Figure 7.88), and crystallized whale oil substituted for tallow in the making of candles. Candlepower was still prevalent in middle-class households until the invention of kerosene lamps during the mid 19th century.

## METALWORKING

During the Neoclassic period, silversmiths worked the metal in a variety of ways to create an assortment of tableware and decorative accessories for upper-class clients. The quality of silver was determined by its purity, with fine silver being 95.84 percent pure, and sterling silver being made of 92.5 percent silver and 7.5 percent copper. When Thomas Bolsover of Sheffield, England, tried to repair the handle of a knife made from copper and silver, he noticed that the two metals fused when heated. His discovery during the early 1740s led to further experimentation of fusing silver sheets over copper sheets to produce silver plate. The invention of silver plate allowed middle-class households to own tea and coffee service, tableware, and ornamental boxes made with the same designs and in the same styles as those made

FIGURE 7.85 This large George III–style cheval mirror is held in a baluster-shaped frame.
© Judith Miller/Dorling Kindersley/Lyon and Turnbull Ltd.

FIGURE 7.86 This Empire–style mahogany looking glass features a reverse-painted upper panel that features three pheasants.
© Judith Miller/Dorling Kindersley/Freeman's.

FIGURE 7.87 An oil lamp invented in 1784 by Aimé Argand. The lamp is made with a hollow, circular wick; glass cover; and an oil tank that produced a brighter flame, bringing more efficient lighting to interiors. Dave King © Dorling Kindersley, Courtesy of The Science Museum, London.

from sterling. Over time, silver plate wears off edges and detailed relief patterns, revealing the copper-formed body.

Before the American Revolution, most silver work made in the colonies came from melted coins to avoid paying a tax to the British Crown. Coin silver is an alloy of 90 percent silver and 10 percent copper. The colonial silversmith Paul Revere, who gained notoriety for his infamous participation in the American Revolution, is equally known for his fine metalwork. Learning the craft from his father, the younger Revere made objects in fine silver for wealthy Bostonians. After the war, Revere began to design a variety of objects priced for the middle-class market. In 1801, he established Revere Copper Products, a company still in business today (Figure 7.89).

## CLOCKS

In 1783, Benjamin Hanks (1755–1824) patented a self-winding clock. Until this time, clocks could run for only eight days at a time before they needed rewinding. The clock Thomas Jefferson owned at Monticello operated with two 18-pound weights. Holes had to be cut into the floor for the weights to drop into the cellar to keep it running for a week at a time. Alarm clocks set to chime at predetermined times appeared during the 18th century; in fact, Napoleon used one at Malmaison. Like all clocks made throughout the periods, clockmakers made the inner workings and cabinetmakers designed cases to coordinate with the popular styles of the period. Commemorative clocks were made for the American market by French clockmaker Jean Baptise Dubac after the French aided the colonists in the Revolutionary War (Figure 7.90). Mantel clocks and wall-hung bracket clocks were designed to reflect the character of Neoclassic interiors.

## TEXTILES

The popularity of imported printed cottons from India led to an increased production of European cottons during the second half of the 18th century. *Toile de Jouy* is a type of printed cotton with a distinctive pattern imitating the scenes found on popular transferware china of the period. The origin of the design came from a small town in France, Jouy en Josas—hence, the French word *toile* means "cloth." The first printed cottons from this factory date to 1760 and were made using woodblocks. Later, copper plates and then copper cylinders were used to transfer the patterns to the cloth. Pastoral scenes were etched onto the copper, then inked and printed onto rolls of cotton. Colors included black on white, blue on white, and red on white, although greens and dark purple were also in fashion (Figure 7.91). These toile fabrics dominated clothing styles, and the fabric was used for upholstery, drapes, and bedding.

Once associated with great wealth, needlework pictures became increasingly popular. These embroideries were framed as artwork in homes. The education of young

girls included mastering the skill of needlework, and the small pieces of cloth they embroidered showed the dexterity of their hands. These practice pieces, called "samplers," showed a variety of stitching techniques applied to ornamental motifs, the alphabet, and numbers (Figure 7.92). Needlework embroideries of the early 19th century became more pictorial, often imitating scenes from fine paintings.

In 1801, Joseph Marie Jacquard (1752–1834) made improvements to the first automated loom (developed in 1745). His invention used a punch card system of weaving to bring speed and consistency to the weaving process, and fabric made this way was known as *jacquard* (Figure 7.93). As mechanization replaced labor-intensive hand weaving, owning well-designed quality textiles was no longer reserved for the elite. Mechanization of the textile industry also affected the making of carpets. The former method of designing a pattern or preparing a cartoon for the weavers to follow was replaced by the jacquard punch card mechanized loom. *Moquette* carpeting was made by sewing woven strips of carpet together in large enough pieces to cover the entire floor surface of a room (Figure 7.94). This form of wall-to-wall carpeting was introduced during the late 18th century, although only the wealthy could afford it.

FIGURE 7.91 This *toile de Jouy* textile dating from circa 1804 features scenes from the story of *Paul et Virginie*, a popular novel published in 1787. © Judith Miller/Dorling Kindersley/Sara Covelli.

FIGURE 7.92 This silk-on-linen sampler is decorated with the alphabet, potted flowers, and birds. It was framed as artwork to display the skill of its embroiderer. © Judith Miller/Dorling Kindersley/Wallis and Wallis.

FIGURE 7.93 This Jacquard-weave bed coverlet designed by Archibald Davidson from the Ithaca Carpet Factory in New York features a field of flowers bordered by deer and trees, American eagles, and buildings. The coverlet dates from 1840. © Judith Miller/Dorling Kindersley/Sloan's.

FIGURE 7.94 This watercolor painting from 1815 depicts two women sitting at a table in a room with wall-to-wall carpeting. Fenimore Art Museum, Cooperstown, New York. Photograph by Richard Walker.

## WALLPAPER

French printer Christophe-Philippe Oberkampf (1738–1815), had produced hand-blocked *toile de Jouy* fabrics as early as 1760. He used his knowledge of printing processes to invent a wallpaper printing machine in 1785. Using cylindrical, engraved copper plates, he printed patterns on continuous rolls of fabric and paper, which was less expensive than hand blocking. Winning the Legion of Honor by Napoleon, Oberkampf's technique enabled upper-middle-class households to afford to wallpaper their homes. Although machine-printed papers were available, hand-blocked papers were still popular among the wealthy. Scenic papers came into fashion during the late Neoclassic period in America, France, and England (Figure 7.95). These hand-printed papers were more expensive than machine-printed papers and were featured in the public areas of houses, such as the front entry hall and sitting room, to impress guests.

FIGURE 7.95 This formal parlor from a Richmond, Virginia, house built in 1810 includes scenic wallpaper imported from France, unassuming draperies, a large carpet, and furniture by Duncan Phyfe and Charles-Honore Lannuier (1779–1819). The Metropolitan Museum of Art, New York, NY U.S.A. Image copyright © The Metropolitan Museum of Art. Image source: Art Resource, NY.

# The Nineteenth Century

## The Industrial Period

At the close of the 18th century, western culture faced enormous change as the Industrial Revolution replaced political revolution, giving power to those capitalizing on manufacturing. Industrialization brought wealth to inventive entrepreneurs who earned substantial profits off the mechanization and distribution of consumer products. The new aristocrats of the Industrial Age were the self-made millionaires such as Cornelius Vanderbilt (1794–1877), who made his fortune in shipping and railroads, and Andrew Carnegie (1835–1919), who supplied the steel needed for machinery, buildings, bridges.

Industrialization displaced tenant farmers as urbanism encroached on agrarian society. People left the hard labor of the fields to work in factories, running machinery for mostly low wages. Moreover, industrialization brought new employment opportunities to educated middle-class workers who could process paperwork in the factories, fill customer orders, direct the shipment of merchandise, and supervise workers. These white-collar, middle-class managers sought a better standard of living for their families. The urban environment changed as more people left farms and moved to industrial cities. Houses built in the city or near factories replaced country villas, offering middle-class families comfortable homes appropriately scaled to fit on narrow plots of land. Because of industrialization, lower cost machine-made goods had appealed to these new white-collar working-class people who wanted nice things for their homes.

## Architecture

The renewed interest in classicism brought on by the rediscovery and excavations of Pompeii and Herculaneum resulted in inventive and eclectic interpretations of the past, as discussed in Chapter 7. In France and England, the Late Neoclassic period included many examples of Greek Revival–style buildings. Likewise, the influence of Thomas Jefferson in creating a national style of architecture had brought the Greek Revival style to the forefront of American design. The style was chosen to represent the new democracy in the design and construction of the many government buildings in the nation's capital, Washington, DC.

The White House was first built in 1792 as a Federal-style home and featured a low roof with a balustrade. When Jefferson became the third president in 1801, he hired Benjamin Henry Latrobe (1764–1820) to remodel the house into the Greek Revival style (Figure 8.1). The north facade reflects this element, with its central portico supported by four ionic columns and a dentil-bordered triangular pediment. The Greek Revival architectural style remained popular in America from the last

FIGURE 8.1 The neoclassical Federal–style home built for presidents of the United States was updated in 1801 in the Greek Revival style. © Albert de Bruijn/Shutterstock

FIGURE 8.2 A rare, early-19th-century trade armchair from Canton, China, is made of Asian hardwood with a caned seat and incorporates Neoclassic designs in the Greek style.
© Judith Miller/Dorling Kindersley/Wallis and Wallis

FIGURE 8.3 A 19th-century rosewood whatnot with tapering square base and brass inlay on the sides features lyre-form upper supports. © Judith Miller/Dorling Kindersley/ Lyon and Turnbull Ltd.

quarter of the 18th century until the 1830s. Interior design incorporated ionic columns, niches became built-in bookcases, and furniture captured the essence of ancient Greece, although in interesting new ways (Figures 8.2 and 8.3).

Diversity and eclecticism in architecture developed as the mood shifted toward a nostalgic reinterpretation of traditional styles. Architectural design projects completed throughout the century produced a wide range of revivalist styles synthesizing key elements of the past—Greek, Gothic, Italianate, Elizabethan, and Romanesque influences, although redesigned for the modern era. Architects and designers of the early 19th century made many visual references to the past in an attempt to create new buildings that looked "old," or as if they were from faraway places.

Between 1815 and 1823, English architect John Nash (1752–1835) expanded the Royal Pavilion in Brighton for King George IV (r. 1820–1830). Nash placed an iron structural framework over the existing classically styled palace to create a pavilion capturing the essence of the Indian Taj Mahal (Figure 8.4). The Pavilion's Hindu-Islamic design reflected the romanticism of 19th-century eclecticism. The dining room had a ceiling designed with a silver dragon holding an oversized chandelier above the dining table set with 20 Regency–style side chairs (Figure 8.5). The proportions of the room are so immense, the furniture appears dwarfed and out of scale. Hand-painted wallpaper show scenes from

FIGURE 8.5 The banquet room in the Royal Pavilion in Brighton features a silver dragon holding an immense chandelier above a long dinner table with Regency–style chairs. Hand-painted wallpaper reveals Indian–inspired landscape designs. © Jim Holden/Alamy

FIGURE 8.4 The Royal Pavilion in Brighton, England, by John Nash, features exotic Oriental designs from India. © stocker1970/Shutterstock

**FIGURE 8.6** This Regency–style bamboo chair featuring Chinese fret motifs was made for the Royal Pavilion in Brighton.
© Judith Miller/ Dorling Kindersley/ Woolley and Wallis

**FIGURE 8.7** This desk in the Moorish style features fretwork motifs and foliate marquetry designs.
© Judith Miller/Dorling Kindersley/Lyon and Turnbull Ltd.

an India–inspired landscape, with Figures wearing exotic clothing. In storybook fashion, the interior furnishings featured Oriental-inspired designs, including a blending of Indian and Chinese motifs, and designs reminiscent of Chinese Chippendale (Figures 8.6 and 8.7).

In 1749, Horace Walpole (1717–1797) began construction on his country villa designed to resemble a medieval castle. At that time, architects thought the Gothic style was most suitable for the English landscape. During the next few decades, work at Strawberry Hill outside London featured a collection of buildings in the Gothic style (Figure 8.8). Furthermore, Chippendale's *Director*, published in 1754, included many Gothic–inspired furnishings and architectural details, documenting England's growing interest in the style. The interiors at Strawberry Hill captured the essence of Gothic design with plentiful tracery, pargework ceilings, and pointed, arched doorways and windows (Figure 8.9).

The rebuilding of the Houses of Parliament in England by Augustus Welby Pugin (1812–1852) and Sir Charles Barry (1795–1860) in 1835 further perpetuated the interest in Gothic styling (Fig. 8–10). Rebuilding the Houses of Parliament in the Gothic style seemed appropriate because they were situated next to the medieval cathedral of Westminster Abbey. The monumental structure blends into the context of the site with its tall spires, Gothic arches, and stained glass windows. The building of the Houses of Parliament perpetuated a formal, Gothic Revival style that remained popular through the 1840s (Figure 8.11).

The Victorian period, named after the 64-year reign of Queen Victoria (r. 1837–1901), is noted for its literal references to historical styles and an emphasis on superfluous decoration. In England and America, Victorian–period houses were designed in the Gothic, Italianate, Second Empire, and Queen Anne styles that followed the current fashions for revivalist designs, although the prototypical Queen Anne home comes to mind when we think of the Victorian style because of its fairy

**FIGURE 8.8** The buildings comprising Strawberry Hill in Middlesex, London, built from 1749–1777 attest to the renewed interest in medieval Gothic styling. akg/Bildarchiv Monheim/Newscom

**FIGURE 8.9** A room in Strawberry Hill is decorated with wallpaper, pargework, and Gothic–inspired woodwork. View of the Holbein Chamber (photo), English School, (18th century)/Strawberry Hill, Middlesex, UK/The Bridgeman Art Library International

**FIGURE 8.10** The Houses of Parliament, with their prominent clock tower, rise above the Thames river in London. Begun in 1835 by Pugin and Barry, the complex perpetuated the renewed interest in the High Gothic style. © S.Borisov/Shutterstock

tale turrets and painted molding designs. Italianate and Second Empire styles blended the Italian and French Renaissance periods with emphasis on mansard rooflines, exaggerated modillions, and the occasional monumental staircase to the front entry (Figure 8.12). Interiors were a mix of classical moldings made of plaster, with elaborate ceiling medallions and Renaissance-inspired furnishings (Figures 8.13–8.15).

In America, Andrew Jackson Downing (1815–1852) published two pattern books: *Victorian Cottage Residences* in 1842 and *The Architecture of Country Houses* in 1850. His books were instrumental in establishing the Gothic Revival style in America. Downing's books featured small cottages designed for the middle class in a style known as *Carpenter Gothic*. The houses were made from wood, not stone or brick like those in England, and were decorated with intricate millwork designs, charmingly called *gingerbread* (Figure 8.16). These smaller homes

**FIGURE 8.11** A 19th-century Gothic interior setting features ornate-style chairs set against richly patterned drapery and carpet. Gothic Revival styling emerged as an attempt to restore the handicraft of the medieval craftsman, and established the basis for William Morris and the Arts and Crafts movement.
Michael Crockett © Dorling Kindersley

**FIGURE 8.12** An Italianate–style home features a prominent tower room, quoins, and classical moldings. © Lisa Eastman/Shutterstock

**FIGURE 8.13** The grand ballroom of the Victorian home Nottoway in southern Louisiana features ornate plaster ceiling moldings and a classically carved marble fireplace mantel. © Corbis Flirt/Alamy

**FIGURE 8.14** A pair of armchairs in the Renaissance Revival style has carved walnut frames with iron head terminal arms and dolphin feet with acanthus carvings. It dates from the early 20th century. © Judith Miller/ Dorling Kindersley/Sloans & Kenyon

**FIGURE 8.15** A Victorian–period walnut and mahogany pier cabinet inlaid with Prince of Wales plumes features term figure side posts in the Elizabethan Revival style.
© Judith Miller/Dorling Kindersley/Gorringes

**FIGURE 8.16** A Carpenter Gothic–style home features a fancy millwork porch and a gabled roof design lined with scalloped bargeboard. © Tom Oliveira/Shutterstock

**FIGURE 8.17** A carved and turned chair in the Gothic Revival style from New York dates from circa 1850. © Judith Miller/Dorling Kindersley/Sloans & Kenyon

**FIGURE 8.18** This Victorian Queen Anne–style house features colorful paint combinations in contrasting colors that accent decorative bargeboard detailing. © Harris Shiffman/Shutterstock

**FIGURE 8.19** This Victorian–period room features dark-green walls, heavy velvet drapes, and a multipatterned carpet and table cover surrounded by furniture of the same period. Doug Traverso © Dorling Kindersley

had minimal interior details compared with the larger-scale Queen Anne–style homes, but they featured tracerylike carvings around fireplace mantels and built-in bookcases. Furnishings reflected more restrained, Gothic influences, with furniture scaled appropriately to fit into small rooms (Figure 8.17).

The quaint designs of Downing's cottages inspired the later Queen Anne homes of the American Victorian period (Figure 8.18). These Queen Anne designs emulated the fancy millwork seen on Carpenter Gothic houses on the eaves, porch, and door frames. In fairy-talelike fashion, these homes sported at least one large turret, a throwback to medieval castles. Paint combinations pushed the visual senses with their bright and contrasting colors accentuating millwork details like icing on a wedding cake. Victorian architecture and its coordinated interior design emphasized the ornamental details on virtually every surface plane. The fancy exterior millwork on Queen Anne–style houses was repeated on the interior hallways, stairwells, and door casements.

The Victorian interior was filled with superfluous ornament. Textiles, wallpapers, carpets, and table coverings with intricate floral patterns created a sense of excitement within dark and dramatic architectural interiors (Figure 8.19). Heavily draped windows concealed the inner sanctum of the home from the outside, offering the inhabitant an escape from the pressures of living in an industrialized world.

Influenced by both the Arts and Crafts movement led by William Morris (1834–1896) and the Aesthetic movement, shingle-style homes were introduced to England and America during the last decades of the 19th century. These homes were large—often two and three stories tall—and featured eyebrow dormers on multiple-gabled roofs (Figure 8.20). Shingle-style homes made rich use of simple, organic materials in design and construction, featuring wood-shake exterior cladding and wood wainscoting, moldings, and flooring throughout the interiors. Interior furnishings maintained the characteristics of the Aesthetic movement, imitating what Morris and Philip Webb (1831–1915) had designed for Red House in Sussex, England—sparse furnishings, wallpapers, and stenciling featuring bird and animal motifs; and Japanese–inspired lacquered furniture (Figure 8.21). The Aesthetic movement focused on the theory of "art for art's sake,"

**FIGURE 8.20** A shingle-style home (also called "stick-style") from the last decades of the 19th century incorporates natural materials such as wood shakes made popular by the Arts and Crafts movement. Treena M. Crochet

**FIGURE 8.21**  William Morris designed this dining room in 1867. It captures the characteristics of the Aesthetic movement in its sparse furnishings, Japanese–inspired wall coverings, and painted wall panels by Pre-Raphaelite artists.  V&A Images, London/Art Resource, NY

**FIGURE 8.22**  A mahogany cabinet by E. A. Taylor has a marquetry top and a mirrored back that is flanked by open shelves. It dates from 1905.  © Judith Miller/Dorling Kindersley/Puritan

emphasizing that the beauty of art should be appreciated, rather than suggest a moral or political message (Figure 8.22).

In America, by the end of the century, smaller homes designed with a sense of economy were being built for the working middle class. The American bungalow was a more modest version of the shingle-style home, incorporating natural materials reminiscent of those used by the English Arts and Crafts designers. Bungalow homes were offered to working-class Americans through mail-order catalogs such as those from Sears and Roebuck. Gustav Stickley (1858–1942) perpetuated the popularity of bungalow-style homes through the publication of his magazine, *The Craftsman*, in 1900 (Figure 8.23). Stickely's magazine offered color renderings of interiors showing rich woodwork, art glass windows, ceramic tile, sparse furnishings, and hand-forged metalwork scaled appropriately for these smaller houses (Figure 8.24).

The 1851 Great Exhibition held in the Crystal Palace in London marked the turning point for architectural design during the second half of the 19th century.

**FIGURE 8.23**  A Sears and Roebuck advertisement selling an American bungalow kit home. The kit was shipped via railroad car and assembled onsite. Courtesy Sears Archives

**FIGURE 8.24**  This color sketch by Gustav Stickley features a bungalow interior with harmonious colors, built-in furniture, and Arts and Crafts–style accessories.  © Judith Miller/Dorling Kindersley/Gallery 532

**FIGURE 8.25** This drawing shows the overall design for the Crystal Palace built for the Great Exhibition in 1851. The interior of the Crystal Palace features daring architectural and engineering feats for the time, with its barrel-vaulted glass ceiling and iron frame mezzanine. © Image Asset Management Ltd./SuperStock

The exhibition was intended to show the world the latest technologies, products, and fashions of the period, and established the format for future "world fairs" (Figure 8.25). With 900,000 square feet of exhibition space, the building reflected structural engineering advancements and new building materials of the age. Built exclusively of iron and plate glass, the Crystal Palace became an icon of the Industrial Revolution, bringing notoriety to its architect, Sir Joseph Paxton (1803–1865). Paxton's only work to this point had been in landscape design and the building of greenhouses for his most important patron, Queen Victoria.

The Crystal Palace, which combined the strength of iron with the delicacy of glass, set the stage for the development of 20th-century architecture with its modern glass and steel-frame buildings. The construction of the Crystal Palace opened up the possibility of using iron to build structures that were taller and more daring in their engineering than structures of the past. The technological advances achieved by using a structural iron framework culminated in the building of the Eiffel Tower for the Paris Exhibition of 1889–1890.

Furthermore, in 1899, Hector Guimard (1867–1942) combined glass and iron in his designs for the entrances to the Paris Metro stations (Figure 8.26). Subways were first built in London in 1868, and the method of transportation quickly spread to other major cities around the world, including Boston, Paris, and New York. Guimard's curvilinear shapes designed for the support columns and petallike lobes of the glass canopy captured the essence of the Art Nouveau style.

As early as 1895, the Art Nouveau style focused on the abstracted beauty inherent in nature, capturing characteristic traits of nature by introducing sweeping lines and whiplash curves through organic forms and free-flowing botanicals. The style emerged in Belgium through works by Victor Horta (1861–1947) and his protégé Gustave Strauven (1878–1919), who designed houses and a large public building in Brussels that featured curvilinear details expressed through elaborate ironwork (Figure 8.27). Interiors avoided 90-degree corners and focused

**FIGURE 8.26** One of the entrances of the Paris Metro designed by Hector Guimard from 1899 to 1905 features the whiplash curves of the Art Nouveau style. © cynoclub/Shutterstock

**FIGURE 8.27** Maison St. Cyr, a house designed by Gustave Strauven in the Art Nouveau style, features ornate wrought iron work on the facade. Demetio Carrasco © Dorling Kindersley

instead on rounded shapes with equally curved moldings around doors and ceilings (Figure 8.28). The furnishings focused on nature-inspired motifs such as flowering vines and rich botanical patterns.

# Furniture

## ENGLISH AND AMERICAN VICTORIAN

Victorian–period interior design took advantage of the abundance of household furnishings available at affordable prices because mechanization kept the costs low. Rooms were filled to capacity with bric-a-brac scattered about on specially designed furniture called "whatnot shelves" (Figure 8.29 and "curio cabinets" to display these *knickknacks* (Figure 8.30). Porcelain bouquets, ceramic birds, and small animals fashioned from molded glass conveyed the presence of nature, whereas an accumulation of these objects reflected the owner's pride in material possessions and indicated his economic achievements.

Adding heaviness to the already visually cluttered interiors, rooms inside Victorian homes were filled with large-scale furniture upholstered in richly colored velvets skirted with fringe (Figure 8.31). These furnishings expressed the essential character of the Victorian period—heavy, cumbersome, and overstuffed. Machine-tufting technology replaced hand-tufting methods, making it more affordable to feature buttoned upholstery on sofas, chairs, and ottomans (Figure 8.32). Increased mechanization and inventive new processes in furniture making allowed middle-class consumers to purchase inexpensive imitations of superior-quality goods. As new processes were developed in furniture making, designers were quick to file patents claiming exclusivity of production rights.

Interior furnishings imitated the Revivalist styles of architecture with a curious blending of historical motifs and modern interpretations (Figure 8.33). In fact, the Great Exhibition at the Crystal Palace featured furnishings manufactured in a variety of styles; Elizabethan Revival, Gothic Revival, Renaissance Revival, and Rococo Revival chairs, settees, and tables were among the new designs manufactured with cutting-edge machine technology. The Rococo Revival was the most popular style of interior furnishings throughout the remainder of the 19th century (Figure 8.34).

Papier-mâché proved to be a suitable material for making furniture and accessory items that evoked fine marquetry inlays produced by 18th-century *ebénistes*, but at reasonable prices (Figure 8.35). The material was used to make small chairs, headboards, tables, and tea trays, and these furnishings were usually placed in

**FIGURE 8.28** **The home of Victor Horta in Brussels features his Art Nouveau interior design and furnishings.** The Dining Room, c. 1894 (photo), Horta, Victor (1861–1947)/Hotel Solvay, Brussels, Belgium/© DACS/The Bridgeman Art Library International

**FIGURE 8.29** **This Victorian walnut whatnot shelf has a pierced gallery, barley sugar twist supports, and movable castors.** © Judith Miller/ Dorling Kindersley/Woolley and Wallis

**FIGURE 8.30** **This pair of pottery Dalmatians on cobalt blue bases with gilt designs dates from 1855.** © Judith Miller/Dorling Kindersley/John Howard—Heritage

**FIGURE 8.31** **A pair of Late Victorian carpet chairs reveals Turkish–style carpet upholstery and gold fringe.** © Judith Miller/Dorling Kindersley/ Lyon and Turnbull Ltd.

**FIGURE 8.32** The overstuffed tufted upholstery on this conversation suite dates from the mid 19th century and is characteristic of Rococo Revival–style furniture. The design of the rounder reflects the strict moral character of the Victorian era; its design prohibits courting couples from bodily contact and enables the chaperone to hear all the conversation. © Judith Miller/Dorling Kindersley/Lyon and Turnbull Ltd.

**FIGURE 8.33** This small cupboard in the Elizabethan Revival style is made from oak and features heavy carving with putti and foliage designs. The unusual leg forms evoke a truly 19th-century interpretation of the style. © Judith Miller/Dorling Kindersley/ Woolley and Wallis

**FIGURE 8.34** A pair of carved walnut side chairs in the Rococo Revival style has curved or *engondole* backs that feature foliate designs and acanthus leaf cresting. Interpretive cabriole legs terminate in whorl feet set on casters. © Judith Miller/Dorling Kindersley/Sloan's

ladies' bedrooms (Figure 8.36). Layers of paper treated with adhesives were applied over a metal form of the desired shape. The objects were then baked until the material hardened. Designs were painted on the surface, or in more elaborate examples, mother-of-pearl inlay was used to create delicate patterns. Finishing with linseed oil and more baking created a high-polish shine.

As new processes were developed in furniture fabrication, furniture designers were quick to file patents claiming exclusivity of production rights. Trained as a master cabinetmaker, Michael Thonet (1796–1871) established a workshop in his native Germany in 1819 where he produced fine furniture. By 1830, he abandoned his skill in marquetry and joinery to experiment with new methods and materials of construction. He first attempted to develop a type of plywood—several layers of wood laminated together with glue—that could be forced into molds that would bend the wood using steam and pressure.

Thonet made a series of furniture out of laminated bentwood and exhibited them publicly in 1841 (Figure 8.37). The chairs caught the attention of the Chancellor of Austria who encouraged Thonet to move to Vienna. Heeding the

**FIGURE 8.35** A pair of papier-mâché side chairs features inlaid mother-of-pearl with gold foliate and botanical designs. Notice the Rococo–inspired cabriole legs, and shaped seat rail. Judith Miller/Dorling Kindersley/Lyon and Turnbull Ltd.

**FIGURE 8.36** A papier-mâché tilt-top tea table features mother-of-pearl inlay and dates from 1860. © Judith Miller/Dorling Kindersley/Sloans & Kenyon

**FIGURE 8.37** A bentwood rocker was designed and made by the Thonet Brothers furniture company. Designed for mass production in the 1860s, bentwood furniture is still in production today. The bentwood features made it easy to produce and assemble by 19th-century standards; the furnishings were crated and shipped worldwide from factories throughout Europe. © 7yonov/Shutterstock

Chancellor's advice, Thonet left for Austria where he opened his own company and patented the steam bending process. A commission to furnish the Lichtenstein Palace prompted Thonet to experiment with other materials. Realizing that laminated wood splintered too easily during the bending process, he substituted solid beech. By comparison, the natural lightness and elasticity of beech enabled the wood to conform to the molds without breaking.

Further success ensued after Thonet's bentwood furniture was included in the Great Exhibition held in London in 1851. As already stated, this event, similar to the modern concept of a world's fair, introduced the general public to the latest technologies and inventions of the century. Thonet's furniture exemplified the capabilities of machine production, although—by modern standards—a great deal of handwork was still required. With applied steam and pressure, beech strips were clamped onto iron forms that shaped them into curvilinear pieces to be used on legs, seats, backs, stretchers, and arms. Handwork was still necessary to assemble frames and weave the cane for seats and backs.

In 1853, Thonet and his five sons established their manufacturing facility in Czechoslovakia and worked under the name Gebruder Thonet. With factories and showrooms in Europe and America, Thonet offered a variety of furniture items and accessories made from bentwood. The success of the company is attributed to Thonet's assembly-line production methods; a high volume of goods was produced daily, thereby keeping the cost within the reach of most household budgets. By the end of the century, and with 26 branch facilities, Thonet produced 15,000 pieces of furniture per day, with nearly 50 million chairs sold. The chairs were so inexpensive that Thonet side chairs appeared in coffee houses and bistros throughout Europe. However, Thonet was not alone in his experimentation with lamination processes or mechanization.

John Henry Belter (1795–1863/65), a German-born and trained cabinetmaker working in New York City, perfected the process for laminating wood. Belter built up several layers of wood, each layer cross-grained and glued in place. He then subjected the wood to steam and pressure until the layers conformed to a mold, giving shape to Rococo-style cabriole legs and serpentine curves. Carved bouquets, vines, and fruit patterns were both hand and machine carved onto the surface, leaving the backside flat. The finished frame was then upholstered and tufted, characteristic of Victorian style (Figure 8.38).

**FIGURE 8.38** This American Renaissance Revival laminated walnut sofa with Rococo–inspired cabriole legs and cartouche-shaped backs features tufted upholstery. Carved details appearing on the laminated back were machine cut using processes patented by John Henry Belter. Belter revolutionized the furniture industry with his patented laminating process. Laminated rosewood was pressed into molds to give it shape, and then the front was machine carved. The back of each piece of furniture was left without any carving. © Judith Miller/Dorling Kindersley/Wallis and Wallis

## THE AMERICAN SHAKERS

One of the first architecture and furniture styles to go against ornamentation and excessive decoration was not attributed to a particular architect or designer, but evolved from a strong religious sect of people known as the Shakers. The Shakers' founder, Ann Lee (1736–1784), grew up working in a textile factory in Manchester, England. Like most factory workers, Anne began working as a young girl. She received no formal education but learned how to be a productive worker and to seek comfort in Christianity. Through her involvement with the Quaker religious order, and because she suffered through an abusive marriage, Anne formulated her own religious philosophy based on celibacy and confession.

In 1774, she left England with a small group of followers and went to America to seek religious freedom. Many members of the group did not know the hardships they would face. On arrival, the Shakers established themselves in upstate New York, where they assembled provisions and built shelter, establishing a self-sufficient and isolated community. The future of the sect depended on converts, and soon Shaker missionaries set out to find them. By the turn of the 19th century, Shaker communities had expanded into New England, Ohio, and Kentucky, and the height of Shaker community development peaked during the 1850s.

Like the first American colonists, the Shakers built temporary shelters until permanent structures could be erected. Shaker religious philosophy emphasized the second coming of Christ and prepared its followers for the millennium. All buildings

# LEARN More

## American Victorian Interior Design

The formal parlor shown in Figure 8.39 dates from around 1850–1860 and is decorated in the Rococo Revival style. The furniture is machine made and incorporates the cabriole legs, cartouche shapes, and delicate curves reminiscent of Louis XV–style furniture. A wide range of decorative accessories including a gas-lit chandelier, rocaille gilt mirror, bric-a-brac, and bold-patterned wall-to-wall carpeting fill the space in the Victorian fashion of superfluous décor. Pierced plaster crown molding and gilt wall panels surround the room and complement the ornate carving of a marble mantelpiece. Last, the oversize windows are corniced with gold-fringed valances and heavy, cascading drapery.

**FIGURE 8.39** This parlor setting depicts furnishings in the style of John Henry Belter and dates from around 1850–1860. Rococo Revival Parlor. ca. 1852. Architectural elements from the La Roque Mansion, 4–17 Twenty-seventh Ave, Astoria, New York; originally owned by Horace Whittemore. Rosewood parlor suite attributed to John Henry Belter (American, 1804–1863), New York City. Gift of Sirio D. Molteni and Rita M. Pooler, 1965. (INST.65.4) The Metropolitan Museum of Art, New York, NY U.S.A. Image copyright © The Metropolitan Museum of Art. Image source: Art Resource, NY

**FIGURE 8.40** A bedroom in this Shaker museum features a single bed, an assortment of chairs, a writing desk, and a wall shelf. Typically, these rooms would be more sparsely furnished; rather, this grouping is intended to show the variety of furnishings in the village. David Lyons © Dorling Kindersley, Courtesy of Fruitlands Museums, Sudbury, Massachusetts

**FIGURE 8.41** An early 19th-century wooden box made by a Shaker features finger joints secured with small brass tacks. © Judith Miller/ Dorling Kindersley/Wallis and Wallis

and furnishings were designed for function and perpetuity (Figure 8.40). Shaker meeting houses, dormitories, shop houses, and barns still stand after nearly 200 years, as reminders of a religious sect that has since disappeared.

Most of the Shaker communities were self-supporting, but they required capital to purchase farming equipment and supplies. To raise money, they made rugs, boxes, brooms, baskets, and furniture that were sold publicly (Figure 8.41). Although the Shakers designed and crafted their own furnishings for communal use, after the Civil War the Mount Lebanon village turned chair making into a thriving business. People of the "world" eagerly purchased the chairs that had a reputation for strength and durability. Earlier versions were often painted or stained in red, blue, or green whereas later examples were either painted or stained black or left in a natural finish. Seats were made from either interwoven cloth strips in contrasting colors or woven rush. The furniture, like the architecture, reflected a rational approach to design. Simplistic in style with clean lines and without unnecessary ornamentation, the Shaker style was the antithesis of eclectic Victorian style.

A variety of local woods were used for the construction of the chair frame; however, oak was more commonly used when available. Workshops complete with foot-powered lathes and hand drills produced a few variations of the basic style: turned uprights, legs, and stretchers with back slats and woven cloth seats (Figure 8.42). Although the chairs made for sale were often stained red, blue, or green, chairs made exclusively for Shaker property buildings were left in natural coloring. The workshops also supplied communal furniture—beds, clothespresses, tables, desks, and cabinets—although most storage units were built directly into the walls.

FIGURE 8.42 A child-size rocker from the Shaker community has a label affixed to the inside of one of the rockers that reads "Shakers no. 1/Trade Mark/MT. Lebanon, NY," and features a white and blue cloth back and seat. © Judith Miller/Dorling Kindersley/Freeman's

FIGURE 8.43 A maple and ash side chair dates from the mid 19th century and features a slat back with turned finials on the uprights. The chair still shows remains of red staining. © Judith Miller/Dorling Kindersley/Sloans & Kenyon

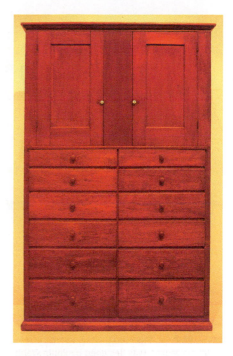

FIGURE 8.44 A tall chest with an upper cupboard features a simple, unadorned cornice and graduated drawers. David Lyons © Dorling Kindersley, Courtesy of Fruitlands Museums, Sudbury, Massachusetts

The tidy appearance of the room and the Shakers' devotion to cleanliness led to the implementation of the Shaker rail—a narrow rail attached to the wall above head height following the perimeter of the room. At regular intervals, small pegs were inserted into the rail that allowed for the hanging of household items, including ladder-back chairs (Figure 8.43). This strategy proved highly efficient as a means of storage, as well as kept the furniture off the floor each evening while it was swept and mopped.

The Shaker style of design reflected the efforts of devoted craftsmen who diligently sought to produce goods that were functional rather than designed for luxury and exuberance. Storage furniture like chests, cupboards, and cabinets were often built into the walls, keeping the room unencumbered by separate pieces of furniture. Freestanding cabinets and chests were designed using panel-and-frame construction with simple hardware of turned wooden knobs (Figure 8.44). Today, many people find beauty in the furniture's restrained elegance. At auction, Shaker furniture began to break records during the 1980s and 1990s. A Shaker rocker taken from a community in New Hampshire sold for $37,400—setting a world record for furniture of its kind.

# The English and American Arts and Crafts Movement

During the second half of the 19th century, proponents for machine-made goods challenged those artisans who still made things by hand, and the economic divide was evident between those who could afford the latter. Concerned with maintaining handmade goods, William Morris supported quality over quantity, rebuking machine-made household furnishings (Figure 8.45). The resulting Arts and Crafts movement was founded on maintaining the spirit of medieval craft guilds that ensured the quality of handcrafted items. The Arts and Crafts movement was supported and perpetuated by John Ruskin (1819–1900), social critic and author of *The Seven Lamps of Architecture* published in 1849. Those working during under the influence of the Arts and Crafts movement sought to adhere to honesty of craft, quality of materials, and devotion to nature.

FIGURE 8.45 This folding screen produced by Morris & Company features silk panels inside an elaborately pierced frame, and dates from 1890. © Judith Miller/Dorling Kindersley/Lyon and Turnbull Ltd.

Morris and his circle of artisans architect Philip Webb and the Pre-Raphaelite brotherhood of artists—Dante Gabriel Rossetti (1828–1882), Edward Burne-Jones (1833–1898), and Ford Madox Brown (1821–1893)—created coordinating decorative accessories for Victorian homes. Under the firm name Morris & Company, they sold quality designed and produced wallpapers and fabrics, furniture, tiles, and carpets (Figure 8.46). Red House was built using indigenous materials on both the exterior and interior, contributing to the articulation and cohesiveness of the total spatial experience. Morris' statement, "Have nothing in your house which you do not know to be useful or believe to be beautiful," summarized his belief that a house should have in it only what was necessary for daily life. His philosophy was in direct opposition to the style of the day, which seemed to reflect a fear of empty spaces through the accumulation of clutter more typical in earlier Victorian interiors.

Followers of Morris sought inspiration from the medieval guilds when crafts were regulated for their quality and craftsmanship. Designs produced during this period reflected the spirit of the Medieval Age in both appearance and construction while maintaining the quality of handcrafted furnishings (Figure 8.47). Furnishings made from oak best represented medievalism, along with stenciled or carved ornamentation. Cabinets, chests, and cupboards incorporated large brass hinges or were accented with ceramic tiles and stained glass, giving the designs a more medieval look (Figure 8.48).

Morris' anti-industrial philosophies were not supported by all of his contemporaries, and many items were machine-made, but with careful consideration to their construction to look handmade. Charles F. A. Voysey (1857–1941) realized that the machine was an integral part of modern society and therefore should be utilized to its fullest potential. Although Morris wanted to do away with the mechanization of furniture production, Voysey saw industrialization as the brain child for future development. Voysey's furniture designs and interiors, however—like Morris—were based on the theory of the elimination of unnecessary ornamentation.

The Arts and Crafts style popular in England had caught on in America under the auspices of the Mission style made popular by the Stickley brothers and the Roycroft Campus (Figure 8.49). American-born Gustav Stickley (1858–1942) and his four brothers manufactured Victorian–style furniture from 1880 to mid-1890 in their factory in Grand Rapids, Michigan. Gustav separated from his brothers in 1895 to establish his own workshop in upstate New York where he could develop

**FIGURE 8.46** This Morris chair, named after William Morris, was designed by Philip Webb in 1865 and features oak-turned framing and Morris–designed upholstery over spring-coiled cushions. The angle of the back changes by moving a wooden rod onto preset rungs on the back frame. © Judith Miller/Dorling Kindersley/ Puritan Values

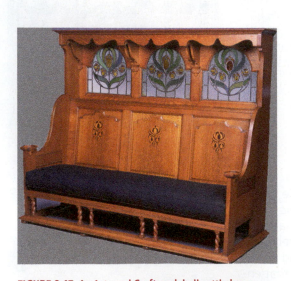

**FIGURE 8.47** An Arts and Crafts oak hall settle has a molded cornice above an ogee-shaped valance framing stained glass panels. The settle features floral inlay, and its bottom frame is supported on barley sugar twist spindles. © Judith Miller/Dorling Kindersley/Lyon and Turnbull Ltd.

**FIGURE 8.48** An Arts and Crafts oak bureau with a slanted fall-front cabinet has ornately designed pierced brass hinges and handles. © Judith Miller/Dorling Kindersley/Lyon and Turnbull Ltd.

**FIGURE 8.49** This slat back rocking chair by Gustav Stickley in the Mission style was made from quarter-sawn oak and features leather upholstery. © Judith Miller/Dorling Kindersley/Wallis and Wallis

his ideas more fully for basic yet functional furniture. In 1898, he traveled to Europe and, while in England and Scotland, Stickley took a strong interest in the hand-crafted quality of William Morris' work and the philosophies of Charles Voysey. On his return to America, he became a proponent for the Arts and Crafts movement in his design of houses and interior furnishings (Figure 8.50).

The 1900 debut of Stickley's trade magazine, *The Craftsman,* introduced Americans to his carefully designed houses and interiors that emphasized clean lines, plaster walls, and exposed beams. Like Morris, Stickley wanted to coordinate the interior with the exterior. *The Craftsman* provided scaled house plans that set the architectural background for his furniture designs. The interior design for the modest-size American bungalow borrowed heavily from the English Arts and Crafts movement. Stickley's color renderings of his bungalow interiors revealed built-in furniture such as window seats, cabinets, and bookcases; finely crafted wainscoting; exposed beamed ceilings; and hardwood floors covered with botanical-patterned carpets. Colors were harmonious and inspired by nature—soft fern green, yellow ochre, terra cotta red, and peacock blue. Decorative accessories fashioned from hammered copper and stained glass, as well as matte-glazed pottery, emphasized a return to nature.

To discourage Americans from buying lesser quality goods, Stickley who was a strong proponent of handmade furniture, published catalogs of his furniture styles. He encouraged do-it-yourselfers by printing detailed drawings of furniture that could be easily made, and supplied kits of leather and other finishing materials to complete the construction. Stickley criticized and rebuked his imitators, including his two brothers, Leopold and John George, who had established their own manufacturing facility in Fayetteville, New York. Unfortunately, Gustav's workshop went bankrupt in 1916, and he joined the workshop of L. & J.G. Stickley.

The magazine and catalogs had clearly helped to establish the American Arts and Crafts style, more commonly referred to as the "Mission style" or "Mission Oak style," names derived from its semblance to ecclesiastical furniture found in southwestern missions. The popularity of the American Arts and Crafts style had extended into the 20th century. A 1908 Sears and Roebuck catalog featured "Mission" furniture for purchase, as by this time there were several companies imitating the work of the Stickley brothers.

As in England, not all furnishings made in America in the Arts and Crafts style were handmade. Furniture manufacturers were quick to adopt a new Arts and Crafts aesthetic based on a popular book *Hints on Household Taste in Furniture, Upholstery, and Other Details* by Charles L. Eastlake (1836–1906), first published in England in 1868. The book featured Eastlake's dissertation against the eclectic styles of the day, and encouraged the purchasing of furnishings that were beautiful and well made. After the book was published in America in 1872, the Eastlake style emerged, appropriating ornamentation seen in the engraved plates from Eastlake's book, into machine-made chairs, tables, and case pieces. The designs emphasized those elements that were easily mass produced, such as spindles and shallow machine carvings (Figure 8.51). Eastlake regretted the association of his name with this popular American style that went against his notion of "well-made" household furnishings.

## THE ART NOUVEAU STYLE

The Art Nouveau style is often referred to as a period of influence rather than a specific stylistic trend. As early as 1890, an attempt to revive beauty while bridging the gap between handicraft and industrialization developed throughout Europe. Unifying stylistic elements from these individual movements, Jugendstil in Germany, Modernismo in Spain, Secession in Austria, and Stile Floreale in Italy were considered the new art of the *fin de siècle.*

Clearly resisting historical reiteration that culminated in the confusion of Victorian eclecticism, architects and designers created less literal interpretations of past styles. Instead, the majority of Art Nouveau designers abstracted the beauty inherent in nature, introducing sweeping lines and whiplash curves through organic forms and free-flowing botanicals. One of the earliest applications of the term "Art

**FIGURE 8.50** This oak sideboard made by Gustav Stickley in 1902 has a raised back with central graduated drawers and side cabinets. The oversized hinges and handles are made from copper. © Judith Miller/Dorling Kindersley/Gallery 532

**FIGURE 8.51** An American Eastlake–style marble-top chiffonier has fanned spindle designs and features low-relief carving (probably machine carved). It dates from 1880. © Judith Miller/Dorling Kindersley/Sloans & Kenyon

**FIGURE 8.52** This fire screen designed by Edward Colonna is made from rosewood and has a front panel of fabric in a stylized floral pattern. The frame features delicate vine-scrolled carvings. © Judith Miller/Dorling Kindersley/Mary Ann's Collectibles

**FIGURE 8.53** This armchair made from cherry was designed by Eugène Gallard in the Art Nouveau style. © Judith Miller/Dorling Kindersley/Mary Ann's Collectibles

Nouveau" is traced to Frenchman Samuel (documented also as Siegfried) Bing (1838–1905). The opening of his innovative *Salon de l'Art Nouveau* in Paris in 1895 was motivated by his recent visit to America. There, he witnessed a fresh and almost naive integration of the decorative arts, unrestricted by national heritage. Bing was particularly interested in the workshop of Louis Comfort Tiffany (1848–1933). Tiffany & Company, established by Louis' father, had organized furniture makers, glassblowers, silversmiths, and ceramists into one workshop where they all strove to achieve a cohesive stylistic direction based on organic form.

With the *Salon de l'Art Nouveau*, Bing sought to establish a gallery where his invited talented designers from France, Belgium, and America (including Tiffany) worked together to create rooms filled with coordinated furnishings and decorative accessories. His attempt to unify all the crafts workers into one collective and cohesive body of artists foreshadowed modern ideology. Bing assembled three superb artists to complete the Pavilion of Art Nouveau for the Paris Exhibition of 1900: Edward Colonna, Eugène Gaillard, and Georges de Feure (Figures 8.52 and 8.53). Six rooms were decorated in the height of Art Nouveau style.

The high style of the Pavilion of Art Nouveau isolated the middle-class consumer because many of the works produced were handmade. French artist Emile Galle (1846–1904) also exhibited at the Exhibition of 1900, and his furnishings showed exquisite craftsmanship in carving and marquetry designs, although he is more recognized for his glassworks (Figures 8.54 and 8.55).

At the same time, Belgian architect Victor Horta completed the Eetvelde House, a masterpiece of Art Nouveau architecture. Just as the Crystal Palace prompted architectural change during the second half of the 19th century, the newly completed Eiffel Tower in Paris challenged modern engineering achievements. Perhaps influenced by the Eiffel Tower, Horta concealed the overt function of the iron support column in its ornateness; reduced to thin, delicate supports, his structural columns terminated into sweeping arches whereas banisters, iron grilles, and door gates were shaped into harmonizing vine patterns. The interiors were equally matched with furnishings with sweeping lines and graceful proportions (Figure 8.28).

**FIGURE 8.54** This walnut and rosewood vitrine designed by Emile Galle features carved vine and leaf designs, and leaf marquetry patterns. © Judith Miller/Dorling Kindersley/Mary Ann's Collectibles

**FIGURE 8.55** This detail from a table designed by Emile Galle features dragonfly motifs in rosewood veneer, and various other woods used in the marquetry designs. Nature-inspired motifs capture the spirit of the Art Nouveau style, with asymmetrical vine patterns and botanicals. © Judith Miller/Dorling Kindersley/Mary Ann's Collectibles

Although there are other fine examples of Art Nouveau architecture spread across Europe and into America, the style itself was more popular in the decorative arts. Complex interiors emphasized exaggerated organic forms that were repeated in furnishings, textiles, art, and accessories. What originally began as a movement to produce a new style of design antithetical to austere Victorian historicism became a movement steeped in elaborate ornamentation.

Although most of the Art Nouveau designers believed in modernization, the intricacies of the style and the fine quality of craftsmanship inhibited its mass production. Because these furnishings were not within the financial reach of the middle class, posters, prints, vases, tea services, and textiles manufactured with the essence of whiplash curves, botanical patterns, and organically inspired motifs were more widespread. The movement that intended to bridge the gap between machine-made and handcrafted furnishings only widened it. As William Morris discovered earlier, handmade goods kept costs beyond the reach of the middle class, and the Art Nouveau style suffered the same fate as Morris' Arts and Crafts movement—demise through elitism (Figure 8.56). Art Nouveau–style architecture, furniture, and decorative accessories prevalent during the last decade of the 19th century appeared old-fashioned and outdated at the turn of the 20th century. As a new century unfolded, designers sought to shed the historicism of the past and create new works that evoked the modern age.

By the early 20th century, designers began to focus on how to design for machine production because handcrafted household items were too expensive for the average consumer. Belgian painter, architect, and designer Henry van der Velde (1863–1957) realized that handcrafted furniture ensured high quality yet isolated all but the wealthy patron who could afford its cost. In his workshop in Brussels, he employed craftsmen who produced furniture using assembly-line methods, although each piece was handmade.

**FIGURE 8.56** This Art Nouveau–style desk by Louis Majorelle features nature-inspired marquetry designs. © Judith Miller/Dorling Kindersley/Sloan's

# LEARN More

## Art Nouveau Interior Design

The early work of architect Victor Horta (1861–1947) (Figure 8.57) featured typical Revivalist styles until a visit to the Great Exhibition in Paris (for which the Eiffel Tower was built) in 1889 influenced him to change to a "modern" style. Horta's home in Brussels, built in 1898, highlighted the emergence of the Art Nouveau style of design in Europe. His interior architectural scheme included rounded shapes over angular ones, and moldings, stairwells, and railings were fashioned into the sweeping movements of growing vines. In contrast to dark Victorian interiors, woodwork was minimized and paint colors lightened to create a freshness for the "new art." Motifs including whiplash curves, growing vines, and flowering botanicals appeared on floor patterns, wall paintings, wallpaper, light fixtures, and furniture designs.

**FIGURE 8.57** Many scholars credit the architect Victor Horta with establishing the Art Nouveau style in Europe with designs such as this one for the Van Eetvelde House, built in 1895 in Brussels, Belgium. Demetrio Carrasco © Dorling Kindersley

**FIGURE 8.58** This oak armchair in the Jugenstil manner attributed to Joseph Maria Olbrich is more geometrical in its design and less fluid than most Art Nouveau examples.
© Judith Miller/Dorling Kindersley/Woolley and Wallis

Van der Velde supported complete unity in design and feared that mass production of household goods with Art Nouveau–inspired designs would be perceived out of context. After moving to Germany in 1900, van der Velde, along with Hermann Muthesius (1861–1927), helped to organize the Werkbund in 1907. The purpose of the Werkbund was to bridge the gap between art and industry by improving "professional work through the cooperation of art, industry and the crafts." With the establishment of the Werkbund, Jugendstil and Secessionist designers shifted toward a more rectilinear interpretation of the Art Nouveau style (Figure 8.58). Consequently, as the 19th century closed, the "art and industry" philosophies of the Werkbund became the root of 20th-century modernism.

# Accessories

## POTTERY

Further developments in pottery making, including mechanized processes, new mold-making equipment, gas-fired kilns, and steam-powered potter's wheels and lathes, made ownership of fine ceramicware more affordable. The Mason family pottery business in London made strong stoneware for the domestic market, and in 1813 patented the name "ironstone." Decorations varied from revivalist designs and motifs to plain and undecorated white versions, simulating the look of bone china. Stoneware pottery, named for its stonelike strength, was made into the most basic kitchen jars, jugs, and saltcellars sturdy enough to handle rough-and-tough daily use (Figure 8.59).

First brought to Europe from the Middle East during the Medieval period, lusterware became increasingly popular during the 19th century. Glazes made with metal oxides gave off an iridescent sheen on ceramics once fired. Pink, blue, and copper lusters were among the favorite colors of avid collectors and were produced by several English factories, including Wedgwood and Staffordshire. The English potter Herbert Minton (1793–1858) displayed an assortment of pottery wares at the Great Exhibition in 1851 that imitated the look of fine Italian majolica. These brightly painted pottery pieces were molded into the shapes of animals, plants, and flowers, and were used on vases, tableware, and knickknacks (Figure 8.60).

Factories such as Sèvres, Staffordshire, Minton, and Worcester continued to produce fine porcelain wares throughout the 19th century (Figure 8.61). Minton developed a process for building up layers of white slip on a porcelain body, then carving away layers to expose the white background, which created a cameo effect called *pâte-sur-pâte*. Worcester and Wedgwood in England produced a range of Parian ceramics made from porcelain. Parian ceramics were left in an unglazed finish—white bisque—so the finished piece looked as though it was carved from marble. Fine Irish belleek porcelain was recognized by its luminous white coloring with gilt accents; it was made in America by the Ceramic Art Company in Trenton, New Jersey, owned by Walter Scot Lenox. In 1906, the company changed its name to Lenox and began producing white creamware under its new name.

The impact of William Morris' Arts and Crafts movement dominated design trends from its inception in the 1860s through the first quarter of the

**FIGURE 8.59** A mid-19th-century American stoneware crock with stenciled letters and hand-painted foliate designs in blue. © Judith Miller/Dorling Kindersley/Pook and Pook

**FIGURE 8.60** This Victorian majolica jardinière and stand features brightly painted sunflowers. © Judith Miller/Dorling Kindersley/Gorringes

20th century. Much of the applied arts were influenced by the Arts and Crafts notion of producing quality handcrafted goods. Artists working in this style sought to recapture the quality of handmade goods, before the crafts were degenerated by the Industrial Age. In effect, these artisans returned to the medieval craft guilds for their inspiration. Rather than fine porcelains, they created earthenware pottery with iridescent glazes featuring designs inspired by their natural surroundings; birds and insects set against fields of flowers appeared in relief or were painted on pottery (Figure 8.62).

In 1880, Maria Longworth Nichol established a ceramic factory in Cincinnati, Ohio, producing matte glaze pottery with botanical motifs in earth-tone colors. In 1902, her company, Rookwood Pottery, created an architectural department supplying tile for various building projects throughout America. Predominantly, her tiles were embossed with flora and fauna designs with matte glazes in green, dark brown, orange, yellow, and pink. Following the success of Rookwood, the Roseville Pottery Company began producing art pottery in 1890, Newcomb in 1895, and Grueby in 1897. These Arts and Crafts–inspired designs remained popular until World War I (Figure 8.63).

Art Nouveau pottery designs emulated the free-flowing floral patterns and whiplash curves found in architecture and interiors. Many examples of Art Nouveau pottery prominently featured young women with long hair blowing in the breeze and wearing flowing gowns (Figure 8.64). These young maidens were essentially ancient classical goddesses recreated for a new era.

## GLASS

The advent of industrialization in the glass-making business brought the price down to manageable levels. Middle-class consumers could not get enough of the wide range of tableware, vases, and figurines that flooded the market during the Victorian period and filled curio cabinets. Colored glass became increasingly popular after the blue cobalt designs introduced by Bristol, and experimentation with adding metallic oxides to glass yielded a variety of colors for modern glassmakers. Adding gold chloride created rich ruby colors for what was called "cranberry glass."

**FIGURE 8.61** One of a pair of Sèvres vases exhibited at the 1851 Great Exhibition at the Crystal Palace by the French government features a portrait of Queen Victoria. © Judith Miller/Dorling Kindersley/Hope and Glory

**FIGURE 8.62** This art pottery vase attributed to John Ruskin is inlaid with engraved silver foliage against an iridescent greenish brown background. © Judith Miller/Dorling Kindersley/Gorringes

**FIGURE 8.63** A green candlestick made by Sarah Sax for Rookwood Pottery. © Judith Miller/Dorling Kindersley/Freeman's

**FIGURE 8.64** This Art Nouveau porcelain compote features a female figure in repose with flowing gown and hair. © Judith Miller/Dorling Kindersley/Lyon and Turnbull Ltd.

FIGURE 8.65 This 19th-century Vaseline glass epergne for holding flowers has three spiraling, clear-glass trumpet-shaped canes with crimped edges and base. © Judith Miller/ Dorling Kindersley/Woolley and Wallis

Chapter 8

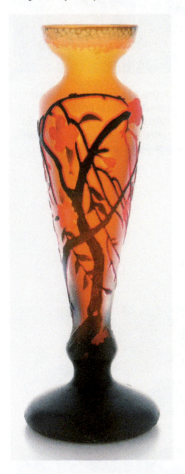

FIGURE 8.67 This amber vase by the French Art Nouveau designer Emile Galle is decorated with tree branches, flowers, and stems made with colored glass threads.
© Judith Miller/Dorling Kindersley/David Rago Auctions

FIGURE 8.66 A Fenton blue carnival glass bowl from 1907 produced in numerous other colors. This popular design features a dragon and lotus pattern. © Judith Miller/Dorling Kindersley/Branksome Antiques

FIGURE 8.68 A Tiffany Favrile glass vase made with iridescent amber glass has green leaf and vine designs. The piece dates from circa 1906 and is inscribed "L.C. Tiffany. Favrile/2352K" and is numbered "14178." © Judith Miller/Dorling Kindersley/Sloans & Kenyon

Vaseline glass, named for its transparent, yellow-green coloring, was made by adding uranium dioxide to molten glass (Figure 8.65). Adding manganese resulted in deep amethyst colors.

The quality of glassware depended on how the pieces were made. Inexpensive glass items were made from molds, which allowed the soft glass to take on any shape, form, or pattern. Cylindrical pieces such as goblets, vases, and pitchers were molded in two pieces and then fused together, leaving a visible seam. Designs once etched by hand or engraved on the wheel were produced more economically by using acid to scratch away at the surface of the glass. By 1907, molded glass was so inexpensive that American glassmaker Frank Leslie Fenton's iridescent glass became known as "carnival glass" because it was given away as free prizes at carnivals (Figure 8.66).

Followers of the Arts and Crafts movement detested the inexpensive knick-knacks, candy dishes, vases, and goblets made from molded glass. For these artists working in the 19th century, making handcrafted glass was another fine art form like painting or sculpture. Considered works of art, highly decorative glass vases featured scenes from nature and captured the design motifs popular with both the Arts and Crafts and Art Nouveau movements, including botanicals, small animals, and the abstracted blossom of a single rose. The intricacies of these styles and the fine quality of artistry precluded mass production, and so the decorative accessories proved too expensive for middle-class society (Figure 8.67).

Louis Comfort Tiffany (1848–1933), the son of jewelry designer Charles Lewis Tiffany (1812–1902), patented his method of making opalescent glass in 1885. Tiffany's glass, called "Favrile," was influenced by the designs of the Art Nouveau movement and featured highly stylized flowers, dragonflies, and other motifs inspired by nature (Figure 8.68). His company, Tiffany Studios, sold lamps, vases, and stained glass window designs along with rugs and textiles.

Nineteenth-century improvements in glass-making celebrated by the construction of the Crystal Palace in 1851 brought about a renewed interest in window glass, whether it was stained, cut, painted, or etched. England repealed a tax on window glass during the second half of the century, and stained glass windows became featured items in newly built Victorian houses. Moreover, the Arts and Crafts movement reintroduced stained glass into the designs of medieval-inspired interiors (Figure 8.69). In 1879, American artist and glassmaker John LaFarge (1835–1910) patented a process for making opalescent glass by fusing small pieces of colored glass to create a milky effect. His window designs followed the prevalent themes of the period, featuring scenes from literature and the Bible surrounded by an abundance of nature. LaFarge's work appeared in churches, libraries, and private homes in and around New England, and rivaled the work coming out of Tiffany Studios.

## MIRRORS

Cylinder glass, inflated with compressed air, could be made in larger sizes because machines could blow more air than humans could. In addition, steam engines powered polishing and grinding machines, relieving workers of the laborious task of hand polishing. These technological advances made the production of mirrors more economical, so they were affordable for all classes of society to own them. Mirrors were soon appearing on whatnot shelves and inside china cabinets to reflect the glistening surfaces of cut-glass and ceramic knickknacks (Figure 8.70). Hall tables and coat racks featured low mirrors just above the floor so women could make sure no petticoat ruffles were showing before they left the house.

Freestanding floor mirrors called "chevals" became a standard feature of bedrooms, allowing women to see their entire figures and make sure petticoats were hidden from the public eye. Frames were designed in Revivalist styles to coordinate with furniture and room décor (Figure 8.71). And, despite the advent of gas and electric lighting in Victorian interiors, the overmantel mirror remained a focal point in the formal sitting room as a stylistic trend, even though its original function as a light reflector was no longer necessary.

## LIGHTING

Considerable improvements in interior lighting came about during the 19th century. The invention of a candle-making machine in 1834 resulted in candles being produced much faster than by hand. Candles were now considerably cheaper. Candleholders were fashioned into the popular styles of the period, designed to coordinate with the interior furnishings (Figures 8.72 and 8.73). By mid century, cleaner burning and odorless paraffin wax was replacing tallow and crystallized whale oil in the making of candles.

Furthermore, lighting interiors with candles became less desirable after improved oil-burning and kerosene lamps, along with the Argand lamp, proved more efficient (Figures 8.74 and 8.75). After that time, candles were used to create atmosphere rather than provide the primary source of light. Lighting changed dramatically when, in 1792, William Murdock (1754–1839) devised a way to light his home using gas as a fuel. Slow to reach the domestic market, gaslights began appearing on the streets of London by 1807, in Baltimore by 1816, and in Paris by 1820. Gas lighting was not available to households and businesses until 1858, and did not become widespread until 1865 (Figure 8.76).

Following on the heels of gas lighting, the incandescent lightbulb, perfected in 1879 by Thomas Edison (1847–1931), opened up the possibility of lighting interiors with electricity. The design of electrical

**FIGURE 8.69** Stained glass windows designed by Edward Burne Jones. Joe Cornish © Dorling Kindersley

**FIGURE 8.70** A pair of Victorian painted and gilt bow-fronted *encoignures*, or corner cabinets, with scrolling mirror backs and marble tops fashioned in the Rococo Revival style. © Judith Miller/Dorling Kindersley/ Lyon and Turnbull Ltd.

**FIGURE 8.71** This copper-framed wall mirror available through the department store Liberty & Company features two flowering plants with blue-glazed circular plaques. © Judith Miller/Dorling Kindersley/Puritan Values

**FIGURE 8.72** A pair of Arts and Crafts–style copper candlesticks designed by Christopher Dresser in 1900. © Judith Miller/Dorling Kindersley/The Design Gallery

**FIGURE 8.73** A bronze Art Nouveau–style candlestick from 1905 is fashioned into a slender maiden holding iris-shaped candleholders. © Judith Miller/Dorling Kindersley/The Design Gallery

FIGURE 8.75 This pair of gilt and cast bronze and cut-glass Argand lamps with bobeche prisms dates from 1825. © Judith Miller/Dorling Kindersley/Sloan's

FIGURE 8.76 This gas chandelier features brass pelicans with curved leaf motifs and white glass shades.
Steve Gorton © Dorling Kindersley

FIGURE 8.74 This Victorian oil lamp with cylindrical hurricane glass and green shade features a clear glass oil reservoir supported by a reeded columnar base. © Judith Miller/Dorling Kindersley/Otford Antiques and Collectors Centre

lighting fixtures varied from a simple exposed bulb hanging by a wire to ceiling-mounted pendants leaving the bulbs exposed to show off their novelty. Later, shades were added to cover the bulb and reduce glare, which created softer, more diffused lighting.

Because electricity was expensive at first, not everyone rushed to have their homes wired. New homes built during the late 1800s were some of the first to feature electric lighting. Designers working during the late 19th century were quick to design table and floor lamps, chandeliers, and wall sconces in styles coordinating with interior furnishings. Arts and Crafts–style lamps featured bases made from hammered copper, shaped wood, or matte glaze pottery with shades made from mica (Figure 8.77). Tiffany Studios began producing electric lamps with stained glass shades in a variety of designs and patterns in the Art Nouveau style. The women in the glass-cutting department at Tiffany's under the leadership of Clara Driscoll (1861–1944) were in charge of fashioning the small pieces of colored glass to make lamp shades, mosaics, and stained glass windows. New research shows that Driscoll was the designer of several important creations formerly thought to be the work of Louis Comfort Tiffany. Her credited lamp shade designs included "Poppy," "Wisteria," and the "Dragonfly"—which won Tiffany a prize at the Paris International Exposition in 1900 (Figure 8.78).

## METALWORKING

The name "Towle" is often used incorrectly to describe silverwork in general (Figure 8.79). The misconception was the result of the Moulton family's silversmith shop set up in Newburyport, Massachusetts. The Moulton family of silversmiths had produced fine silver since prerevolutionary times until 1857, when one of the sons sold the company to Towle Silversmiths. After the sale, "Towle" erroneously became the catch-all term to describe silver work, regardless of maker.

One of the leading silversmiths of the 19th century was Charles Lewis Tiffany. In 1837, Charles Lewis Tiffany and John B. Young opened their doors in New York City selling fine stationery and accessories. In a few short years, Tiffany & Company had

FIGURE 8.77 A lamp designed by Dirk van Erp has a mica shade and hand-hammered copper base and dates from circa 1910. © Judith Miller/ Dorling Kindersley/Geoffrey Diner Gallery

FIGURE 8.78 A rare Tiffany wisteria laburnum-patterned chandelier made from purple, blue, and white mottled glass pieces features a ruffled edge that was difficult to make. It dates from 1910. © Judith Miller/Dorling Kindersley/Sloans

earned a reputation for offering high-quality sterling silver tableware, dresser jars, and jewelry to upscale clients. Tiffany took full control of the company in 1853 and expanded into the retailing of clocks, picture frames, and, by the end of the century, fine china and crystal. The Tiffany name became synonymous with refinement and good taste. Tiffany's retailing of sterling silver through his *Blue Book* catalog enabled him to compete in European markets. The company still operates today, and its silverwares are packaged in their infamous light blue box.

Christopher Dresser (1834–1904) earned a place in history as a botanist, a designer, and a sort of renaissance man living in Victorian England. The author of three books on botany, Dresser left his post as a college lecturer to work as a designer of household objects. The Design Museum in London named Dresser the "first independent industrial designer," recognizing the importance of his designs in textiles, glassware, wallpaper, metalwork, furniture, and ceramics. In 1862, Dresser published *The Art of Decorative Design,* in which he made connections between nature and design. His interest in botany and his nature-inspired designs aligned him with the emerging Arts and Crafts movement in England (Figure 8.80).

Unlike William Morris and his followers, Dresser became a proponent for mass production by creating designs in consideration of how they would be manufactured. Before managing his own retail business in 1880, Dresser consulted and designed for established companies such as Wedgwood, Minton, and Hukin and Heath, which produced silver plate and new electroplate tableware. After a visit to Japan in 1877, Dresser's designs became less aligned with Victorian taste. Instead, he began opting for a streamlined approach to ordinary household accessories. The Art Furnishers Alliance, a group of designers with whom Dresser worked, was short-lived and was sold in 1883 to Liberty & Company of London. Liberty & Company opened its doors in 1875, offering imported goods from Japan to curious clients wishing to purchase exotic carpets, fabrics, and household accessories. Archibald Knox (1864–1933), who worked with Dresser, became a leading designer for Liberty & Company in 1897.

In 1895, Elbert Hubbard (1856–1915) started a small publishing company in East Aurora, New York, as a way of printing works under his authorship. He called it "Roycroft," after 17th-century book publishers Samuel and Thomas Roycroft. Hubbard saw an opportunity to expand his business when construction started on a local inn and he organized workers to create the interior furnishings for the project. Dard Hunter (1883–1966) arrived at Roycroft in 1904 and became the primary designer of stained glass windows for the Roycroft Inn. Sculptor and metalworker Jerome Conner (1874–1943) began designing and making copper items in 1906. He remained at Roycroft for four years, later returning to his native Ireland to work. The Roycroft Campus quickly became a consortium of artisans working in the Arts and Crafts style made popular by the work of Gustav Stickley, and they supported their craft by selling household copperware to the public (Figure 8.81).

From as early as 1890, characteristic traits of the Art Nouveau movement developed throughout Europe, with each country interpreting the "new art" in its own regional manner. These regional components shared a connecting thread of design inspired by nature. Many of the whiplash curves seen on railings were integrated into

**FIGURE 8.79** These Victorian repoussé vases feature delicate flowers and leaf designs. © Judith Miller/Dorling Kindersley/Law Fine Art Ltd.

**FIGURE 8.80** This Victorian cloisonné vase made by Minton in the style of Christopher Dresser. It features butterflies and stylized foliage against a blue background. © Judith Miller/Dorling Kindersley/ Gorringes

**FIGURE 8.81** This copper vase made by the Stickley brothers features hammered copper pitting, a typical metalworking technique of Arts and Crafts–style artisans. © Judith Miller/ Dorling Kindersley/Freeman's

FIGURE 8.82 A French Art Nouveau brass fireplace surrounded with pierced floral designs and whiplash vine patterns. © Judith Miller/Dorling Kindersley/Mary Ann's Collectibles

FIGURE 8.83 A late-19th-century American clock with a perpetual calendar, by Seth Thomas, patented in 1876, features white enamel dials in a mahogany case with a plinth base. © Judith Miller/Dorling Kindersley/Jacobs and Hunt Fine Art Auctioneers

the metalwork of decorative accessories and interior furnishings, which completed the interior scheme (Figure 8.82).

## CLOCKS

Centuries before the clock tower known as "Big Ben" was erected outside the Houses of Parliament in London in 1859, civic buildings and churches proudly featured large clocks chiming on the hour and sometimes the half hour (Figure 8.10). With the increasingly present railroad transporting people from city to city and running tight schedules, the measurement of time became much more important during the 19th century than in the past. The Industrial Revolution gave rise to the mass production of clocks so that nearly every household could afford one. In America, Seth Thomas (1785–1859) began mass producing clock movements in wood by making up to 500 at a time (Figure 8.83). Another American, Eli Terry (1772–1852), relied on mechanical means to mass produce die-cut and stamped clock dials, hands, and gears so that the parts were interchangeable with a variety of clockworks. The clock shifted from being a status symbol of the wealthy to a commonplace item found in most middle-class households.

Victorian superstition instigated the practice of stopping the movements of a hall or mantel clock when someone died in the home; it was supposed to ward off bad luck for the surviving family members. In 1875, Henry Clay Work (1832–1884) wrote a popular song, "Grandfather's Clock." From that time on, Americans adoringly called the long case clocks a grandfather clock (Figure 8.84).

### My Grandfather's Clock by Henry Clay Work

*My grandfather's clock*
*Was too large for the shelf,*
*So it stood ninety years on the floor;*
*It was taller by half*
*Than the old man himself,*
*Though it weighed not a pennyweight more.*
*It was bought on the morn*
*Of the day that he was born,*
*And was always his treasure and pride;*
*But it stopped short*
*Never to go again,*
*When the old man died.*

The advent of standardization in clock making coupled with the establishment of uniform time zones throughout the world in 1884 revolutionized timekeeping. Furthermore, with clock movements now being mass produced, clock sales were ensured by designing the cases to coordinate with the room décor of the period (Figure 8.85).

FIGURE 8.84 This Victorian Renaissance Revival tall case clock made from walnut with burr walnut panels emphasizes the inner pendulum workings contained behind a glass door. © Judith Miller/Dorling Kindersley/Freeman's

FIGURE 8.85 This Arts and Crafts–style mantel clock features oak and brass details with exaggerated designs. © Judith Miller/Dorling Kindersley/The Design Gallery

The three clocks shown here represent a variety of styles that were popular at the time they were made, although they are most telling about the social standing of women during their respective periods. The women depicted in these clocks embody the image of the classical goddess through hairstyles, nudity, or diaphanous clothing, and the presence of Greek and Roman design motifs such as festoons, the urn, and the lyre make reference to ancient traditions. Figure 8.86 shows a Parian clock from the late 19th century and features three nude maidens, with hair piled in knots on the tops of their head, standing around a column supported by an urn that doubles as the clock's dial. The maidens appear to be draping a floral garland around both the column and urn in poses reminiscent of statues of classical Greek goddesses.

The second clock, in the Art Nouveau style, features a maiden leaning over the face of the clock, which is shaped like a monument and covered with vines, leaves, and dragonflies (Figure 8.87). The maiden's long, flowing hair cinched with a clip cascades down her back, exposing a bare shoulder. Her dress clings to her body, hinting at nudity in the same manner as artists in classical Greece used wet drapery styles to reveal the female form in a more demure manner.

The third clock, in the Art Deco style, features a maiden playing a lyre as she stands on a marble base that holds the dial (Figure 8.88). Her costume reflects the new styles in women's fashions in the 1920s: short skirt, rolled stockings, and short hair.

Although the depictions of women vary in each clock, they are linked by the representation of women throughout the history of the decorative arts as modern goddesses. These three clocks reflect the social structures and attitudes toward the women of their time: nudity exposes the feminine vulnerability of late-19th century women, the youthful maiden in seductive pose and clothing represents man's temptation, and the inspiring muse offers strength and support.

**FIGURE 8.86** This late-19th-century Parian figural clock features classical nude maidens.
© Judith Miller/Dorling Kindersley/Sloan's

**FIGURE 8.87** This Art Nouveau metal mantel clock with circular enameled dial features a willowy maiden among swirling vines. © Judith Miller/Dorling Kindersley/Lyon and Turnbull Ltd.

**FIGURE 8.88** A maiden plays a lyre on top of this mantel clock in the Art Deco style. © Judith Miller/Dorling Kindersley/Freeman's

## TEXTILES

The invention of the steam engine and Jacquard loom spurred competition among factories seeking to offer quality fabrics for clothing and household furnishings at reasonable prices. The Great Exhibition at the Crystal Palace was the impetus for competition among countries to corner the market on the textile industry. Exhibits

featured not only the beautiful textiles manufactured by various factories, but also some of the mechanisms for producing them, inspiring creative inventors to come up with new and more advanced methods of production. Synthetic *aniline dyes*, first developed in 1856 by W. H. Perkin from England, were incorporated into textile manufacturing by 1862. Furthermore, roller-printing machines could print up to eight colors at a time by 1860, and 20 colors at a time before the end of the century (Figure 8.89).

Apart from technological advancements, textile fashions for home furnishings followed the popularity of eclecticism of the 19th century. England remained fixated on styles reminiscent of the past; Gothic Revival and Renaissance Revival were still in fashion at the time of the Great Exhibition. However, France maintained a strong connection to the Neoclassic styles of the previous century. Although in England and America, pictorial tapestries were no longer fashionable, France maintained its production of Aubusson and Savonnerie carpets (Figure 8.90). The French Revolution had interrupted advancements in textile production in France, but the industry soon recovered during the Second Empire under the reign of Napoleon III (r. 1848–1870).

William Morris prided himself as a weaver, mixing his own dyes from organic pigments to create woolen cloth for curtain panels, bedding coverlets, and tapestries (Figure 8–91). Using hand-carved wooden blocks, he printed cotton fabrics and wallpapers one color at a time. His favorite motifs incorporated organic forms based on flowers, birds, and vine patterns, which he printed in vivid colors on his woven textiles, wallpaper, and fabric.

Not all of Morris' British contemporaries supported his anti-industrial philosophies. As mentioned, Charles F. A. Voysey (1857–1941) believed the machine was an integral part of modern society and therefore should be used to its fullest potential. In fact, Voysey saw industrialization as the driver of future development. His furniture, textile, and wallpaper designs had the organic focus of the emerging Art Nouveau style; flowers and foliage intertwined in curvilinear forms (Figure 8.92).

## WALLPAPER

Mechanical methods of producing wallpapers led to two new types of wall coverings during the last quarter of the 19th century—*Lincrusta* and *Anaglypta*. Lincrusta

**FIGURE 8.89** This framed wall hanging made from printed cotton panels depicts George Washington and the shield of the United States. © Judith Miller/Dorling Kindersley/Sloan's

**FIGURE 8.90** This Aubusson carpet from the late 19th century features acanthus leaves and scrolls in a Rococo Revival style. © Judith Miller/Dorling Kindersley/Sloan's

**FIGURE 8.91** Morris & Company's "Honeysuckle" patterned textile panel in printed and embroidered wool features honeysuckle, bellflower, poppies, and sinuous vine patterns, and dates from 1876. © Judith Miller/Dorling Kindersley/Lyon and Turnbull Ltd.

**FIGURE 8.92** This Wilton woolen carpet designed by Charles F. A. Voysey, retailed through Liberty & Company, features scrolling foliate motifs against a deep blue background. © Judith Miller/Dorling Kindersley/Lyon and Turnbull Ltd.

was invented in 1877 by Frederick Walton (1833–1928), who took the idea from his already successful product, linoleum. He used mechanized roller machines to engrave relief designs on linseed and resin pulp paper to emulate fancy plasterwork (Figure 8.93).

In 1887, one of Walton's former employees, Thomas Palmer, had the idea to lower costs by using the same mechanized process on rolls of built-up paper pulp and cotton. The resulting Anaglypta was lighter and more flexible than the heavier Lincrusta, and both wall coverings could be painted. Mass production contributed to the overabundance of wallpapers in homes built during the mid 19th century onward. During the late Victorian period, wallpaper was used on walls and ceilings, with elaborate border designs separating the two surfaces (Figure 8.94).

Hand-blocked wallpaper was made by artists working in the Arts and Crafts and Art Nouveau styles. Morris & Company sold hand-blocked wallpapers designed by William Morris and his team of designers to upper-class English households (Figure 8.95). Hand-made wallpapers were also made by Art Nouveau designers for an affluent clientele seeking one-of-a-kind designs.

FIGURE 8.93 The entrance to the Gibson House in Boston features Victorian Lincrusta wallpaper in the Italianate style. Embossed designs of vines, fruits, and flowers are enhanced with gold paint over a slate blue background. Linda Whitwam © Dorling Kindersley. Courtesy of the Gibson House, Boston

FIGURE 8.94 Landis house museum features Victorian furnishings in a wallpapered room from 1870. © Travel Division Images/ Alamy

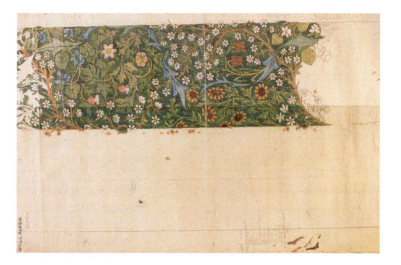

FIGURE 8.95 An original watercolor design for William Morris' "Blackthorn" patterned wallpaper produced by Morris & Company in 1892. Sanderson has been printing Morris' wallpaper designs since 1864. © Judith Miller/Dorling Kindersley/ Lyon and Turnbull Ltd.

# The Twentieth and Twenty-First Centuries

## The Modern Movement

The long-lasting reign of Queen Victoria ended with her death in 1901, and as a new century began, the Victorian period ended. The new technologies that emerged near the turn of the 20th century were the underlying force behind the modern cultural movement. Modern culture embraced the development of electricity, telephone and telegraph communication, and rapid transportation made possible by railroads, automobiles, and eventually airplanes. This new century of technological progress marked the beginning of worldwide pragmatic political issues that resulted in two world wars before midcentury.

World War I, or the First World War as it was known in Britain, began in 1914 as increasing tensions caused by European imperialism culminated in war. Ultimately, 32 countries would become involved in the war, with the Central powers of Germany, Austria-Hungary, Bulgaria, and the Ottoman Empire fighting against the Allied powers of the British Empire, Russia, and France. Italy joined the Allied powers in 1915, and the United States joined in 1917. In 1917, Russia withdrew from the war under the pressure of increasing civil war at home and the rising Bolshevik-led revolt. The war, which claimed an estimated 10 million lives, caused the demise of imperialism in Germany and Austria-Hungary and the collapse of the Ottoman government. The signing of the Treaty of Versailles in 1919 brought an official end to the war and redistributed political boundaries across Europe. World War I was the first war to embrace modern technological advances such as airplanes and wireless telegraphy. In addition, as a result of Thomas Edison's contributions to the motion picture camera, millions sitting in movie theaters throughout developed nations watched newsreel images of the progress and subsequent end of the war.

During World War I, manufacturing shifted toward producing only those items relevant to fighting the war, such as tanks, artillery, ships, submarines, and airplanes. The halt in the manufacturing of domestic goods and, more important, the exportation of the nations' gross national product—whether industrially based or agriculturally based—resulted in high inflation worldwide after World War I ended.

Further destabilizing the economic situation were inconsistencies in the gold standard currency markets. Finally, when the U.S. stock market crashed in 1929, the effects were felt all over North America and Europe, upsetting international trade and increasing unemployment. For the next decade, the Great Depression affected the world economy. President Franklin Roosevelt's New Deal in America and an increase in the manufacturing of military goods during World War II brought economic stability.

World War II began when Germany invaded Poland in 1939; by 1941, 26 Allied countries were fighting against German-led Axis powers. With all the major powers of the world involved in the conflict, the devastating war lasted through 1945. Postwar conferences among the United States, Great Britain, and the Soviet Union held at Yalta and in Potsdam in 1945 accelerated the Cold War between the United States and Russia over divergent political ideologies in post–World War II Europe.

In addition to the two world wars, many social reforms took place during the first half of the 20th century, including labor reform and women's suffrage. The industrialists of the late 19th century, who had exploited factory workers, were now faced with labor laws and unions that were established to curtail the abuse of human rights. Women's rights movements occurred throughout the world because women who had kept the economy going during World War I by performing jobs previously held by men demanded equality. Countries such as India, Great Britain, Canada, Norway, and Denmark gave women the right to vote before the war ended in 1919.

Moreover, the Treaty of Versailles of 1919 included a clause ensuring that women would be given equal pay to men when performing the same jobs (although this condition of the treaty was ignored by most countries). Women everywhere were exerting their independence in male-dominated societies. Fashions changed drastically from the Edwardian styles popular before the first war: women cut their hair (long hair was hazardous in operating machinery), shortened their hemlines, and wore trousers in public for the first time.

# Early Modernism

Architects working toward progressive changes in design discovered that the Neoclassic, Neo-Gothic, and Victorian styles popularized throughout most of the 19th century no longer fit into the 20th century, with its technological advancements. The styles of the 19th century were considered too old-fashioned and out of place within the context of this new contemporary culture. Instead, designers chose to strip away historicism and nationalism from their work, which led the way for a new International Style.

For the first time, modern architects put materials such as steel, glass, and reinforced concrete to innovative uses in commercial, industrial, and residential design projects. Architects expressed form using these new materials without regard to historical context. The Viennese architect Adolf Loos (1870–1933) wrote: "To find beauty in form instead of making it depend on ornament is the goal towards which humanity is aspiring." His statement typifies the efforts of early modern architects, whose exclusionism introduced unadorned, minimalist structures (Figure 9.1).

The events of World War I led designers to develop a style of architecture apart from location or culture. People started thinking globally after watching newsreels in local theaters on the war. The need to furnish the interior with styles equally reflective of the new architecture led to the design of modern furniture. In the beginning, modern furniture styles followed geometric formulas that mimicked the cubist form of architecture. At the same time, the designs also accommodated machine fabrication. By the start of World War I, machine aesthetics prevailed over the distinctive curvilinear styles of the Art Nouveau movement and replaced the excessive scrolls and curlicues seen in Victorian designs.

**FIGURE 9.1** Adolf Loos designed the Mueller House in Prague. The house exemplifies the modern architectural movement by shedding historicism and focusing on form, structure, and materials. © Inavan Hateren/Shutterstock.

**FIGURE 9.2** J. Herbert MacNair designed this table-cabinet in 1901, ignoring the whiplash curves of the currently popular Art Nouveau style and emphasizing instead straight lines and geometric arcs and semicircles.
© Judith Miller/Dorling Kindersley/Lyon and Turnbull Ltd.

**FIGURE 9.3** This view of the expansion for the Glasgow School of Art, designed by Charles Rennie Mackintosh, reveals modern features that incorporate a geometrical arrangement of architectural elements and subtle Art Nouveau motifs. Stephen Whitehorn © Dorling Kindersley.

**FIGURE 9.4** Two high-backed chairs arranged in front of a square table are set against the stark interior setting of the House for an Art Lover designed by Charles Rennie Mackintosh and Margaret MacDonald. The built-in cupboards, pendant light fixtures, and wall stencil designs characterize the couple's penchant for subtle Art Nouveau details amongst bare, minimalist interiors.
Stephen Whitehorn © Dorling Kidersley.

**FIGURE 9.5** This elaborate piano was designed by Charles Rennie Mackintosh for the House for an Art Lover. Stephen Whitehorn © Dorling Kindersley.

# GLASGOW SCHOOL

Students at the progressive Glasgow School of Art in Scotland were exploring stylistic changes in the currently popular Arts and Crafts and Art Nouveau styles. The school's most celebrated student at that time was Charles Rennie Mackintosh (1868–1928). Mackintosh took classes at night and worked in an architectural office in the daytime, first with John Hutchinson and later in the practice of Honeyman and Keppie. Both firms worked in the contemporary Art Nouveau style of the times. Mackintosh formed a friendship with J. Herbert MacNair (1868–1955), who worked with him and studied at the school in the evenings. A teacher at the Glasgow School of Art introduced the two men to artist Margaret MacDonald (1864–1933) and her sister, Frances (1873–1921), who were day students at the school. Ultimately, Charles and Margaret married, as did Herbert and Frances. Joining creative talents, they were known as the Glasgow Four, first exhibiting their art and furniture designs in the 1896 Arts and Crafts Society Exhibition held in London (Figure 9.2). In a manner that embodied the spirit of an uncomplicated, simplified interior, The Four designed china and tableware, textiles, carpets, and murals with the popular whiplash curves and organically inspired motifs of the Art Nouveau style. These curves appeared as delicate counterpoints to the rectilinear architecture and furniture styles that were sleek and vertical, emphasizing a front elevation that expressed geometrical negative spaces (Figure 9.2).

In 1897, Mackintosh won a design competition for the expansion of the Glasgow School of Art (Figure 9.3). The exterior only hinted at Art Nouveau decoration; the mass of the building was visually reduced by the placement of oversized glass windows on the facades. Mackintosh and MacDonald collaboratively worked on designs for the interior, which featured large open spaces and double-volume ceilings. The expansive geometry of their interiors illuminated by the oversized industrial windows and massive skylights earned the two a reputation for innovative modernism in design.

Charles and Margaret entered a competition to design a "House for an Art Lover" sponsored by a German design magazine (Figure 9.4). The house was built in 1989 and completed in 1994 based on the complete portfolio of drawings made by the couple in 1901. It stands as a testament to the truly timeless modernistic style envisioned over a century ago and features the collaborative work of husband and wife. For the exterior of the house, Mackintosh drew on traditional Scottish architecture. The house features a gabled roof and cubic forms arranged with projecting rooms and balconies. Window muntins are arranged in a tight grid pattern, and the same motif is carried through on the interior furnishings (Figure 9.5).

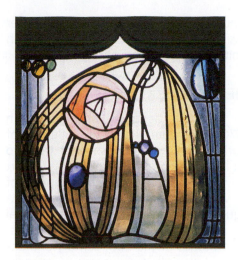

FIGURE 9.6 This stained-glass panel inside the House for an Art Lover, designed by Charles Rennie Mackintosh and Margaret MacDonald, breaks down conventional Art Nouveau whiplash curves, bringing more control to both the rose and vine designs. Stephen Whitehorn © Dorling Kindersley.

FIGURE 9.7 A pair of Glasgow School brass wall sconces, dated from 1900 attributed to Agnes Bankier Harvey (1873–1947); each is embossed with profiles of Art Nouveau maidens flanked by tendrils and poppy seed pods. © Judith Miller/Dorling Kindersley/Lyon and Turnbull Ltd.

Striking contrasts between light and dark surfaces and furniture designed with stark minimalism were an extreme departure from Victorian fashions of the past century (Figure 9.6). Margaret's artistic hand appears in the interior design as well; her stencil patterns adorn walls, art glass panels feature delicate Art Nouveau–inspired botanicals, and grid-patterned textiles complement the austerity of the architecture.

Commissions for the Hill House in 1902 and a series of tearooms owned by Kate Cranston in Glasgow brought the Mackintoshes' design into the public eye and introduced to modern culture a shockingly stark minimalism that would be developed further by leaders of the Bauhaus in Germany during the 1920s. The Four worked on designs for the Ingram Street Tea Room and the Willow Tea Room in 1900 and 1904, respectively, creating modern interiors that featured white walls, Art Nouveau–style murals, and straight-lined furniture. Tablecloths, silverware and tea services, light fixtures, and hat racks were designed in accordance with the interior architectural setting.

The work of the Glasgow Four mixed Art Nouveau and Celtic motifs, although to place these designers in the category of Arts and Crafts or Art Nouveau designers would be misleading; their work embodied freshness by creating light and bright interiors that pushed design into the modern age, lifting the darkness of the Victorian era.

Furniture was stained in a dark brown or dark green that contrasted with creamy white interior walls or were painted white to create a seamless interior. The designs of other artisans working in a similar direction, now referred to as the Scottish School, evoked a similar mood by mixing Art Nouveau styling with Celtic motifs (Figures 9.7, 9.8, and 9.9). All the while, the team's work was not in great demand by the general public, and after winning a few more competitions, Mackintosh and the Four faded into history until resurrected by modern

FIGURE 9.8 This Scottish School brass mirror features repoussé work with a band of poppy seed heads with whiplash stems. © Judith Miller/Dorling Kindersley/Lyon and Turnbull Ltd.

FIGURE 9.9 A Glasgow school stained beech wood clock case with a brass dial designed by Margaret Thompson Wilson in the form of two female figures dates from 1900. © Judith Miller/Dorling Kindersley/Lyon and Turnbull Ltd.

FIGURE 9.10 A set of Secessionist black lacquer nesting tables designed by Josef Hoffmann with spindle supports on runners.
© Judith Miller/Dorling Kindersley/Lyon and Turnbull Ltd.

FIGURE 9.11 Josef Hoffmann's *Sitzmaschine*, "machine for sitting," recliner designed in 1905 has a reclining mechanism based on the Morris chair. Sitzmaschine, adjustable lounge chair, produced by J. & J. Kohn, 1908 (stained bentwood, plywood and brass), Hoffmann, Josef (1870–1956)/Private Collection/Photo © Christie's Images/The Bridgeman Art Library International.

enthusiasts. In 1975, Italian manufacturer Cassina began reproducing the Mackintosh furniture line.

## WIENER WERKSTÄTTE

The Viennese designer Josef Hoffmann (1870–1956) came under the influence of Charles Rennie Mackintosh after the two met in 1903. Hoffmann broke from the Art Nouveau tradition under the auspices of the Viennese Secession to explore a rectangular style employing severe geometrical shapes. His work embodied the progressive attitudes of the 20th century and anticipated the strict geometry of modern art (Figures 9.10 and 9.11). Hoffmann's

---

## COMPARISONS    The Grid

The two chairs have similar design features and it is reasonable to assume that the same person created them. However, the chair in Figure 9.12 was designed by Charles Rennie Mackintosh in 1904 for a house he designed, Hill House. The ebonized sycamore chair has a slightly curved back filled with vertical slats extending from the crest rail to the lower stretcher. The upper back features horizontal slats intersecting a central, vertical panel of squares also running from the crest rail to the lower stretcher. The drop-in upholstered seat is trapezoidal with the broad side facing front and is supported by squared legs connected with stretchers.

- Other than the fact that one chair is a side chair and one is an armchair, how does the design of this chair differ from the one in Figure 9.13?
- What characteristics are similar?

The chair in Figure 9.13 was designed by Josef Hoffmann in 1908. It is made from black-stained ash and poses a simple geometric arrangement of horizontal and vertical slats. The chair features metal studs around the seat of the chair and a leather seat pad. Both designers placed dark-stained furniture in rooms with light walls, often white, to achieve contrast between furnishings and architecture. Hoffmann's chair was designed to contrast against his interior design, which focused on bright interiors and adhered to geometric architectural elements.

FIGURE 9.12 An ebonized sycamore chair designed by Charles Rennie Mackintosh in 1904.
© Judith Miller/Dorling Kindersley/Lyon and Turnbull Ltd.

FIGURE 9.13 Josef Hoffmann designed this chair made from black-stained ash in 1908. Modern in design, the simple geometry features an apparent grid pattern on the back. A black leather cushion replaces traditional upholstery. © Judith Miller/Dorling Kindersley/Sloan's.

interest in uniting architecture and design resulted in the formation of the Wiener Werkstätte in 1903.

Along with Koloman Moser (1868–1918), Hoffmann organized the Wiener Werkstätte, which brought artisans together in a workshop environment who would work to produce goods in the more progressive modern spirit (Figure 9.14). The workers focused on handcrafted items that reached wealthy patrons (Figure 9.15). In 1925, Hoffmann designed the Austrian pavilion for the *Exposition Internationale des Arts Décoratifs et Industriels Modernes* held in Paris, which brought recognition to the group. The *Exposition* launched the Art Deco styles of the 1920s and 1930s. By 1932, a dwindling supply of patrons forced the workshop to close, because workers could no longer compete against increasingly available mechanized goods.

## FRANK LLOYD WRIGHT

In America, Frank Lloyd Wright (1867–1959) helped to introduce a new style of design comparable in theory to the honest purity of the Glasgow Four, one that broke with an adherence to traditional design full of historical references. Wright studied engineering from 1885 to 1887 at the University of Wisconsin before apprenticing in the offices of Adler and Sullivan in Chicago. In 1896, Wright opened his own architectural practice and began designing residences in the fashionable Oak Park, Illinois, neighborhood where he lived.

Wright's residences emphasized the horizontal plane expressed as geometric solids. Intrinsically, Wright broke away from the restricting bulk of the Victorian style and chose to articulate the contradiction of form and materials. Mass opposed void spaces, smooth poured concrete contrasted with the harsher textural qualities of brick and mortar, and light values visually advanced from darkened backgrounds. Unlike Mackintosh whose flat spatial relationships were best appreciated from a two-dimensional perspective, Wright's architecture leaped into three-dimensional space through these manipulations of mass and void, textural contrasts, and value changes.

The Meyer May House built in Michigan in 1908 and fully restored in 1987 captures Wright's fresh architectural style and attention to interior details, which were deeply rooted in the Arts and Crafts movement (Figure 9.16). In 1909, Wright completed designs on a house in Chicago for the Robie family. Like the May House, the Robie House epitomized Wright's interest in the horizontal plane and the dichotomy of mass and void through its cantilevered flat roof that offered shade to balconies and recessed windows. The design of the Robie House anchored Wright's Prairie style (houses designed to "hug" the earth with flat roofs and horizontal emphasis), setting the stylistic direction for future projects and shattering the verticality of seemingly old-fashioned Victorian Queen Anne houses.

FIGURE 9.15 A terra-cotta figurine made at the Weiner Werkstätte with polychrome glaze; it features a mother and child both wearing exotic costumes. © Judith Miller/Dorling Kindersley/Lyon and Turnbull Ltd.

FIGURE 9.14 This silver flower vase (the glass liner is missing) by Josef Hoffmann from 1904–1906 was produced during his time at the Wiener Werkstätte. The basket and handle feature Hoffmann's strong grid motif. © Judith Miller/ Dorling Kindersley/Lyon and Turnbull Ltd.

FIGURE 9.16 The Meyer May House in Grand Rapids, Michigan, designed by Frank Lloyd Wright and completed in 1909, features characteristic Prairie-style architecture with its low profile, deep-shaded eaves, and horizontal emphasis. Jon Spaull © Dorling Kindersley.

**FIGURE 9.17** This dining room set designed by Frank Lloyd Wright and George Niedecken for the Robie House emulates Arts and Crafts styling with its straight lines and unornamented oak. The straight-backed chairs emphasize the strict formality of dining for the period, forcing erect posture while eating. Side lanterns of stained glass at each corner of the table create subdued lighting. Andrew Leyerle © Dorling Kindersley. Courtesy of Frank Lloyd Wright Home and Studio Foundation.

Severely contemporary for its time, the Robie House demanded interior furnishings equally modern in design. Wright complied by assembling a team of artisans who followed his designs to produce furniture, textiles, carpets, lighting fixtures, and stained-glass windows. The unique open-plan interior of the Robie House enabled Wright to use a system of built-ins and carefully placed chairs and tables that ingeniously separated space with minimal walls or room dividers. Tall-backed chairs created a visual screen around the dining tables and separated the eating area from adjoining spaces.

Wright's designs for furniture and textiles were explicitly connected to the structures he built. The Arts and Crafts movement and the American Mission style influenced his handmade oak furniture, although it was often criticized for being too heavy and cumbersome. George Niedecken (1878–1945) worked on several significant Wright-designed homes including the Robie, Meyer May, Avery Coonley, and Susan Lawrence Dana houses. He worked for Wright in his Oak Park studio completing designs for furniture, murals, and rugs from 1909 to 1913 (Figure 9.17). Niedecken maintained his own practice designing and producing furniture and completing interior design projects throughout his lifetime, working once more with Wright in 1916.

Although several other architects worked in the Prairie style and its closely related Craftsman style of architecture, Wright's work stands out as innovative for breaking down the barriers of tightly planned and enclosed interior spaces. He went on to design many more residential and commercial buildings, each carefully

# LEARN More

## Frank Lloyd Wright Interior Design

Frank Lloyd Wright designed this Prairie-style house located in Grand Rapids, Michigan, for the Meyer May family in 1908. Consistent with the characteristics found in Wright's other Prairie-style designs, low walls and freestanding partitions act as dividers within an open-plan interior. This interior view reveals Wright's selective layering of contrasting colors and materials to emphasize the horizontal. Notice how the quarter-sawn white oak millwork stands out against a background of warm ochre, giving linear dimension to the wall planes. In 1987, the house underwent complete restoration after extensive research in the Prairie Archives at the Milwaukee Art Museum produced crucial information regarding the original specifications for construction and interior furnishings.

**FIGURE 9.18** Frank Lloyd Wright designed this Prairie-style house located in Grand Rapids, Michigan, for the Meyer May family in 1908. Courtesy Steelcase, Inc., Grand Rapids, Michigan.

FIGURE 9.19 The Schröder House in Utrecht, the Netherlands, designed by Gerrit Rietveld in 1924, still holds its modern appeal and is considered the purest expression of De Stijl architecture. Schroeder House, built in 1923–24 (photo), Rietveld, Gerrit (1888–1964)/Utrecht, Netherlands/© DACS/The Bridgeman Art Library International.

FIGURE 9.20 The main floor of the Schröder House shows a combined living and dining space, expansive glass windows, ceiling tracks that accommodate movable wall panels, and the Rood Blau (Red Blue) Chair, designed in 1918. This is a restored interior of Gerrit Rietveld's architectural masterpiece. Gerrit Rietveld (1888–1964). First floor, 1987, view of the stairwell/landing and the living-dining area. In the foreground is the Red and Blue chair. Rietveld Schroderhlis, 1924, Utrecht, The Netherlands. Centraal Museum Utrecht/Rietveld-Schroder Archive.

orchestrated from the inside out to create a sense of harmony and balance between indoor and outdoor settings. For the most part, Wright's legacy is the introduction of modernism into the American vernacular of residential design.

## DE STIJL

Dutch artist and architect Theo van Doesburg (1883–1931) founded the De Stijl movement after collaborating with painter Piet Mondrian (1872–1944) and architect Gerrit Rietveld (1888–1964). The group adopted specific design characteristics that embodied the De Stijl movement, including the extensive use of geometric form; the primary colors of red, blue, and yellow; and asymmetrical spatial relationships. They designed without historical expressiveness and created imaginative structures that required equally inventive interior furnishings. Analogous to Frank Lloyd Wright, De Stijl architects incorporated engineering innovations and new technological advances available in building construction into their work.

In 1924, Rietveld received a commission that gave him complete creative freedom to design a residence that unified both architectural structure and interior space. The Schröder House in Utrecht, the Netherlands, allowed him to fully explore his theories on modernism. The house is still considered a milestone achievement in modern design and exemplifies the purest expression of De Stijl architecture (Figure 9.19). The recently restored house was designed for interior designer Truus Schröder-Schräder (1889–1985) and features projecting cantilevers, balconies, and flat rectangular planes that create interesting areas of mass and void. The color palette was restricted to the white surface treatment of the concrete accented by red, blue, and yellow with black on columns, windows, and doorframes.

An open-plan interior features sliding panels that close and separate spaces (Figure 9.20). The furniture is designed with geometric austerity. The house made Rietveld's 1918 design for the Rood Blau (Red Blue) Chair famous; his chair expresses the three-dimensional sculptural aspects of a Mondrian De Stijl painting with an emphasis on geometry and the integration of primary colors. Rietveld continued to design after the completion of the Schröder House, adapting his designs to children's toys and furniture.

Although Rietveld was trained in custom joinery and had learned the skill of cabinetmaking at 11 years of age, he was a proponent of mass production. He was

**FIGURE 9.21 A painting in the Cubist style features the geometricizing of ordinary objects.** © B Christopher/Alamy.

convinced that machine fabrication was the only affordable way to reach the masses, and his designs were finally produced by the Netherlands-based Mertz and Company in the 1930s.

## INTERNATIONAL STYLE

By 1917, European architects had succeeded in removing architecture from traditionally based revivalist designs. Instead, they initiated a purely geometric approach to design and adopted structural innovations that relied on steel and reinforced concrete and non-load-bearing walls. Called the International Style by American architect Philip Johnson (1906–2005), the style is identified by its ability to escape the regional vernacular by adhering to geometrical form and avoiding applied ornamentation. Instead of relying on historical references, architects introduced a rational approach to design that emphasized international unity and crossed cultural boundaries. The end of World War I was the first in a series of events that began to globalize the world. For the first time in history, newsreels crossed cultural boundaries to bring news and information to the public through powerful visual images. Capturing the zeitgeist, the modern architectural movement continued to dominate European design throughout the 1920s and 1930s.

As early as 1906, European Cubist painters represented the world as a collage of forms reduced to simplified geometrical shapes that shattered the traditional laws of spatial order (Figure 9.21). Through the accomplishments of Pablo Picasso (1881–1973) and Georges Braque (1882–1963), other European painters sought to purify form and remove art from the context of traditionalism. By 1917, European architects excelled in removing architecture from traditionally based revivalist design. Instead, they initiated a purely geometrical style of design based on the principles of Cubism.

Structural innovations, specifically the non-load-bearing walls that employed industrially engineered materials such as steel and reinforced concrete, enabled the fragmentation of interior space. Coupled with Cubist, Fauvist, and Futurist artists of the avant-garde, industrial designers delighted a rising social class of aesthete elitists eager to commission works for the sole purpose of proclaiming an appreciation of ultra-modern art and design.

Charles-Édouard Jeanneret-Gris, nom de plume Le Corbusier (1887–1965), a native-born Swiss, was another advocate of modern design. Even though most of his training was from a local art school, at age 17 he designed his first house. In 1907, he took a grand tour of Europe and the Middle East where he sketched numerous ancient monuments. During these travels, he met Josef Hoffmann, who exposed him to the work of the Wiener Werkstätte. Over the next four years Le Corbusier worked as an apprentice in the architectural firms of Peter Behrens in Germany and August Perret in France. As a leading proponent of modern architecture, Behrens collected European publications of Frank Lloyd Wright's work and kept them in his atelier. Here, Le Corbusier was first exposed to Wright's design philosophies. It was also in the studio of Behrens that Le Corbusier met two other apprentices, Walter Gropius (1883–1969) and Ludwig Mies van der Rohe (1886–1969) who would later influence the Bauhaus school.

In 1917, Le Corbusier relocated to Paris and began his own practice. After legally changing his name to Le Corbusier in 1920, he began to write extensively on modern design while developing a style of architecture that was truly purist in nature, including massive three-dimensional sculptures of geometric form. His International Style exteriors and interiors lacked decoration, emphasizing instead sleek modernism in the use of concrete, glass, and steel (Figure 9.22). Encompassing the avant-garde theories of Cubism, his forms were

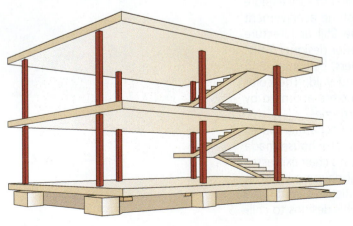

**FIGURE 9.22 A drawing of Le Corbusier's concept behind the Domino House of 1914.**

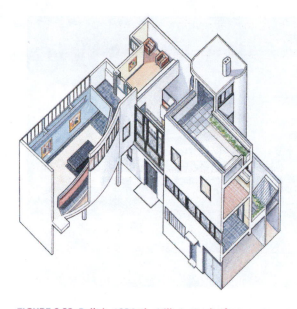

FIGURE 9.23 Built in 1924, the Villa La Roche features Le Corbusier's "machine for living." Kevin Jones and Associates © Dorling Kindersley.

FIGURE 9.24 Villa La Roche, designed in 1924 by Le Corbusier, features stark, minimalist interiors with modern furniture and art of his own design. Dorling Kindersley © 2005 Artists Rights Society (ARS), New York/ADAGP, Paris/FLC.

reduced to geometrical solids emphasizing a machine aesthetic that supported the use of reinforced concrete and steel. Le Corbusier's claim that "the house is a machine for living in" summarized his more rational approach to design.

The 1925 *Exposition Internationale des Arts Décoratifs et Industriels Modernes*, the first of a series of expositions that continued through 1937, introduced furniture and decorative arts designed for mass production. Le Corbusier's Pavilion de l'Esprit Nouveau showed attendees the architectural possibilities of mechanization and standardization. His method of using uniform measurements for doors, windows, and walls revolutionized residential construction. In 1926, Le Corbusier and his architect cousin, Pierre Jeanneret (1896–1967), published a manifesto detailing their architectural philosophies titled, "Five Points Towards a New Architecture." In it, the two detailed their architectural aesthetic: structural *pilotis* carry the load of the house, leaving an open-plan interior without the need for load-bearing walls, and a continuous band of ribbon windows and a generous roof terrace expand the outdoor space. The manifesto solidified the International Style of architecture in theory, and the completion of a home for Raoul La Roche, Villa La Roche, became the manifestation of their ideology (Figures 9.23 and 9.24). Begun in 1923, the house was designed with a stark minimalism to show off the client's art collection. The next project, Villa Savoye, completed in 1929, features an elevated living space supported on slender pilotis.

Charlotte Perriand (1903–1999), one of the founding members of the Union des Artistes Modernes, was so inspired by Le Corbusier's ideology that she invited him to see her own work at the Parisian Salon d'Automne in 1927. The resulting collaboration between Perriand, Le Corbusier, and Jeanneret would last until Le Corbusier's death in 1965. At the 1929 Salon d'Automne, the now infamous tubular steel furniture collection introduced furnishings that fit within the context of the architecture. The steel supports on chairs and tables mocked the pilotis used to elevate Villa Savoye's main living area above the ground (Figure 9.25). The furniture support mechanism and body of the piece were treated as two separate entities, each depending on the other to function. Tubular steel, black leather, and pony hide and cowhide were basic materials used by the three in the design of their furniture. Cushioned black leather or stretched pony hide kept the body from coming into direct contact with the supporting framework, creating comfortable furnishings that were not dependent on traditional upholstery methods.

FIGURE 9.25 Le Corbusier, Perriand, and Jeanneret's Grand Comfort chair (available in two sizes with a matching settee) is manufactured with a separate steel frame that holds cushions in place to form the seat, back, and sides. © Judith Miller/Dorling Kindersley/Freeman's.

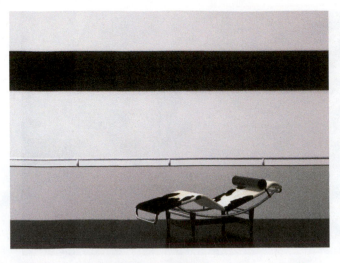

**FIGURE 9.26** In 1929, Le Corbusier, Perriand, and Jeanneret exhibited their newly designed furniture collection at the Salon d'Automne in Paris. Their efforts to treat the function of the supporting frame separate from the body of each piece, along with their use of tubular steel, are characteristic of their unique style of design. The back on this chaise longue designed in 1927 adjusts from an upright to reclined position by simply moving the arc-shaped frame along its detached base. © andrés arias/Shutterstock.

**FIGURE 9.27** Walter Gropius designed the buildings at the Bauhaus in Dessau, Germany, in 1925. Following the tenets of modern architecture, the building lacks historical references or applied ornamentation, focusing instead on construction materials, such as concrete, glass, and steel. © c./Shutterstock.

The furniture satisfied both comfort and function, but was small in scale since Le Corbusier chose to emphasize the architectural interior; he viewed furniture as sculpture—artwork that completed the overall integrity of the space. Along with tapestries, paintings, and sculptures, furniture became an accessory because he preferred that his clients live in the space rather than among furniture (Figure 9.26).

## BAUHAUS

In Germany, under the direction of Walter Gropius, a school called the Bauhaus ("build-house") opened its doors in 1919. The Bauhaus became the first school to recognize the importance of training artisans to design products for mass production. The design of the buildings at the school exemplified the intent of the school; they were radically modern by current architectural standards. Designed by Gropius in 1925, the Bauhaus school buildings were rectangular structures with flat roofs and glass and concrete walls, without ornamentation or references to the historical past (Figure 9.27). Steel columns supported the structures allowing for large expanses of glass curtain walls.

Students at the Bauhaus were considered apprentices under the guidance of their instructors. They were encouraged to experiment with the materials of construction before working through the problems of design. Gropius and his colleagues believed it was important for students to understand how the materials of construction functioned relative to the design process. This clearly expressed the working philosophy of Gropius, and "form follows function" became the motto of the Bauhaus. Some of the most important names in 20th-century art and architecture were connected with the Bauhaus. Students included Marcel Breuer (1902–1981), who later became director of the furniture shop at the Bauhaus; Mart Stam (1899–1986); Marianne Brandt (1893–1983), who replaced László Moholy-Nagy (1895–1946) as director of the metal shop; Anni Fleischmann Albers (1889–1994), who studied weaving; and her future husband, Josef Albers (1888–1976), who taught painting classes. Other instructors included painters Piet Mondrian, Wassily Kandinsky (1866–1944), and Paul Klee (1879–1940), and architect Mies van der Rohe who directed the architectural department from 1930 to 1933.

The Bauhaus led the way for an avant-garde style of teaching that emphasized cooperation between artist and machine. At first students were trained in the arts of painting and sculpture. Eventually, industrial arts and home product design—textiles, tableware, wall coverings, lighting, and furniture—were introduced into

FIGURE 9.28 Marianne Brandt designed this clear glass teapot for the Schott & Gen glass company of Jena, Germany, glass company. Inventive for its time, the teapot was made of a new heat-resistant glass. © Judith Miller/Dorling Kindersley/Graham Cooley.

FIGURE 9.29 A wool rug in the Constructivist style features geometric elements over a solid ground. © Judith Miller/Dorling Kindersley/Freeman's.

the curriculum (Figures 9.28 and 9.29). Like Anni Albers, Gunta Stölzl (1897–1983) began her career as a textile weaver, first as a student at the Bauhaus. She later became the director of the weaving shop. After the school's closing in 1933, she established her own workshop in Zurich where she produced curtains, wall hangings, and fabrics for commissioned clients through the 1960s. Throughout Stölzl's career, her designs never wavered from the lively patterns and bold colors of the Cubist and Fauve artistic movements.

In 1920, Marcel Breuer came to the Bauhaus as a student in the cabinetmaking shop. There he was introduced to the cubical angularity of the De Stijl movement, specifically the work of Gerrit Rietveld. Breuer's first chairs were constructed entirely out of flat planes of wood. Soon after, he designed a chair that had an open wood frame with stretched canvas providing the structural support for seat and back. Breuer discovered that the stretched canvas supported the body without heavy upholstery and it was quite comfortable.

After additional experimentation with various other materials, Breuer encountered something unique in the design of the bicycle he rode to the workshop. As he studied the bicycle, he noticed the frame was strong yet lightweight due to its tubular steel construction. Breuer also noticed that the curvilinear shape of the handlebar was created by bending the bar of tubular steel. He reasoned that this same process could be adapted to the design and manufacture of furniture (Figure 9.30). Breuer quickly arranged for tubular steel bars to be sent to his workshop, and finally, in 1925, the first chair made from bent tubular steel was introduced.

One of the most influential products to come out of the Bauhaus was a chromium-plated tubular steel chair designed by Breuer in 1928 (Figure 9.31). The Cesca Chair (named after his daughter Francesca) was made from bent tubular steel and had a cantilevered frame fitted with a cane back and seat instead of traditional cloth upholstery. The chair was too expensive to produce until proper tube-bending equipment could be developed. By 1930, the chair identified as the B 32 appeared in the Thonet catalog. Before long, Breuer's furniture designs and those of his Bauhaus colleagues, Mies van der Rohe and Mart Stam, revolutionized the concepts of furniture manufacturing and inspired designers throughout the 20th century as chromium steel replaced wood as the dominant material in furniture construction.

In 1928, a department of architecture was added to the Bauhaus curriculum. Mies, a longtime acquaintance of Walter Gropius, became Director of Architecture at the Bauhaus from 1930 to 1933. Mies quickly introduced his own theories on architectural design, which emphasized glass curtain walls supported by a steel skeletal frame. When asked to design a pavilion for the 1929 World's Fair held

FIGURE 9.30 Marcel Breuer designed this chair in 1925 for his friend and Bauhaus colleague, Wassily Kandinsky. The chair's tubular steel construction with leather strapping instead of upholstery gave the design a modern theme and emphasized machine aesthetics. © Judith Miller/Dorling Kindersley/Freeman's.

FIGURE 9.31 Marcel Breuer designed the Cesca chair (named after his daughter, Francesca) in 1928 using natural materials of beech wood and cane integrated with sleek tubular steel. The cantilevered design revolutionized modern furniture and machine-produced furniture. © frotos/Shutterstock.

FIGURE 9.32 The German Pavilion built in 1929 and designed by Mies van der Rohe was based on his concept of an all-glass house. © Treena Crochet.

FIGURE 9.33 The steel frame on this chair designed by Mies van der Rohe with its graceful, sweeping curves supports leather webbing that holds tufted cushions that form the seat and back. © Adam Filipowicz/ Shutterstock.

FIGURE 9.34 Mies van der Rohe designed the MR chair with a cantilevered base made from stainless steel that supports an upholstered seat and back. Like many other Bauhaus furniture designs, the chair did not go into mass production until after the war. © Thomas Hernandez/Shutterstock.

in Barcelona, Mies complied by building a spectacular glass and steel structure known as the German Pavilion (Figure 9.32). The glass curtain walls were void of ornamentation and illustrated Mies's design philosophy, "Less is more." His achievements in International Style architecture advanced the cause of modernism and set forth a new direction in residential design.

The significance of the German Pavilion led to the popularity of a chair designed by Mies specifically for its interior. The Barcelona chair quickly became a modern furniture classic, even though its construction was not conducive to mass production due to a complicated design that required special welding (Figure 9.33). Mies and Lily Reich (1885–1947), his collaborator on many of his designs including the MR chair, continued to design significant architectural structures and complemented their interiors with coordinating furnishings, including several versions of cantilevered tubular steel chairs (Figure 9.34). These furnishings are currently reproduced through The Knoll Group and are seen as icons of the 20th century.

Members of the school dispersed throughout Europe and America when the National Socialist Party shut down the Bauhaus in 1933. Walter Gropius, who had left as director of the Bauhaus in 1928, went to England in 1934, worked there briefly, and then moved to the United States in 1937 accompanied by Marcel Breuer. Both became professors in Cambridge. Gropius eventually became director of the school of architecture at Harvard and Breuer went to the Massachusetts Institute of Technology. The two combined their architectural talents and built several homes in New England. Their work in residential design brought Bauhaus styling to the American vernacular (Figure 9.35).

Although Breuer went on to establish his own architectural practice in New York, Gropius remained in Cambridge and formed The Architects Collaborative in 1945. Open-plan dwellings catered to the changing American lifestyles brought about by the economic depression of the 1930s. Mies arrived in America a year after Gropius and Breuer. He settled in Chicago and became the Director of Architecture at the Armour Institute (renamed the Illinois Institute of Technology), where he contributed to the design of many campus buildings. Mies's "glass box" architectural style dominated city skylines with high-rise steel buildings with glass curtain walls.

FIGURE 9.35 The living room of the Walter Gropius home in Lincoln, Massachusetts, features furniture designed by Marcel Breuer. View of the Living Room of Gropius House in Lincoln, Massachusetts, built in 1938 (photo), Gropius, Walter (1883–1969)/Historic New England, Boston, Massachusetts, USA/The Bridgeman Art Library International.

# Art Deco and Art Moderne

Often referred to as the Jazz Age, the 1920s was an era in which people embraced change like no other decade in history. Music, dance, clothing, and hairstyles resonated with the modernization exemplified in Erté's (1892–1990) graphic illustrations for *Harper's Bazaar* magazine. Evidence of this new direction in art and design appeared shortly after the end of World War I. The effects of the modern architectural movement continued to dominate European design throughout the 1920s and 1930s. As the appreciation of modernity became fashionable among bourgeois elitists, remarkable cultural change took place.

The discovery of the tomb of King Tutankhamen in Egypt by the archaeologist Howard Carter (1874–1939) in 1922 had influenced modern styles from architecture and interior design to clothing and hairstyles. Artifacts taken from the tomb caused a renewed interest in the styles of the past and of an exotic nature, which lead to the superfluous use of ornamentation. The 1925 Paris *Exposition Internationale des Arts Décoratifs et Industriels Modernes* expressed the new style of Art Deco, which evolved from an appreciation of machine aesthetics coupled with lavish ornamentation, rich color, and whimsical interpretations of space and form. Although this exposition introduced the world to Art Deco, the term was not widely used until 1966. The Art Deco furniture styles of the 1920s emphasized exotic woods and high-quality artisanship that included inlays of equally exotic materials such as shagreen, ivory, tortoiseshell, and eggshell (Figure 9.36). Like the Art Nouveau movement beforehand, Art Deco led to elitism, because only a select few could actually afford these lavishly designed objects (Figure 9.37).

At the Paris Exposition, a special pavilion was devoted to the exotic furnishings of Jacques-Èmile Ruhlmann* (1879–1933), who revived the opulence of cabinetwork unequaled since the French Baroque period in the 17th century (Figures 9.38 and 9.39). Ruhlmann himself expressed the attitude of Art Deco even before the Paris Exposition took place:

> A clientele of artists, intellectuals and connoisseurs of modest means is very congenial, but they are not in a position to pay for all the research, the experimentation, the testing that is needed to develop a new design. Only the very rich can pay for what is new and they alone can make it fashionable. Fashions don't start among the common people. Along with satisfying a desire for change, fashion's real purpose is to display wealth.**

The designer-turned-architect Eileen Gray (1879–1976) successfully combined the more decorative Art Deco styling with Bauhaus machine aesthetics and Le Corbusier industrialism. Often overlooked, but nonetheless important, Gray made significant contributions to the field of design. After studying drawing and learning the craft

*There are contradictions in monographs as to the sequence of Ruhlmann's first and middle names; Èmile-Jacques also appears in print.
**Kellar, Harold. "Twentieth Century Design: Jacques-Emile Ruhlmann." Picture Framing Magazine, July 1998.

**FIGURE 9.36** This screen by Paul Etienne Saln (1904–1995) is made from lacquered wood; each panel is attached with brass hinges. © Judith Miller/Dorling Kindersley/Freeman's.

**FIGURE 9.37** Carlo Bugatti designed this vellum-covered box decorated with frogs and lily pads; it is valued between $10,000 and $15,000. © Judith Miller/Dorling Kindersley/Mary Ann's Collectibles.

**FIGURE 9.38** Jacques-Èmile Ruhlmann's brown velvet armchair features burr amboyna wood with ebony details and gilt metal footings. © Judith Miller/Dorling Kindersley/DeLorenzo Gallery.

**FIGURE 9.39** This cabinet designed by Jacques-Èmile Ruhlmann is rosewood veneer with ivory inlay swirling designs and dates from 1919. © Judith Miller/Dorling Kindersley/DeLorenzo Gallery.

The Twentieth and Twenty-First Centuries

FIGURE 9.40 The Transat chair designed and patented by Eileen Gray and Jean Badovici in 1927 has a lacquered wood frame with leather upholstery. Notice the adjustable headrest. © Judith Miller/Dorling Kindersley/ John Jesse.

FIGURE 9.41 This Art Deco side table features a black glass circular top with chromium-plated supports on an ebonized base. © Judith Miller/Dorling Kindersley/Lyon and Turnbull Ltd.

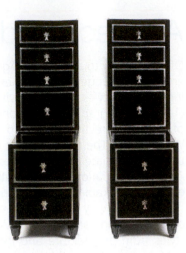

FIGURE 9.42 A pair of American Art Deco skyscraper cabinets made from black-lacquered and gilted wood rests on nickel feet and dates from the 1930s. © Judith Miller/Dorling Kindersley/High Style Deco.

of Japanese lacquer work in London, she left for Paris in 1902 to further develop her interest in lacquering techniques. While in Paris, Gray was trained in this ancient art by the Japanese cabinetmaker and lacquer worker, Sugawara.

She began her career as a designer of exotic lacquered screens for wealthy Parisian patrons. These designs were so successful that, in 1922, Gray opened her own workshop and gallery to produce and sell her collection. During this time, Gray expanded the content of her work to include wood furniture, lamps, mirrors, and handwoven textiles. Her early works depict a definitive Art Deco styling exemplified through the use of shiny finishes, bright colors, and exotic materials—rich inlays of ivory, colored enamels, and ebony.

After Gray saw the work of Le Corbusier in 1922 at a Parisian exhibition, her designs evolved to reflect the theories of Le Corbusier, the Bauhaus, and the De Stijl movement. In 1926, Gray received a commission to design and build a house on the Côte d'Azur in France. From 1926 until 1929, Gray and her partner, Jean Badovici, devoted most of their time and attention to the Maison E.1027. Designing every last detail from the outside structure to the interior, Gray and Badovici created furniture that transformed the Art Deco designs into those epitomizing the International Style. (Figure 9.40).

The Metropolitan Museum of Art in New York City had also made significant contributions to promoting modern design. The museum's American Industrial Art Exhibition, held annually from 1917 to 1940, introduced the sleek styling of a streamlined age of industrial glamor. The name Art Moderne exemplified the blending of art and industry in aesthetically designed objects that lacked the harsh angularity of early modern designs. Also, the harder edges of ziggurats were softened by incorporating a series of circles and arcs into interiors accentuated with sleek and glossy furnishings (Figure 9.41). Materials emphasized chrome and glass rather than ornate and expensive marquetry designs.

In the 1930s, modern skyscrapers were becoming a reality as New York City led the world in building high-rises with steel frames, modern elevators, and rudimentary air-conditioning systems. America fell in love with the skyscraper (Figure 9.42). The latest skyscrapers such as the Chrysler Building, Empire State Building, and Rockefeller Center in New York City incorporated Aztec, Gothic, and Egyptian motifs along with images of classical gods and goddesses and primitive African designs (Figures 9.43 and 9.44).

FIGURE 9.43 Rockefeller Center in New York City consists of a central plaza surrounded by 14 skyscrapers designed by Raymond Hood in the Art Deco style. Begun in 1931, the buildings feature ziggurat profiles and applied decoration inspired by ancient civilizations. The sculpture of the Greek god Prometheus is located in the central plaza. Dave King © Dorling Kindersley.

FIGURE 9.46 This hotel in South Beach, Miami, epitomizes the American Art Moderne style of architecture. © Tony Arruza/CORBIS.

FIGURE 9.45 This armchair designed by Jean-Michel Frank is reflective of Art Deco styling with its arched back and rounded arms. Courtesy Palazzetti.

FIGURE 9.44 The elevator doors inside the Chrysler Building in New York City feature papyrus blossoms in metal and wood inlay. Dave King © Dorling Kindersley.

The streamlined designs of such notable industrial designers as Norman Bel Geddes (1893–1958), who designed furniture as well as automobiles, and Raymond Loewy (1893–1986) helped create a shift from looking at the past in awe (spurred by the discovery of King Tutankhamen's tomb) to looking toward the future. An increased use of Bakelite, a hard plastic that was easily formed into a variety of shapes and sizes, made streamlined industrial products and cheap decorative objects more affordable to the general public. In fact, actors Fred Astaire and Ginger Rogers danced on Bakelite floors on the sets of several movies throughout the 1930s and 1940s.

Marrying art with industry, Jean-Michel Frank (1895–1941), a leading French designer, created opulent interiors for high-end Parisian clientele. More known for his overstuffed furnishings immortalized by his Lipstick chair, and his materialization of the Lip sofa, Frank set the direction for the slick Hollywood set designs of the 1930s (Figure 9.45). The Art Deco style and overlapping modernism of the period became increasingly popular in the United States throughout the 1930s, reaching its pinnacle by the end of the decade. The ensuing Art Moderne style captured the American scene through Hollywood movie sets and was epitomized in the architectural style of South Beach, Miami (Figure 9.46).

The 1939 World's Fair held in New York City focused on the future, averting attention from the economic hard times of the Great Depression (Figure 9.47). The theme "Building the World of Tomorrow" introduced fairgoers to the latest technologies, including Loewy's design for the fastest train on record for the time and New York City's first television broadcast showing off RCA TV sets. Bel Geddes designed Futurama for General Motors, an exhibit that gave attendees a glimpse into the future—what the country would look like in 1960 with modern

FIGURE 9.47 Postcards issued during the 1939 World's Fair in New York City feature some of the Art Moderne buildings designed for the theme "The World of Tomorrow." © Judith Miller/Dorling Kindersley/Tony Moran.

highways and skyscrapers. Other futuristic-looking buildings designed for the fair emphasized smooth and rounded corners in the Art Moderne style. The fair's main exhibit, a diorama revealing industrial designer Henry Dreyfuss's (1904–1972) vision for a utopian future, was housed inside the Perisphere. The motif of a Perisphere was repeated in future World's Fairs of the 20th century (Figure 9.48). The fair ended in 1940, when optimism about the future was overshadowed by the escalation of World War II in Europe.

**FIGURE 9.48** This Perisphere-shaped frosted green and uncolored Saturn lamp with internally painted stars and planets was made to commemorate the 1939 World's Fair in New York City. © Judith Miller/ Dorling Kindersley/Deco Etc.

# Accessories

## POTTERY

Art Deco and Art Moderne ceramics included a wide range of designs for decorative and functional purposes alike. Egyptian motifs, influenced by the opening of King Tutankhamen's tomb, were featured on pottery vases resembling canopic jars (Figure 9.49). Figurative ceramics featured popular subjects ranging from the modern woman to mythological goddesses. Figurines of women wearing the current fashion in poses of lively dance were widely available. The flapper of the 1920s epitomized the carefree and independent woman; she had short bobbed hair and wore newly marketed cosmetics influenced by Hollywood movie stars and short skirts revealing rolled-down stockings. It is clear that the figurines were produced in great quantities to adorn interiors, because many originals currently come up for auction or are available through dealers. Although high-quality porcelains were made by recognized factories such as Royal Worcester, Royal Doulton, and Goldscheider, mass-produced and painted plaster cast figurines found their way into the consumer market, offering cheap substitutes.

One of the most innovative ceramicists of the Art Deco period was Clarice Cliff (1899–1972), who began working in a pottery factory in England as a young teenager. As an adult, she attended art classes at night while continuing to work as a pottery painter in the factory. After World War I, Cliff was given the chance to create some of her own designs and began to learn more about the shaping of pottery. Her unusual shapes and painted designs, which reflected the current interest in Cubism, Fauvism, and Futurism, were popular among consumers (Figure 9.50). Cliff produced some of her most interesting pieces, called "Bizarre" ware by critics and the public alike, during the Art Deco period.

**FIGURE 9.49** This Carlton Ware vase features a pharaoh figurehead on its lid and Egyptian motifs. Made in 1927, the design was inspired by the treasures removed from King Tutankhamen's tomb in 1922. © Judith Miller/ Dorling Kindersley/Woolley and Wallis.

**FIGURE 9.50** This Clarice Cliff inverted ziggurat vase features a brightly colored tree in the fashion of the Fauvist painters. © Judith Miller/Dorling Kindersley/Woolley and Wallis.

## PLASTICS

Despite William Morris's denouncement of "shoddy machine-made goods," mass production took hold of design culture in the early part of the 20th century. New methods, processes, and materials were explored to create a wide range of products for middle-class consumers. A synthetic plastic first created by Dr. Leo Baekeland in 1909 led the way for the production of molded goods using a phenolic resin. The plastic known as Bakelite could be molded into virtually any shape and size, making products such as radios, telephones, and decorative objects more affordable.

The hardness and durability of Bakelite, along with its heat-resistant qualities, made it the perfect material for table- and kitchenware. The material also found its way into the manufacture of jewelry, office equipment, and household appliances. By the 1930s, competitors developed other plastics, such as Catalin and Melamine, which could be colored any hue. Soon, all plastics from this era through the 1950s were referred to by the catchall trade name Bakelite.

## GLASS

As William Morris feared, the machine eventually muddled the lines between the fine art of craft and inexpensive substitutions of inferior quality. The dichotomy between quality-made goods and cheap ones continued throughout the 20th century. Glass-making was no exception as a wide range of press-molded glassware flooded the market. As Fenton had proven with his carnival glass, these machine-made, pressed-glass candy dishes, pitchers, vases, and compotes were attractive to middle-class consumers, who could buy them at next-to-nothing prices. Depression glass, as we call it today, was a press-molded glass made by machine. Advertisers used cheap glassware as free giveaways to entice consumers into their supermarkets, gas stations, and banks during the Great Depression.

Similarly, French artist René Lalique (1860–1945), who began his career as a jewelry designer, contributed to the advancement of the decorative arts. His creations in crystal evoked the feeling of the Art Deco style and embodied central themes seen in the graphic illustrations of Erté. Known for his fine-quality glass and crystal designs, some of his first works in glass took the form of perfume bottles he designed for Coty. These exquisite Lalique designs brought elitism to the perfume industry. His work on the glass pavilion at the 1925 *Exposition Internationale des Arts Décoratifs et Industriels Modernes* brought Lalique's work to the forefront of Art Deco design. Lalique's designs were created by hand pressing soft glass and crystal into shaped molds. After cooling, the pieces were then hand polished or acid etched to create beautiful patterns. The finished glass was often given a wash of color to enhance the relief designs (Figure 9.51). Although there were many hand processes involved in Lalique's glass, the molds allowed mass production of the same designs.

In addition to Lalique, well-established companies such as Baccarat captured the feeling of the Art Deco style by producing high-quality glass to be sold in high-end department stores. Designs included the stark geometric patterns inspired by Cubist paintings as well as nature motifs and young maidens. In competition with Lalique, Daum, a manufacturer of fine glassware located in Nancy, France, had its beginnings in the third quarter of the 19th century. Without formal training in glass manufacturing, the family-run business became a leading producer of glass in the Art Nouveau style in the early 20th century. Daum began creating designs influenced by the Cubist painters, after seeing the work shown at the 1925 *Exposition Internationale des Arts Décoratifs et Industriels Modernes*.

## MIRRORS

With a boom in the cosmetics industry spurred by Hollywood, wearing makeup became an accepted part of modern culture for the new independent woman of the 1920s. Many pocketbook-sized compact mirrors were produced at this time for ladies to carry in their pocketbooks to touch up their makeup. In addition to wall-hung mirrors and cheval mirrors, small dressing tables specifically designed for women to apply their makeup featured built-in mirrors. Moreover, Art Moderne style furniture featured mirrored surfaces and inset panels in their designs (Figure 9.52).

**FIGURE 9.51** This Art Deco–style vase by René Lalique from 1924 features press-molded fish enhanced by a blue wash of color. © Judith Miller/Dorling Kindersley/David Rago Auctions.

**FIGURE 9.52** This small occasional table from the 1930s in the Art Moderne style is veneered on all sides, the top, and the legs with cut mirror glass. © Judith Miller/Dorling Kindersley/Lyon and Turnbull Ltd.

FIGURE 9.53 This French Art Deco frosted glass and metal table lamp from 1925 features the signature of Lalique on the press-molded shade. © Judith Miller/Dorling Kindersley/Sloans & Kenyon.

FIGURE 9.54 A Marcel Bouraine cast bronze figurine supports a lamp and stained-glass globe shade. © Judith Miller/Dorling Kindersley/Sloan's.

FIGURE 9.55 The spire of the Chrysler Building in New York City is clad in stainless steel sunburst patterns with gargoyle accents. Designed by William van Allen in 1930. © Gary718/dreamstime.

FIGURE 9.56 This detail from an Art Deco building in New York City captures the mood of the period with its highly decorative detailing and depiction of Neptune. © Vtphotos/Dreamstime.

## LIGHTING

Electricity had revolutionized how interiors were lit, and in the 20th century, many Art Deco and Art Moderne designers included lighting fixtures in their vast design repertoires (Figure 9.53). Jacques-Èmile Ruhlmann designed lamps for his clients, and Jean-Michel Frank commissioned the sculptor Alberto Giacometti (1901–1966) to sculpt lamp bases for his interior design projects. René Lalique provided the glass designs for the luxury cruise ship the *S. S. Normandie (Normandy)* that included lit skylights and 15-foot illuminated columns.

Marius Sabino (1878–1961) founded a glass-making company whose designs were similar to those of Lalique. His designs were evocative of the Art Deco period, and like Lalique, he produced light fixtures for the *S. S. Normandie*. For the more mainstream clientele, low-end manufacturers copied the beauty of Lalique's and Sabino's inspired designs and produced pressed-glass lampshades as less expensive substitutes. Marcel-Andre Bouraine (1886–1948) was a sculptor working in bronze creating statues of Art Deco style nudes. His lamp design features a female nude supporting a decorative shade (Figure 9.54).

## METALWORKING

The Chrysler building in New York would not be the same without its pinnacle top clad in shimmering steel (Figure 9.55). Moreover, Rockefeller Center is known throughout the world by its oversized gilded bronze sculpture of Prometheus created by Paul Manship (1885–1966), who also produced Art Deco architectural details in the surrounding area (Figure 9.56). A key hallmark of the Art Deco style, the use of metal is incorporated into the design of furniture details, vases, clocks, light fixtures, and sculptures. Fine metalworking throughout the period featured

FIGURE 9.57 These French Art Deco vases are cast in bronze and feature an Aztec ziggurat shape and stylized floral motif; they date from circa 1925. © Judith Miller/Dorling Kindersley/Moderne Gallery.

FIGURE 9.58 This unusual U-shaped chrome-plated aluminum candlestick on a ziggurat Bakelite base made by the Dole Vale Company of Chicago was exhibited at the 1939 World's Fair in New York City. © Judith Miller/Dorling Kindersley/ High Style Deco.

characteristic Art Deco motifs including ziggurats, figural sculptures collected as knickknacks around the home, candle holders, and bookends (Figures 9.57 and 9.58).

The Danish silversmith and sculptor Georg Jensen (1866–1935) began creating small works of art and jewelry until he forged a working relationship with Johan Rohde (1856–1935) to produce flatware in 1905. The success of their company was apparent, and Jensen soon expanded his business. Harald Nielsen began apprenticing with Jensen in 1909 and later began designing his own pieces under the Jensen name. Jensen's company of silversmiths took the Grand Prix prize at the 1925 *Exposition Internationale des Arts Décoratifs et Industriels Modernes* for their designs, and their reputation for making fine silver and hollowware led to their winning numerous other awards. The pyramid series featured trays, bowls, boxes, teapots, and tureens with an Art Deco–inspired stepped design.

To meet the demands of the middle-class market, American companies such as Chase Brass & Copper, the Dole Vale Company of Chicago, and Alcoa Aluminum hired freelance industrial designers to develop products their companies could easily mass-produce. Chase Brass & Copper got its start by making buttons in the 19th century, and then realized the potential of using its resources and machinery to produce household products. Industrial designer Ruth Gerth and her architect-husband William were contracted by Chase to design collections of tableware made from copper and chromium that would appeal to the middle-class market (Figure 9.59).

FIGURE 9.59 This Chase Brass & Copper Company copper bud vase designed by Ruth and William Gerth has four asymmetrical tubes bound by a Bakelite collar and mounted on a stemmed circular base. The copper napkin holder also features a Bakelite handle. Both are from the 1930s. © Judith Miller/Dorling Kindersley/Freeman's.

## CLOCKS

Advancements in clockworks in the early part of the 20th century included the introduction of battery-operated and electric clocks. The ever-popular mantel clock was offered in a wide range of designs in the Art Deco style (refer back to Figure 8.88). Streamlined shapes made from wood offered high style to middle-class consumers. Industrial designers also designed clocks from Bakelite. More elaborate models catered to a higher-end market; Lalique offered exquisite glass clock cases with the clock movements made in Switzerland (Figure 9.60). In 1926, the Howard Miller Clock Company of Zeeland, Michigan, began manufacturing mantel clocks in more traditional styles that appealed to more mainstream consumers.

## TEXTILES AND WALLPAPER

Mohair velvet was favored by Art Deco designers as a popular choice for upholstery on chairs and sofas. The wool fibers resisted crushing and were woven into solid and patterned textiles. Most textiles and wallpapers

FIGURE 9.60 This Art Deco frosted blue glass mantel clock fashioned after the designs of Lalique features partially nude maidens surrounded by flowering vines. © Judith Miller/ Dorling Kindersley/Lyon and Turnbull Ltd.

**FIGURE 9.61** A French Art Deco–style low stool from 1928 has an upholstered cushion set in a rosewood frame with zebrawood banding. The textile is a woven design of stylized machine parts such as wheels and axles in typical Art Deco geometry. © Judith Miller/Dorling Kindersley/Jazzy Art Deco.

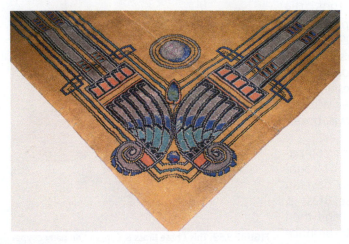

**FIGURE 9.63** This close-up detail of an Art Deco machine-woven carpet shows the influence of Egyptian motifs following the discovery of King Tutankhamen's tomb. © Judith Miller/Dorling Kindersley/Lyon and Turnbull Ltd.

**FIGURE 9.62** Ruth Reeves's reputation for representing American culture from the 1920s to the 1940s is perfectly illustrated by this Art Deco block-printed, polychrome cotton "tapestry." Designed for W & J Sloane, and entitled "The American Scene," it's a montage of scenes and activities from everyday American life. c. 1930. © Judith Miller/Dorling Kindersley/Alan Moss.

reflected the jazziness of Art Deco and Art Moderne designs with Cubist-like geometry and bold Fauve colors (Figures 9.61 and 9.62). The primitive forms of Egyptian, Aztec, and African designs appeared after the opening of King Tutankhamen's tomb, which brought about an interest in the exoticness of these cultures and were incorporated into fabric and rug designs. (Figure 9.63).

# Scandinavian Design

Although architects and designers in Europe and America in the 1920s and 1930s became increasingly accepting of industrialization and synthetic materials, designers from the Scandinavian countries looked to their own natural resources for inspiration. Combining mechanized production methods with hand-finished detailing, furniture designers from this region used teak, birch, and maple instead of the chromium tubular steel introduced by the Bauhaus. The warmth of natural fiber textiles used on seat cushions and in upholstery complemented the softer contours of Scandinavian furniture design.

Alvar Aalto (1898–1976) and Aino Marsio (1894–1949), Scandinavian designers from Finland, were both architects who began working on projects together when they married in 1924. The Aaltos formed Artek, a company that fabricated their unique furniture, glassware, and lighting fixtures (Figure 9.64). Aalto's process for bending laminated birch which he patented in 1933, led to the design of his famous stacking stool and lounge chair (Figure 9.65). Aalto's design for a stacking stool was exhibited at the New York World's Fair in 1939, launching the popularity of Scandinavian design in America. The natural lightness of beech, birch, and ash along with the soft contours of Scandinavian furniture designs helped set the tone for the Contemporary style throughout the postwar decade.

Original Aalto furniture is still produced by the Artek company following his exact specifications for production, including both mechanical and hand-finishing processes. Aalto's accomplishments with bending laminated woods inspired Marcel Breuer to create his own version of an organically designed chaise lounge in 1935. Also noteworthy is Aalto's influence on American designer Charles Eames (1907–1978). Eames introduced his rendition of a molded plywood chair in 1940. In fact, during the 1950s, the "Danish Modern" style of design was popularized through an aesthetic focusing on natural woods and fabrics, textural contrasts, and sleek modernism.

**FIGURE 9.64** The Savoy Vase originally designed by the Aaltos in 1936 celebrates biomorphic form. © Judith Miller/Dorling Kindersley/Mum Had That.

# Contemporary Culture and the Postwar Period

Although the Great Depression started in America with the crash of the New York stock market in 1929, economic ramifications were worldwide. The number of unemployed reached record numbers in America and abroad. But the slogan for the 1930s became "Brother, can you spare a dime?" Lack of work forced many Americans from their hometowns in search of employment. Consequently, temporary living quarters in rooming houses and small apartments kept household furnishings to basic essentials. This change in American culture inspired the need for easily transported, lightweight furniture produced using sophisticated technology. Mass-produced furniture fit more appropriately into the budgets of American families. Almost prophetic in a lecture given at the Technical University in Delft in 1931, Breuer commented, "A few simple objects are enough, when these are good, multi-use, and capable of variation. We avoid thus the slavish pouring of our needs into countless commodities that complicate our daily lives instead of simplifying them and making them easier." America's economic recovery from the Great Depression in the 1930s was slow. Government intervention through the Works Progress Administration and the New Deal introduced by President Franklin Roosevelt (term, 1933–1945) boosted manufacturing and gave Americans the necessary means to support economic recovery.

While Americans dealt with the Great Depression, independent European countries watched cautiously the activities of the National Socialist Party in Germany. Adolf Hitler's leadership as chancellor of Germany in 1933 led to the stronghold of Nazi power, which infiltrated Austria and Czechoslovakia. Before the year ended, concentration camps began filling up with resisters and persecuted Jews. Those who could leave the country did so, many fleeing to England and the United States. In 1939, Hitler ordered the invasion of Poland, which launched World War II. The war accelerated over the next two years, engulfing most of Europe, Great Britain, parts of Russia, Greece, North Africa, and the Pacific Islands.

At the onset of the war, the European governments involved restricted manufacturing to shift all efforts toward the production of wartime equipment. On December 7, 1941, the Japanese bombed Pearl Harbor. As the United States declared war the next day, American manufacture of consumer goods virtually shut down and geared up for military production. The government placed restrictions on manufacturing that limited the use of raw materials, including timber and metal.

**FIGURE 9.65** This molded plywood chair was developed for the Paimio Sanatorium by Alvar Aalto between 1930 and 1933 and is still in production today. Although the chair is constructed entirely from wood, the rounded contoured seat and back make it comfortable to sit in. Paimio armchair, 1931–32 (bent & laminated birch and lacquered bent plywood), Aalto, Alvar (1898–1976)/The Israel Museum, Jerusalem, Israel/Purchase, Palevsky Fund/The Bridgeman Art Library International.

Instead of refrigerators, automobiles, and washing machines, metal was used to manufacture bombs, tanks, and munitions. America was brought out of the Depression through an increase in government spending on the war. Wartime restrictions and a shortage of raw materials led to the development of such new materials as plywood, galvanized rubber, fiberglass, synthetic fibers, and PVC plastics. Turning to these resources, inspired designers created interior furnishings in new Contemporary styles, which were put to good use when the war ended.

## ORGANIC DESIGN IN HOME FURNISHINGS

America had not yet entered the war in 1940, and therefore was not limited in resources and had no government-imposed manufacturing restrictions. In an attempt to promote creative development in America, the Museum of Modern Art (MoMA) in New York sponsored a competition with the central theme "Organic Design in Home Furnishings." Furniture, textile, and lighting designers were encouraged to send in entries, and the winners were promised manufacturing contracts to have their works produced. Distribution of the work was to be handled through the 12 department stores and furniture stores who co-sponsored the exhibition. The results launched the Contemporary style of design in America and introduced casual and affordable interior furnishings designed with style and taste.

Charles Eames and Eero Saarinen (1910–1961) won the prize for furniture design with a living room entry that combined modular furniture units with an informal grouping of chairs around a low, round table. The entry had fulfilled the intent of the competition. Eames and Saarinen created organically designed home furnishings offering modern conveniences for the new American lifestyle. The working partnership of Eames and Saarinen was short lived; however, their accomplishments changed American design for the next two decades. Their furniture revolutionized the American living room by reducing the bulk of heavy upholstered goods that cluttered newer small houses.

St. Louis–born Eames studied architecture at Washington University and worked for a local architect after graduation. He worked privately until 1937 when hired by Eliel Saarinen to head the Experimental Design department at the Cranbrook Academy of Art. The Finnish architect and designer Eliel Saarinen brought the International Style to America when he was commissioned to design a building to house a new experimental school near Detroit in Bloomfield Hills, Michigan. Consequently, the Cranbrook Academy of Art opened its doors in 1932 offering an apprentice-style education in art and design fashioned after the Bauhaus. The Saarinen home on the Cranbrook campus was the result of the joint efforts of Eliel and his wife, Loja (1879–1968), who was a textile designer and sculptor. In addition to the Saarinens' modern architectural style, the couple's home featured rich veneers and marquetry-patterned furniture, geometric rugs and upholstery fabrics, and leaded-glass windows—an interior characteristic of the prevailing Art Deco style. Eliel Saarinen had remained president of the school until 1948.

It was here that Eames met Eliel's son, Eero. Eero came to the United States with his family in 1923 after his father won second place in the design competition for the Chicago Tribune Tower. Eero attended art school in Paris before returning to the United States to study architecture at Yale University. Upon graduation, Eero earned a scholarship enabling him to travel throughout Europe for two years; he returned in 1936 to teach at the Cranbrook Academy of Art.

Instructors and students associated with the Cranbrook Academy of Art before the United States entered World War II in 1941—specifically Charles Eames, Ray (Bernice Kaiser) Eames (1912–1988), Eero Saarinen, Florence Schust Knoll (b. 1917), and Harry Bertoia (1915–1978)—brought America into the forefront of world design, setting the tone for the Contemporary style of design in the decades that followed.

Although Eames and Saarinen won the Museum of Modern Art design competition, when the United States entered the war in 1941, the production of the furnishings was interrupted as war rationing and government restrictions halted the production of unnecessary domestic objects. The winners of the competition had to wait until after the war before their impact on American design could be realized.

Because raw materials were scarce during the war, experimentation with new and recyclable materials led to significant discoveries that benefited the production not only of military equipment, but of home furnishings as well. Plywood, laminated cross-grained layers of thin wood, produced a lightweight but durable substitute for solid lumber. Eames and his wife, Ray (Bernice Kaiser) Eames, spent the war years making wooden leg splints for the Navy. As they experimented with molding plywood to make the splints, they continued to perfect the winning chair design. The chair was designed with a separate seat, back, leg, and supporting frame out of molded plywood (Figure 9.66). Once formed, the seat and back attached to the plywood support frame with galvanized rubber disks, which Eames added as shock absorbers, between the molded plywood and the frame.

The war finally ended in 1945. By 1946, the Museum of Modern Art exhibited new furniture designed by Charles Eames in a show of the same title. Herman Miller, Inc., a major furniture manufacturing company based in Zeeland, Michigan (operated by the father of Howard Miller, who produced clocks), purchased the production rights from Eames and went on to manufacture all of Eames's designs. In 1948, Eames introduced another version of the molded plywood chair. Aluminum was substituted for the molded plywood of the support frame and leg in the previous design. Both versions were easily manufactured through assembly-line production and provided comfort to the newfound American consumer. Eames's molded plywood chairs became an icon of American popular culture of the 1940s and 1950s.

Following the war, Europe was faced with rebuilding its bombed-out cities. In Great Britain, the government stepped in and established an emergency relief fund for bombing victims. Those left without home furnishings could purchase new items through a catalog of basic utilitarian furniture regulated by the Board of Trade. Utility furniture was the only style of furniture produced in Great Britain during the 1940s, as the manufacture of wartime equipment took precedence over furniture production. In Britain, rationing remained in effect well into the 1950s.

At the end of World War II, the United States faced a housing shortage as thousands of veterans returned to hometowns across America eager to secure civilian work and begin family life. In 1947, the American landscape was changed forever as suburban developments offered inexpensive, mass-produced housing. Money earned from military service coupled with available mortgage financing enabled a newly emerging middle class to purchase the American dream—a new home. Tract homes built in the early 1950s offered affordable housing to returning veterans. Soon, suburban America grew out of developer-planned communities.

In the January 1945 issue of *Arts & Architecture* magazine preselected architects were challenged to come up with a solution to the housing shortage by designing affordable houses that captured the zeitgeist of the period and that could be economically duplicated throughout the country. The Case Study housing project encompassed the work of what would become the leading architects of the postwar era: Charles Eames, Richard Neutra (1892–1970), Eero Saarinen, Craig Ellwood (1922-1992), and Pierre Koenig (1925–2004), among others. The magazine required that the houses be designed and built with a sense of economy, feature materials new or old, and stay within a specified budget. Some of the homes were built from prefabricated materials, concrete, and steel. The homes featured informal living spaces that created a casual atmosphere and interior furnishings that were designed to be equally casual and inexpensive for the time. After completion, the homes (which were mostly built in southern California) were opened to the public for viewing. The program lasted from 1945 to 1962 and perpetuated modern residential design in America.

The "California" style or ranch style home exemplified the quintessential American tract home. Designed and built with a sense of economy, these homes featured flat roofs, a carport, and a patio for outside entertaining. Generally, the homes had two or three bedrooms with one or two bathrooms, prefabricated kitchen components, and a combined living and dining space. The more informal living and dining space opened onto the patio through sliding glass doors.

**FIGURE 9.66** This Charles and Ray Eames plywood chair made by Herman Miller in 1946 features the award-winning design of the 1940 Organic Design in Home Furnishings competition sponsored by the Museum of Modern Art in New York. © Judith Miller/Dorling Kindersley/Freeman's.

FIGURE 9.67 These armchairs designed by Florence Knoll feature tufted leather cushions supported on a chromium steel frame and were produced in 1954.
© Judith Miller/Dorling Kindersley/Freeman's.

This created a more casual atmosphere that allowed for flexibility in indoor and outdoor entertaining. The furniture also had to be flexible. Modular furniture fit well into the interior scheme because of its adaptability; storage units, bookshelves, and cabinets could be modified by restacking or reconfiguring the arrangement. The furniture designed by Eames and Saarinen was well suited to this environment and manufacturers of their designs by Herman Miller and Knoll Associates, Inc., respectively, capitalized on supplying modern furnishings for these more modern homes.

Florence Schust, born in Michigan in 1917, remains as the leading figure in the formation of Knoll Associates, Inc., and the company's vision to perpetuate modern design in the postwar era. Schust met Eames and Saarinen while she was an architectural student at the Cranbrook Academy of Art. She later studied at the Illinois Institute of Technology under the leadership of Mies van der Rohe. After her marriage to the German furniture designer Hans Knoll (1914–1955), the husband-and-wife team formed Knoll Associates, Inc., in 1946. Their goal was to merge furniture and textile design into one complete manufacturing package, promoting a collection of interior products designed by Florence and others. At that time, Knoll signed on some of the leading furniture designers of the 20th century, including Saarinen and Mies van der Rohe. Florence Knoll herself was a brilliant designer working under the latest styles that reflected easy living (Figure 9.67).

Knoll signed on another designer affiliated with the Cranbrook Academy of Art, Harry Bertoia. Bertoia began his career as a student at Cranbrook and eventually became a member of the faculty. Early experimentation with designing furniture resulted in Eames-inspired molded plywood types; however, Bertoia's interest had previously been in metal sculpting. He quickly abandoned wood and returned to working with metal. Bertoia's ability to sculpt and mold metal greatly influenced his future as a designer of furniture (Figure 9.68). He commented that when "it came to rod or wire, whether bent or straight, I seemed to find myself at home. It was logical to make an attempt by utilizing the wire." In 1952, Knoll introduced the Bertoia collection of wire chairs. Bertoia analyzed the connection between sculpture and furniture. He summarized this ability to translate one concept into the other in describing the wire chairs: "Chairs are studies in space, form, and metal too. If you look at these chairs, you will find that they are mostly made of air, just like sculpture. Space passes right through them."

Eero Saarinen's furniture designs were also manufactured through Knoll Associates, Inc.; he was paid royalties on each item sold. Compared with Eames's designs, Saarinen's were equally organic in form, but he chose to work with different materials. Like Bertoia, Saarinen's experimentation with molded plywood was brief; he chose instead to work with plastics. In 1946, Saarinen introduced a chair made from a press-formed plastic shell supported by a steel structural framework (Figure 9.69). Instead of traditional upholstery, the plastic shell was made more comfortable for the sitter with a covering of foam rubber

FIGURE 9.68 This Harry Bertoia wire chair frame, called the Diamond chair, is shown here without the leather seat cover. © Judith Miller/ Dorling Kindersley/Lyon and Turnbull Ltd.

FIGURE 9.69 Designed in 1946 by Eero Saarinen, this chair was given the name Womb chair by Florence Knoll, who quickly attested to its comfort. The chair utilized two new postwar materials in its fabrication process: plastic and foam rubber. Traditional upholstery methods that had depended on coil springs and stuffing for support were replaced with a molded plastic shell layered with foam rubber and covered in a wool fabric. Courtesy Knoll, Inc.

(another new material developed during the war) encased between the plastic shell and woven fabric. This reduced the weight of the chair by nearly one-half compared with a chair made with traditional upholstery methods. As Florence Knoll sat in the chair, she appropriately named it the Womb chair because of its comfort. The body of the chair raised on slender steel legs expresses Saarinen's disgust with the cluttering of architectural spaces with unnecessary elements. In a speech given to the Society of Industrial Designers, he explained himself: "The undercarriage of chairs and tables in a typical interior makes an ugly, confusing, unrestful world. I wanted to clean up the slum of legs."

In 1951, Eames introduced a shell-type chair made out of thermoset resin-reinforced glass fibers. The seat unit was formed out of this colored fiberglass-reinforced plastic and shaped so the seat, back, and sides were one continuous piece. The plastic seat shell was supported by a thin steel framework of legs that was held in place by characteristic galvanized rubber disks (Figure 9.70). Eames continued to design furniture throughout the 1950s, expanding into the commercial market by introducing tandem seating for airport terminals. Herman Miller, Inc., continued to sell Eames-designed plastic shell chairs and the molded plywood chairs, along with molded plywood coffee tables, stools, and screens for the residential market. In 1956, Eames added another design to his collection: a lounge chair and an ottoman. This chair came to encapsulate the achievements of molded plywood and was the perfect chair for a new American pastime, TV watching (Figure 9.71).

First thought to be an invention that would not amount to much, television became increasingly popular during the 1950s when the price of a set was within reach of the typical middle-class family. A radio could be anywhere in the room, with family members reading a book, sewing, or working a jigsaw puzzle. The radio provided hours of entertainment and news as long as the listener was within earshot. A television set, however, was something that had to be looked at. This new invention quickly altered the arrangement of the family living room. Now the furniture was arranged to face the TV set. American lifestyles changed from formal sit-down meals to quick TV dinners and a more relaxed, casual existence.

The Eameses and Saarinen continued their contracts with Herman Miller and Knoll, respectively. Each designer considered comfort and functional flexibility as a key factor in successful designs. Although the Eameses chose to work in plywood, Saarinen preferred to work with human-made materials and approached the structural aspects of furniture similarly to his architectural designs. Recalling the Womb chair, slim steel legs seemed to effortlessly support the upholstered molded shell, giving the design a sense of weightlessness (Figure 9.72). American Contemporary styles were organic in form, yet featured some of the latest synthetic materials. Press-formed plastic, molded plywood, and fiberglass, along with foam rubber, aluminum, and plastic laminate were popular materials used in the manufacturing of home furnishings in the postwar period.

**FIGURE 9.70** A fiberglass chair supported on thin metal legs designed by Charles and Ray Eames introduced consumers of the postwar era to ultralight, casual home furnishings.
© loukia/Shutterstock.

**FIGURE 9.71** The Eames lounge chair and ottoman made from molded rosewood plywood has tufted leather upholstery and an aluminum frame. Galvanized rubber disks (visible on headrest and back) are still employed, connecting the frame to headrest, back, and seat. © style67/Fotolia.

**FIGURE 9.72** Eero Saarinen designed the Tulip chair in 1957 using molded fiberglass and plastic, aluminum, and foam upholstery. His designs for table and chairs feature a delicate pedestal support that gives the furniture the effect of weightlessness. Courtesy of Knoll, Inc.

FIGURE 9.73 Eero Saarinen's design for Dulles Airport reveals the core of his gravity-defying structural designs. The original terminal, designed in 1961–1962, was constructed using slender columns that seem to effortlessly support the roof as they penetrate through the massive concrete. Saarinen applied this visual dichotomy to his furniture designs as already seen with the Tulip chair, Womb chair, and Saarinen tables. © Steveheap/dreamstime.

FIGURE 9.74 An aluminum frame supports the Swan chair designed by Arne Jacobsen for Fritz Hansen in 1957. The chair is covered in wool fabric over a foam and plastic shell. © Marko Bradic/Shutterstock.

When the Tulip collection, introduced in 1957, was combined with Saarinen-designed tables, the furniture grouping created a similar feeling of lightness, as if the mass was suspended in space. The organically shaped seats supported by slender legs or pedestals compare with Saarinen's architectural designs for two airport terminals: the TWA terminal at JFK Airport in New York and Dulles Airport serving Washington, D.C. (both airports completed the year after his death). The biomorphic interior of the TWA terminal and the gravity-defying sloped concrete roof of Dulles reflect a common attitude of the 1950s—a fascination with futuristic design (Figure 9.73).

Scandinavian designer Arne Jacobsen (1902–1971) incorporated the unique influences of organic modernism and new materials such as foam rubber and plastics with stainless steel into sculptural statements in furniture. The Swan chair, Egg chair, and Ant chair collections feature the precarious balance between mass and frame; they were sculptural seats supported on thin, stainless steel frames (Figures 9.74 and 9.75).

The influence of the Organic Design in Home Furnishings launched by the MoMA exhibition in 1940 crossed into almost all of the decorative arts by the mid-1950s, appearing in everything from ceramics to lamps. Isamu Noguchi (1904–1988) incorporated the Japanese heritage of his father into his designs for paper lamps (Figure 9.76). The sculpted paper over wire framing became interior sculptures in modern design. By the end of the decade, the hard-edge geometry of the Bauhaus and De Stijl movements was quickly becoming passé. The new style, called the Danish Modern style, ushered in a combination of organic designs made from natural materials and fabrics (Figure 9.77).

FIGURE 9.75 Arne Jacobsen's Ant chair, designed in 1952 for Fritz Hansen, once revolutionary for its single-shell construction, remains the quintessentially modern, industrially produced, everyday chair. The shell is molded plywood with a smooth lacquer finish and the legs are made of tubular steel. The chairs can be stacked or attached in tandem. © Danicic Milan/Shutterstock.

FIGURE 9.76 Isamu Noguchi created paper-shaded light fixtures based on Japanese influences mixed with Contemporary style. © Judith Miller/Dorling Kindersley/Freeman's.

FIGURE 9.77 Heywood Wakefield produced affordable furniture for American homes during the 1950s in the new, Danish Modern style, but the company had its roots in machine-made furniture as early as 1826. © Judith Miller/Dorling Kindersley/Freeman's.

FIGURE 9.78 An unusual building in Brussels built in 1958 for the World Expo is in the shape of the molecular structure of an atom. © Sikirillova/Dreamstime.

FIGURE 9.79 The Ball Clock by George Nelson, originally designed for Howard Miller in 1947, features a radial display of orange balls emulating the molecular structure of an atom. © Judith Miller/Dorling Kindersley/Freeman's.

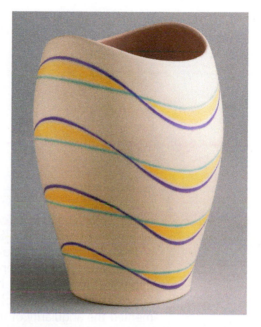

FIGURE 9.80 This free-form vase from Poole Pottery designed between 1955 and 1959 features a double helix design. The first scientifically correct drawing of the double helix of DNA was released in 1953. © Judith Miller/Dorling Kindersley/Art Deco Etc.

Additionally, designs were inspired by the postatomic age; the bombs dropped on Hiroshima and Nagasaki to end the war created an interest in science and technology (Figure 9.78). The home furnishings industry eagerly adopted motifs resembling exploding atoms, amoeba-like biomorphic shapes, and molecular structures influenced by the discovery of the double helix of DNA in 1953 (Figures 9.79 and 9.80).

# A New Generation

## POP CULTURE

Most Americans were eager to put World War II behind them, but the Cold War was an ever-present reminder of living in the atomic age. In 1957, scientific research and development propelled human beings toward space with the Russian launch of *Sputnik*, the world's first satellite. Landmark events in space exploration that occurred during the 1960s and 1970s influenced the current generation of designers fascinated with speed and space travel. Space-age designs took over; boomerang

**FIGURE 9.81** The air traffic control tower at Los Angeles International airport is designed in a futuristic, space-age style emulating a "flying saucer." © Karin Hildebrand Lau/Shutterstock.

**FIGURE 9.82** This vase from Orrefors was created using a two-step process of glassblowing that gives the colored area the appearance of floating above its translucent base. © Judith Miller/ Dorling Kindersley/Nigel Benson.

**FIGURE 9.83** This table lamp features a saucer-shaped base on spindly metal supports and has a pleated plastic shade. © Judith Miller/Dorling Kindersley/Manic Attic.

patterns, spaceship-inspired architecture, and futuristic automobiles reflected this latest look of modernism. Streamlined products with push-button controls gave the appearance of gliding through space.

Popular culture was enthralled with the possibilities of living on the moon. The geodesic dome, inspired by architect and industrial designer Buckminster Fuller, hinted at what a space colony might look like. Circular, biomorphic shapes supplemented the angularity of the 1950s. In anticipation of this new way of life, the late 1950s and early 1960s experienced drastic change in design trends once more. The organic designs that enveloped the early 1940s took on an entirely new direction. As humans ventured beyond the earth's atmosphere, buildings began to look like space stations and spaceships (Figure 9.81).

Home accessories were designed with a feeling of lightness, as if mass were suspended in space (Figures 9.82 and 9.83). Boomerang and biomorphic shapes replaced the rectangular styles of the Early Modern movement. American-born Isamu Noguchi was one of the first designers to translate this science fiction attitude into futuristic furnishings for the home. Bizarre biomorphic-shaped sofas and tables based on the aerodynamic shape of a boomerang were considered too extreme when first introduced in the late 1940s and were not mass produced until the 1950s (Figure 9.84). Other designers followed Noguchi's lead. Noguchi worked as a freelance designer selling work to both Herman Miller and Knoll (Figure 9.85). Eventually, both the Herman Miller Company and Knoll focused more on the manufacture of office and commercial furniture and discontinued many of their postwar production designs. As the next decade unfolded, these icons of contemporary design were replaced with new furniture designed for a rapidly changing consumer-based American culture. Only recently have the

**FIGURE 9.84** This "Angelo" sofa designed by Edward Wormley for manufacturer, Dunbar, features a prominent 1950s boomerang shape. © Judith Miller/Dorling Kindersley/Freeman's.

**FIGURE 9.85** A table in the style of Isamu Noguchi but sold as "Danish Modern" features an interconnecting teak base with freeform glass top. © Judith Miller/Dorling Kindersley/Freeman's.

**FIGURE 9.86** The massive globe sculpture *Unisphere*, from the 1964 World's Fair in New York City, shows the earth with rings tracking the orbits of the astronauts of the time. © evantravels/Shutterstock.

classics of modern furniture been reintroduced to an enthusiastic public, eager to own an "original" 20th-century classic piece of furniture.

What was science fiction and a dream for the future in the 1950s became a reality in the 1960s. American president John F. Kennedy felt that the future lay in space and joined the Russians in a race to the moon. Now more than ever, the dream that humans could someday walk on the moon meant that life on earth also would change. The World's Fair in 1964 held in New York City perpetuated the notion of space exploration. Attended by over 50 million people, the fair's theme, "Peace through Understanding," focused on the global community symbolized by a 140-foot steel sculpture of Earth. The *Unisphere* globe was placed at the end of the entrance promenade, giving viewers a peek at how the earth—tilted on its axis—would look from six thousand miles out in space (Figure 9.86).

Space-age gimmicks were prevalent throughout the 1960s and 1970s in the design of household furnishings (Figure 9.87). Other industries responded by producing goods that suggested the future of space (Figure 9.88). Eero Aarnio's (b. 1932) Ball Chair, designed in 1963, reflected the growing interest in planetary exploration (Figure 9.89). Furthermore, Expo '67 in Montreal, Canada; director Stanley Kubrick's (1928–1999) landmark movie *2001: A Space Odyssey*, released in 1968; and the U.S. moon landing in 1969 kept space-age designs in the forefront of popular culture through the early 1970s.

Adaptable housing, inspired by the prefabricated mobile home, was more conducive to a temporary lifestyle and was well suited to change. Prefabrication was considered the wave of the future. Architect Moshe Safdie (b. 1938) designed *Habitat* for Expo '67, a futuristic housing project made from prefabricated building materials (Figure 9.90). Each room was a self-contained "pod" made in a factory, which was then shipped to the site and connected to other pods. The concept enabled the housing units to be expanded by adding more pods—a precursor to the concept behind the International Space Station of today.

During the 1960s, the explosion of youth culture from the baby boomers—children of postwar veterans—led to yet another shift in design. An emphasis on the temporary here-and-now dominated everything from housing design to furniture to clothing. Culture was something that was used to change—rapid change that evoked a sense of the disposable aspects of daily life.

**FIGURE 9.87** These mirrors show the influence of space; one has a bubble border design and the other features the rings of Saturn. © Judith Miller/Dorling Kindersley/Freeman's.

**FIGURE 9.88** Lava lamps contain two liquids that will not blend together; when subjected to the heat of the lamp, the colored liquids float as if defying gravity. © Steve Bower/Shutterstock.

**FIGURE 9.89** The orange Ball chair designed in 1965 by Eero Aarnio creates the whimsical feeling of sitting inside a sphere. The upholstery fabric is Dacron polyester, the latest in synthetic fibers. © Judith Miller/Dorling Kindersley/Lyon and Turnbull Ltd.

FIGURE 9.90 The *Habitat* housing project by Moshe Safdie for the Montreal Expo in 1967 features prefabricated "pods" assembled on-site. © Jeffrey M. Frank/ Shutterstock.

FIGURE 9.91 An inflatable chair designed in 1967 for furniture company Zanotta was intended to be temporary furniture. The chair's designers also designed an inflatable house. Steve Gorton and Karl Shone © Dorling Kindersley.

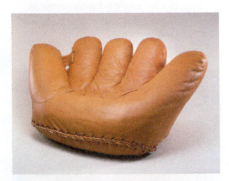

FIGURE 9.92 The Joe Sofa, named for American Baseball legend Joe DiMaggio in 1971, captures pop culture's interest in designs with a gimmick. Joe Sofa, designed by Gionatan de Pas (1932-91), Donato D'Urbino (b.1935) and Paolo Lomazzi (b.1936), 1971 (leather, polyurethane and metal), Italian School, (20th century) / Museum of Fine Arts, Houston, Texas, USA / Gift of the Houston Astros Baseball Club and Drayton McLane / The Bridgeman Art Library International..

What was here today most often was gone tomorrow, and popular culture capitalized on the disposable consumerism that dominated American life.

An easier lifestyle centered on a seemingly younger generation—one that never saw the Great Depression or suffered through the rationing of World War II. More and more goods were available and at lower prices, thanks to sophisticated manufacturing processes and the wonder material, plastic. Soon, cheap goods replaced well-built, more expensive ones. The generation grew up on the belief that once used up, throw it out. Furniture became more disposable as well. Buy a plastic chair, use it, and when it no longer performs, throw it out with the plastic milk cartons (Figure 9.91). Emphasis was placed on the chair or adaptable seating unit, and round, organically shaped modules manufactured out of plastic materials prevailed.

Inspired by the pop art movement, designers evoked in their work whimsy, fantasy, and gimmick, along with the notion of someday living in outer space. Pop art first appeared in London and New York with British artist Richard Hamilton (b. 1922) leading the way with his iconographic collage from 1956, *Just What Is It That Makes Today's Homes So Different, So Appealing?* Hamilton's collage summarized popular culture and its unusual curiosities. The scene is set with the image of a glowing moon hovering above a living room outfitted with the latest in modern conveniences. A woman wearing a dress and high heels cleans a staircase with a new space-age vacuum cleaner, the Hoover Constellation, which actually hovered above the floor by the force of its exhaust. A bodybuilder holds a giant Tootsie Pop next to a coffee table that bears a canned picnic ham. The appearance of a film marquee, a comic book page, and a television set along with a reel-to-reel tape recorder subliminally reminds viewers how often they are bombarded with images and sound. Completing the scene, a nude woman sits on a modern designed sofa wearing a spoof of the lampshade hat made popular by Parisian couture.

The pop art movement captured the interest in consumerism provoked by television, magazine, and billboard advertisements integrated into popular culture. Artist Andy Warhol (1927–1987) turned ordinary consumer objects such as the Campbell Soup can and Coca Cola bottles into art through oversized and colorful silk screens. By the 1960s, it appeared that the more gimmicky the idea, the more of a reaction it received from the public (Figure 9.92). Pop art capitalized on this and influenced a new generation of designers.

Soon the younger generation, who questioned everything that had been established by the previous generation, found themselves living in a society that felt that life was disposable, too. Increasing American involvement in the conflict in Vietnam gave this younger generation a platform on which to rebel. As the Vietnam conflict ended, the 1970s saw a return to a more stabilized, secure society. In the 1960s, the world was considered disposable; when things got too polluted, too used up, there was always the belief that humankind would find a new existence somewhere else. The Greenpeace movement, however, had given people a new outlook on their world, one that emphasized the fact that when things on earth did get too polluted, or used up, there would be nothing to sustain life here on earth. Consequently, human existence would cease. Aptly titled, Robert Hughes's (b. 1938) book *The Shock of the New*, published in 1981, chronicled the changes in modern art and its impact on society in the 20th century.

Home furnishings matched wits with pop art by providing high-style ceramics and glassware with designs that followed the characteristics of modern art. The work of Warhol and artist Peter Max (b. 1937) influenced designers to create abstracted city scenes in bright transfer-printed colors and stylized flower patterns that appeared on home accessories. The Midwinter pottery factory in Great Britain produced a collection of dinnerware for the hip new lifestyle of young homeowners. High-end collections were hand painted, and Midwinter retained artists to meet the demands of a burgeoning market. Madoura Pottery, located in France, was fortunate enough to pique the interest of world-renowned modern artist Pablo Picasso (1881–1973). Its exclusive pottery collections painted by Picasso appealed to the high-end collector and were produced from 1947 to 1971 (Figure 9.93).

Brightly colored tableware, vases, and knickknacks with stylized or abstracted designs were also produced in glass. Artist Peter Max captured the bright, psychedelic colors and bold patterns of the era in his silk-screen paintings, which were turned into inexpensive and easily purchased posters and transferred onto household accessories (Figure 9.94). Although the Chance glass factory in Great Britain had been around since the early 19th century and supplied the glass for the Crystal Palace in London, their collection of designs from the 1950s, 1960s, and 1970s set new directions for hip style and innovative manufacturing processes. Chance began applying the transfer process, which had been used for two centuries by potters, to print intricate designs onto glass. This process brought the cost within financial reach of young consumers.

The slogan "Flower Power," first coined in 1965, captured the carefree attitudes of a young generation that fought against government establishments and the accelerating crisis of the Vietnam War. Warhol created a series of silk screens of larger-than-life poppies, the flower symbolizing the remembrance of war veterans since World War I. To the young generation of the 1960s and 1970s, flowers symbolized peaceful solutions to world problems (Figure 9.95).

The high-tech style of design set the direction both architecturally and in interior design. Objects that normally were used in factories or in an industrial setting were now used in the home: dome lighting, galvanized steel, and rubber flooring. Glass block made a comeback, creating interesting walls that accentuated the sleekness of fabricated materials. Nothing was sentimental or suggested anything prior to the extreme modernism seen in the early 20th century.

**FIGURE 9.93** This pottery jug painted in bright yellow and black by artist Pablo Picasso features an abstracted face. © Judith Miller/Dorling Kindersley/Woolley and Wallis.

**FIGURE 9.94** This glass dish features a screen-printed decoration designed by Peter Max. © Judith Miller/Dorling Kindersley/Wallis and Wallis.

**FIGURE 9.95** This patterned fabric features the bright colors of abstracted poppies. © Judith Miller/Dorling Kindersley/Luna.

## MINIMALISM

The set designs from the movie *2001: A Space Odyssey* featuring futuristic, stark white and bare interiors made popular a new trend in design aptly called minimalism. Architect Richard Meier (b. 1934) captured the essence of minimalism in the residences he began designing in the 1960s (Figure 9.96). The Smith House, built between 1965 and 1967 in Connecticut, features an all-white exterior punctuated by expansive glass revealing gleaming white interiors. Minimalism was a throwback to the designs of the Bauhaus and De Stijl movements, bringing back a sense of geometrical massing and clean lines. White walls, stair rails, columns, and furniture juxtaposed against the richness of natural hardwood floors emphasized Meier's geometrical organization of shape and mass.

Minimalism quickly became the latest new fashion in design. Interior spaces left white and uncluttered were accented by brilliantly colored accessories featuring the form of the object rather than its decoration (Figure 9.97). The bright, psychedelic colors

**FIGURE 9.96** Richard Meier's interior designs feature minimalist interiors with understated furnishings, gleaming white walls, and imposing architectural elements. © Arcaid Images/Alamy.

**FIGURE 9.97** Mold-blown vases from the 1970s feature simple concentric circular forms shaped from colored glass. © Judith Miller/Dorling Kindersley/Mum Had That.

of the 1960s were replaced with earthy undertones such as burnt orange, avocado green, sienna brown, and creamy white (Figure 9.98). The organic shapes of the postwar era were fashioned into furniture and decorative accessories that proved the malleability of plastics (Figure 9.99). Moreover, as plastics took over as the new wonder material, high design was available to a younger generation with limited funds. Through synthetic materials and sophisticated manufacturing processes, more and more goods were now available at lower prices (Figure 9.100).

Italian designer Joe Colombo (1930–1971) and Danish designer Verner Panton (1926–1998) began designing furniture and household accessories to be manufactured out of plastic. With Colombo's vision for the "habitat of the future" and Panton's idea of the "total environment," both designers focused on using plastics to create all-in-one, completely coordinated interiors. Colombo first studied painting and sculpture before turning his artistic talents into designing furniture. His attempts to make plastic furniture using injection-molding processes responded to the period when plastic was considered the wonder material of the future (Figure 9.101). Colombo's Universale chair, introduced in 1965, was finally mass produced in 1967. His product designs were manufactured by Kartell, a company founded in 1949 specifically to produce plastic products for the home. Colombo designed several innovative products, including a rolling trolley, a fully adjustable chair (by removing and reconnecting parts), and lamps (Figure 9.102).

Panton had also experimented with plastics in his native Denmark. He was the first to develop a chair made from one piece of molded plastic in 1968 (Figure 9.103). These stackable chairs were made using injection molding by Vitra, a company in Switzerland founded in 1950. Vitra produced several of Panton's designs as well as works by the leading industrial designers of the day, including George Nelson (refer back to Figure 9.79) and Mario Bellini (b. 1935).

Plastics revolutionized the home furnishing industry. Thermoset plastics were used to make dinnerware (melamine) and laminate (such as name brand Formica) for the table tops (Figure 9.104). This is a type of brittle plastic that uses heat and adhesives to make, but once cooled it resists melting from heat. Thermoplastic, a malleable plastic used in injection-molding processes, is a more pliable material but will melt when exposed to heat (Figure 9.105). Products made with plastics were affordable and stylish for the period. The long-term environmental effects of using petroleum-based plastic products would not be realized until decades later.

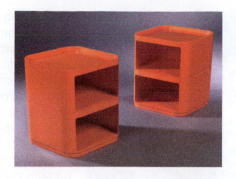

FIGURE 9.104 A pair of orange plastic tables designed by Anna Castelli (b. 1920) for Kartel dates from the 1960s. © Judith Miller/ Dorling Kindersley/Lyon and Turnbull Ltd.

FIGURE 9.105 Designed in 1969 by Giancarlo Piretti (1920–2006) these chairs, called the Plia, are an icon of design. They feature a stainless steel frame and clear plastic back and seat. © Judith Miller/Dorling Kindersley/Freeman's.

# Postmodernism

The 1960s and early 1970s was the era of plastics and Pop; however, by the approaching 1980s, more emphasis was placed on individual creativity rather than cultural genres or kitschy design. There was a dualism in the 1970s of taste and style. As the computer age influenced the functioning of everyday life, some designers reinterpreted the sleekness of the industrialized materials of the Bauhaus era, whereas others sought a back-to-basics approach with a renewed interest in craft and traditional materials. As designers began to look to the past for their inspiration, natural materials were popular once again and the colors of the earth, such as the celadon of plants, the umber of soil, and the blue of sea. A diversity of design characteristics resulted, with each designer choosing what aspect suited him or her best: high-tech design based on the advances of an automated world or styles that were connected to a sense of place.

Bauhaus theories were the doctrine for instruction at major universities in Europe and the Americas during the postwar era. However, as the Modern architectural movement had taken hold during the 1950s, some began to question the strict adherence to Modernism in design as early as the 1960s. The Late Modern style of architecture emerging in the late 1970s had taken the Miesian glass box and twisted it, turned it, and cut off the tops at daring angles in an attempt to create interest (Figure 9.106). This new generation of architects and students began to criticize the sterility of Modern buildings with their perceived cold steel and hollow, reflective glass and to question how this related to the human aspects of society.

Moreover, by the mid-1970s, whimsical pop art and space-age designs were considered kitsch. The contemporary designs of the postwar era had relinquished their hold over popular culture. Architect Robert Venturi (b. 1925), in his groundbreaking book *Complexity and Contradiction in Architecture*, published in 1966, proposed a vernacular approach to design, incorporating the local character of "place" and a return to the architectural elements of historicism rather than the nondescript rationalism associated with the Early Modern and International Styles. His book put the wheels in motion for the Postmodern movement of the 1980s.

Charles Jencks's book *The Language of Postmodern Architecture*, published in 1977, raised an awareness of the importance of designing architecture that could be understood by the broad spectrum of society. Jencks felt that design needed to "communicate with the public" and pushed for a responsible approach to urbanism that he felt

FIGURE 9.106 The reflective glass Lippo Towers in Hong Kong designed by Paul Rudolph (1918–1997) in 1988 exemplifies the sculptural style of the Late Modern period. Chris Stowers © Dorling Kindersley.

**FIGURE 9.107** The Portland Building, designed by Michael Graves in 1980, indicates an emerging Postmodern style. Bruce Forster © Dorling Kindersley.

**FIGURE 9.108** This collection of chairs designed by Robert Venturi and Denise Scott-Brown (b. 1931) in 1984 reinterprets the traditional English designs of the 18th century with a Postmodern flavor. Courtesy Knoll, Inc.

was lacking in current "glass box" architecture. Perhaps an understanding of the preservation of the earth and the basic human needs of society led to a more responsible approach to urbanism. In the end, Postmodern designers often turned toward a romantic, sometimes sentimental interpretation of the past.

Michael Graves (b. 1934) was one of the first architects to explore Postmodernism in his design for the city of Portland, Oregon (Figure 9.107). The building, shocking when first completed in 1980, appeared as a pop art interpretation of Neoclassicism—overscaled pilasters, flattened festoons, and a sympathetic treatment of classical massing of structure that emphasized distinct base, middle, and top sections that all appeared in bright colors. Graves designed other projects in a similar style for Disney, and critics began calling his work "Disneyesque."

As the decade of the 1980s began, designers working in a Postmodern approach began to interpret historicism in unique ways. Venturi designed a collection of chairs for Knoll based on styles of the past, including Chippendale, Hepplewhite, and Art Deco, among others. Unlike the designs from the Rococo and Neoclassic periods, his were made from laminated bentwood and featured bright colors with bold patterns; some critics described them as "cartoon-like" fashion (Figure 9.108).

Ettore Sottsass (b. 1917) led a group of young designers in forming Memphis, a Milanese-based furniture studio in 1980. Loosely based on an interest in popular punk culture, the Memphis style became the latest shock to the design industry. Charged with imagination and emotion, Memphis designers challenged the way materials were used. A contradiction existed between high style and high tech, as the rationale of traditional wood furniture was transformed into that of wood and plastic laminate. The multitalented Sottsass had succeeded in creating Postmodern furniture without resorting to historicism; however, the work was considered more of a fad and the group disbanded in 1988.

On the other hand, the work of French furniture designer-turned-architect Philippe Starck (b. 1949) reflects an avant-garde approach to pop culture. Known for his commercial appeal, Starck has designed everything from hotel interiors to toothbrushes. The popularity of his work results in its accessibility to the public. Starck gained world renown with the completion of the Paramount Hotel in New York City in the 1990s.

Reminiscent of old Hollywood, the lobby space features a retro Art Deco look. Starck relieved the banality of small, cramped rooms and dull architecture with imaginative furniture and accessories on the cutting edge of design and clever, oversized reproductions of Baroque period paintings (Figure 9.109). Like Venturi and Graves, Starck reinvented styles of the past into a fresh new aesthetic without resorting to Victorian revivalist conceptions.

Little did William Morris know that the "shoddy machine-made goods" of the late 19th and early 20th centuries would find their places among the most elaborate handmade items in the history of the decorative

**FIGURE 9.109** The view into this guest room at the Paramount Hotel in New York City reveals an interesting juxtaposition of modern and traditional design. Designed by Philippe Starck in 1990, the hotel was one in a series of "boutique" hotels for Ian Schrager. © Ed Malitsky/CORBIS.

**FIGURE 9.110** Michael Graves's iconic tea kettle designed for Alessi in 1985 features a whimsical bird-shaped cap that whistles when the water boils. Clive Streeter © Dorling Kindersley.

arts. Yet, designers working at the *fin de siecle* of the 20th century, like those working at the end of the 19th century, still debated the issue between craft and quality. Both Graves and Starck designed high-end domestic products for the Italian company Alessi (Figure 9.110). Their designs captured an enthusiasm for freshness, and both went on to design for other high-end companies—Graves for Steuben and Lenox, and Starck for O. W. O. and Vitra (Figure 9.111).

When Target department stores launched a new campaign, "Design for All," in 1990, both Graves and Starck embarked on designing affordable goods for Target's middle-class consumer market. The concept of achieving high style in affordable domestic products was first introduced by Charles and Ray Eames in the 1940s and industrial designers such as Norman Bel Geddes and Henry Dreyfuss. By the end of the century, retail stores such as Target and IKEA became leaders in providing well-designed household furniture and accessories within the financial reach of the average consumer (Figure 9.112).

**FIGURE 9.111** Philippe Starck's Miss Sissi Lamp, designed for Flos in 1991, is made of plastic. Steve Gorton © Dorling Kindersley.

**FIGURE 9.112** Chairs of sculpted foam covered in leather, a metal table, and built-in shelves complete this minimalist interior. © Antoha713/Shutterstock.

**FIGURE 9.113** Marc Newson's interior design for the Hotel Puetra America in Madrid features fluid architecture and minimalist furniture. © View Pictures Ltd/ SuperStock.

As the 20th century approached and society wondered what the future might bring, designers in the 19th century looked to the past for inspiration and stability. Modernism, on the other hand, for all practical purposes, gave artists the license to be as creative as possible, embracing a culture that welcomed change, diversity, and individualism. Now, after a century of progress and rapid change, present-day designers are equipped with the realization that anything is possible and obtainable. No longer restricted by the mandates of a patron, whether public or private, the designer works with the freedom of an artist, creating for the sake of creation. As young designers looked inward for answers, practicality and function no longer hindered the creative mind.

As society moves further into the 21st century, and with a growing acceptance of multiculturalism, design no longer has restrictions or boundaries, because an individual's personal taste is reflective of the freedom to choose. The work of designers such as Karim Rashid (b. 1960), Marc Newson (b. 1963), and brothers Ronan Bouroullec (b. 1971) and Erwan Bouroullec (b. 1976) to create a wide range of home furnishings is the culmination of the practices and principles of 20th century design. This design is based on aesthetic and function for the current generation and relies on machine production, which no longer threatens the designer but allows the designer to be as creative as possible (Figure 9.113). The Bouroullec brothers were voted "Designers of the Year" at the Salon du Meuble in 2002 for their innovative designs produced by such notables as Kartell, Alessi, and Vitra.

# Design for the Twenty-First Century

At the turn of the 21st century, the urban landscape was dazzled by the daring architecture of Canadian architect Frank Gehry (b. 1929). His highly charged designs first appeared in the house he designed for himself in Santa Monica, California, in 1978, in which he experimented with wildly projecting walls clad with corrugated metal and chain link. His fascination with the sculptural massing of a building with shiny, metal-clad surfaces was revealed in several projects in the late 1990s, including the Experience Music Project in Seattle, Washington; the Guggenheim Museum in Bilbao, Spain; and his recently completed Walt Disney Concert Hall in Los Angeles, California (Figure 9.114).

Gehry's exploration of architecture as sculpture paved the way for ultimate freedom in design and creativity for the new century. His brilliant architecture encouraged designers to be as creative as possible and realize that anything is achievable in the realm of style and taste (Figure 9.115). His architectural boldness earned him the Pritzker Architecture Prize in 1989. Computer technologies advanced to the point where Gehry's free-form sketch for the 1997 Guggenheim Museum in Bilbao was generated into complex three dimensional working drawings for construction guidelines leaving other designers with the conviction that any design could be built.

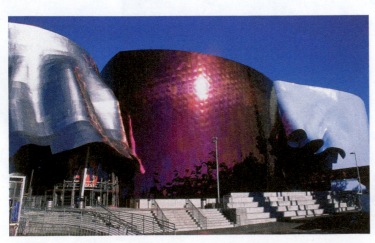

**FIGURE 9.114** The exterior of the Walt Disney Concert Hall with its billowing stainless steel walls of sculptural intensity was designed by Frank Gehry and opened in 2003. Scott Pitts © Dorling Kindersley.

FIGURE 9.115 The cafeteria for the headquarters of Conde Nast Publications by Frank Gehry is a three-dimensional sculptural experience of form, color, and rhythm. Michael Moran Photography, Inc.

FIGURE 9.116 Zaha Hadid's design for a winery in Spain reflects her penchant for unusual but inspiring architecture. age fotostock/Robert Harding

FIGURE 9.117 Hadid's interior design for a winery features built-in shelving and seats, with Verner Panton stacking chairs in white. age fotostock/Robert Harding.

Following the vein of unabashed creativity, Zaha Hadid (b. 1950) has set a new direction for futuristic design that fits right into the modern landscape. Hadid cut her architectural teeth in the mid-nineties, with the Vitra Fire Station in Germany in 1994. The oversized canopy and slanted walls hinted at Gehry's work but what was to come next for her career set her apart from all the others. The first female to win the Pritzker Prize in Architecture in 2004, her London-based practice is far from her upbringing in formerly liberal Iraq when she left there in the 1970s. Designs for buildings and furnishings feature streamlined shapes, gravity defying in some and solidly hugging the ground in others (Figures 9.116 and 9.117). Since winning the Pritzker, her sketchbook is filled with projects either already completed, under construction, or in the form of computer generated models, with numerous other projects still in free form sketches left on the drawing board. The new global culture of the 21st century welcomes change, diversity, and individualism without restrictions or boundaries; ultimately, for this new generation of designers, being part of a trend is no longer trendy.

# Furniture
## Construction

## The Ergonomics of Design

Ergonomically and anthropometrically designed furniture can be traced back to the Egyptian period when the first raking-back chair was introduced in the palaces of the pharaohs. Ergonomics, a scientific approach to design, is based on the relationship between humans and their environment. In furniture design, the relationship is based on the function of the object and how the body responds to it. The Egyptian chair with a raking back aligned the sitter in a more appropriate, somewhat reclined position, rather than a vertical, upright manner. The seat height was designed according to the physiological length between knee and foot so the feet would not dangle in midair. Remember, in Greek and Roman times, some chairs were equipped with a footstool.

Ergonomically designed furniture takes into consideration the seat depth, back height, and seat-to-back tilt ratios as well as how adaptable the chair is to a change in the body's position (Figure 10.1). The tilt of the back and pitch of the seat are important factors. In designing most general-purpose chairs, the seat and back are kept perpendicular to each other. When the seat is pitched 5 degrees off the horizontal plane, the back is automatically tilted. Would this be comfortable?

By increasing the angle between the seat and the back from 90 degrees to 105 degrees, the seated person is made more comfortable because pressure is relieved from the tuberosities and distributed to the back. Keeping the back-to-seat angle at 105 degrees, the designer can vary the pitch of the seat off its horizontal plane from the standard 5 degrees to 15 degrees, ideal for an easy chair or recliner. Leaving the pitch at 0 degrees, or in a direct horizontal position, is seen in the design of a stool or a drafting chair where it is necessary to lean forward. Designing special-needs furniture obviously deviates from these formulas.

The spinal column is an undulating shape: shoulder blades out, lumbar in, buttocks out. Another concern for the seated person is the weight distribution of the body. The posterior ischial tuberosities maintain the body's balance and take the shock of the entire weight of the body bearing down on the seat (Figure 10.3). The depth of the seat must be correctly adjusted to the body's seated position because of the sensitive areas behind the knees. Blood circulation can be cut off if there is too much pressure on this area. Also, if the seat is too short, the body becomes cantilevered without proper support and may lose its balance.

How do furniture designers know the correct proportional relationship between chair and sitter? The science of anthropometrics studies the measurement of the human body. The Greek's philosophy of "man is the measure of all things" came to life with Leonardo da Vinci's studies of anatomy. The proportional relationship between head and hand, hand and foot, and foot and overall body height was illustrated in his well-publicized drawing of the man in the square/circle.

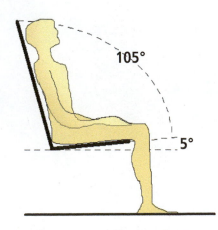

**FIGURE 10.1** A general-purpose chair is designed with a seat-to-back ratio of 105 degrees, and the seat is pitched 5 degrees off the horizontal plane. © David Vleck.

# LEARN More

## Ergonomics

Because different chairs are designed for different tasks, the design of each type of chair will require different ergonomic solutions. An office desk chair will be designed with adjustable features allowing changes for the seat height, back tilt, and seat pitch. A reading chair might be oversized with plush upholstery and soft cushions. The main function of a chair, whether for office workers or for relaxing and reading, is to provide support for the lumbar area of the back. The designers of the Queen Anne spoon-back chair noticed that a seated person does not have a straight and vertical spine, or a straight and slanted one; it is curved (Figure 10.2).

Study the drawing of a Queen Anne dining chair. Based on the information provided on ergonomics, how did the designer alter the seat-to-back ratio and seat pitch to accommodate the seated body for formal dining? Considering the shape of the "spoon" back, how has the designer responded to the lumbar region of the spine? Lastly, how does the design of this chair differ from chairs designed before the 18th century?

**FIGURE 10.2** A drawing of an 18th-century Queen Anne side chair originally designed as a dining chair. David Vleck.

Designers study anthropometric data to determine how high a chair seat should be from the floor, the placement of the armrest above the seat, and the width of chair seat. An incorrect system of figuring these calculations would be to base the dimensions on an "average" size. Instead, the designer should concentrate on the "normal"-sized individual.

The normal sizes are determined by decades of studies that recorded the measurements of a cross section of individuals from various countries and in specific age groups. Once the information is compiled, a figure is determined reflecting the percentage of the population that fits these measurements. For example, if 95 percent of the adult male population has a shoulder breadth of 19 inches and only 5 percent of the population has a breadth of 17 inches, then the average size of 18 inches would not be a successful compromise. If so, then only 5 percent of the adult male population could sit comfortably (or fit) in a wing chair that had a breadth of 18 inches, whereas 95 percent of the population would be eliminated. The designer should study anthropometric data for the larger percentile range of the population rather than working from averages.

By designing a wing chair 20 inches in breadth, it satisfies a functional requirement for 95 percent of adult males and accommodates a larger percentage of the population. When the data for women are included, again this becomes a concern of the furniture designer. Do you compromise? If so, how?

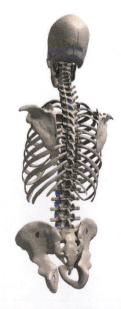

**FIGURE 10.3** The natural shape of the spinal column creates a distinctive lower back undulation called the lumbar region that must be supported while seated. Moreover, the weight of the upper body rests on two small ischia tuberosity that take the shock of the entire weight of the body bearing down on the seat. © Sebastian Kaulitzki/Shutterstock.

**FIGURE 10.4** These samples show the coloring and grain of the more common woods. From left to right: cherry, oak, walnut, and mahogany. © s74/Shutterstock.

**FIGURE 10.5** This cross section of a log shows the growth cycles with the pith at the innermost center. © Hydromet/Shutterstock.

**FIGURE 10.6** Lengthwise cut of log shows discoloration due to new and old growth called sapwood and heartwood, respectively. © MARGRIT HIRSCH/Shutterstock.

# Woods

Furniture and millwork are constructed from two types of woods. Hardwoods derived from deciduous trees supply the best types of wood for furniture construction because of their strength. Deciduous trees have a broad leaf and typically drop their leaves in the winter. Softwoods, taken from coniferous trees having needles or cones, are sometimes used in furniture construction. These woods, however, are less durable than hardwoods.

Oak, walnut, cherry, and mahogany are only a few examples of hardwoods used in furniture construction, and as history records, were most commonly used by cabinetmakers for centuries (Figure 10.4). Softwoods, such as pine, were used by English and American furniture makers as the body material, covered with a finer walnut or mahogany veneer. The differences between hardwoods and softwoods reflect the density of the physical makeup of the wood. Because wood is from a natural, living substance, it is important to realize the material's strengths and limitations. Both types of wood will warp and crack over time.

Woods are chosen for their different characteristics. Some are more conducive to stain finishes, whereas others require painted finishes due to the grain patterns. The most important aspect of using wood, whether for furniture construction or millwork construction, is the curing process it goes through. When most timber is cut, it dries briefly at the lumberyard before it is sent to the kiln. It would take a piece of wood five years to dry completely using air-drying methods. Instead, lumber mills use kilns to dry the wood, some reaching a temperature between 110 and 180 degrees. This is necessary to remove the moisture from the wood, which, over time, causes the lumber to warp or crack. The moisture content of cured wood usually ranges from 6 to 11 percent.

Kiln-drying methods also kill any diseases or insects embedded in the wood, as well as drying resins commonly found in most trees. The drying process is important because it helps prevent warping. Wood constantly expands and contracts, resulting in large and small fissures known as cracks and checks, respectively.

Whether hardwood or softwood, the physical makeup of the tree determines how responsive the material will be in fabrication. A cross section of a tree reveals various layers from the bark to the center (Figure 10.5). The cambium layer is just under the surface of the bark and is made of new growth cells. The next layer, sapwood, distributes water to the roots and is a soft wood with light coloring. Moving toward the center, the heartwood is the hardest core of the tree. Heartwood is darker in color than sapwood because these cells have matured, creating compact deposits (Figure 10.6). When using pine or other coniferous wood in construction, heartwood is most desirable since it is denser and more durable. Often, trade names given to wood products allude to the differences in coloration of wood taken from the same species. White birch is sapwood, whereas red birch is the heartwood. The pith is the very center of the tree and is not used in the construction of furniture.

The veneering of wood dates back to Egyptian times, even though it was not widely used until the 18th century. Veneering is a process of removing layers from the log or branch of the tree in thin sheets, then applying these layers to the surface of another material with glue. A *flitch* is bought and sold based on its appearance and quality of graining. Size, figuring, color, and naturally occurring marks can make the veneer more or less desirable, depending on the overall characteristics. Naturally occurring marks such as graining depend on the wood's growth over time. Graining is the pattern caused by the growth rings that develop over the life of the tree and reflects the composition of the wood fibers. Figuring refers to the depth or three-dimensional appearance of the grain and depends on the contrast between light and dark values. Contrast occurs when the tree experiences natural deviations from a normal growth cycle. For example, if a tree suffers through a drought, the grain of the wood is permanently altered.

Character marks such as wormholes, branch knots, injuries to the bark, or mineral deposits can bring added beauty to the veneer (Figure 10.7). For example, burl walnut is taken from a tree that has suffered injuries or bruising to the bark during the growth cycle. Mending of the injured bark takes place, creating small spirals of contrasting grains. In many cases, injuries to the tree are often deliberately made to force a burl effect. Other irregularities, such as knotholes, can create interesting effects as seen in knotty pine used in the construction of country furniture or panel products.

Another contributing factor to the character of a veneer is from what part of the tree the flitch is cut. Crotch mahogany, a desirable veneer for its irregular grain pattern, is cut from the intersection of two branches. Also, different methods of removing the layers of wood from the trunk or branch can emphasize character marks, graining, and figuring (Figure 10.8). Likewise, various veneer-matching processes such as book match, slip match, and diamond match are commonly used to enhance the wood's decorative qualities.

The most economical way of removing layers from the tree is the plain sawn method. By cutting the log in a straight path from top to bottom, resulting grain patterns emphasize more separation between figuring. This method also produces wider veneer strips. Quarter sawing produces the straightest grain because the log is first quartered then sliced; however, this process yields smaller veneer widths (Figure 10.9). Quarter-sawn veneers give the appearance of cathedral or peaked figuring with a flaking effect. Frank Lloyd Wright preferred this trait, and most of his furniture was constructed from quarter-sawn oak.

Rift cuts are similar to quarter sawn; however, cuts made into the quartered log are cut like slices of a pie. This results in even widths and cuts down on the flaking produced with a direct quarter-sawn process. The rotary method basically shaves the wood from the log as it is turned. This method often results in uneven grain patterns, making matching more difficult (Figure 10.10). However, because the entire log is cut, one continuous veneer sheet is possible. Half-round slicing is a method of cutting the log into halves first, then rotary slicing from the half log. The veneer's graining has a visual appearance between that produced by rotary and plain slicing.

When matching the veneer's grain and figuring, the book match produces the most symmetrical pattern. Slip matching creates the visual effect that the grain and figure continue, whereas the diamond match radiates the grain around a center point. End matching produces a similar effect to slip matching because the veneers are placed end to end and side to side. Random matching is often done where the continuity or symmetry of the match does not matter, such as the inside or on the back of a case piece (Figures 10.11 and 10.12).

Different species of woods are more conducive to yielding larger or smaller net footage sheets. Lengths of veneer sheets can range from 9 to 12 feet, also depending on the species. The thickness of veneer sheets can be anywhere from 1/28 to 1/42 inch thick with 1/32 inch most commonly used for furniture veneering. Flexwood is cut at 1/100 inch and is used as wall paneling that requires the flexibility necessary to be formed around curves.

Veneers are laid onto a core material with either urea or melamine resins (moisture resistant) and are aesthetically pattern matched. Cores are usually solid wood, plywood, or particleboard. Particleboard, once thought to be inferior, proves to be much stronger and more durable than solid core or plywood. Because particleboard is composed of a fusion of wood chips and glues, it is less likely to warp or crack. Particleboard is available in low, medium, and high densities and should be selected for its strength according to its appropriate application.

FIGURE 10.7 Knots are character marks naturally occurring in trees, and the wood is chosen for its unusual beauty. © David Lee/ Shutterstock.

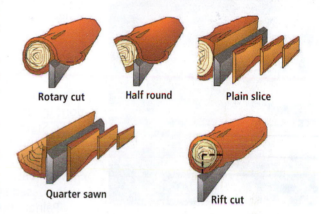

**Rotary cut**    **Half round**    **Plain slice**

**Quarter sawn**    **Rift cut**

FIGURE 10.8 Methods for removing veneers from a log each yield a different graining effect for the veneer. © David Vleck.

FIGURE 10.9 A quarter-sawn oak features a straight grain with some flaking. © James M Phelps, Jr/Shutterstock.

FIGURE 10.10 This mahogany veneer shows the irregularity of the grain pattern caused by rotary cutting. © Ozger Aybike Sarikaya/Shutterstock.

 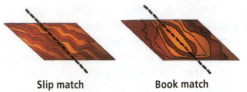

| Diamond match | Random match | Slip match | Book match |

**FIGURE 10.11** Veneer-matching techniques produce a variety of grain effects. © David Vleck.

Veneers are adhered to the core material using pressure and adhesives. The veneer is placed over the core in crossbanded patterns, or at 90-degree angles to the direction of wood grains. This gives the veneer and the piece of wood more stability against warping, cracking, or checking, which may cause separation. As one layer expands in one direction, the other expands opposite, thereby providing more stability to the piece.

A distinction is made between the face veneer and the back veneer. Whenever a veneer is applied over a core material, careful consideration is made to the final appearance of the furniture item. A case piece should be constructed with the most decorative grain and figured veneer panels on the front and sides of the piece. The back, which is usually placed against a wall, often will have a less expensive piece of veneer. Types of woods, sizes, and defect ratings are supplied in *Architectural Woodwork Quality Standards* as grades I, II, and III. Grade I has a higher quality of veneer selection based on color and graining, whereas grade III has no matching requirements.

## FINISHES

The use of finishes on woods also dates back to Egyptian times. Modern applications of stains bring out the beauty of the grain and accentuate the wood's natural color. Stains, enamels, oils, lacquers, and varnishes are used to treat woods. Each has a distinctive purpose and resulting finish. Stains are usually transparent, tinted with color, and dissolved in either a chemical solvent or water (Figure 10.13). Solvent-based stains are used most often because they are more durable than water-based stains.

Paints and enamels are usually opaque and require that the wood be sealed before application. The brand name Kilz is a primer often applied to raw, unfinished wood before painting. A finishing seal is added to protect the painted surface, guarding against nicks and scratches. Shellac, lacquer, and varnish create an indelible finish over the stained or painted wood surface. Most are polyurethane based and will not yellow over time.

Toners, wash coats, and wiping stains can create interesting visual effects such as distressing or white washing. Faux finishes have become popular once again, creating marbleized patterns, white-washed woods, and crackle finishes that provide alternatives to regular stained or painted finishes.

# Construction Techniques

## JOINTS

In addition to the type of wood and core material used, the quality of a piece of furniture also depends on its method of construction. Custom joinery techniques used to hold the piece of furniture together can be more expensive to produce and purchase. Nevertheless, these items will last much longer than an inferior item and will not need to be replaced as often. Deciding which joint to use in furniture construction depends on the type of furniture, how it is to be used, and, in many cases, what the final wholesale price will be. It is more expensive to use traditional joinery methods, and the final price point for the finished piece will be determined by the quality of construction.

**FIGURE 10.12** The veneers in this panel of Brazilian rosewood were laid up using the end-match patterning. Brazilian rosewood is now an endangered species of trees.
© Sevil Ozkavak/Shutterstock.

**FIGURE 10.13** A stain is applied with a brush to enhance the natural color of this teak table. The quantity of stain applied and the length of time it remains on the surface before wiping are critical to achieving even coloration. © SmarterMedium/Shutterstock.

# FRAMES

All wood furniture is made from the frame up. Upholstered goods depend on the frame to set the design style and provide a foundation for building up the layers of materials required in the upholstering process. The frame is created from several supporting members or elements that strengthen the frame and determine the furniture's design. Seats, legs, backs, arms, and wings serve an ergonomic purpose and can be enhanced depending on the upholstery foundation (Figure 10.14).

Open frames are commonly used for upholstery, because the open cavity allows for the platform of springs for seats and padding for the back and arms (Figure 10.15). Exposed frames are only partly upholstered. Slip frames are exposed wood with an independent piece that is upholstered and attached separately to the supporting frame. Open frames can be made from metal, plastic, or wood.

Wooden frames should be made from kiln-dried, straight-grained woods that are free of knots and selected based on the desired furniture finish. Stained wood, used in the construction of exposed frames, must have a visible grain pattern. Cut widths of 1⅛ to 1½ inches are common, and most manufacturers will use poplar or maple, although oak is most desirable.

Leg construction and its attachment to the furniture frame are equally important in determining quality (Figure 10.16). Better-grade furniture manufacturers will fabricate the front legs into the seat rail and incorporate the rear legs into the uprights or stiles. This reduces the chance of breakage and stabilizes the overall frame.

# UPHOLSTERY

In traditional upholstery methods, webbing made from wooden slats, jute, metal, polypropylene, or rubber provides the support for coil springs that shape the contour of seats and backs (Figure 10.17). Since the introduction of coil springs in the mid-18th century, various other types have been introduced and used in the construction of upholstered furniture. Using coil springs requires either a four-way or eight-way hand-tied process. Hand tying the springs secures the loose edge of the wire, keeping it from puncturing through the upholstery fabric. The tying process also determines the contour of the unit, depending on how tight the coil is tied. The firmness of the support is connected to the gauge of wire used along with the size, type of coil, and number of coils used. After the coils are set, burlap is stretched over the springs and the unit is ready for the stuffing.

Although traditional conical or cylindrical coil springs are still common, the modern zigzag spring offers a faster method of providing the supporting foundation for upholstery. Today, many manufacturers use zigzag springs because they do not need to be tied and can be quickly stapled to the frame and covered with layers of stuffing and padding. Loose stuffing materials can be made from animal hair (dating back to the Renaissance), natural fibers such as moss (typically found in furniture constructed in the South), down and feathers (90 to 10 percent blend is desirable because down has a tendency to flatten; feathers are more resilient), or synthetic Dacron fibers. Compact stuffing such as foam rubber (introduced in the 1940s), rubberized hair formed into cushions, or polyfoam (higher-density foam is used for the seats, whereas lighter-density foam is used for the arms) are used more often in today's upholstered goods. Once the stuffing is in place, a felted pad, either cotton or polyester, is placed over the stuffing and the piece is then covered with muslin.

**FIGURE 10.14** A woodworker uses a lathe to turn a block of wood into a furniture leg. The leg will be integrated into the seat rail for extra strength. © r.martens/Shutterstock.

**FIGURE 10.15** These open-frame chairs are ready for upholstery that will be applied to the seat and back. © Judith Miller/Dorling Kindersley/ Lyon & Turnbull, Ltd.

**FIGURE 10.16** These cabriole legs were carved with corner blocks that will be integrated into the seat rail to create a sturdy support. © MARGRIT HIRSCH/ Shutterstock.

**FIGURE 10.17** This unique mockup shows how a chair is upholstered using traditional methods, including eight-way hand-tied spring coil seat, zigzag spring back, stuffing and padding, muslin lining, and finish fabric. Dorling Kindersley Media Library.

This muslin cover prepares the piece to receive the decorative fabric and helps to protect it from unnecessary wear. The muslin keeps the decorative fabric from rubbing on the support materials. After the covering fabric is attached to the frame, a variety of methods are employed to finish the piece. Channeling or fluting creates parallel grooves or furrows, whereas tufting divides the surface into diamond-shaped pockets. Boxing creates a finished edge on a cushion, whereas welting—double, contrasting, or self—adds additional fabric to the seam. Finally, banding is the process of hand sewing small pieces of fabric over the tacking used to secure the decorative fabric to the frame. Skirts are applied on more traditional styles and are box pleated, gathered, or shirred.

Decking is used on the underside of loose seat cushions or over springs to conceal the inner workings of the upholstery. Decking may be made from an inferior material or the same decorative fabric. Self-decked cushions, although more expensive due to increased fabric costs, allow the flexibility of "turning over" the seat cushions, maintaining more even wear. Other concealing materials are added to the bottom of the unit. An inferior, lightweight fabric similar to what is found on a box-spring mattress is stapled to the underside of the upholstered good, keeping dust away from the inner springs.

Although upholstery refers to the construction of a piece of furniture from the frame up, the process of recovering a piece of furniture pertains to the replacement of the decorative fabric. Fabrics used as decorative coverings are chosen for their durability. It is important to consider the wear and use of a piece of furniture and select a finishing fabric accordingly. A good rule of thumb is to know the thread count—the tighter the weave of individually colored threads, the greater the fabric wears. Good-quality upholstered furniture should exhibit a uniform pattern match of fabrics, especially on the backs in case the furniture is not placed against the wall.

## CASE GOODS

In addition to upholstered furniture, case good construction should be examined closely to determine its quality. From outside appearances, check the veneer match of the piece from the front and side. There should be an even match and consistent coloring. If the front of the case piece has glass doors, the veneer used on the inside back should also show careful selection and match to insure the overall unity of design. The inside of the cabinet should reflect the same quality as the outside. Glass doors should be secured inside the case piece as well as on the outside, and the glass should be beveled or sturdy enough not to rattle when opening or closing the door. Glass shelves should be a standard 3/8-inch thick or more and easily glide in and out from the stabilizers that support them.

A trained artisan can use drawings and templates to execute precisely detailed carvings using tools that remain unchanged since the Medieval period (Figure 10.18). Although the tools are still a part of our modern culture, the necessary skills to create fine specimens of carved furniture are not. Long, arduous apprenticeships as well as extensive training in European schools have enabled artisans to carry on the tradition. Check for a sharpness to the carving. This will determine whether the ornamentation was actually carved or created from a mold. There is an obvious difference in wholesale pricing, as quality constructed pieces will never use plaster or melamine casts.

When examining the joinery, the best indication of quality is to remove a drawer (Figure 10.19). If the drawers are held together with dovetail joints, then, more than likely, the remainder of the piece will be constructed using custom joinery (Figure 10.20). The tongue and groove joins two pieces with the tongue form fitted to the groove. *Mortise-and-tenon* joints are used most often when attaching two pieces of wood at right angles. A *dado* is used to attach two pieces of wood in a perpendicular arrangement. *Dowels* are separate cylindrical pieces of wood that are fitted into recessed holes on the wood to be joined. These are often reinforced with glue. Finger joints are used to attach two pieces of wood end to end. These joints help to extend the length of wood segments. Minimum joint visibility is obtained by

**FIGURE 10.18** A highly skilled woodworker carves a delicate detail using some of the same tools that medieval cabinetmakers relied upon. © Chris Shackleford/Shutterstock.

**FIGURE 10.19** A side view of this drawer reveals dovetail joinery, an indication of quality construction. © robcocquyt/Shutterstock.

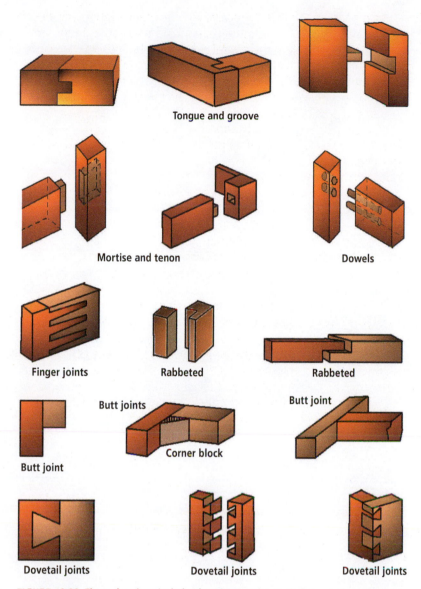

**Tongue and groove**

**Mortise and tenon**

**Dowels**

**Finger joints**

**Rabbeted**

**Rabbeted**

**Butt joints**

**Butt joint**

**Butt joint**

**Corner block**

**Dovetail joints**

**Dovetail joints**

**Dovetail joints**

**FIGURE 10.20** These drawings include plan views and extruded views of specific types of joints used to secure pieces of wood. © David Vleck.

using a wood filler and painting. Rabbeted joints are used to create a flush overlapping of two pieces of wood. Examples of these can be found on shutter or cabinet doors. A butt joint is secured with glue or sometimes screws. Extra reinforcement is obtained with the insertion of a corner block. Dovetail joints are commonly used on drawers and create a durable bond between two pieces of wood that does not need additional gluing. While the drawer is removed, check the body of the piece to see whether dust covers are included between the drawer openings. As the drawer is put back into the piece, check the ease of the slide. A drawer should fit tight, but not stick. This could be a sign of warpage or improper construction. Again, a good rule of thumb is to compare wholesale price points, because a lower-quality case good is less expensive.

# GLOSSARY

## A

**Adamesque** In the style of Robert Adam.

**Alabaster** A natural calcite or gypsum material of translucent, creamy white coloring suitable for carving; was used in windows before glass panes.

**Ambry** An English wardrobe or cabinet.

**Amphitheater** In Roman times, a circular or oval-shaped, open-air arena with tiered seating where people gathered to watch sporting events.

**Amphora** An egg-shaped Greek vase designed with a long neck and side handles used to store liquids.

**Amulet** An Egyptian talisman or charm used to bring good luck or ward off evil.

**Anaglypta** The brand name for an embossed wallpaper with patterns in low relief.

**Aniline dyes** Dyes made from a synthetic material derived from coal tar.

**Antefix** An ornamental finial positioned along the ends of a clay tiled, gabled roof on ancient Greek temples.

**Anthropomorphic pottery** A type of pottery fashioned with human features.

**Apron** Decorative skirting attached to the underside of a seat rail, tabletop, or case piece.

**Arabesque** A free-flowing motif using flora, vines, or foliate patterns.

**Architectonic** Having architectural characteristics. In furniture design, architectonic features such as the cornice and frieze, columns, pilasters, and modillions are used.

**Architrave** The lower part of the entablature; architectural molding placed above the capital of a column.

**Arcuated architecture** A form of architecture that uses arches to carry the load of a building or structure.

**Armario** A large Spanish case piece used to store articles of clothing.

**Armoire** A case piece originating in the Medieval period used to store arms and suits of armour. Also a wardrobe cabinet.

**Armoire à deux corps** Literally translated from the French, "armoire of two bodies" refers to a case piece designed in two sections used to store articles of clothing and miscellaneous household goods.

**Aubusson** A flatly woven carpet, rug, or tapestry usually in soft pastel colors featuring floral and foliate designs. Patterns have an enlarged scale with colors generally light in tone. Also it is the name of a type of rug with a flat weave.

**Axminster** A pile carpet with a stiff jute back; the weave permits a variety of colors and designs. Also the name for an English machine-woven rug.

## B

**Bakelite** A plastic-like substance made from phenolic resins.

**Balconet** A pseudo-balcony; a low ornamental railing to a window, projecting but slightly beyond the threshold or sill.

**Baldachin** An Italian term describing an architectural canopy supported solely by columns.

**Baluster** A turned form used as a furniture support and in the construction of railings. The baluster is commonly formed in the shape of an elongated vase, but not exclusively.

**Banded banding** A narrow border in a contrasting veneer that follows the perimeter of table tops, drawer fronts, and cabinet doors to emphasize its surface.

**Bandy** An American term used to describe a cabriole leg. The word "bandy" refers to a shape that is bent or curved.

**Bargeboard** Ornamentally carved boards appearing on the gabled ends of a roof as a form of decoration.

**Beam** Any horizontal structural supporting member.

**Bergère** A French upholstered armchair with closed-in sides.

**Bergère en gondole** A French upholstered armchair having curved sides that meet to form the back.

**Biscuit ware or bisque** Generally unglazed ware; pottery that has been fired once and has no glaze or a very thin glaze.

**Black figure technique** A technique in ancient Greek pottery decoration where the positive shapes appear in black against a red or terra cotta colored background.

**Block front** A façade treatment on case furniture whereby the center vertical structure is recessed between its two sides.

**Bobbin lace** Handmade lace made using wooden bobbins for managing the threads while weaving the lace.

**Bolection molding** A molding projecting beyond the surface of the work it decorates; often used to conceal a joint where the joining surfaces are at different levels.

**Bombé** A French term describing the gentle curve or swell applied to the front and/or sides of furniture case pieces. The use of the bombé is typically found on furniture of the Rococo period.

**Bone china** Porcelain with bone ash added to strengthen the clay and keep it from chipping once fired.

**Bonheur du jour** The French reference for a small desk with a compartment top used by ladies in their daily correspondences. The French word means "happiness of the day."

**Bonnet top** A singularly arched pediment used on the top of case pieces; also referred to as a "hooded top." A double bonnet or double hood refers to the presence of two arched pediments.

**Boulle work** A type of marquetry named after the cabinetmaker who introduced it, using tortoiseshell and silver or brass.

**Bracketed knee** Makes the transition between the top of a cabriole leg and the front and side rails on a chair or case piece.

**Brass** An alloy of copper and zinc.

**Breakfront** Case furniture having recessed and projecting sections on its façade.

**Bric-a-brac** Small decorative objects collected for their sentimental or aesthetic value.

**Brocade** A textile (originally silk) having fluid foliate and arabesque patterns woven into the fabric in contrasting values or colors.

**Broken rangework** Stone masonry laid in horizontal courses of different height, any one course of which may be broken (at intervals) into two or more courses.

**Bronze** An alloy of copper and tin.

**Bronze doré** The French term for ormolu.

**Bulbous form** A swelling form.

**Bureau à caissons latéraux** Literally translated from the French, "desk with lateral compartments" refers to a desk with drawers.

**Bureau à cylindre** Literally translated from the French, "desk with cylinder" refers to a rolltop desk.

**Bureau à dos d'âne** Literally translated from the French, "desk with a donkey back" refers to a ladies writing table designed with a curved storage compartment.

**Bureau du roi** Literally translated from the French, "desk of the king" refers to rolltop desks designed for the French monarchs.

**Bureau plat** Literally translated from the French, "flat desk" refers to a writing table. Some bureau plats were fitted with drawers on both sides and used from either side.

**Burnishing** Polishing a metal surface to make it shine or bring out the patina.

**Buttress** An exterior architectural support for a wall designed to alleviate outward thrust created by the compression of the roof.

## C

**Cabriole** A leg formed to resemble the stylized front leg of a capering animal. The cabriole leg with its distinctive knee form is a strong characteristic of the Rococo period.

**Calcite** A mineral of calcium carbonate.

**Cameo glass** Decorative glass formed by laminating together two or more layers of glass, often in varying colors, which are then wheel-carved or etched to expose the colors underneath, creating a design in relief.

**Canapé** A French sofa or settee.

**Candelabra** A candleholder with multiple cups or branching arms.

**Canopic jar** A jar made from stone or pottery used as a storage container for the mummified internal organs of ancient Egyptians.

**Cantilevered** A horizontal projection supported by a downward force behind a support of free rotation without external bracing; appears to be self-supporting.

**Cap** Usually, the topmost member of any vertical architectural element.

**Capital** The top or uppermost element of a column, usually decorated.

**Caquetoire** A derivative of the French word "caqueter," meaning "to chatter"; refers to a conversation chair.

**Caravansary, caravanserais** A shelter built for traveling caravans for overnight lodging.

**Carpenter Gothic** In 19th-century American architecture, the application of Gothic motifs, often elaborate, by artisan-builders in wood.

**Cartibulum** The Latin term used to describe a rectangular table.

**Cartoon** A preliminary drawing or sketch used as a pattern for paintings, tapestries, or carpet designs.

**Cartouche** A rounded or oval form with a convex surface usually surrounded by ornamental scrollwork.

**Carving** The process of cutting into the surface material either wholly or in part to create pattern, texture, or relief.

**Caryatid** A column in the form of a woman usually depicted wearing ancient Greek clothing or drapery.

**Case good, case piece** Any nonupholstered furniture item used for storage, including bookcases, bureaus, chests, china cabinets, and armoires.

**Casket** A small chest or a large box.

**Cassapanca** The Italian term for a bench-like couch.

**Cassone** The Italian term for a chest or trunk.

**Casting** Giving three-dimensional shape or decoration to an object by pouring molten materials into a mold.

**Cellulosic fibers** Fibers obtained from plants or grasses.

**Ceramics** A generic term referring to articles made of earth materials such as clay, processed by firing or baking. The objects are formed, and then hardened by exposing them to heat. This firing process makes the material hard and impervious.

**Certosina** The Italian term used to describe light-colored wood, bone, or ivory inlaid against a dark background.

**Chaise longue** Literally translated from the French, "long chair" refers to a chair with an extended seat used for lounging.

**Chalice** A drinking cup.

**Chasing, chased** The process of cutting, embossing, or incising metal to create design or pattern.

**Château** A castle or imposing country residence of nobility in old France; now, any French country estate.

**Cheval** A freestanding floor mirror.

**Chiffonier** A French small chest of drawers.

**Chinoiserie** A French term describing design motifs possessing distinctive Chinese styling.

**Chintz** A textile of woven cotton finished with wax and starch glaze that leaves a shiny surface.

**Clapboard** A wood siding commonly used as an exterior covering on a building of frame construction; applied horizontally and overlapped, with the grain running lengthwise; thicker along the lower edge than along the top.

**Claw-and-ball** A furniture foot form shaped to resemble a bird's claw clutching a pearl.

**Clay** A naturally occurring mineral substance consisting of hydrous aluminum silicates. When wet, it can be molded or shaped and then heated at high temperatures to harden the material.

**Cloisonné** A type of enameling in which the design is created by fusing copper bands onto a surface. These cells maintain color separation through the firing process. The object is cooled and then polished to give the copper the appearance of gold.

**Concrete** A building material made from cement and aggregate materials.

**Continuous stretcher** Connecting members between all legs of a chair or case piece used to strengthen the construction of the frame.

**Corinthian** A Greek column dating to the Classical period featuring a slender shaft and a carved acanthus leaf capital.

**Cornice** The uppermost part of the entablature; a molding with a projecting profile.

**Course, courses, coursing** Rows of brick or stone laid one layer on top of the other. Often used to build a wall.

**Cove ceiling** A ceiling having a cove at the wall lines; the junction of the wall to the ceiling is curved, not at a right angle.

**Creamware** Fine white earthenware developed after 1750.

**Credenza** A small piece of furniture fitted with drawers or cupboards used for storage.

**Crest rail** The top horizontal member on a chair frame; also referred to as the top rail.

**Cristallo** The Italian word for crystal.

**Crockets** Ornamental finials resembling the foliate patterns found on handles of medieval swords. Architectural embellishments on a Gothic cathedral.

**Crossbanded, crossbanding** Banding inlaid at a 90-degree angle to the grain.

**Crown** Any upper terminal feature in architecture; the top of an arch including the keystone.

**Crystal** A clear and transparent quartz resembling ice; an imitation of this material made in glass. Colorless glass of high quality.

**Cubiculum** The Latin word identifying a bedroom within an ancient roman dwelling.

**Cuneiform** An ancient form of writing using wedge-shaped characters to represent words, syllables, or ideas.

**Curule** Having an X-form base.

**Cyma recta** The Latin word identifying a type of projecting architectural molding in the shape of the letter "S".

## D

**Dado** The middle parts (sometimes all parts) of a protective, ornamental paneling applied to the lower walls of a room above the baseboard.

**Dais** A raised platform or base.

**Damascene** A style of ornamentation whereby gold or silver is inlaid into a contrasting metal ground.

**Damask** A flatly woven textile with a reversible pattern in monochromatic colors.

**Dantesca** An upholstered Italian armchair having a short back, open sides, and an X-form base. Dantesca is also referred to as a Dante chair named for the 14th-century Italian poet.

**Delftware** Production of ceramics in Delft, Holland; having a brilliant and heavy glaze, noted for blue colors and decorations on a white field.

**Diamond work** Masonry construction in which pieces are set so as to form diamonds on the face of a wall.

**Diaper pattern** A design motif identified by its distinctive diamond-shaped patterns.

**Diphros okladias** The Greek term used to describe an X-form folding stool.

**Disk, disk turning** A flat, tapered, circular shape.

**Domus** A Latin term used to describe houses for the upper classes.

**Doric** A column dating to the ancient Greek period featuring a thick, tapering shaft and a simple disk-carved capital.

**Double cove** A term used to describe the contoured seat on an Egyptian chair or stool. Also called a dipped seat.

**Dowels** Cylindrical pegs used to join two pieces of wood. Each receiving member has a drilled hole with a combined diameter and length of the dowel. Glue or epoxy is often used to strengthen the joint.

**Dressoir** A French sideboard or dresser. Originally the dressoir was placed in the great hall of a medieval castle and used for storage and display.

**Drop seat** A shaped upholstered seat designed to rest securely within the framework of the seat rail. The seat was easily removed for seasonal recovering. Also referred to as a slip seat.

**Drum** In ancient architecture, the individual circular disks stacked one on top of the other to form a column. In Egyptian furniture, a small tapering cylinder positioned beneath a paw foot.

## E

**Earthenware** Pottery fired at low temperatures, often making it coarser and more porous than other ceramics.

**Ébéniste** The French term for a cabinetmaker.

**Embossed** A raised design created by stamping, molding, or carving.

**Embroidery** The process of creating a design or pattern on cloth using thread and a needle.

**Enamel** A glassy substance used for painting on pottery and porcelain after it has had a preliminary coating of glaze. After the pattern is finished, the piece is fired again and the enamel is fused with the original glaze. The colors are made from gold, silver, iron, tin, lead, and other compounds.

**Engondole** The French word used to describe a curving chair back.

**Entablature** An architectural term used to describe a grouping comprised of the cornice, architrave, and frieze areas on an ancient temple.

**Escutcheon** The French term for a protective key plate.

**Etching** The process of scratching into the surface of a material to create pattern or texture.

## F

**Façade** In architecture, the face of a building; usually the main entrance or side bearing architectural significance.

**Faience** A type of pottery made originally at Faenza, Italy. A glassy paste usually applied over earthenware or pottery to give the object the appearance of glass once fired.

**Fanlight** A semicircular window over the opening of a door, with radiating bars in the form of an open fan; also called a sunburst light.

**Farthingale chair** An upholstered, box-form English side chair. The chair accommodated fashionable 16th-century ladies wearing hooped skirts called farthingales.

**Fauteuil** A French upholstered armchair with open sides.

**Festoon** A rope of flowers or vines draped in garlands or any motif that resembles this design.

**Finial** An upright, decorative object formed in a variety of shapes.

**Firing** Subjecting an object to heat, as in pottery or cloisonné work.

**Flatware** Completed metalwork having a thin surface as in plates, platters, forks, knives, and spoons.

**Flax** The plant from which linen is made.

**Fleur de lis** A French term translated as "flower of the lily;" a design motif of a stylized lily.

**Flitch** The series of veneer cuts taken in sequence from a log.

**Fluted, fluting** Concave cut parallel grooves used as a decorative surface treatment. The process of fluting originated from Greek architecture; column shafts were decorated with this treatment.

**Flying shuttle** A threaded device used to weave weft fibers into the warp fibers on a loom.

**Formwork** A temporary platform or mold used for pouring a malleable material to form a shape until hardened.

**Frailero** A Spanish box-form armchair typically used in monasteries (the name is a derivative of "friar"). Most chairs of this type had a stretched leather seat and back tacked to a wooden frame. The chair could be folded lengthwise and carried from room to room.

**Fresco** A wall painting done on wet plaster.

**Fruitwood** Wood from apple, cherry, or pear trees.

**Fulcrum** A scroll-shaped object placed at one or both ends of a Roman lectus and used as a headrest or armrest.

## G

**Gable** The pitch or slope of a roof, pediment, or wall. Also the slope or pitch of the top of a chest or other piece of furniture.

**Gadroon** A design motif featuring a series or rows of convex patterns sometimes resembling curved tear drops (thinner at the top and wider at the bottom).

**Gallery** In architecture, an upper balcony of a building protected by handrails or a balustrade.

**Gauged arch** An arch of wedge-shaped bricks that have been shaped so that the joints radiate from a common center.

**Gauged work** A precise brickwork in which bricks are cut or sawn to shape and then rubbed to an exact size and smooth finish.

**Gesso** Plaster mixed with glue used as an undercoating for painting or gilding.

**Gilding** The process of applying gold leaf to a prepared surface such as wood or plaster.

**Gilt** An object that has been coated with gold.

**Gilt furniture** Furniture that has gold leaf applied to its surface.

**Gingerbread** The highly decorative woodwork applied to Victorian and Gothic revival style houses, or the like.

**Glaze** In ceramics, a coating applied to the surface of clay to give color or gloss. The glaze is activated by firing.

**Goddard foot** A short, ogee-shaped foot form named after the 18th-century cabinetmaker, Daniel Goddard.

**Gold leaf** Thin sheets of flattened gold used to decorate surfaces.

**Goldsmith** A metalsmith trained to work with gold.

**Gooseneck arm** A crook-shaped arm support imitating the neck of a goose.

**Great hall** The largest room in a medieval castle.

**Greco-Roman** Characteristics shared by both the ancient Greeks and Romans.

**Grillwork** Any design fashioned from open metalwork.

**Gros point** Lacework featuring large-scale designs; needlework created with large stitches.

**Gueridon** The French term for a small decorative table or stand.

**Guilloche** A decorative motif of interlocking circles with or without further embellishments.

### H

**H-form stretcher** A structural support between two or more legs on furniture forming the letter "H".

**Hallmark strike** The insignia of the maker; seen on metalware and pottery.

**Hard-paste porcelain** A term applied by European potters to a type of clay made with kaolin, a material used by the Chinese in making true porcelain and not discovered in Europe until 1709. Also, porcelain made from a ceramic material with good plasticity that holds its shape through firing, offering maximum sculptural capabilities.

**Hieroglyph, hieroglyphics** An ancient Egyptian form of writing using pictures or symbols to represent words or thoughts.

**Hollowware** Metalwork in modeled shapes, such as a teapot, bowl, or pitcher; the opposite of flatware, which refers to forks, spoons, knives, and so on.

**Hydria** A Greek term used to describe a three-handled vessel for holding water.

**Hypostyle** In architecture, interior columns that support the roof in an Egyptian building.

### I

**Impluvium** The recessed area located directly under the atrium of a Roman house used to collect rainwater.

**Impost block** In architecture, a wedge-shaped block placed between the capital and that which it supports.

**In situ** In its original location.

**Incising** Digging into the surface of an object with a sharp tool.

**Incurvate** A concave or inward shape; in furniture the concept is usually applied to the shape of the arm rest or arm post.

**Inlay** In furniture, the process of imbedding a variety of materials including contrasting woods, bone, ivory, metal, and/or semiprecious stones into the wood's surface to create a decorative effect.

**Insula** A Roman dwelling containing several units or apartments.

**Intarsia** The Italian term for inlay of different colored woods.

**Ionic** A column dating to the ancient Greek period featuring a slender, tapering shaft and a volute-shaped capital.

**Iridescent** Containing the bright luster of color on a surface.

**Ivory** The teeth or tusks of an animal.

### J

**Jacquard** A mechanized loom that uses a punch card system for creating an even and consistent pattern.

**Japanning, japanned** A paint and varnish process that imitates oriental lacquerwork.

**Jasperware** A hard biscuit ware pottery popularized by Wedgwood in the 18th century; essentially, unglazed porcelain.

### K

**Keystone** The uppermost block of an arch that locks the structure in place.

**Kiln** A large oven-like chamber used to heat pottery using controlled temperatures as a means of hardening the clay.

**Kline** A Greek reclining couch or bed.

**Klismos** A Greek side chair having a concave back and saber legs.

**Knickknacks** Small decorative objects collected for their aesthetic value.

**Krater** A two-handled piece of Greek pottery used as a mixing bowl.

**Kylix** A footed-style Greek drinking cup, with or without handles.

### L

**Lace** A type of needlework that leaves open areas as part of the design.

**Lacquer** A glossy finish made from a natural or synthetic substance.

**Ladder-back chair** A chair with horizontal back slats resembling the rungs of a ladder.

**Lambrequin** A decorative hanging usually appearing on a shelf edge or at the top of a window opening.

**Lappet** A narrow piece of lace usually attached to clothing.

**Lathe** A machine used to turn and cut a block of wood, giving it a rounded shape.

**Lead crystal** Crystal with lead added for strength.

**Lectus** A Roman reclining couch or bed.

**Lekythos** A Greek term used to describe a handled vessel for holding oils, perfumes, or wine.

**Limoges** Fine-quality porcelain produced in the vicinity of Limoges, France.

**Lincrusta** The brand name for an embossed wallpaper with patterns in low relief.

**Linear B texts** An ancient form of writing used by Aegean cultures, which is currently undecipherable.

**Lit à colonnes** The French term for a four-post canopy bed.

**Lit à la polonaise** The French term for a dome-shaped canopy bed.

**Lit à travers** The French term for a bed placed sideways against a wall.

**Long gallery** A gallery in the upper stories of an Elizabethan or Jacobean manor house; often used as a promenade or family room.

**Longcase clock** A type of clock large enough to stand on the floor.

**Loom** A weaving apparatus with a framework for attaching warp and weft yarns.

### M

**Majolica, maiolica** Italian and Spanish pottery coated with a tin enamel and painted with bright colors.

**Manchette** The French term used to describe a small upholstered arm pad attached to the armrest.

**Marquetry** A decorative treatment whereby colored woods, ivory, mother-of-pearl, metal, or tortoiseshell is inlaid into a veneered surface.

**Megaron** A large rectangular room used by the Minoans and Mycenaeans for ceremonial or religious purposes.

**Meissen** A factory established in Germany to produce porcelain ware in the early 18th century.

**Melamine** A plastic made from resin.

**Mensa** A Latin term used to describe a small table.

**Millefleur** Translated as "thousand flowers," the term refers to the appearance of a field of flowers in a design; often seen in tapestries.

**Millwork** Woodworking including moldings, trim, stairs, window sashes, and doors.

**Minstrel gallery** A small balcony on the inside of a church or manor house hall, usually over the entrance.

**Modillion** An architectural bracket located under the cornice. Also, a decorative motif used on furniture.

**Moquette** Carpeting made by sewing sections of woven carpet together to cover a room from wall to wall (18th and 19th centuries).

**Mortar** A bonding agent consisting of cement, sand, and lime used to set concrete, stone, or brick.

**Mortise and tenon** A type of joint consisting of peg and hole configuration. The projecting member (tenon) from one piece of wood is fitted into the cavity (mortise) of another.

**Mosaic** A decorative wall or floor covering created by placing small pieces of colored stone, glass, or tile in a mortar or cement ground.

**Mother-of-pearl** The iridescent layer inside certain seashells.

**Motif** A recurring design.

**Mudéjar** A style of ornament based on a combination of Spanish Christian and Moorish influenced designs.

**Mural** A wall painting.

**Murano glass** A type of high-quality glass produced in the Italian municipality of Murano.

## N

**Nave** A wide, rectangular central space flanked by narrower side aisles and running the length of building.

**Needlepoint** Embroidery using threads to create a design or pattern on a canvas or open weave cloth.

**Newel post** A tall and more or less ornamental post at the head or foot of a stair, supporting the handrail.

## O

**Objets d'art** Literally translated from the French, "art object" refers to any small art object.

**Obsidian** A natural siliceous (glass) substance formed from volcanic eruptions.

**Ogee arch** A pointed arch composed of reversed curves, the lower concave and the upper convex. On furniture, a decorative detail that resembles this type of arch design.

**Ormolu** Brass or bronze mounts applied to furniture and other decorative accessories.

## P

**Palladian** In the style of Andrea Palladio.

**Papelera** A small Spanish cabinet with fitted compartments or drawers used for the storage of important papers and writing implements.

**Papyrus** A flowering plant that grows along the Nile in Egypt. The stalk was used to make an early form of paper.

**Parapet wall** The part of a wall that is entirely above the roof.

**Parcel gilt** Gilding applied to specific parts of a carved or flat design.

**Pargework** A decorative treatment using molded or carved plaster; usually used on ceilings.

**Pâte-sur-pâte** A decorative treatment on porcelain used to achieve the look of cut-glass cameo.

**Pediment** The triangular section of a gabled roof; usually appears on the short ends of a building.

**Pendant** An ornamental knob that hangs vertically.

**Petit point** Lacework featuring small-scale designs; needlework created with small stitches.

**Pewter** A metal alloy of tin and lead.

**Piano nobile** The Italian translation, "great floor" refers to the main floor of a large house or building.

**Pier table** A table placed between two doors.

**Pierced tracery** Tracery with open cutwork designs.

**Pietra dura** Literally translated from the Italian, "hard stone" refers to colored marble mosaic.

**Pilaster** A squared column with one side attached to a background.

**Pillow lace** Handmade lace made by pinning the work to a pillow while weaving.

**Pilotis** The free-standing columns or posts that support a building, raising it above ground level.

**Piqué** An inlay design using metal and combinations of ivory, tortoiseshell, and stone.

**Pithos, pithoi** Stone or pottery storage jars used by ancient Aegean cultures.

**Plaster** A mixture of lime, sand, and water.

**Plinth** A small block placed at the base of a column, pilaster, or pedestal, or anything resembling this feature.

**Point d' Angleterre** A type of bobbin lace featuring foliate patterns with needlework embellishments.

**Point de France** A type of lace featuring floral designs over a hexagonal background.

**Polychrome** Having many colors.

**Porcelain** One of the three principal types of ornamental pottery. A hard, translucent clayware body that differs from china in composition and manufacturing process.

**Porringer** A small, shallow bowl.

**Post-and-lintel construction** A construction method for buildings and structures relying on posts or columns and lintels or beams to support the load.

**Post, posts** Any vertical structural supporting member. Also called a column.

**Pottery** A porous and not very durable form of clayware made of crude clay and fired at low temperatures.

**Pottery shards** Pottery fragments taken from excavated sites.

**Puente** A Spanish arcaded stand used to support a vargueño.

**Pulvinar frieze** A convex-shaped frieze. The frieze is a wide band of molding placed between the architrave and cornice.

**Putti** The Latin term used to describe figures of baby boys with wings; their images derived from the Roman god Cupid.

**PVC** Polyvinyl chloride; used to make plastics.

## Q

**Quatrefoil** A design motif with four lobes or foils dating from the Medieval period.

**Quoins** Masonry blocks placed at the exterior corners of a building.

## R

**Raking back** A chair with a slant back.

**Red figure technique** A technique in ancient Greek pottery decoration where the positive shapes appear in red or terra cotta color against a black background.

**Reed** A grasslike stalk of cellulosic material.

**Reeded, reeding** Decorative, convex grooves carved into the shaft of an architectural column or anything that resembles this.

**Refectory** A room used for dining.

**Reinforced concrete** Concrete with increased tensile strength produced by iron or steel mesh or bars embedded in it.

**Relief** A raised design created by carving, molding, or repoussé work.

**Repoussé** Metalwork designs created by hammering one side of an object to create a relief effect on the opposite side.

**Ridgepole** A longitudinal member at the apex of a roof that supports the upper ends of the rafters.

**Romayne** A medallion-enclosed portrait resembling those used on Roman coins.

**Rose point** A type of finely worked needlepoint lace with roses and small loops.

**Runner** A horizontal connecting member used between the legs of a chair or case piece to strengthen its construction. Unlike a stretcher, the runner rests on the floor.

**Rush** In furniture, a type of grass used to make chair seats.

## S

**Saber legs**  A term used to describe concave-shaped furniture legs.

**Saltire stretcher**  A structural support between two or more legs on furniture forming an X.

**Sandwich glass**  A type of press-molded glass originating from a factory in Sandwich, Massachusetts, or anything resembling these patterns.

**Sarcophagus, sarcophagi (plural)**  A coffin made from a variety of materials including stone and wood.

**Savonarola**  An Italian Renaissance chair constructed from multiple wooden staves in an X-form configuration that collapses lengthwise for easy mobility.

**Savonnerie**  A high-quality knotted pile carpet or rug originally from a French rug manufacturer; first woven in 1618; the pattern is usually slightly higher than the field. Also the name of a type of a pile rug with warp linen fibers and weft wool fibers.

**Scratch carving**  Shallow or deep scratching on a surface to produce pattern or decoration.

**Scrimshaw**  Objects made from whale bone or ivory.

**Seat rail**  The horizontal member on a chair, sofa, or settee frame that forms the seat.

**Secrétaire à abattant**  The French term for a fall-front secretary.

**Secretary, secretaire**  A tall fall-front writing desk with storage compartments above and drawers below.

**Sedia**  An Italian Renaissance box-form upholstered armchair.

**Sella curulis**  The Latin term used to describe an X-form folding stool.

**Settle**  A term applied to a bench-like couch during the Medieval period.

**Sèvres**  A French ceramic factory.

**Sgabello**  An Italian Renaissance wooden chair designed with two trestle supports, an octagonal seat, and inverted triangular back.

**Shagreen**  Sharkskin used as a veneer on surfaces of Art Deco furniture and accessories.

**Shingle style**  An American eclectic style, primarily in domestic architecture during the second half of the 18th century; characterized by extensive use of unpainted wood-shingle covering for roofs as well as for walls.

**Shoe**  A furniture term describing a small round disk that supports a decorative foot.

**Side light**  A framed area of fixed glass alongside a door or window opening; also called a wing light, margin light, or flanking window.

**Sillón de caderas, sillón de tijera**  A Spanish Renaissance armchair with an X-form base.

**Silver plate**  Items made from an application of silver over copper.

**Silversmith**  A metalsmith trained to work with silver.

**Singerie**  The French term describing design motifs depicting frolicking monkeys.

**Slat**  A wide, horizontal wooden member used in furniture construction. Slats can be decorative or plain.

**Sleeping chairs**  Chairs designed with reclining backs.

**Slip**  Clay mixed with water to create a creamlike consistency. Slip acts as a bonding agent to join two pieces of clay before firing, or as a decorative treatment if colored.

**Slip seat**  A shaped, upholstered seat designed to rest securely within the framework of the seat rail. The seat was easily removed for seasonal recovering. Also referred to as a drop seat.

**Soft-paste porcelain**  A term applied by European potters to describe a mixture of clay and ground glass used to make imitation porcelain before the widespread use of kaolin. It is a porcelain made from a ceramic material with low plasticity, which limits its sculptural capabilities and is more translucent and fragile than hard-paste porcelain.

**Solium**  The Latin term used to describe a ceremonial throne chair.

**Spindle (furniture)**  An elongated, turned member in a variety of shapes used as decoration in millwork and on furniture. Split spindles are cut lengthwise, the flat side affixed to the surface of case pieces for decoration.

**Spindle (weaving)**  A shaped rod used to carry the weft yarns through a loom.

**Spinning frame**  A machine used to twist fibers into yarns.

**Spinning jenny**  A machine used to twist fibers into yarns with the ability to handle multiple units.

**Splat back**  A wide, vertical wooden member used as a back support on chairs or settees. Splats can be decorative or plain.

**Splayed**  Legs or trestle supports designed with an outward slant.

**Spoon-back chair**  A chair with a shaped splat that follows the curvature of the spine.

**Staffordshire**  English earthenware produced in a provincial character.

**Stained glass**  Glass created by applying color with pigment.

**Steel**  An alloy of iron and carbon.

**Sterling silver**  An alloy of 92.5 percent silver and 7.5 percent other metals.

**Stoneware**  Pottery fired at high temperatures to give it strength.

**Stretcher**  A horizontal connecting member used between the legs of a chair or case piece to strengthen its construction. Unlike runners, stretchers do not touch the floor.

**Stringing**  Thin bands of inlay appearing on furniture.

**Strut**  A connecting member from the seat to the stretcher that provides additional structural support.

**Stucco**  A mixture of lime, sand, cement, and water.

## T

**Table à ouvrage**  A French work table.

**Tabouret**  A French stool.

**Taffeta**  A lightweight woven fabric with a crisp hand and high sheen.

**Tapestry**  A medium- to heavy-weight woven textile with the decorative pattern or design worked into the looming process.

**Taquillon**  The Spanish term for a chest of drawers.

**Taracea**  Spanish inlay work using contrasting woods, bone, ivory, metal, and/or other semiprecious materials for decorative effect.

**Term figure**  A rectangular-shaped column fashioned with a human head and paw feet.

**Terra cotta**  A hard-baked pottery extensively used in the decorative arts as a building material. This coarse clay maintains its reddish coloring after firing.

**Tesserae**  Small pieces of colored stone, glass, or tile used in mosaics.

**Tester**  The overhead canopy of a bed.

**Textiles**  Woven fabrics, carpet, upholstery, or tapestry.

**Thatch**  Straw, reed, or grasses bundled together and used as a building material.

**Thronos**  The Greek term used to describe a ceremonial throne chair.

**Toile de Jouy**  A printed cotton textile made in Jouy en Josas, France, and popularized during the 18th and 19th centuries.

**Tole**  Enameled or painted metalwares.

**Top rail**  The top horizontal member on a chair frame, also referred to as the crest rail.

**Torchère**  A lamp large enough to stand on the floor.

**Tortoiseshell**  Hawksbill turtle shell with a reddish brown and yellow mottled appearance.

**Trabeated**  In architecture, post-and-lintel construction whereby horizontal beams are supported by vertical posts.

**Tracery**  In architecture, decorative stone mullions used in windows such as those that hold the stained glass in a Gothic cathedral. In furniture, a decorative carving that imitates this cut stonework. Pierced tracery is a decorative cut-through carving.

**Transferware** A type of ceramic with a design produced from inked paper.

**Transom** A horizontal bar of wood or stone across a window; the cross-bar separating a door from the fanlight above it.

**Treenware** Small household objects made by carving or hollowing out wood.

**Trefoil** A design motif with three lobes or foils dating from the Medieval period.

**Trestle** A type of support used on chairs and tables in the place of traditional legs.

**Triclinium** The Latin room identifying a dining room within an ancient Roman dwelling.

**Tripod table** A table supported on three legs.

**Trompe l'oeil** Literally translated from the French, "fool the eye" refers to a type of illusionistic painting giving the appearance of three dimensions.

**Truss** A structure composed of a combination of members, usually in some triangular arrangement so as to constitute a rigid framework.

**Tudor arch** A four-centered pointed arch common in the architecture of the Tudor style in England.

**Turkey work** A handmade textile made to simulate the appearance of an oriental rug.

**Turning, turned** A process used to shape a block of wood into a uniform, cylindrical design. First, a wooden block is securely fastened to a lathe. As the lathe rotates the block, a cutting implement is moved in a forward and backward motion giving the wood its shape.

## U

**Unguents** Perfumed ointments, lotions, or salves used by the ancient Egyptians.

## V

**Vargueño** A Spanish drop-front writing cabinet.

**Velvet** A woven textile with a cut pile.

**Verdure tapestry** Woven tapestry featuring vegetative patterns.

**Vernacular architecture** A mode of building based on regional forms and materials.

**Vernis Martin** A term describing a type of varnish used on French furniture of the 18th century named for the cabinetmaker who developed it.

**Vitrine** A glass-enclosed cabinet designed to display fine accessories such as figurines, porcelains, china, or knickknacks.

**Voyeuse** A type of French chair having an arm rest along the crest rail for game watching.

## W

**Wainscot chair** A chair having a solid wood paneled back; introduced during the Renaissance period.

**Wainscot, wainscoting** The lower half portion of a wall covered with wood paneling or anything that resembles this treatment.

**Warp** The vertical yarns on a loom or in a weaving.

**Wattle-and-daub** A wall finishing material consisting of the application of a mixture of mud and clay over a framework of wood twigs or boards.

**Weaving** The process of interlacing fibers or yarns using an over-under method or similar variation or process.

**Webbing** Latticed leather, jute, burlap, rubber, or metal used as a support for upholstery, whether coil springs or loose cushions.

**Wedgwood** Josiah Wedgwood's jasperware; fields of blue, olive green, black, lilac, or sage with white classically inspired Greek motifs or figures.

**Weft** The horizontal yarns on a loom or in a weaving.

**Wicker** Straw, reed, or grasses woven together to form baskets, furniture, or other domestic items.

**Wilton carpet** A type of looped pile carpeting woven on a loom.

**Window seat** A seat built into the bottom inside of a window; a seat located at a window.

**Woad** A plant grown in the areas surrounding the Mediterranean; its leaves are used in the production of blue dye.

**Wrought iron** Iron with a low carbon content, making it easy to shape. The iron is hammered or forged into a decorative shape while the metal is either hot or cold.

## Y

**Yoke** In furniture, a distinctive shaped crest rail resembling the yoke on a team of oxen. Also a device used by African tribes as a type of pillow support that raises the head several inches from the mattress during sleep.

This bibliography offers a selection of the most current publications on the decorative arts. The list avoids collector-type books, focusing instead on publications representing scholarly research. For monographs on individual designers, it is best to consult Internet bookstores. This list is a testament to the fact that more scholarly research and publication in the field of the decorative arts is needed. Furthermore, several scholarly publications on the decorative arts are out of print and are excluded from this compilation of titles.

## GENERAL STUDIES

Aav, Marianne, and Nina Stritzler-Levine, eds. *Finnish Modern Design: Utopian Ideals and Everyday Realities, 1930–97*. New Haven: Yale University Press, 2000.

Arwas, Victor. *Art Nouveau: The French Aesthetic*. London: Andreas Papadakis Publishers, 2002.

Blonston, Gary, and William Morris. *William Morris: Artifacts/ Glass*. 1st ed. New York: Abbeville Press, 1996.

Campbell, Gordon. *The Grove Encyclopedia of Decorative Arts*. Oxford: Oxford University Press, 2006.

Cherry, Deborah, and Katie Scott, eds. *Between Luxury and the Everyday: French Decorative Arts in the Eighteenth Century*. Oxford: Blackwell Publishing Limited, 2006.

Eversmann, Pauline. *The Winterthur Guide to Recognizing Styles: American Decorative Arts from the 17th through the 19th Centuries*. 1st ed. Winterthur, DE: Winterthur, 2001.

Greenhalgh, Paul. *Art Nouveau, 1890–1914*. New York: Harry N. Abrams, 2000.

Gruber, Alain, ed. *The History of Decorative Arts: Renaissance and Mannerism in Europe*. New York: Abbeville Press, 1994.

J. Paul Getty Museum. *Summary Catalogue of Decorative Arts in the J. Paul Getty Museum*. Los Angeles: Getty Trust Publications, 2002.

Krill, Rosemary Troy. *Early American Decorative Arts, 1620–1860: A Handbook for Interpreters*. Rev. ed. Lanham, MD: AltaMira Press, 2000.

Luchs, Alison. *Western Decorative Arts: The Collections of the National Gallery of Art Systematic Catalogue*. Cambridge: Cambridge University Press, 1994.

Ostergard, Derek E., ed. *The Sevres Porcelain Manufactory: Alexandre Brongniart and the Triumph of Art and Industry, 1800–1847*. New Haven: Yale University Press, 1997.

Pons, Bruno, Johan R. Ter Molen, Ursula Reinhardt, Robert Fohr, and Alain Gruber, eds. *Classicism and the Baroque in Europe: History of Decorative Arts*. New York: Abbeville Press, 1996.

Riley, Noel, and Patricia Bayer, eds. *The Elements of Design: A Practical Encyclopedia of the Decorative Arts from the Renaissance to the Present*. New York: Free Press, 2003.

Snodin, Michael, and John Styles. *Design and the Decorative Arts*. London: V & A Publications, 2001.

Snodin, Michael, and John Styles, eds. *Design and the Decorative Arts: Georgian Britain 1714–1837*. London: Victoria & Albert Museum, 2004.

Tise, Suzanne, and Yvonne Branhammer. *Decorative Arts of France 1900–1942*. New York: Rizzoli, 1990.

Troy, Nancy J. *Modernism and the Decorative Arts in France: Art Nouveau to Le Corbusier*. New Haven: Yale University Press, 1991.

Wood, Ghislaine. *Essential Art Deco*. 1st North American edition. Boston: Bulfinch, 2003.

Woodham, Jonathan M. *Twentieth-Century Design*. Oxford: Oxford University Press, 1997.

## CLOCKS

Cipolla, Carlo, and Anthony Grafton. *Clocks and Culture: 1300–1700*. New York: W. W. Norton & Company, 2003.

Dohrn-van Rossum, Gerhard, and Thomas Dunlap, trans. *History of the Hour: Clocks and Modern Temporal Orders*. Chicago: University of Chicago Press, 1998.

## FURNITURE

Aronson, Joseph. *The Encyclopedia of Furniture*, Third Edition. New York: Clarkson Potter, 1961.

Calloway, Stephen, Alan Powers, and Elizabeth C. Cromley. *The Elements of Style: an Encyclopedia of Domestic Architectural Detail*. London: Mitchell Beazley, 2007.

Habegger, Jerryll, and Joseph H. Osman. *Sourcebook of Modern Furniture*. New York: W.W. Norton &, 2005.

Litchfield, Frederick. *Illustrated History of Furniture: From the Earliest to the Present Time*. Charleston, SC: Nabu, 2010.

Miller, Judith. *Furniture: World Styles from Classical to Contemporary*. London: DK Publishing, 2011.

Morley, John. *The History of Furniture: Twenty-five Centuries of Style and Design in the Western Tradition*. Boston: Little, Brown and, 1999.

Postell, James Christopher. *Furniture Design*. Hoboken, NJ: John Wiley & Sons, 2007.

Stimpson, Miriam F. *Modern Furniture Classics: [a Sourcebook of Styles, Designers, and Manufacturers from 1855 to Today]*. New York: Whitney Libr. of Design, 1987.

## GLASS

Arwas, Victor, and Susan Newell. *The Art of Glass: Art Nouveau to Art Deco*. New York: Rizzoli International Publications, 1997.

Brown, Sarah, and David O'Connor. *The Glass-Painters (Medieval Craftsmen)*. Toronto: University of Toronto Press, 1991.

Curtis, Jean-Louis, Jacques Boulay, and Jean-Michel Tardy. *Baccarat*. New York: Harry N. Abrams, 1992.

Fleming, Stuart James. *Roman Glass: Reflections of Everyday Life*. Philadelphia: University Museum Publications, 1997.

Gable, Carl I. *Murano Magic: Complete Guide to Venetian Glass, Its History and Artists*. Atglen, PA: Schiffer Publishing, 2004.

Gudenrath, William, and Veronica Tatton-Brown. *Catalogue of Greek and Roman Glass in the British Museum: Non-Blown and Early Blown Glass*. London: British Museum Press, 2006.

Hatch, Carolyn. *Deco Lalique: Creator to Consumer*. Toronto: Royal Ontario Museum, 2007.

Macfarlane, Alan, and Gerry Martin. *Glass: A World History*. Chicago: University of Chicago Press, 2002.

Mentasti, Rosa Barovier. *Venetian Glass*. 1st ed. Venice: Arsenale Editrice, 2007.

Netzer, Nancy, and Hanns Swarzenski. *Medieval Objects in the Museum of Fine Arts Boston: Medieval Enamels and Glass*. Boston: Museum of Fine Arts Boston, 1986.

Nicholson, Paul T. *Egyptian Faience and Glass*. Buckinghamshire, England: Shire Publications, 1999.

Orrefors Glasbruk, Kerstin Wickman, eds. *Orrefors: A Century of Swedish Glassmaking*. Stockholm: Byggforlaget, 1999.

Ricke, Helmut, Jan Mergl, and Johann Lötz Witwe. *Lötz: Bohemian Glass 1880–1940*. Ostfildern, Germany: Hatje Cantz Publishers, 2003.

Ricke, Helmut, and Eva Schmitt, eds. *Art Nouveau Glass: The Gerda Koepff Collection*. Munich: Prestel Publishing, 2004.

Saliba, George, Linda Komaroff, and Catherine Hess, eds. *The Arts of Fire: Islamic Influences on Glass and Ceramics of the Italian Renaissance*. Los Angeles: Getty Trust Publications: J. Paul Getty Museum, 2004.

Stern, Marianne, Sylvia Funfschilling, and Johan Grimonprez. *Roman, Byzantine and Early Medieval Glass: Ernesto Wolf Collection*. Ostfildern, Germany: Hatje Cantz Publishers, 2001.

Tait, Hugh, ed. *Five Thousand Years of Glass*. Rev. ed. Philadelphia: University of Pennsylvania Press, 2004.

Turander, Ralf, Claes Britton, and Tom Rafstedt. *Gunnel Sahlin & Kosta Boda*. Corte Madera, CA: Gingko Press, 2000.

Warmus, William. *The Essential Rene Lalique*. New York: Harry N. Abrams, 2003.

## LIGHTING

Dilaura, David L. *History of Light and Lighting*. New York: Illuminating Engineering, 2006.

Eidelberg, Martin, Alice Cooney Frelinghuysen, Nancy McClelland, and Lars Rachen. *The Lamps of Louis Comfort Tiffany*. New York: Vendome Press, 2005.

## METALWORKING

Bigelow, Francis Hill. *Historic Silver of the Colonies and Its Makers*. Whitefish, MT: Kessinger Publishing, 2005.

Hayes, John W. *Greek, Roman, and Related Metalware in the Royal Ontario Museum*. Toronto: Royal Ontario Museum, 1984.

Hornsby, Peter. *Pewter of the Western World, 1600–1850*. Atglen, PA: Schiffer Publishing, 1983.

Kauffman, Henry J. *Early American Copper, Tin & Brass: Handcrafted Metalware from Colonial Times*. Mendham, NJ: Astragal Press, 1995.

Pina, Leslie, and Donald-Brian Johnson. *The Chase Era: 1933 & 1942 Catalogs of the Chase Brass & Copper Co*. Atglen, PA: Schiffer Publishing, 2000.

Rainwater, Dorothy T., and Donna Felger. *American Silverplate*. 3rd ed. Atglen, PA: Schiffer Publishing, 2000.

Schroderti, Timothy. *English Domestic Silver: National Trust Book of English Domestic Silver and Metalware 1500–1900*. Reprint ed. London: Penguin, 1990.

Scott, Jack L. *Pewter Wares from Sheffield*. Baltimore: Antiquary Press, 1980.

Young, W. A. *The Silver and Sheffield Plate Collector*. London: Hesperides Press, 2006.

## POTTERY

Adams, Elizabeth. *Chelsea Porcelain*. Rev. ed. London: British Museum Press, 2002.

Birch, Samuel. *History of Ancient Pottery: Egyptian, Assyrian and Greek V1*. Whitefish, MT: Kessinger Publishing, 2006.

Bradshaw, Peter. *Derby Porcelain Figures, 1750–1848*. London: Faber & Faber, 1990.

Cook, R. M. *Greek Painted Pottery*. 3rd ed. Oxford: Routledge, 1997.

Cooper, Emmanuel. *Ten Thousand Years of Pottery*. 4th ed. Philadelphia: University of Pennsylvania Press, 2000.

Coutts, Howard. *The Art of Ceramics: European Ceramic Design 1500–1830*. New Haven: Yale University Press, 2001.

Elliott, Charles Wyllys. *Pottery and Porcelain*. Whitefish, MT: Kessinger Publishing, 2003.

Garner, Phillipe. *Emile Galle*. Rev. ed. New York: Rizzoli, 1990.

Greer, Georgeanna H. *American Stonewares: The Art and Craft of Utilitarian Potters*. 4th ed. Atglen, PA: Schiffer Publishing, 2005.

Hildyard, Robin. *European Ceramics*. Philadelphia: University of Pennsylvania Press, 1999.

Karmason, Marilyn G., and Joan B. Stacke. *Majolica: A Complete History and Illustrated Survey*. Rev. ed. New York: Harry N. Abrams, 2002.

Menzhausen, Ingelore. *Early Meissen Porcelain in Dresden*. New York: Thames & Hudson, 1990.

Peña, J. Theodore. *Roman Pottery in the Archaeological Record*. Cambridge: Cambridge University Press, 2007.

Poole, Julia E. *English Pottery*. Cambridge: Cambridge University Press, 1995.

Snyder, Jeffrey B. *Rookwood Pottery*. Atglen, PA: Schiffer Publishing, 2005.

Stevenson, Greg. *Art Deco Ceramics*. Buckinghamshire, England: Shire Publications, 1999.

van Dam, Jan Daniel. *Dutch Delftware 1620–1859*. Zwolle, The Netherlands: Waanders Uitgevers, 2007.

Wardell, Sasha. *Porcelain and Bone China*. Wiltshire, England: Crowood Press, 2005.

Whittle, Alasdair. *Europe in the Neolithic*. Rev. ed. Cambridge: Cambridge University Press, 2003.

## TEXTILES

Brédif, Josette. *Toiles de Jouy: Classic Printed Textiles from France, 1760–1843*. London: Thames & Hudson, 1989.

Bremer-David, Charissa. *French Tapestries & Textiles in the J. Paul Getty Museum*. Los Angeles: Getty Trust Publications, 1997.

Broudy, Eric. *The Book of Looms: A History of the Handloom from Ancient Times to the Present*. New York: Van Nostrand Reinhold, 1979.

Cavallo, Adolfo Salvatore. *The Unicorn Tapestries in the Metropolitan Museum of Art*. New York: Metropolitan Museum of Art Publications, 2005.

Day, Susan. *Art Deco and Modernist Carpets*. San Francisco: Chronicle Books, 2002.

Delmarcel, Guy. *Flemish Tapestry*. New York: Harry N. Abrams, 2000.

Faraday, Cornelia Bateman. *European and American Carpets and Rugs: A History of the Hand-Woven Decorative Floor Coverings of Spain, France, Great Britain, Scandinavia, Belgium*. 2nd ed. Suffolk, England: Antique Collectors' Club, 1990.

Hackenbroch, Yvonne. *English and Other Needlework: Tapestries and Textiles in the Irwin Untermyer Collection*. Cambridge, MA: Harvard University Press, 1960.

Harris, Jennifer, ed. *Textiles, 5,000 Years: An International History and Illustrated Survey*. New York: Harry N. Abrams, 1993.

Jenkins, David, ed. *The Cambridge History of Western Textiles*. 2 vols. New York: Cambridge University Press, 2003.

Levey, Santina M. *Lace: A History*. London: Victoria and Albert Museum, 1983.

Parry, Linda. *Textiles of the Arts and Crafts Movement*. New York: Thames & Hudson, 1988.

Schoeser, Mary, and Kathleen Dejardin. *French Textiles: From 1760 to the Present*. London: L. King, 1991.

Schoeser, Mary, and Celia Rufey. *English and American Textiles: From 1790 to the Present*. New York: Thames & Hudson, 1989.

Sherrill, Sarah B. *Carpets and Rugs of Europe and America*. New York: Abbeville Press, 1996.

Synge, Lanto. *Art of Embroidery: History of Style and Technique*. Woodbridge, England: Antique Collectors' Club, 2001.

Wallace, Ann. *Arts & Crafts Textiles: The Movement in America*. Layton, UT: Gibbs Smith Publishers, 1999.

## WALLPAPERS

Hoskins, Lesley. *The Papered Wall: The History, Patterns and Techniques of Wallpaper*. 2nd ed. London: Thames & Hudson, 2005.

Lynn, Catherine. *Wallpaper in America: From the Seventeenth Century to World War I*. New York: W. W. Norton & Company, 1980.

Oman, Charles, and Jean Hamilton. *Wallpapers: A History and Illustrated Catalogue of the Collection of the Victoria and Albert Museum*. London: Philip Wilson Publishers, 1982.

Warner, Joanne K. *Landscape Wallcoverings*. London: Scala Publishers, 2006.

## INFORMATIVE WEBSITES

The high cost of permissions fees for printing color photos in publications limits the quantity of images used in this book due to budget constraints. These websites offer high-quality images for students to get a closer look at room settings, furniture details, and accessories.

| | |
|---|---|
| **The Art Institute of Chicago** | **www.artic.edu/aic** |
| *Search online collections* | *ARCHITECTURE AND DESIGN* |
| | *Thorne miniature rooms* |
| | *European decorative arts* |
| | *Textiles* |
| **Brighton Pavilion** | **www.brighton-hove-rpml.org.uk** |
| *Click on:* | *About the Palace* |
| **Château de Fontainebleau** | **www.musee-chateau-fontainebleau.fr** |
| *Click on: the British Flag for English* | *EXPLORE THE CHÂTEAU* |
| | *History* |
| | *Architecture* |
| | *The Apartments* |
| | *The Galleries and Theatre* |
| | *The Chapels* |
| | *The Four Museums* |
| | *Collection Masterpieces* |
| | *Courtyards and Gardens* |
| **The Getty Museum** | **www.getty.edu/museum** |
| *Click on: Collection* | *Browse* |
| | *Architecture and Room Elements* |
| | *Decorative Objects and Vases* |
| | *Furniture* |
| **Harewood House** | **www.harewood.org/house/state-rooms** |
| *Click on:* | *"State Rooms" to explore individual rooms as listed.* |
| **The Metropolitan Museum of Art** | **www.metmuseum.org** |
| *Click on: Collection Database* | *European Sculpture and Decorative Arts* |
| **The Museum of Modern Art** | **www.moma.org/explore/collection/index** |
| *Click on: Architecture and Design* | *Sort by: Date earliest first* |
| | *Architecture and Design With Images* |
| **The National Trust UK** | **www.nationaltrust.org.UK** |
| *Search by House Name* | *Osterley Park* |
| | *Wimpole Hall* |
| | *Ham House* |
| | *Croome Court* |
| | *Claydon House* |
| **PBS** | **http://www.pbs.org/marieantoinette/life/queen.html** |
| **Strawberry Hill House** | **www.strawberryhillhouse.org.uk** |
| *Click on:* | *About the House* |
| **Versailles** | **http://en.chateauversailles.fr/homepage** |
| *Click on: Explore the Estate* | *The Palace* |
| | *The Garden* |
| | *The Hall of Mirrors* |
| | *The Grand Trianon* |
| | *Marie-Antoinette Estate* |

| The Victoria and Albert Museum | www.vam.ac.uk |
| --- | --- |
| Click on: Collections | ARCHITECTURE (then click Objects in the Architecture Collection) |
| | *FURNITURE* |
| | *Galleries* |
| | *Objects in the Furniture Collections* |
| | *Objects in the Ceramics Collection* |
| | *Objects in the Furniture Collections* |
| | *Past Exhibitions* |
| | *Exhibition: Thomas Hope* |
| | *Thomas Hope, Family, Grand Tour & Book* |
| | *Duchess Street* |
| | *Interior Decoration, Deepdene & Influence* |
| | *Thomas Hope Objects in the V&A* |
| | *Things to Do: Design a Room* |
| | *Tickets & Visitor Information* |
| | *Thomas Hope Events* |
| | *GLASS VIDEOS* |
| | *Art Nouveau Glass* |
| | *Glass Features* |
| | *Stained Glass* |
| | *Stained Glass Periods and Styles* |
| | *Objects in the Textiles Collection* |
| | *HISTORY, PERIODS & STYLES FEATURES* |
| | *Festivals of Light* |
| | *History of the V&A* |
| | *Understanding Styles* |
| | *Art Nouveau: A Study Room Resource* |
| | *The Great Exhibition* |
| | *Role & Status of Women 1900–1939: A Study Room Resource* |
| | *Architecture Features* |
| | *Arup Associates Campus Model* |
| | *Islamic Architecture* |
| | *Architecture in the Arts* |
| | *Architects' Sketchbooks* |
| | *Architects' Drawings and Ideas: A Study Room Resource* |
| | *VIDEOS: FURNITURE* |
| | *The Adam Interior* |
| | *Williams Burges's Washstand* |
| | *Is this a Chippendale Chair* |
| | *Video: Discover . . . Oriental Carpets* |
| | *The Great Bed of Ware* |
| | *Video: Installing the Leistler Bookcase* |
| | *A Musical Automaton Clock* |
| | *Rebuilding the Melville Bed* |
| | *A Rococo Writing Table* |
| | *A Royal Writing Desk* |
| | *Country Houses* |
| | *Water Gilding* |
| | *FURNITURE LINKS* |
| | *Conservation Journal Articles: Furniture Collections* |